toward
the
understanding
of
st. paul

toward
the
understanding
of
st. paul

toward
the
understanding
of
st. paul

DONALD JOSEPH SELBY

Professor of Religion
Catawba College

PRENTICE-HALL, INC.

Englewood Cliffs, N.J.

pReface...

The study of St. Paul has carried his interpreters into several distinct fields of investigation, each of which has produced an extensive literature. In his quest for a knowledge of the life and letters of Paul, the modern reader must therefore grapple with such matters as Paul's background—Jewish and Graeco-Roman; his place in the history of the Primitive Church; his biography; the literary problems concerning his letters; and the orientation, pattern, and interpretation of his thought. This book, by surveying these various aspects of the study of Paul, is intended to help the reader toward a better understanding of Paul and his contributions to the life and thought of Christianity.

Of necessity, such a survey as this must leave many matters to the reader's further investigation. I have attempted, however, to describe the important problems involved in Pauline studies and the significant answers that have been proposed.

A bibliography or selected list of readings has not been included. The footnotes will guide the reader to the literature on the various topics under discussion, and they have the advantage of indicating more specifically the bearing of the work cited on those topics than would the general comments in an annotated bibliography. The literature on Paul is virtually endless. What I have included in the footnotes indicates my judgment as to the more important, representative works which in turn may guide the reader further into the field.

With one unavoidable exception all works cited are available in English. I have also tried as much as possible to confine my references to books which are in print. Thanks to the ever-increasing number of basic works which have long been unavailable but are now being reprinted in paperbacks—a most commendable trend—this attempt is becoming easier. The out-of-print books I have cited can be found in most college and university libraries.

In the study of Paul many problems remain unsolved and many passages are still obscure; but if this book succeeds in helping the reader toward a better understanding of the Apostle to the gentiles, it will have served its purpose.

acknowledgments . . .

In a book of this kind, intended as a survey of the results of accumulated learning in a specific field, the writer's debt, although incalculable, is obvious. Happily, I have the opportunity to acknowledge my debt to the many direct and indirect, known and unknown sources of ideas and information from which the material in this book has been drawn. The maze of learning is intricate, indeed, and reaches out in many directions far beyond our vision. To sense the vastness of our debt to the cooperative labors of innumerable scholars is a humbling but enriching experience. My specific indebtedness is, I trust, adequately acknowledged in the footnotes. I especially wish to thank the publishers and authors who have generously granted me permission to use materials from their works.

Gratefully I own my obligations to those whose interest, suggestions, and labor have been indispensable in bringing this book to completion. My colleagues, Dr. Raymond Jenkins of the English Department and Dr. C. Gregg Singer of the History Department, have read and criticised the entire manuscript. Dr. David E. Faust of the Religion Department and Professor John C. Carey, now Chaplain of Florida State University, Tallahassee, Florida, have given helpful suggestions and criticisms. Two of my students, Mr. and Mrs. Harry F. Ray, have read and cross checked the many footnotes. Mrs. Raeia Maes of Prentice-Hall, Inc., has been most helpful through her suggestions and editorial skill in preparing the manuscript for publication. The maps came from the skillful hands of Felix Cooper. Assisted by my former student, Mr. Teryl V. Schweitzer, York, Pa., my friend, The Rev. Joseph M. Trask, Rector of St. James' Episcopal Church, Laconia, N.H., has compiled the index. My friend, the Rev. H. Hunt Comer, of St. Paul's Episcopal Church, Salisbury, has assisted with the reading of the proofs. Finally, by her typing of the manuscript and with her help in many ways, my wife has shared with me another of our projects. To all of these friends ---and others---credit is due for many corrections and improvements. The weaknesses and errors I must accept as my own.

Salisbury, North Carolina   DONALD J. SELBY

contents ...

vii

PART III   *MY MESSAGE*

8   his letters are weighty . . . 235

9 we do impart wisdom ... 296

APPENDICES

introduction

a slave of jesus christ...

*Paul, a servant [Greek: slave] of
Jesus Christ, called to be an apostle, set apart for the
gospel of God. (Romans 1:1)*

1 so paul wrote to you...

So also our brother Paul wrote to you according to
the wisdom given him, speaking of this
as he does in all his letters. There are some
things in them hard to understand, which the ignorant
and unstable twist to their own destruction,
as they do the other scriptures. (II Peter 3:15b–16)

Nineteen centuries have passed since Paul penned or, more likely, dictated the letters with which we are concerned. They were written to meet one emergency, to solve another problem, or to bare his heart in response to a sacrificial gift from friends. How amazed he would have been to discover that these occasional letters were to become the most widely circulated correspondence in history and the subject of widespread study even today. As a matter of fact, he did not anticipate any such continuum of time at all:

That after centuries some of these confidential letters would still be in existence Paul neither intended nor anticipated. His glowing faith never reckoned on coming centuries. Spanning apostolic Christendom, like the sultry sky of thunderous weather, was the hope that the present age of the world was hastening to its close, and that the new world of the kingdom of God was just about to appear.[1]

That Paul was not consciously writing scripture must be kept in mind throughout this study. He was writing genuine letters to meet real situations. If we are to understand these letters, we must seek, insofar

[1] Adolf Deissmann, *Paul*, trans. William E. Wilson (New York: Harper & Bros., Torchbook edition, 1957), p. 13.

3

as possible, to understand the situations and the people to whom they were written.

Yet to many thousands of readers of Paul's letters in every age it has seemed as though he were writing to them. The universality of his letters is among their most surprising qualities. We are probably not so surprised as Paul would have been had he known that they were to become so prominent a part of Christian scriptures.

Paul's letters were among the first Christian writings to be regarded as scripture in the growing New Testament canon. Many scholars date II Peter, from which the quotation at the beginning of this chapter is taken, as late as the middle of the second century. It is evident that by that time several things had happened: 1) The collected letters of Paul had been published and were rather widely known, at least in Asia Minor. 2) They had become regarded as scripture to such an extent that they could be spoken of in the same manner as the Old Testament. It is to be remembered that from the first, the Bible of the Christians had been the Old Testament. It is undoubtedly the Old Testament that is meant by "the other scriptures." 3) Already by the time of II Peter, Paul's letters were providing difficulties for the interpreter and were the subject of controversies.

Paul's Influence on Later Christian Writings

The story of Paul's letters in history begins with the verses from II Peter which stand at the head of this chapter. The situation depicted was to be duplicated many times. It may not be too much of an exaggeration to say that the history of Christian theology can be told by tracing the history of these writings. It is not within the scope of our study to trace that history, but a few significant high points may demonstrate the importance of Paul's letters.

Paul had been enjoying a kind of popularity from the time his collected letters first began to circulate. Scholars generally believe that his letters had been copied and placed in circulation during the latter part of the first century. Their influence, for instance, is detected in I Peter. The epistle, or letter, form of the later so-called Catholic Epistles in the New Testament may well be due to the influence of the circulation of Paul's letters.

The writings of the Apostolic Fathers not only quote from his letters in such a way as to show the reverence they had for him, but also in several cases pay him the sincere flattery of imitating his letter form. However, this group of writings demonstrates the way in which Paul was revered and his authority invoked while the real meaning of his thought was almost wholly misunderstood or neglected. Paul's heroic figure, his moral admonitions, and the devotional aspects of his letters occupied their exclusive attention.

The influence of Paul's letters on Christianity received its great impetus, however, from the rise of a heresy that for many years threatened the very life of the Church. It is with this event that the real prominence of Paul actually begins.

Shortly before the middle of the second century a Christian teacher, Marcion, arrived in Rome from Pontus, near the Black Sea. His teaching soon aroused a storm of opposition, and as a result he has become known in history as one of Christianity's first and greatest heretics.

Marcion's importance lies in his choice of scripture. Rejecting the God of Judaism as a morally inferior god, unworthy of Christian worship and, therefore, not the God of Jesus Christ, and also rejecting the entire Old Testament, Marcion was left without a scripture. To replace the Old Testament, which until then had been the sacred writing of Christians, he created a canon of scripture in which he used ten of Paul's letters and an expurgated version of Luke's Gospel. Although II Peter 3:15–16 seems to indicate that Paul's letters had already begun to be regarded as scripture in some sense, Marcion's action greatly accelerated the process.

In defending itself against Marcion, the orthodox Church was forced to apply itself seriously to the task of establishing an authoritative canon of Christian documents to be placed alongside those of the Old Testament.[2]

Marcion's canon is significant in two ways. First, Paul and his writings were familiar enough at Rome to make their authority useful to

[2] Frederick C. Grant calls this developing New Testament a "Christian supplement to the Greek Old Testament . . . which was the original Bible . . . of the Greek-speaking Christian church." *An Introduction to New Testament Thought* (New York: Abingdon Press, 1950), p. 81.

Marcion and to cause the orthodox serious concern when they were thus employed by a heretic. Second, Marcion had succeeded in focusing the Church's attention on these letters to such an extent as to help achieve for them the prominence they now enjoy in the New Testament.

Paul as the Starting Point for Christian Theology

It was the service of Marcion to call attention to the more theological and profound side of Paul. Although he distorted Paul's thought in the interest of his own theories, he at least came to grips with it in a way that has forced the orthodox Church to reckon with it ever since.

Two names stand out in the controversy that followed: Tertullian and Irenaeus. In several ways these men, who lived and wrote in the latter part of the second and early part of the third centuries, mark the beginning of systematic theology. With the coming of Augustine in the latter part of the fourth century the basic structures of systematic theology were established and Paul's position as the fountainhead of theology was fixed.

The letter to the Romans in particular came to be regarded—and still is—as the source book of theology. It has sometimes been said that either Romans or the Sermon on the Mount (Matthew, chapters 5–7) is the basis for every period of revival or reform in Christian history. Certainly they are the two poles around which Christian thought has always revolved. The prominence given to Romans by both Luther and Calvin in the Protestant Reformation illustrate again the importance of this document for Christianity. In our own time it was the publication of his commentary on Romans that started Professor Karl Barth toward the eminent place he occupies among contemporary theologians.

Paul and Greek Ideas

While the Apostolic Fathers were copying Paul's moral teachings and while Marcion was calling attention to his theological significance, other forces were at work which were to lead Paul's influence in a different direction. For one thing, early in the course of the spread of Christianity in the Roman World the gentile constituency began to dominate. As Paul's answer to the problem of how gentiles were to be admitted to the church became more and more the accepted pattern, a bitter antagonism grew up between Christianity and the parent religion, Judaism. Christianity was no longer a Jewish sect; it was gentile, or perhaps better, a universal religion. Gradually its Judaic presuppositions began either to be called into question or to be related to what appeared to be corresponding Greek ideas.[3]

The Greek influence on Christian thought took place largely, though by no means exclusively, through the medium of Paul's letters. That his letters lent themselves to such a process has led to the charge, quite popular in the nineteenth century, that Paul derived many of his ideas from the Greeks, but it is clear now that almost the reverse is true. It was Paul's terminology, quite innocently used to communicate with his gentile and Hellenistic Jewish converts, that opened the way for the entrance of Greek ideas in the thinking of the philosopher-theologians of the second and third centuries.

Thus, Christianity ran headlong into the whirlpool of metaphysical speculation so popular in that time. Speculations as to the nature of Christ in relation to both God and the world were rife. Heresies springing up on the right and left precipitated one of the worst periods of ecclesiastical controversy, which reached its climax in the Nicene Council in 325 A.D. In the course of the controversies Paul was summoned to the support of the various contenders. So once again, as in Acts 23:10, he found himself being pulled asunder by contending parties.[4]

Two results of this period are worth noting: 1) Many basic theological issues were settled; and concepts, many of them derived from Greek thought, found a permanent place in Christian thought. 2) Some of the ritual practices and interpretations influenced by the mystery religions have left their impress on Christian worship to this day.

[3] For an excellent treatment of this process, see Edwin Hatch, *The Influence of Greek Ideas on Christianity* (New York: Harper & Bros., Torchbook edition, 1957). A good brief description of the prevailing situation in Greek thought is given in Howard Clark Kee and Franklin W. Young, *Understanding The New Testament* (Englewood Cliffs, N.J.: Prentice-Hall, Inc., 1957), pp. 15–24.

[4] One might almost take this story as symbolic of the theological fate of Paul to this very day!

Thus, it turns out that the indirect influence of Paul as a gateway for Greek ideas in many respects is as significant as his more direct influence.

Reasons for Paul's Continuing Influence

Undoubtedly, there are many reasons for the great influence Paul has exercised over Christian life and thought. It will be necessary to list only a few of the more obvious ones.

Perhaps the first reason is that Paul was an heroic figure.[5] Whatever may have been their reaction to his teaching or their dislike of his exercise of authority over the churches, those who knew him could hardly have failed to admire the astounding courage and endurance of this "Apostle to the Gentiles." Paul was not above appealing in this way to his own example: "With far greater labors, far more imprisonments, with countless beatings and often near death . . ." (II Corinthians 11:23) was his boast to an arrogant group in the Church at Corinth who attempted to discount his authority and teaching. It is not difficult to see how such an heroic example would prove useful to the early Christian exhorter, particularly in the difficult and dangerous days which followed Nero's onslaught against the Church. This aspect of Paul's influence was aided greatly by the publication of Acts, which quickly spread the reputation of the indefatigable missionary beyond the circle of influence of his own churches and permanently imbedded him in Christian tradition.

In spite of the curious fact that Paul's own account of his sufferings for the gospel exceeds that of Acts, it is noteworthy that the emphasis in Acts is on this side of Paul's career rather than on his thought. Acts may be partly responsible for the strange neglect of the latter by the Apostolic Fathers. They found his heroic example inspiring; they imitated his letters; they copied his moral exhortations; but they left aside "the depth of the riches and wisdom and knowledge of God" in his interpretation of Christ.

They needed his example and they found his exhortations useful. In-

[5] See *I Clement,* V.

deed, both these elements found fertile soil in the Hellenistic world. The way had been well prepared for the reception of such material by the sophists. Schools of rhetoric, found in nearly all the leading metropolises of the time, were busy turning out lecturers, commonly known as sophists, who would "set up shop" in a town by hiring a hall and sending out invitations to the would-be intelligentsia to provide themselves with an audience.[6] Others became itinerant lecturers and wandered from town to town giving lectures in public places, at festivals, anywhere they could assemble an audience.

These sophists customarily expounded on one or another of two themes. On the one hand, they vied with one another in giving colorful orations on the heroic periods and personages in the history of Greece. On the other hand, they harangued their audiences with moral discourses, called diatribes, which moved from one subject to another in a loose fashion by a chain of association.[7] Insofar as ideals and teaching are concerned, the first century was not as morally destitute as is sometimes supposed.[8] The willingness of audiences to suffer the meagre talents of one would-be philosopher after another clearly indicates the moral hunger of the time.

Christian preachers of the first and second centuries found ready audiences both for their accounts of Paul's adventures in establishing churches and for expositions of his moral teaching.[9]

The significance of Paul's conversion as a useful example for the early Christian evangelist may be indicated by Acts relating it three

[6] The Hall of Tyrannus in Ephesus, which Paul made use of after withdrawing from the synagogue, may be an example of one such rhetorician's place of business. The sincerity of these sophists was sometimes called into question. Cf. Epictetus, *Discourses*, III, chaps. 21, 23. For a good discussion of the sophists and their relation to the practices of the Christian ministry see Hatch, *The Influence of Greek Ideas on Christianity*, chap. IV. Augustine in his *Confessions* tells of his own training and later practice as a rhetorician.

[7] The canonical Epistle of James offers an example of the diatribe pattern of moral exhortation.

[8] The similarity between the teachings of these moralists and Christian moral admonitions has often been noted, especially that between the Stoics and Paul. Epictetus, whose teachings, thanks to Arrian, have survived to us, was one of the best of these moralists.

[9] Acts 17:21 is Luke's rather cynical picture of one such hearing given Paul himself.

times in detail. These pious uses of Paul's example established his fame in later tradition.

In the years immediately after Paul's death, his churches occupied a position of some prominence among the churches of the Empire. The influence of the leaders of these churches naturally played a very important role in establishing Paul's apostolic authority. This was especially true in the period during which the Church, struggling with the growing menace of heresy, came to attach great importance to those teachers and leaders who had actually been associated with an apostle.[10] Such a direct succession of the tradition was the orthodox Church's best guarantee of the purity of its teaching.

Throughout his letters Paul names a number of young men whose leadership after his death would perpetuate his influence. Timothy and Titus are the two most prominent among these younger leaders. The attractive theory, if it is true, that Onesimus, Bishop of Ephesus early in the second century, was the slave on whose behalf Paul wrote the letter to Philemon provides an important example of the way in which Paul's influence was carried over to the next generation.[11]

The most important factor contributing to the abiding influence of Paul, however, is the intrinsic worth of the letters themselves. Whatever the Church's needs, his letters have helped to find an answer. Moral instruction, courageous example, hope, exhortations to true piety, profound theological ideas—they are all there. To be sure, his was not a finished theological system, but no document in Christian history has furnished the theological stimulus or shaped theological thinking as have these letters. Although the shape of systematic theology is Greek in origin, its inspiration and much of its material have come from the Pauline letters. The influence of that inspiration and that material has never weakened.

[10] The words of Papias, quoted by Eusebius, seem to provide an example of this attitude: "If, then, anyone came, who had been a follower of the elders, I questioned him in regard to the words of the elders,—what Andrew or what Peter said. . . For I did not think that what was to be gotten from the books would profit me as much as what came from the living and abiding voice." *Church History*, Bk. III, chaps. 39, 4. Philip Schaff and Henry Wace, eds. *Nicene and Post-Nicene Fathers*, trans. A. C. McGiffert, Second Series (New York: The Christian Literature Company, 1890), I, 171.

[11] Cf. John Knox, *Philemon among the Letters of Paul*, 2nd ed. rev. (New York: Abingdon Press, 1959), pp. 98–108.

Values of the Study of Paul

Many readers of Paul will undoubtedly agree: "There are some things in them hard to understand" (II Peter 3:16). This difficulty has caused many to discount the value of Paul for present-day Christianity, but I suspect most of us would be surprised to discover how prominent a place he occupies among our favorite passages in the New Testament. Perhaps the first step in learning to appreciate Paul is to give attention to those phases of his life and letters which we do understand.

Certainly one of the values in a systematic study of Paul is that such a study not only can deepen our understanding of and appreciation for the clearer and more familiar passages, but also can, to a great extent, reduce the areas of difficulty. In some respects we are in the position of one finding an old letter in the attic written by a former resident unknown to him. Much of the letter is unintelligible to him because he has only one side of the conversation. When he is able to trace down the circumstances that occasioned the letter, he can understand it. To a large extent this is our task; its value is apparent.

Our survey of the important place Paul has occupied in the development and history of Christianity should make clear the importance of understanding him in order to understand the history and present-day complex of Christian thought. The place of these letters in the Canon is so prominent that it is impossible to escape their influence. It is surprising how much Paul has unconsciously colored our interpretation and understanding of Jesus. To make this influence more explicit is important enough to justify our study.

Aside from the influence of his thought, Paul's contribution to a knowledge of the character of first century churches makes a study of him indispensable to the student of Christian beginnings. Except for a few brief glimpses of the life of the Jerusalem Church—in several ways a unique situation—provided in the early chapters in Acts, no information whatever outside these letters has come down to us of the actual life of the earliest churches. Without the Corinthian letters, for example, how impoverished our knowledge would be.

The serious student of Paul will find deeper treasures. He cannot fail to find inspiration in so dedicated and heroic a life. He will recognize Paul's insight into human nature. The profound meanings of an experience of Christ disclosed by his life and letters should help to add a new dimension to our own religious life.

"So Paul wrote to you." In a sense neither intended by II Peter nor anticipated by Paul, we may feel justified in interpreting these words by including ourselves in the "you." Paul wrote better than he knew. The very "occasional" nature of his letters has only added to their value. He who understands Paul will agree that his letters belong where they are, in the center of the New Testament.

2 the least of the apostles...

*For I am the least of the apostles, unfit to be called
an apostle, because I persecuted
the church of God. (I Corinthians 15:9)*

To the modern reader of the Bible, Paul often appears
as a strange mixture of greatness and obscurity. From the story of his
life in Acts we gain a picture of a man of inimitable stature. As a missionary, founder of churches, and hero of the faith, he has never failed
to command interest and admiration in every age. From the perspective of the intervening centuries, we are inclined to estimate Paul's
apostleship differently from his humble self-estimate: "The least of
the apostles." It is far more usual to call him the greatest of the
apostles.

Yet many, thus fascinated by Paul the missionary, feel themselves
left quite in the dark by Paul the theologian. In many passages among
Paul's letters, the reader feels himself to be in a strange world, at times
incredible, at other times incomprehensible. There is another Paul
whom many have discovered to their enrichment—Paul the devout.
How many readers, after wading through his tortured interpretation of
some Old Testament passage have rejoiced to come upon passages of
unsurpassed beauty such as the hymn to love in I Corinthians, chapter
13, or the hymn of praise of Romans 11:33–36. All three are the same
Paul. If we are to understand him in any of these roles, we must endeavor to understand him in all.

Paul and the Jerusalem Apostles

To understand Paul's letters it is first necessary, insofar as possible, to understand the man who wrote them. The question of the importance and influence of his letters, therefore, leads to the question of Paul's place in the beginnings of the Church, and especially his relation to the other Apostles.

"I am the least of the apostles" is one estimate of the matter from Paul's own pen. This verse is not false modesty. Paul is quite capable of a more affirmative estimate of himself: "I think that I am not in the least inferior to these superlative apostles" (II Corinthians 11:5). Probably "apostles" in the latter verse does not refer to the leaders of the original Jerusalem Church, and certainly I Corinthians 15:9 was not intended to refer to Paul's prominence in or importance to the development of apostolic Christianity. Both of these verses do, however, indicate Paul's consciousness of his somewhat oblique relationship to the original Jerusalem Apostles.

In more ways than one Paul might be called the thirteenth Apostle —a fact which his many conflicts with other church leaders made abundantly clear. The Jerusalem Apostles had been restored to the revered number of twelve by the election of Matthias to replace Judas Iscariot (Acts 1:15–26). From the point of view of this group Paul was something of an outsider. Yet it is that very obliqueness which makes Paul's place in the growth and development of Christianity so remarkable.

Paul in the New Testament

Two names contain in themselves the primitive history of Christianity: the names of Jesus and Paul.

Jesus and Paul—these two do not stand side by side as first and second. From the broadest historical standpoint Jesus appears as the One, and Paul as the first after the One, or—in more Pauline phraseology—as the first in the One.[1]

These words with which Adolf Deissmann begins his justly famous study of Paul may be an overstatement, but the reader of the New Testament cannot help feel that there is a large measure of truth in them. In the first place one-fourth of the New Testament itself is at-

---

[1] Deissmann, *Paul*, p. 3.

tributed to him. Even if we conclude, as many scholars do, that Paul did not write the Pastoral Letters (I and II Timothy and Titus), he remains second only to Luke in the amount of material contributed to the New Testament by one man. He is the center of interest in the major portion of Acts and in the New Testament appears second only to Jesus in prominence. In the light of this prominence, it is not surprising that early Christians were later inclined to assign even the anonymous Epistle to the Hebrews to Paul.

Paul's nearest rival is Peter, the hero of the early part of Acts and the leader of the disciples in the Gospels, but Peter runs Paul a poor second. Later tradition, undoubtedly influenced by Acts, linked these two Apostles much closer than they appear to have been in the New Testament. Eusebius, the church historian writing about 325 A.D., placed Peter and Paul in a joint leadership of the Church at Rome and said that they were martyred there under the Emperor Nero.

Nor does the interest in Paul on the part of the early Christian writers of the first and second century—known to us as the Apostolic Fathers—show any decline of his importance. No part of the New Testament had a more obvious influence on the Apostolic Fathers than the letters of Paul. Along with the churches in Egypt and North Africa, the churches either founded by or visited by Paul or addressed by him in a letter dominate the Christian scene for many years.

It is frequently pointed out that Paul in this later period was seriously misunderstood. In the very Aegean world in which he had worked and written, Christianity had sometimes taken a legalistic turn quite foreign to Paul's great emphasis on grace and new life in the Spirit. At other times his doctrine of freedom from the law had degenerated into libertinism. But if Paul was misunderstood, at least he was not neglected.

The almost exclusive use made of Paul's writings by Marcion indicates a process which had its roots deep in first century Christianity.[2] Therefore, we quite naturally find it easy to agree with Professor Deissmann's estimate of the place of Paul in first century Christianity.

Yet we must not overlook the fact that the real foundation of this

[2] See "Paul's Influence on Later Christian Writings" in Chap. 1.

impression is the bulk and prominence of Paul's letters in the Canon
of the New Testament. Written records of that time are sketchy. Is our
picture of the situation correct? Were there not, perhaps, others even
more prominent and influential in the first stages of the development
of Christianity who are lost to us simply because they did not write, or
if they did, their writings were not preserved? These are questions
which we cannot answer with any finality. Yet there are indications
that the spread, development, and establishment of Christianity were
not as exclusively the work of Paul as has often been assumed.

Parallel Developments of Christianity

To begin with, there is a significant number of churches listed
in the New Testament obviously not founded by Paul. Several of them
were there to meet him. There were Christians in Damascus, his intended victims, who had the honor of receiving him into the fellowship
of those of "the Way." The church which ordained him a Christian
missionary—the church in which the name "Christian" originated—
was there before Paul. The summary statements in Acts, chapter 8, indicate missionary activity which surely must have yielded some permanent results. Believers are indicated in Samaria and Caesarea at the
very time Paul was "breathing threats and murder against the disciples of the Lord."

When we go farther afield into the Roman world the same situation
meets us. The opening verses of Acts, chapter 19, read as though a
church had sprung up in Ephesus independent of Paul. The churches
in Colossae and Laodicea also were not founded by Paul, although they
may have been founded by a disciple of Paul and therefore indirectly
were a result of his work, but there is no certainty of this. On the
other side of the Mediterranean churches very early appear about
whose founding we know nothing at all. The Ethiopian eunuch has
sometimes been credited with the establishment of the church in Egypt,
but the only evidence is that he was traveling south, toward home,
when Philip encountered him. This theory hardly accounts for the
churches along the coast of North Africa. Finally, there was the very
important church in Rome itself, to whose existence we owe the most

influential letter we have from Paul. It is impossible to know who founded this church. Concerning the founding of these churches we can only say that there were apostles other than Paul whose mission it was to spread the "Good News" around the Empire.

While it is true that the oldest documents in our New Testament are from the hand of Paul, there are reasons to believe that other Christians were writing material, some of which was finally destined to find its way into the Gospels.

Students of the Gospels generally agree that the first three, at least, were compiled from earlier sources, which must have been written within Paul's lifetime. The story of the crucifixion and resurrection as told in all four Gospels displays a homogeneity and body of common material which has persuaded some scholars that it once existed as an independent document and was the first piece of Gospel material to be written. A collection of the teachings of Jesus, comprising about two hundred verses which Matthew and Luke have in common, is generally supposed to have come from an early writing, now for the lack of a better term called, Q.[3] If there was such a document, it possibly was written before Paul wrote Romans.

There can be no doubt that by the time Paul's letters had been collected and circulated, Mark and probably Matthew had been published and were in use in their respective areas. At least one New Testament scholar has suggested that it was the publication of Acts that aroused the interest in Paul which finally led to the collection of his letters.[4]

These observations have been made at the outset of our study to place Paul in proper perspective. Studies of Paul have frequently left the impression that Paul was the effective founder of Christianity, that he single-handedly succeeded in establishing throughout the Empire a religion based on an obscure Galilean who, but for him, would quickly have been lost to history.

[3] Eusebius quotes a second century writer, Papias, as saying that "Matthew wrote the oracles (sayings) in the Hebrew language." *Church History,* III, 39, 16. Schaff and Wace, *Nicene and Post-Nicene Fathers,* Second Series, p. 173. These oracles, or logia as they are frequently called, are thought by a number of scholars to be identical with the lost document Q. The designation Q for this material is derived from the German word, *Quelle,* meaning source.

[4] Edgar J. Goodspeed, *The Formation of the New Testament* (Chicago: The University of Chicago Press, 1926), p. 21.

Paul and the Origin of Christianity

There have been those who, either because of a dislike for classical Christian teachings or a misunderstanding of Paul's own thought, have blamed him for muddying the pure stream of the "simple gospel" of Jesus. He has been called an obscurantist, a fanatic, whose abstruse theories—sometimes thought to have been borrowed from the oriental mystery religions—lie at the base of all the bitter theological controversies that have plagued Christian history. The origin of Christian doctrines which some in the modern temper find objectionable have been laid to his charge. Christianity without Paul, so some argue, would have been a lovely, simple thing—the beautiful, poetic ideals of a charming Galilean prophet. They forget that the greatest hymn to Christian love was written by Paul.

Others, with perhaps slightly less prejudice, have contended that Jesus and the religion based on him would never have survived but for Paul. That neither of these impressions is true, I believe, is demonstrated by the recognition of the parallel developments of Christianity which were quite independent of him.

But would not Christianity have been a far different affair without his dominant influence? Here again the answer must be no. Paul's conflict with the more reactionary elements within the Church, which indicates the existence of a widespread and virile Christianity that owed nothing to him, may help to demonstrate this.

That Paul's dispute with the reactionary factions in the Church, with which we shall be concerned in detail later, occupies so prominent a place in the New Testament may well be due mainly to historical accident. Without this dispute some of Paul's earliest letters might never have been written. At the outset, Christians were not concerned with writing for posterity; indeed, they seem to have believed that there would be no posterity. Hence the letters of Paul were purely occasional, called forth by the ever-present problems and conflicts in his churches. The large areas of agreement, as a result, were left out of account. Only later do they come into view.

It may be worthwhile to anticipate here a later discussion by pointing out that areas of disagreement in the conflict between Paul and the Judaisers, as they are usually called, are quite limited. In Paul's discussion of them, they concern entirely the question of the inclusion of the Jewish Law in the New Faith. As important as this matter proved to be in the logical development of Christian theology, it did not involve the denial of the messiahship of Jesus, his resurrection, or the divine revelation that was made in him. These are cardinal beliefs which are placed in the foreground by every witness in the New Testament who speaks on these matters at all.

Paul's main argument against his opponents is that their continuing dependence on the Law is inconsistent with the logical consequences of these beliefs. It is significant that Paul's victory was not altogether complete, as is shown by the large amount of legalism in the Christianity of the second century.

In Acts Luke sought, near the end of the first century, to place this conflict in a clearer perspective. Perhaps Luke went too far and painted the picture in softer tones than the facts warranted, but it is instructive that at the same time he pictures the large amount of harmony among the Apostles, including Paul, he seems to ignore those teachings peculiar to Paul which appear prominently in his letters. Luke, at least, represents a Christianity not created by Paul which is, nevertheless, not very different.

The Gospels bear out the same point. In fact, the major portion of the New Testament shows that Christianity was not the creation of Paul, but developed with not a few variations along the general lines in which he gladly shared. Paul's claim not to have received his gospel from men (Galatians 1:12) is often taken too seriously. We shall have occasion later to study the considerable extent to which he reflects the traditions about Jesus which are later recorded in the Gospels.

One other evidence that Christianity is not a one-man creation is the large place assigned in later tradition to the Twelve Apostles. The luxuriant growth of fanciful legends which sought to supply the lack of actual information about them, the increasing interest in Peter— finally exalted as the "Prince of the Apostles"—and even the traditions surrounding the origin of the Apostles' Creed, all bear witness to the fact that at least Christian writers in the succeeding centuries were not aware that Paul had single-handedly founded the Church.

To deny that Paul founded Christianity is not to make Paul seem unimportant but rather to see his importance in its true perspective. In some ways it makes his prominence all the more remarkable. The Jerusalem Church could not have planned the spread of Christianity in such a fashion. The spontaneity of the growth of the Church can hardly be better illustrated than by the story of the conversion of their arch-enemy into its most remarkable ally. His greatness is by comparison. "I have labored more than they all," he wrote. No student of his life will doubt him, but by that very token he is not to bear either the praise or the blame, as the case may be, for the basic character of the Christian Faith. In the areas of Asia Minor and the Aegean world, Christianity's chief exponent, he nevertheless was not its inventor or perverter.

Paul as an Interpreter of Christ

What, then, are the abiding contributions of Paul? Two suggest themselves: First, there is that incalculable value which every devoted student of Christian biographies knows by experience, the ability of the spirit of a great personality to transmit itself even through the written word and across the centuries to other persons and help them to greatness. Underneath the surface of every great epoch in Christian history we can find, if we look for it, the power of his spirit. Second, his is the first written interpretation of Christ of which we have any knowledge—probably the first to have been written and for many his is the greatest.

Not the least of the values of his interpretation of Christ is the fact that it was made in the process of meeting problems of every-day living. Some of these problems were peculiar to the time in which he lived, but many of them were more universal. Most of them were basically the same as those which Christians have faced in every age. Here is no ivory tower ideology. It was hammered out on the anvil of life in a difficult and exceedingly complicated age.

Furthermore, Paul's interpretation of Christ was not the backward look of an historian. Christ was for him a living, present reality. This is a key to his thought. Yet he did not, as we shall see, ignore the "historical Jesus." The present reality always depends on the reality of the earthly ministry of Jesus. The past is in that regard not merely past but a living present as well; that is its significance.

Finally, Paul interpreted Christ in terms of vital religious experience. Not only his experience of conversion on the Damascus Road—though undoubtedly it began there—but also his daily consciousness of the living reality of Christ in his own life was the basis for understanding Christ. If Paul spoke of the incarnation, it was to exhort his readers to "have this mind among yourselves, which you have in Christ Jesus." When he thought of the crucifixion, it was to say, "I have been crucified with Christ." Was he thinking of the resurrection? It was in order "that I may know him and the power of his resurrection."

We will understand Paul better if we begin by recognizing that his interpretation of Christ began, not with doctrine, but with experience. Indeed, the goal of his life was that those to whom he ministered "might walk in newness of life." "For if we have been united with him in a death like his, we shall certainly be united with him in a resurrection like his." Therefore "you also must consider yourselves dead to sin and alive to God in Christ Jesus."

Such a method of interpreting Jesus makes demands on more than the intellect of those who would understand it. To those who would understand the true depths of his teaching as well as to those who would know the secret of his strength Paul beckons to follow him in that mystic experience of the living Christ of which he speaks as being "in Christ." If Paul is really to be understood, there is no other way.

I have captioned this introductory section with Paul's own description of himself, "A Slave of Jesus Christ." This is how he is to be understood. From the standpoint of the revered number of the "Twelve" he was indeed the "least of the apostles." There were those who insisted that he was no apostle at all, but he could without any feeling of undue arrogance claim a place equal to any of them, for his election was not by the Jerusalem Church but by the Lord himself. He could demand obedience. He could challenge all human authority. He could even shamelessly invite others to imitate him, for he had been commissioned by Christ himself. He was Christ's personal slave.

the traditions of my fathers...

And I advanced in Judaism beyond many of my own age among my people, so extremely zealous was I for the traditions of my fathers. (Galatians 1:14)

𝟹 a son of pharisees . . .

*But when Paul perceived that one part were Sadducees
and the other Pharisees, he cried out in
the Council, "brethren, I am a Pharisee, a son
of Pharisees; with respect to the hope and the
resurrection of the dead I am on trial."* (Acts 23:6)

No man can entirely escape his own background
whether he consciously remains within it or he rebels against it. The
thought forms, the presuppositions, the frame of reference, the subtle
influences of his mother tongue all remain his birthright throughout
his life. Thus, one cannot be understood apart from his heritage.
Clearly, then, it is with Judaism, especially Pharisaical Judaism, that
we must begin in our attempt to understand Paul. Indeed this is what
he himself invites us to do.

"A son of Pharisees." The phrase locates Paul definitely in the major
party within the sectarian structure of Judaism. Whatever may be our
impression of the authenticity of speeches such as this attributed to
Paul in Acts,[1] this description of him is easily confirmed by his own
letters. The words in Galatians 1:14, "so extremely zealous was I for
the traditions of my fathers," the statement in Philippians 3:5, "as
to the law a Pharisee"; his constant appeal to the authority of the
Jewish Scriptures, provide sufficient proof of this.

Judaism was more than a background for Paul; it was the framework within which he lived and worked throughout his entire life. The
point can hardly be overemphasized. It is crucial, for instance, in un-

[1] On the problem of the speeches in Acts see Henry J. Cadbury in F. J.
Foakes Jackson and Kirsopp Lake, *The Beginnings of Christianity* (London:
Macmillan & Co., 1933), V, 402-27.

derstanding the familiar controversy over the admission of gentiles into the Church. Paul always remained under the discipline of the synagogue as is clear from his reference in II Corinthians 11:24 to having received five times "at the hands of the Jews the forty lashes less one." But more than this, his interpretation of his call and ministry and the meaning of Jesus as the Messiah was within the framework of the Judaism in which he was reared and schooled.[2]

It may appear from Philippians 3:6-11 that Paul's Pharisaism has been overstated. Is it not apparent that Pharisaism is among the things Paul has "counted as loss"? Further, is not Paul largely responsible for the separation of the Christian Church from Judaism? That he played a significant role in the development of Christianity which eventually established it as a separate and universal religion is not to be denied. But that separation was not consummated in his day nor was he conscious of its inevitability. It is too easy for us to read such passages as this one from his Philippian letter in the light of the later independence of Christianity and to view his Damascus Road experience as a "conversion" from one religion to another.

Actually, all this is properly to be understood within the framework of Judaism because for Paul Christ was the new and final event in God's historical dealings with Israel. It was to this that he was "converted." Because of this he "counted as loss" all his achievements "under the Law." Therefore it is precisely within the setting of Pharisaic Judaism that Paul's position becomes most clearly intelligible. It is not simply that modes of thought and expression and methods of argument which had long been habitual with him continued to find expression in his letters or that he wove into the fabric of his Christian theology a considerable number of strands of Pharisaical doctrines. Rather he saw himself as standing at the threshold of the final denouement of Israel's destiny. It was as the ultimate meaning of Israel's *raison d' etre,* not as a repudiation of it, that he argued for the inclusion of the gentiles without the requirements for the proselyte.

[2] "What the boy Saul learned in the school of the Pharisees, that determined Paul the Christian's thoughts and feelings in decisive hours, although to himself he seems to have become a 'new creature.'" H. Weinel, *St. Paul, The Man and His Work,* trans. G. A. Beinemann (New York: G. P. Putnam & Sons, 1905), p. 21.

From this it is clear that a knowledge of Judaism is important for the study of Paul not only as background but also as the prevailing frame of reference.

Paul, however, was a Diaspora Jew. As such he was brought into inevitable involvement with the gentile world in a way more influential and determinative than were those who remained within the confines of Palestinian Judaism. It will be necessary, therefore, to survey the Greek culture as it was known in the Levant and the shape that the Roman Empire had given to the world into which Paul was born and in which he carried out his historic mission.

In this section we shall attempt such a survey beginning with Judaism as that part of Paul's background at once closest to him and throughout his life the most relevant and determinative. In the succeeding chapter we shall consider the relevant aspects of the Graeco-Roman world.

The Origin of the Pharisees

The Pharisees appear by name quite suddenly in history in connection with the reign of John Hyrcanus I (135–105 B.C.). Josephus mentions them as a party of great popular influence with whom Hyrcanus became disaffected because of an ill-advised comment on his ancestry made by one of their number.[3] The incidental manner in which Josephus introduces them and refers the reader to his description of the party in an earlier writing suggests that they had already been in existence for some time. However, since we hear nothing of the Pharisees during the Maccabean revolt some thirty years before, the name at least must have arisen in the interim. Yet it is evident from Josephus' description of their influence and popularity that the Pharisees did not arise as a completely new phenomenon in the period between the Maccabean revolt and the time of John Hyrcanus.

That there is some connection between the Pharisees and the Hasi-

---

[3] *Antiquities of the Jews,* XIII, 10. He mentions the Pharisees five chapters earlier and discusses their relationship to the Sadducees and Essenes with regard to their attitude toward a doctrine of fate, but since he evidently does not know of any actual connection they may have had with history then, it appears doubtful that he is right in introducing them in the time of Jonathan. In any case, the mention in Chapter 5 is very indefinite and vague.

dim (meaning pious) among the early Maccabean supporters is hardly to be questioned,[4] but both rabbinic tradition and the later connection of the Pharisees with the Oral Law require that their story begin far earlier.[5] To this beginning we shall now turn.

The Exile and the Torah   The establishment of a written code of law (621 B.C.) by Josiah, King of Judah, had gone far toward preparing the Exiles for national and religious survival in an alien country as well as laying the foundation for the development of a legalism that has characterized Judaism ever since. It is customary to cite Josiah's code as the real beginning of Judaism, but the impetus given it during the Exile and again under Ezra and Nehemiah was of far reaching and decisive importance.

Under the conviction that the disaster that had befallen them in the Fall of Jerusalem (586 B.C.) was caused by their disobedience to God, the Exiled Jews in Babylon applied themselves diligently to the study of the Law in order that they might know more precisely God's will and thus be enabled to keep it more faithfully. In this, they believed, lay their salvation. Under the leadership of Zerubbabel and Joshua Ben Jehozadak the first group returned from Babylon after its conquest by Cyrus (538 B.C.). With almost fantastically high hopes inspired in the main by the predictions of the exilic prophets, they set about to restore Jerusalem and the sacrificial cultus. By anointing Zerubbabel as king it was their hope to restore the monarchy. But the Persians, though not interfering in religious matters, prevented this obvious bid for independence and retained suzerainty until it was wrested from them by Alexander the Great (334–331 B.C.).

---

[4] On the problem of that relationship see Foakes Jackson and Lake, *Beginnings of Christianity*, I, 88–89.

[5] W. O. E. Oesterley believes the differences between the Pharisees and Sadducees go back ultimately to the conflict between the house of Abiathar, David's priest and that of Zadok, whom Solomon appointed to replace him. Thus, the Sadducees represent the descendants of Zadok and the Pharisees are the followers of the house of Abiathar who was exiled to Anathoth. With considerable ingenuity Oesterley traces the ancestry of the Pharisaical party back through Ezra and Jeremiah to David's priest and ultimately to Aaron! W. O. E. Oesterley, *Jews and Judaism in the Greek Period, The Background of Christianity* (New York: The Macmillan Company, 1941, also London: Society for Promoting Christian Knowledge, 1941), p. 248.

Some eighteen years later, under Haggai and Zechariah, the Temple was rebuilt (520 B.C.). But as Malachi clearly shows the decline and consequent disillusionment of the struggling community brought about a serious decline in religious interest and observances. If it were not for the reforms of Ezra and Nehemiah this decline might well have presaged the end of the Post Exilic Jerusalem community.

It was from Babylon, then, where the creative interest in the Law had continued unabated, that, nearly a century after the first return under Zerubbabel, the new stimulus to the study of the Law came. Both Ezra and Nehemiah are credited with this. It will not be necessary to go into the complicated critical problems surrounding the relation of Ezra and Nehemiah to one another nor to the Jerusalem community.[6] Coming from Babylon with the Law in his hand and a sizeable assembly of leading Babylonian Jews, Ezra introduced a new concern for the Law and doubtless initiated a new stage in its development. Eventually it was ratified by the Jerusalem community in a public ceremony.

Meanwhile the redoubtable Nehemiah armed with a firman from Artaxerxes arrived in Jerusalem to rebuild the city wall and set matters straight generally (444 B.C.). The new life thus injected into the Jerusalem community changed the course of Jewish history and was responsible in large degree for the Judaism that meets us in the New Testament times. The fact that the entire Pentateuch was finally canonized within a half century or less after this, and the fact that within approximately another half century II Chronicles could ascribe it to Moses, suggests that what was ratified at this time was substantially the Torah itself.

Ezra and the Scribes   The activity which brought about the Torah did not

---

[6] For a discussion of these problems see Robert H. Pfeiffer, *Introduction to the Old Testament* (New York: Harper & Bros., 1948), pp. 813–38. The prominence of Ezra in the later tradition and the persistence of that tradition in associating him with the Torah and the rise of the Scribes make it impossible for me to share Dr. Pfeiffer's disbelief concerning Ezra's role as a scribe. The argument that there could be no scribe until after the canonization of the Pentateuch seems to me to ignore the fact that part of it existed as early as 621 and further Ezra may well have had considerable to do with the final stages of its development while in Jerusalem. Cf. Charles Foster Kent, *Makers and Teachers of Judaism* (New York: Charles Scribner's Sons, 1911), pp. 132–33.

stop there. Laws need to be interpreted. Changing circumstances make old laws obsolete and new ones necessary. Ambiguities and apparent conflicts require clearing up and in the study of religious law piety finds many occasions for edifying admonitions. Thus the process that produced the written Torah continued until it had produced a parallel tradition in the form of the Oral Law that all but nullified the original. Eventually Jewish tradition was to assign this Oral Law as well as the Torah to Moses.[7] It was apparently the tradition that Moses had given the Oral Law to be preserved as such which retarded the process of recording it in written form.[8] Paul, therefore, had to learn this weighty body of tradition by rote from his teachers.

Ezra and Nehemiah are of interest to us at this point in two ways. In the first place neither of them was a product of the environs of Jerusalem. Ezra from Babylonia and Nehemiah from Susa are evidence of the continuing virility of Mesopotamian Judaism. The great interest shown by the Exiles in the Law and Traditions of Israel apparently had continued with little abatement throughout the century between the first return of the Exiles under Zerubbabel and Nehemiah's time. Also, the place which Jerusalem still occupied in the thinking of Babylonian Judaism is shown by the concern for the Holy City by both Ezra and Nehemiah. This was an early instance of a continuing creative influence exerted by Mesopotamian Judaism on that of Palestine. Hillel, one of the greatest of the ancient Rabbis and grandfather of Gamaliel under whom Paul studied, was a product of this influence. And, of course, the very important Babylonian Talmud was a final gift of Persian Jewry.

In the second place Ezra and Nehemiah mark the beginning of a new period of religious development in Palestine which was to eventuate in the elaboration of the Oral Law and its interpretations. In this development the origin of the Pharisees is discovered.

Rabbinic tradition divides the time between Ezra and the School of

[7] Cf. W. O. E. Oesterley and G. H. Box, *The Religion and Worship of the Synagogue* (London: Sir Isaac Pitman and Sons, Ltd., 1907), pp. 50–51. Oesterley, *The Jews and Judaism*, p. 58, gives the rabbinic exegesis of Exod. 34:27 by which this theory was supposed to be substantiated.

[8] See Heinrich Graetz, *History of the Jews* (Philadelphia: The Jewish Publication Society of America, 1946), II, 608.

Jamnia (after 70 A.D.) into three periods during which the Oral Tradition began to take written form: the Sopherim, or scribes; the
Zugoth, meaning pairs; and the Tannaim, meaning teachers. The first
of these periods extends roughly to the time of the Maccabees. Ezra,
the ideal scribe (cf. Ezra 7:10), is supposed to have been the original
member and founder of this group. The tradition is closely associated
with that of the "Great Synagogue" to which was credited the work
of editing and canonizing of Scripture along with the regulation of
prayers and other matters of worship.

The historical and chronological problems raised by this tradition
make it difficult to take this tradition literally. Yet there can be no
doubt that such work was actually carried on and that in that work
the scribes had a leading part.[9] This is the truth to which the tradition
undoubtedly points. According to Finkelstein, the scribes arose in the
period of the Exile when priest and prophets, forced by economic
necessity to seek gainful employment, turned to the work of a notary
and public secretary.[10]

In consequence of this development these men, now skilled in such
matters, were called upon to act as custodians and copyists of the
growing body of religious literature of their own people. Such an one
was Ezra. The copyist not only reproduced the manuscripts, but he
also soon became an expert on its contents. He was called upon to
read it (Nehemiah 8:4 ff). He also had a hand in the development of
any new legislation.

In time the roles of priest and scribe were separated. Subsequently
the scribes came from and represented the laity.[11] An antagonism grew
up between the two groups which gathered force from the difference
in their social and economic status. Thus it came about that the
scribes became the spokesmen for the popular middle class while the

[9] Louis Finkelstein believes such a "Great Assembly" did actually exist but
confines it to the time of Simon the Just, who according to the tradition was
the last of its members. See his *The Pharisees*, 2nd ed. rev. (Philadelphia: The
Jewish Publication Society of America, 1940), II, 576 ff.

[10] Finkelstein, *Pharisees*, I, 262.

[11] Since Simon the Just—traditionally the last of the "Men of the Great
Synagogue"—was also high priest, this separation presumably was not finally
effected until after the period of the Sopherim, i.e., about the time of the
Maccabees.

priests remained the representatives of the aristocratic and wealthy minority.[12] Soon the scribes were surrounded by a large following of the pious with whom they had many affinities. It is within this class, whose daily problems made the need for interpretation and adjustment of the Torah more apparent, that the Oral Tradition developed. Thus a society known as the Hasidim came into being.

In the meantime the conquests of Alexander the Great and, upon his death (328 B.C.), the subsequent division of his Empire among his generals finally brought Palestine under the control of the Ptolemies of Egypt where it remained until Antiochus the Great, one of the Seleucid rulers of Syria, brought it under his domain (198 B.C.).

Deeply religious and thoroughly devoted to the Torah as interpreted to them by their scribes, the Hasidim were the first to perceive the threat to the whole structure of Israel's faith in the wave of enthusiasm for Hellenistic culture that swept over Palestine under Antiochus the Great. When, later, Antiochus Epiphanes, in a thorough-going attempt to Hellenize the Jews, desecrated the Temple, attempted to destroy all copies of the Torah, and proscribed all Jewish religious observances (168 B.C.), it was from among the Hasidim that the resistance movement, led by Judas Maccabeus, arose to win back the Temple and the freedom to continue the practice of their faith.[13] However, once their religious life was again secure they lost interest in the struggle for independence and withdrew their support.[14] Within two decades, nevertheless, the Syrian yoke was broken (143 B.C.) and John Hyrcanus, a nephew of Judas Maccabeus, became the first Jewish king since the Fall of Jerusalem in 586 B.C.

It is at this time that Josephus introduces the Pharisees by name.[15] The source of this name is a matter of conjecture.[16] The word itself, from *Perisha*, apparently means "separate" or "separated one." One plausible theory is "that it was originally applied to the Asidaeans

---

[12] Finkelstein uses the terms, "patrician" and "plebeian" for this distinction, *Pharisees*, I, iii, n. Cf. Josephus, *Ant.*, XX, chap. 10.

[13] I Macc., 2:42.

[14] *Ibid.*, 7:13.

[15] See "The Origin of the Pharisees" and note 3 in this chapter.

[16] See George Foot Moore, *Judaism*, (Cambridge: Harvard University Press, 1927), I, 60–61.

(Hasidim) who separated from Judas Maccabeus when freedom of religion was achieved and a legitimate high priest succeeded Menelaus."[17]

The Pairs

The reign of the Maccabees corresponds to the traditional period of the Zugoth. The Zugoth, or pairs, refer to five generations of popular religious leaders who, according to the tradition, served as president and vice-president, respectively, of the Sanhedrin,[18] and hence the term "pairs." It is probably too early to apply the title Rabbi to these men but this tradition points to the link between the early Sopherim and the later Rabbis. That these pairs were actually the leaders of the Sanhedrin is doubtful, but the tradition in the period preceding New Testament times certainly points to the popular religious leadership of the middle class Pharisees.[19]

The last and most famous of these pairs, Hillel and Shammai, is of particular interest to us.[20] They mark the beginning of two opposing schools within Pharisaism. Shammai is noted for his violent temper and strict interpretations of the Law, while Hillel's far broader and more tolerant teaching coupled with his great humility and piety made him the leading teacher of his time and founder of the dominant school in later Pharisaism. He is familiar to New Testament students for having given in negative form the golden rule as representing the essence of the Law.

---

[17] *Ibid.*, p. 61.

[18] The Jewish high court composed of 70 elders. Its actual origin is obscure and need not concern us here.

[19] Evidence of the power of the Pharisees is seen in the story of their restoration to power under Alexandra following the deathbed advice of her husband, Alexander Jannaeus, in Josephus, *Ant.* XIII, chaps. 15, 16. That the High-Priests were the actual heads of the Sanhedrin seems evident from Josephus, *Ant.* XX, Chap. 9. Cf. John 11:47.

[20] For a good characterization of these two men and their respective schools, see Finkelstein, *Pharisees*, I, 83–85. See also Montefiore in Foakes Jackson and Lake, *The Beginnings of Christianity*, I, 42, 74, *passim*. According to the *Pirke Aboth*, I, 12, Hillel said: "Be of the disciples of Aaron, loving peace and pursuing peace, loving mankind and drawing them to the Torah." By permission of Judah Goldin, trans. *The Living Talmud*, (Chicago: The University of Chicago Press, 1957), p. 65. Cf. Moore, *Judaism*, I, 79.

Hillel, of all the rabbis, is the most familiar name to most Christians. He owes this reputation to the anecdotes which illustrate his genial temper and to the fine religious and moral aphorisms that are quoted from him; but his great significance in the history of Judasim lies not so much in these things as in the new impulse and direction he gave to the study of the Law, the new spirit he infused into Pharisaism.[21]

We shall return to Hillel later. Now, it will suffice to note that his grandson, Gamaliel I, later head of the Hillel school and prominent member of the Sanhedrin (Cf. Acts 5:33–40), was Paul's teacher. Paul, therefore, was a Hillelite and as such an heir to generations of earnest piety occupied with the study of, interpretation of, and obedience to the Torah.

The Tannaim   A radical change in the fortunes of the Jews ushered in the third period, that of the Tannaim. From the time of Pompey's invasion (63 B.C.), Palestine had been under the control of Rome. In 38 B.C. Herod with the support of Roman legions achieved the position of "King of the Jews" conferred upon him earlier by Rome. The Maccabean rule, which had been practically dead for some time officially ended. At the time of Herod's death (4 B.C.) Palestine was divided into tetrarchies ruled over by his sons, Philip, Antipas, and Archelaeus. After ten years of misrule over Judea, Archelaeus was banished, and Judea was placed under Roman procurators. The excesses of Florus, the last of these, and the appearance of the Zealot, John of Gischala, signaled the revolt which eventuated in the Fall of Jerusalem and destruction of the Temple by Titus in 70 A.D.

Johanan ben Zakkai, who escaped during the siege of Jerusalem by having himself carried out of the city in a coffin, began the period of the Tannaim.[22] Having obtained permission from the Romans to settle in Jamnia on the Palestinian coast, he established a school there which became of the greatest importance not only because of its work in fixing the limits of the Hebrew Canon, but also in its influence on the liturgy of the synagogue and the organization and recording of the Oral Law. We are dependent on the work of the Tannaim and that of

[21] Moore, *Judaism,* I, 81.
[22] See Graetz, *History of the Jews,* II, 323–24.

their successors, the Amoraim, for much of our information concerning this Oral Tradition and the Pharisees.

The Oral Law and Jewish Literature

Although from the time of Ezra and Nehemiah the Pentateuch, or Torah as it is called in Hebrew, has been the vital center of Judaism, there grew up alongside the Torah an enormous body of literature which by supplementing and interpreting stands in the closest relation to it.[23] Since the role of the Pharisees in Judaism is most intimately bound up with the growth of this literature, it will be helpful to survey it briefly.

The Talmudic Literature   This extra-canonical, legal literature consists in general of two parts: *halakah* and *haggadah*. *Halakah*, meaning a rule, refers to additional rules and definitions by which the Torah was applied and kept abreast of the requirements of changing social and political situations as well as removing ambiguities and apparent conflicts inherent in the Torah itself. *Haggadah*, meaning narrative, refers to materials designed to supply illustrations, sermonic materials, examples of legal precedent, and the like. The heart of this literature is the Mishna (meaning to repeat and hence to learn).[24] The term refers primarily to a collection consisting principally of halakah, made by Judah ha Nasi[25] and preserving the best of the work of the Tannaim. It consists of sixty or more tractates divided into six sections by themes.

[23] A Talmudic saying runs: "As the sea has little waves between the large ones, so the Torah has many details of Oral Law affecting commandments of the Written Law" (*Shekalim* 6, 1). Louis I. Newman, *The Talmudic Anthology*, (New York: Behrman House, Inc., 1945), p. 510. Also a thirteenth century saying finds the relation of the two Torahs symbolized in the Creation Story: "The upper waters are the Torah of the Scripture; the lower waters are the Torah of Tradition" (*Tekkune Zohar*, 60 b). Newman, *Talmudic Anthology*, p. 33. Cf. Gen. 1:6-9.

[24] Apparently the term refers to the monotonous process of recitation by which successive generations of pupils had learned by rote this massive body of material. Such is the meaning of Paul's words, "at the feet of Gamaliel," Acts 22:3.

[25] Literally, Judah the Prince. He was the grandson of Gamaliel II, hence a descendant of Hillel. See Isaac Landman, ed., *The Universal Jewish Encyclopedia* (New York: Universal Jewish Encyclopedia Co., Inc.), VI, 229-30. On Judah's Mishna see Emil Schürer, *The Jewish People in the Time of Jesus*

A parallel body of material is contained in the Tosephta, meaning additions, regarded by some scholars as containing even older traditions.[26] Beside these two collections stands another body of materials by way of commentary on the Torah known as Midrashim. Since the fourth century the most authoritative collections are the two Talmuds: The Palestinian (often wrongly called the Jerusalem) Talmud and the Babylonian Talmud. They date respectively from the fourth and fifth century A.D. These consist of expositions (Gemara) on several levels based on the Mishna. Of the two, the Babylonian is the more complete and authoritative.

The Targums

One other collection deserves mention. As the classical Hebrew fell into disuse in post-Exilic Judaism, it became necessary to follow the reading of the Torah in the synagogue with a translation into Aramaic, the common language of the day. These translations were not to be read from written notes but were to be given extemporaneously. Gradually, however, they became crystallized and handed down in definite forms. In some cases they were close paraphrases, in others they were more interpretative. After the Fall of Jerusalem in 70 A.D. these, too, were written down and thus preserved.

The Targums are important not only for the light they throw on Jewish theology, but also, especially, as a *Thesaurus* of ancient Jewish exegesis; in this way they frequently offer matter of interest in relation to the Old and New Testament writings; in particular it can be shown that the New Testament often agrees with the ancient Synagogue in interpreting certain passages messianically which later were expounded differently in orthodox Jewish circles.[27]

Christ (New York: Charles Scribner's Sons, n.d.), I, 119–30; S. M. Jackson, ed., *The New Schaff-Herzog Encyclopedia of Religious Knowledge* (New York and London: Funk & Wagnalls Company, 1908), Vol. XI, 256–57; Isadore Singer, *The Jewish Encyclopedia* (New York: Funk & Wagnalls Company, 1907), VII, 333–37.

[26] There were, of course, traditions usually called Baraita (meaning external) which were not incorporated in either the Mishna or Tosephta but were included in the Gemara, or comments in the Talmuds.

[27] W. O. E. Oesterley and G. H. Box, *The Religion and Worship of the Synagogue* (London: Sir Isaac Pitman and Sons, Ltd., 1907), p. 50. The Septuagint (the Greek translation of the Old Testament made in Egypt dur-

Although the literary activity which produced this mass of material began with the school at Jamnia, the material it contains is, in large part at least, much older. All of this material was developed and handed down by the Rabbis and the scribes before them in one of the most creative periods in Jewish history. In theory, at least the material was not committed to writing until the time of the Tannaim. Thus it is often referred to as the Oral Law. In the Gospels it is called the "Tradition of the Elders." It was in this fluid state that Paul learned the Oral Law "at the feet of Gamaliel."

Hillel's Rules of Interpretation   Inevitably such a painstaking preoccupation with the Law must establish methods of interpretation. The oft-quoted saying attributed to "the men of the Great Synagogue": "Be deliberate in judgment, raise many disciples, and make a hedge about the Torah"[28] was interpreted to mean that the requirements of the written Torah were to be safeguarded by careful interpretation and delimiting rules so that there would be no danger of infractions through ignorance or misunderstanding. In theory the interpreters were merely making explicit that which was already implicitly contained in the Law. This, of course, led to many subtleties of exegesis that were often more ingenious than convincing. As time went on and this activity became more extensive and self-conscious some definitions of method became necessary. Hillel, the grandfather of Gamaliel, appears to have been the first to attempt to systematize the principles of interpretation in his famous "Seven Rules." In a sense these were principles of rabbinic logic. The meaning of some of these rules is obscure, but a few observations concerning them will be of interest.[29]

---

ing the last two centuries before Christ) may have served Greek speaking Jews as a Targum. It is not clear that it ever actually supplanted the Hebrew text in the official reading in the synagogue service. See Moore, *Judaism*, I, 288 and Graetz, *History of the Jews*, II, 386. For opposite view see Oesterley *Jews and Judaism*, p. 214 and Hans Leitzmann, *The Beginnings of the Christian Church*, trans. Bertram Lee Woolf, 3 ed. rev. (London: Lutterworth Press, 1953), pp. 87–91.

[28] *Pirke Aboth*, I, 1, Goldin, *The Living Talmud*, p. 43.

[29] See the article on Hermeneutics in *The Jewish Encyclopedia*, XII, 30–33 for the list and explanation of these rules as well as their later modification into thirteen rules by R. Ishmael. See also Moore, *Judaism*, I, 80.

Hillel's rules were a serious attempt to bring some order and consistency into rabbinic teaching. They required, for instance, that decisions applied in a given instance must be binding in all similar cases. Definitions of words must be consistently maintained in the various instances. In the argument from the less to the greater, familiar to us from the teaching of Jesus, he laid down the logical principle that the conclusion must not contain anything not contained in the major premise. Also, his rules were designed to curb extreme and fanciful interpretations by restricting and defining the use of arguments from analogy.

His rule that if two cases can be shown to be similar the legal decision binding on one holds for the other calls to mind Paul's use of this principle in Romans 7:1-6, where he argues from the principle that the "law is binding on a person only during his life" to the conclusion that, since the Christian has "died to the law through the body of Christ," he is "discharged from the law."

How generally these rules were observed is impossible to say. Their survival, however, in Rabbinic tradition is not only a tribute to the great esteem in which Hillel was held but also an indication of their influence. A further evidence of their importance is that later, in the Tannaim period, a generation after Paul, Hillel's seven rules were modified in opposite directions by R. Akiba and R. Ishmael. The latter elaborated them in his famous thirteen rules which became a standard for rabbinic exegesis.

The argument between these two Rabbis is of interest to us. R. Akiba contended that the Torah, unlike other human writings in which style and rhetoric play a part, contains not so much as a sound that is not essential to the meaning. Hence every word and syllable is capable of yielding treasures of hidden truth. R. Ishmael, however, contended that "the Torah speaks in the language of men."[30] Therefore he became known as the "clear thinker" because of his common sense approach to the interpretation of the Torah.[31]

At some points Paul seems to have anticipated R. Akiba's position. A clear instance of this is his exegesis of Genesis 12:7 (Galatians

[30] *The Jewish Encyclopedia*, XII, 31.
[31] Cf. Graetz, *History of the Jews*, II, 355-56.

3:16), in which he bases his whole argument on the singular number of the noun "offspring" (*spermati*).

In the meantime a radically different method (allegorical) of interpreting the Torah was being developed under Hellenistic influence which seems to have had its center in Alexandria in Egypt. This method is usually associated with Philo who was certainly its greatest and most influential exponent.

Probably Philo was not its originator. Indeed, he, like Hillel among the Palestinian teachers, may have had a restraining influence on its excesses.[32] Philo maintained that the Torah had two meanings: The literal sense, which is the body; and the spiritual sense, which is the soul. By this means he attempted to show that the truths of Greek philosophy, particularly Platonism, were already spoken by Moses long before Plato's time! Here again we find affinities with Paul's exegesis. Allegory apparently is Paul's favorite method. One notable example is his treatment of Abraham's two sons, Isaac and Ishmael, in Galatians 4:21–31.

Jewish religious interest and creativity, however, were by no means exhausted by their preoccupation with the Torah, as is evident from the rise of two widely divergent types of literature in the two centuries or so before Christ; since there is evidence of the influence of both of these in Paul's writings, they deserve some attention.

The Wisdom of Solomon   Toward the end of the Persian period and particularly during the Greek period there appeared a number of writings which, because of their primary concern with wisdom, are classified as Wisdom Literature. Proverbs, Job, and Ecclesiastes in the Old Testament belong to this class along with Ecclesiasticus, by Jesus ben Sirach and The Wisdom of Solomon in the Apocrypha.

Wisdom Literature in general is similar to the *haggadah* in the later Talmuds and Midrashim. Alternating between sundry bits of prudential advice and essays on the supreme worth of wisdom, it addresses itself primarily to the individual and his immediate, every-day life. It is ethical rather than theological and holds before the reader the goal

[32] *Ibid.,* pp. 208–15.

of happiness or blessedness rather than righteousness.

Egyptian influence in this literature may be seen in the importance attached to wisdom. Nevertheless, the definition of wisdom is strictly Jewish: "first they identified it with their own religion and ethics (Proverbs), then with the Law of Moses or the Pentateuch . . ."[33] The identification of wisdom with the Law indicates that although this literature arose independently of the development of the Oral Law, it was not antagonistic or unrelated to it. It may be regarded simply as a different phase of Scribal activity arising, as did the Oral Law itself, among the Pharisees and their spiritual forebears.

Among these writings the Wisdom of Solomon is of particular interest to us because some scholars have found evidence that Paul was considerably influenced by it.[34] While a closer examination of the evidence reveals that the influence of the Wisdom of Solomon was by no means as great as has sometimes been claimed, it is probable that Paul was familiar with it, especially since it undoubtedly stood in the Greek Scriptures (Septuagint) which he used. What is more noteworthy is that he reflects so little influence from the rest of this literature. Actually, the similarities between Paul's writings and the Wisdom of Solomon are more formal than basic. While in several instances the figures and phraseology bear striking resemblances, an examination of the thought will show that the differences in ideas are equally impressive. The conclusion is inescapable that it is not to the Wisdom Literature that we are to look for the source of the basic concepts of Paul's thought.[35]

[33] Robert H. Pfeiffer, *History of New Testament Times* (New York: Harper & Bros., 1949), p. 64.

[34] See T. R. Glover, *The World of the New Testament* (New York, The Macmillan Company, 1931), p. 129 and Edgar J. Goodspeed, *Paul,* (New York, Abingdon Press, 1947), pp. 150, 205; and others; following a number of German scholars around the turn of the century took this position. Professor Goodspeed, however, dates the document so late as to exclude it from Paul's Septuagint. He believes that Paul knew it as an independent, recently published book.

[35] William Sanday and Arthur C. Headlam, *Romans, International Critical Commentary,* 13th ed. (New York: Charles Scribner's Sons, 1911), pp. 51–52 and 267–69 give a careful and detailed analysis of the main passages in question (cf. Romans 1:18 ff. with Wisdom of Solomon 13:1 ff. *passim;* Romans 9:21 ff. with Wisdom of Solomon 15:7–8). Of course, in light of the popularity of the Wisdom of Solomon, the possibility must not be ruled out that Paul learned

The character of the Wisdom of Solomon may be seen in the ways by which the author sets about to accomplish the three purposes he has in mind: To the pious Jews who in spite of their continued faithfulness are beleaguered by misfortunes and persecution he holds forth the assurance of reward in the after life; to the worldly, apostate Jews he directs a warning of final judgment, "for horrible is the end of the unrighteous generation" (3:19); to the pagans he addresses a strong and sometimes satirical polemic against idols and pagan worship in general.[36] In its broad outline and, formally, in some of its phraseology, Paul shows affinities with this work. Its importance, nevertheless, as an influence on Paul can easily be exaggerated.

Apocalyptic Writings   At the opposite extreme is another type of literature known from its characteristic claim to reveal otherwise hidden information concerning the future as apocalyptic or revelation. It is a Greek term meaning to disclose that which is covered or hidden. The relevance of the apocalypse for understanding Judaism, particularly Pharisaical Judaism, has sometimes been questioned, but the arguments are not convincing. The weight of scholarly opinion seems to incline toward the opposite direction. The fact that the Bar Cochba Rebellion (132– 135 A.D.) with its disastrous outcome and similar ill-advised movements was apparently influenced by this literature helped to bring it into disfavor and led to its repudiation by rabbinic Judaism. This, however, confirms rather than denies its earlier prominence. The fact remains that numerous eschatological references and ideas in rabbinic Judaism are inexplicable without this literature. The later attitude of the Rabbis is reflected in the saying of an anonymous sage in the Talmud: "May the curse of heaven fall upon those who calculate the date of the advent of the Messiah, and thus create political and social unrest among the people."[37]

---

these figures of speech and similes second-hand from popular currency. Cf. J. Gresham Machen, *The Origin of Paul's Religion* (New York: The Macmillan Company, 1928), p. 200.

[36] Pfeiffer, *History of New Testament Times*, p. 334. For an excellent detailed study of the Wisdom of Solomon see pp. 313–51.

[37] *Sanhedrin*, 97 b. Newman, *The Talmudic Anthology*, p. 277. Cf. Oesterley and Box, *The Religion and Worship of the Synagogue*, pp. 42–43; Moore,

The apocalyptic writings began to make their appearances in the time of the Syrian domination of Palestine (after 200 B.C.) and continued until the end of the first century A.D. They represent a rather decidedly different strain of Pharisaical thought from that of the Wisdom Literature. Although we can point to no specific books, apocalyptic influence on Paul's writing is manifest. The imagery, for instance, in II Thessalonians 2:1–12 is clearly apocalyptic.

The invariable theme of the apocalypse is the end of the present age, the coming of the final day of judgment, and the establishment of a perfect new age to follow. This denouement is always viewed as being in the immediate future of the book's publication. The ethical implications of the prospects of the advancing Day of Judgment are, of course, the real purpose of these writings. In this denouement the authors see the vindication of the faithfulness of the righteous and the manifestation of divine justice in the awful fate of the wicked.

In point of view the apocalypse is cosmic rather than individualistic. It places little confidence in human action to effect the betterment of man's lot, but rather places its hope entirely on a final divine act in judgment and deliverance. There is no Messiah, in the strict sense of the term, in this material. Some—Daniel and Enoch, for example—speak of the "Son of Man" as the agent of God's action. The role of this figure is not always clear and is never central in the program. In any case, he is a superhuman figure and bears little relation to the anointed scion of David to whom the term messiah more properly refers.

Drawing heavily on the increasingly glorious visions of the supermundane future of Israel in the later prophecies of the Old Testament, the apocalypses describe the coming events by means of abstract but standardized images often in bizarre combinations. In spite of the standardization of this symbolic language, the recipient of the "visions," which comprise the apocalypse, needs to have them explained to him at each point. The explanation is given by the angelic guide who is

---

Judaism, I, 127–32; R. H. Charles, *Religious Development between the Old and the New Testament*, (New York: Holt, Rinehart & Winston, n.d.), p. 44; Foakes Jackson and Lake, *The Beginnings of Christianity*, I, 135–36; Charles Guignebert, *The Jewish World in the Time of Jesus*, trans. S. H. Hooke (New York: E. P. Dutton & Company, 1939), pp. 133, 150.

conducting him through his "tour of the future." The apocalypses are usually pseudonymous. Ascribed to some outstanding personage in Israel's past, they purport to have been hidden (sealed) until they should be miraculously "discovered" and published at the end of time.

As strange and often fantastic as these writings appear to the modern mind, they, nevertheless, gave to pious Jews, caught in the web of what must have appeared as hopeless circumstance, profound expression to their faith in the righteousness of God. Far more than an assertion of the rightness of the writers' own causes or their confidence in personal vindication, apocalyptic was another way of affirming the truth annunciated by the prophets before them, a truth which finds its finest expression in the letters of Paul—that God's ultimate purpose in creation must finally issue in a world of unimaginable glory and perfection. Only such an outcome of history is worthy of the God they worshiped and in whom they placed their fullest trust. Like the Pharisees generally, they were essentially pacifists and followed faithfully the admonition of Isaiah: "In quietness and in trust shall be your strength" (Isaiah 30:15).

The Synagogue

According to the Book of Acts, Paul's regular procedure in beginning his work in a new city was to enter a synagogue on the Sabbath. There he would take advantage of the privilege, enjoyed by any faithful adult male Jew, of participating in the Service. Inevitably, his Gospel would raise dissension and he would be forced to continue his preaching elsewhere.[38] Perhaps this pattern is being referred to in his own words, "to the Jew first and also to the Greek" (Romans 1:16). For this reason and also because the patterns of Christian worship have come from the synagogue it will be helpful for us to survey briefly the nature of the synagogue and its place in Judaism.[39]

Origins of the Synagogue   The actual origins of the
                                  synagogue (Greek: assembly

[38] The account in Acts 17:2 ff. may be taken as typical.

[39] It would not be amiss to speak of Paul's churches as Christian synagogues. Except for the introduction of certain ecstatic elements, and, of course, the development of certain distinctively Christian practices, the worship was a continuation of the Jewish synagogue liturgy.

or congregation) are lost to history. The prevalence of the Greek name seems to suggest a beginning in the Greek period (i.e., after Alexander the Great) and among Greek speaking Jews outside Palestine. The term, however, is not invariable. Twice in Acts the synagogue in Philippi is called a "place of prayer" (16:13, 16). Psalm 74:8 surely refers to the synagogues and calls them "the meeting places of God in the land." The incidental way in which synagogues are referred to and their prevalence by New Testament times suggest their origins must reach far back into the Persian period.[40]

In all probability the synagogue grew out of the voluntary assemblies of the Jews in Babylon during the Exile. Left without a temple or sacrifice, yet stimulated to a new devotion to God and His Law, they by necessity developed a form of worship built around prayer, fasting, and reading of the Law rather than the sacrificial rituals of the Temple (Cf. Zechariah 7:3). Thus, they laid the foundations for an institution which was to determine the structure of Christian worship and to be of inestimable worth in preserving Judaism from the Fall of Jerusalem in 70 A.D. down to our own day.

During the Persian period after the Exile these assemblies were probably overshadowed by the restored Temple, but with the scattering of Jewish communities around the world,[41] it was natural that they should reappear and develop into the institution we know as the synagogue. Furthermore, those who lived within Palestine at a distance far enough from the Temple to forbid frequent attendance at its ceremonies would likewise find in the synagogue an answer to their spiritual needs. Ultimately, synagogues appeared within Jerusalem itself, though the Talmudic claim that there were some 480 synagogues in this city cannot be taken seriously.[42]

Functions of the Synagogue   Its worship was no longer a mere substitute for the Tem-

---

[40] Synagogues appear in Egypt as early as the third century B.C. See *The Universal Jewish Encyclopedia*, X, p. 120. Josephus mentions one in Antioch shortly after the time of Antiochus Epiphanes (171–164 B.C.). The incidental way in which he uses the term makes it clear that synagogues were not uncommon at that time, *Wars of the Jews*, VII, 3.

[41] See "The Diaspora" in this chapter.

[42] *Schaff-Herzog Encyclopedia*, XI, 213. Cf. Acts 6:9; 24:12.

ple ritual but became an independent institution in its own right whose influence on the Pharisaical attitude toward the Temple ritual was to have far reaching consequences.[43] The synagogue performed three important functions: a means of worship; a school for teaching the Torah; and, especially outside Palestine, a community center for the Jews of the village or city.[44] The value of such an institution for preserving the identity, faith, and traditions of Jews scattered throughout the pagan world is apparent.

Organization of the Synagogue   The synagogue was essentially a lay organization. Not until much later did the rabbi begin to function as a pastor. If there chanced to be a priest at a service, he was called upon to pronounce a blessing. In other respects any capable adult male Jew might lead the worship. A minimum of ten male Jews was required to constitute a synagogue.

Two officers of the synagogue are mentioned in the New Testament. In Acts 13:15 the "rulers of the synagogue" invited Paul and his companions to deliver the homily after the reading of the "Law and the Prophets." In Luke 13:14 a "ruler of the synagogue" objects to Jesus' healing of the woman with an infirmity on the Sabbath. Such an one was Jairus whose daughter Jesus healed (Mark 5:22 ff., Luke 8:41 ff.). Sosthenes, who was beaten before the court of Gallio (Acts 18:17) was such an officer as was Crispus, one of Paul's converts in Corinth (Acts 18:8). The "ruler" appears in these passages to have been a presiding officer. The plural in Acts 13:15 suggests that in some cases the leadership may have resided in an official board rather than in a single individual. The other officer is mentioned only once, in Luke 4:20, where Jesus handed the scroll to the "attendant." Probably this refers to a custodian, one of whose duties was the care of the scrolls.

Worship of the Synagogue   The synagogue worship had its center in the reading of

[43] Cf. Moore, *Judaism*, I, 284–86. Also Foakes Jackson and Lake, *The Beginnings of Christianity*, I, 160, Pfeiffer, *History of New Testament Times*, p. 49.
[44] *Ibid.*, p. 180.

the Law.[45] In later times the readings were scheduled so that the entire Pentateuch would be covered in a given period. In Palestine the Pentateuch was read through every three years; in Babylon it was done in a single year. According to the New Testament, the Law was followed by a selection from the Prophets. Although the Prophets were accepted as canonical, they never occupied the place in Judaism accorded the Law. The reading from the Prophets, therefore, would be by way of further elucidating or expounding the meaning of the Law.

Regularly the worship included two other important elements: 1) The *Shema,* which may be described as a confession of faith as well as a succinct statement of Jewish religious obligations, and is comprised of Deuteronomy 6:4–9, 11:13–21, and Numbers 15:37–41. 2) The prayers, often called benedictions because of the benedictory response at the end of each of them. Early in the second century these prayers were arranged in a series called *Shemoneh esreh,* "eighteen benedictions." A number of these, though not all, unquestionably go back to pre-Christian times. One writer contends that prior to the second century there were six prayers called H'middah.[46] In any case established prayers, often patterned after the Psalms, were a vital part of the service. In addition, if there was someone present capable of doing so, the readings for the day were followed by a homily or exposition—the ancient counterpart of our modern sermon. Both Jesus and Paul were invited to give such homilies (Luke 4:16 ff., Acts 13:14 ff.). Undoubtedly, the synagogues outside Palestine tended to elaborate their services with elements of the Temple ritual.[47] This elaboration may have included the use of Psalms which was apparently not an established part of the services in the Palestinian synagogues. More than likely Paul's churches felt free to improvise in their worship, yet Paul's mention of Psalms in that connection (I Corinthians 14:26, Ephesians 5:19, Colossians 3:16) may indicate their use in the synagogues of Asia Minor and Achaia.

[45] Paul refers to this in II Cor. 3:15.
[46] N. Levison, *Jewish Background of Christianity,* (Edinburgh: T. & T. Clark, 1932), pp. 139–40. Cf. Moore, *Judaism,* I, 290–92. On the synagogue and its service see the old but still useful description in Alfred Edersheim, *The Life and Times of Jesus the Messiah,* 8th ed. rev. (New York: Longmans Green, and Co., 1899), I, 430–50.
[47] Moore, *Judaism,* I, 290.

The Diaspora

In an extended quotation from the famous Greek geographer, Strabo, Josephus has the following oft cited description of the distribution of Jewish settlements around the world: "Now these Jews have already gotten into all cities; and it is hard to find a place in the habitable earth that hath not admitted this tribe of men, and is not possessed by them."[48] The phenomenon referred to here is of the greatest importance for our understanding of Paul's mission. It must therefore be included in our survey of Judaism. We have already noted the regularity with which Acts begins the story of Paul's work in each city with the synagogue. The fact that even as far west as Corinth— and Rome, for that matter—Paul could find a synagogue in every city to which he came calls for some explanation. The fact is that the existence of Jewish communities in cities throughout the ancient world is one of the prominent features of Judaism in New Testament times. It is customary to refer to these scattered Jewish communities as The Diaspora. The word itself is of Greek derivation and means a scattering or dispersion (from the verb meaning to sow or scatter as of seeds).[49]

The story of the Diaspora begins as far back as Nebuchadnezzar's capture of Jerusalem (597–582 B.C.). With his deportation of the populace of Jerusalem to Babylon a Judaism was established in Mesopotamia that was to survive with remarkable vitality and under Persian rule, to find its way into Media and Persia as well.

In Egypt   About the same time (582) a group of Jews migrated into Egypt (Jeremiah 43:1–7), but these may not have been the first to do so. The pro-Egyptian sentiments of many of the Jerusalem citizens are well known from Isaiah. At any rate we know from the Elephantine Papyri that there existed a Jewish settlement very early on an island in the upper Nile across from Assuan.[50] This settlement

---

[48] Josephus, *Ant., XIV,* chap. 7 (Whiston's translation).
[49] Actually the term is not common in the New Testament. In fact, of the three occurrences (James 1:1, I Peter 1:1, John 7:35) only one, John 7:35, can be taken to refer to the Jewish dispersion. Acts' term for this is "the Jews who are among the Gentiles" (21:21).
[50] For examples of these papyri and a description of this community see

appears to date as far back as the sixth century B.C. It possessed a temple which was destroyed in 410 B.C. Its relation with Jerusalem is evidenced in a letter for aid in securing permission to rebuild its temple.

Much later, in the latter part of the fourth century B.C., Alexander the Great settled a Jewish colony in Alexandria which, being strengthened by frequent voluntary migrations under the later Ptolemies, grew to very large and influential proportions.[51] We have already noted some of the influences of Alexandrian Judaism. Philo was an Alexandrian and the Septuagint, the Greek translation of the Old Testament from which Paul habitually quoted in his letters, originated here. It may be that the Wisdom of Solomon which we discussed earlier was also written here.[52] Probably nowhere on earth were the Jews so well situated as in Alexandria. In wealth, in status, and in numbers they enjoyed an enviable position. It is hardly to be wondered at that Strabo could suppose that "the Jews were originally Egyptians."[53]

In Asia Minor   How or when the migration
                                   of Jews into Asia Minor
took place is impossible to say. It is likely that Jews began to move into the larger cities during the later Greek period when under the sovereignty of the Seleucids, enthusiasm for Greek culture ran high among the upper-class Jews. Jewish settlements in Antioch and in the gentile cities of Coele-Syria were established in this period. Seleucus Nicator I, Josephus tells us, granted citizenship to the Jews in Asia, Lower Syria, and Antioch.[54] Later in the same chapter he describes with obvious pleasure the amicable relations between Antiochus the Great and the Jews after he gained possession of Palestine from the Egyptians. It may be that his expedition through Asia Minor into Greece had encouraged further Jewish migrations. Again, after the death of Antiochus Epiphanes, "did those that succeeded him in the kingdom, restore all the donations that were made of brass to the Jews of An-

---

D. Winton Thomas, *Documents from Old Testament Times* (London: Thomas Nelson and Sons Ltd., 1958), pp. 256–69.

[51] Cf. Josephus, *Ant.*, XIX, chap. 5.

[52] Foakes Jackson and Lake, *The Beginnings of Christianity*, I, 153.

[53] Josephus, *Ant.* XIV, chap. 7.

[54] *Ant.*, XII, Chap. 3.

tioch . . . and granted them the enjoyment of equal privileges of citizens with the Greeks themselves."[55]

Jews were present in significant numbers on the island of Cyprus (Acts 13:4–6), Antioch of Pisidia (13:14–45), Iconium (14:1 f.), and Ephesus (19:8 ff.). Doubtless there were synagogues in Lystra, Derbe and other such cities as well which Luke found unnecessary to mention.

How or when Jewish communities appeared in Macedonia and Greece is hard to guess, but Paul found synagogues in Philippi (Acts 16:13), Thessalonica (17:1), Beroea (17:10), Athens (17:17), and Corinth (18:4 ff.).

In Rome

The important Jewish community in Rome may possibly go back to the delegation sent to Rome by Judas Maccabeus.[56] Certainly the presence of Jews in Rome goes back as far as the time of Pompey who returned with a number of them as captives. Their life in Rome became at times turbulent, as is evident in their expulsion from the city by Tiberius and then by Claudius.[57] The latter is of interest to us particularly because it resulted in Priscilla (Prisca) and Aquila moving to Corinth where they became Paul's hosts and co-workers (Acts 18:1–3). On the other hand, the Herods long enjoyed the favor of the Roman court and Josephus, friend of Vespasian and Titus, retired to Rome to write his famous historical works, or perhaps better, apologies for Judaism (his autobiography might be called an apology for Josephus).

Homogeneity of Judaism

The surprising thing about the Diaspora is the remarkable homogeneity which it manifested. The Jews not only maintained their national identity in resisting the tendency to be absorbed into the surrounding gentile population, but according to both Acts and Paul's

---

[55] Josephus, *Wars*, VII, chap. 3 (Whiston's translation).

[56] I Macc. 8:17–32. Morton S. Enslin questions this in his *Christian Beginnings*, 4th ed. (New York: Harper & Bros., 1938), p. 91.

[57] Acts 18:2. Suetonius says that this was due to an uprising at the instigation of one Chrestus. *Claudius*, 25. The name Chrestus has raised the speculation that he actually meant Christus and was describing a Jewish-Christian controversy. Cf. Josephus, *Ant.*, XVIII, chaps. 3 and 5.

letters, they preserved considerable uniformity in their religious character.

Several factors contributed to this homogeneity, chief among which unquestionably is the synagogue. Schooled as they had been in the ways of survival in an alien land by the Exile, the Jews found in the synagogue not only a place of worship in lieu of the Temple, but a school and a community center as well. Favored by special concessions from the Roman government, they were free to develop their own exclusive community life and, within limits, their own self-government (see Acts 18:14–15). The heart of the synagogue life, of course, was the Law. It was, as we have seen, a central feature of the worship. It was the subject of instruction in the school and the basis for regulating the life of the community. Indeed, among the Diaspora the Law, the "portable fatherland" of the Jew, had already gone far toward replacing the Temple as the real heart of religion.

The Septuagint played a considerable part in maintaining the distinctive character of these Diaspora communities. Whether or not the Septuagint actually was substituted for the Hebrew in the liturgical reading, it was the only intelligible Scripture of those who long ago had adopted Greek as their mother tongue. Since the majority of the Old Testament quotations in Paul's letters came from this translation, it shows that his early training in the Law was from the Septuagint.

At the center of world Judaism stood the Temple. Although the opportunity was never afforded to many in the Diaspora to fulfill the dream of making a festal pilgrimage to the Holy City, the possibility of the dream itself gave a sense of oneness. The list of nations represented in the multitude on Pentecost (Acts 2:5–11) may indicate the geographical distribution typical of those of the Diaspora for whom the dream had become a reality.[58] It is difficult to take the astounding figures of Josephus literally; nevertheless, his claim that at least 2,700,-200 Jews ate the Passover feast in Jerusalem at one time during the reign of Nero does indicate that many did find the means to make the sacred journey.[59]

[58] Henry J. Cadbury and Kirsopp Lake, partly for textual reasons, believe that these are to be taken as gentiles rather than Diaspora Jews. *The Beginnings of Christianity*, V, 67–68 and 113–14.

[59] *Wars*, VI, chap. 9. The normal population of Jerusalem has been estimated to be between 200,000 and 250,000.

Of course, every loyal adult male Jew wherever he might dwell, had a more direct tie to the Temple in the form of the half-shekel Temple tax which was paid annually for the support of the Temple services.[60] Beyond this was the consciousness, which helped to bind far-flung Judaism into one Commonwealth, that, however far from Jerusalem one might be, there at the Temple the smoke from the sacrifices continued to rise toward heaven in his behalf. Jerusalem was still his capital and there God was worshiped according to the prescriptions of the Law. His annual tax was his share in this. He could look to Jerusalem and know that God was with him because God dwelt in Israel in the Holy Place.

The Character of the Diaspora   In all probability the Diaspora Jew was more urbane and in subtle ways more influenced by the gentile culture and ideas around him than his Palestinian brothers. The adoption of Greek as his mother tongue was bound to carry with it subtle changes of thought.[61] Philo's influence—and surely he was not alone in his interest in Greek ideas—was "in the air." Yet in a general way, at least, the Diaspora Jew can be classified with the Pharisees. While lacking the rigidity and, likely, the organization of Palestinian Pharisees, he nevertheless centered his religion in the Law. Essentially pacifistic by necessity, he shared the Pharisaical hope for the resurrection, a divine act bringing judgment upon the wicked and the new age for the righteous. The real center of his religious life, the synagogue, was an essentially Pharisaic institution. His attitude toward the gentiles, to judge from Acts and Paul's letters at least, hardly differed from that of the Palestine Pharisees. Paul the Pharisee was no exception among Diaspora Jews.

Paul and the Diaspora   Diaspora Judaism was both Paul's immediate back-

---

[60] Edersheim has a good description of this tax and its connection with the money changers whom Jesus drove from the Temple in his *The Life and Times of Jesus the Messiah*, I, 367-70.

[61] There were instances, of course, in which the changes of thought were not so subtle. On the fringes of the Diaspora were Jews who succumbed to the syncretism of the time. The itinerant exorcists in Acts 19:13 may have been among these.

ground and foreground. He was born a Diaspora Jew. Undoubtedly, he received his first training in the Law in a Tarsus synagogue, but it was also to the Diaspora that he first addressed his Gospel. "To the Jew first," in practice at least, meant for him the Diaspora.

The Diaspora was important, however, for more than simply a representation of Judaism in the pagan world. It was not merely the passive recipient of the Palestinian faith, but as Philo and Alexandrian Judaism abundantly show, it exercised its own creative influence on that faith. It is not at all likely that this creativity was confined to Egypt. If the following quotation from a lecture delivered before an international meeting of Old Testament scholars in 1927 is an exaggeration, at least there is enough truth in it to make it worth repeating: "Jerusalem was a center into which all the ideas and ideals of Jewry flowed, and while it was the seat of authority, and its stamp was required for orthodoxy, yet the Diaspora was the original home of the great thoughts of Judaism."[62] Paul could never hope to obtain the stamp of Jewish orthodoxy, but if the Diaspora had done no more than produce him, its claim to creativeness would be justified.

Proselytes and God-Fearers

Whatever they may indicate about the motives and character of proselytes to Judaism, the words of Jesus to the Pharisees: "You traverse sea and land to make a single proselyte," points to an important feature of the Judaism of the Greek and Roman periods. Because of its importance for understanding the early spread of Christianity, we cannot leave this survey of Pharisaical Judaism without a brief discussion of the attraction of gentiles to Judaism as converts (proselytes, from the Greek word for alien or newcomer) or at least as sympathizers.

The amazingly large number of Jews living in the Diaspora at the beginning of the first century has as its most plausible explanation the likelihood that a considerable number of these were actually proselytes. Charles Guignebert estimates that the Diaspora population must have been between four and seven million.[63] The zeal for proselyting had

[62] Professor Causse of Strasbourg, quoted in Levison, *Jewish Background of Christianity* (Edinburgh: T. & T. Clark, 1932), p. 137.
[63] Guignebert, *The Jewish World in the Time of Jesus*, pp. 214–15. See also

borne fruit abundantly. Apparently proselyting took place principally in the Diaspora. Although Jesus' words indicate that it was far from uncommon in Palestine.

Motives for Proselyting   In an earlier time, the Maccabean period, there had occurred a wave of proselyting that had considerably increased the Jewish Commonwealth. Alexander Jannaeus, for example, had offered the Idumeans the alternative of circumcision or moving out of their land. They chose circumcision.[64] Such actions, it must be acknowledged, stemmed from a rather different motive from the first century "missionary" activity with which we are concerned. The Maccabees were seeking to "restore the borders of Israel" inspired, perhaps, by such prophetic passages as Obadiah, verse 19. Their political security as they saw it lay in the subjugation of the surrounding nations. They were eliminating the "strangers in the land" by forcing them to become Jews.

In the Roman period, especially under the Judean procurators and in the Diaspora, there was no room for such objectives. Rather, the religious purpose of winning the gentiles to the worship of Israel's God spurred the new movement. Under the conviction, inspired no doubt by such prophets as II Isaiah (49:6; 60:1-3 *passim*) and Zechariah (8:20 ff.), that the future must inevitably bring the nations to the worship of the One True God, they welcomed every manifestation of interest shown their faith by the gentiles. How actively they solicited proselytes is hard to say. It is unlikely that they campaigned in any such fashion as the early Christian missionaries, but their very existence and activities among the gentiles became a source of great attraction to many of the latter.[65]

The times were auspicious. The attraction that Judaism held for the Graeco-Roman world was a part of the awakening interest in things

---

Graetz, *History of the Jews*, II, 215–21 and Levison, *Jewish Background of Christianity*, p. 182.

[64] Josephus, *Ant.*, XIII, chap. 9.

[65] Robert V. Moss believes that they may have employed missionaries and that possibly Paul was training for such a role. See his *The Life of Paul* (Philadelphia: The Christian Education Press, 1955), p. 7. Cf. F. M. Derwacter, *Preparing the Way for Paul* (New York: The Macmillan Co., 1930), ch. III, 41–60, also 86–94. This entire book is a valuable study of Jewish proselyting.

oriental, particularly religious. In a later chapter we shall take notice of the welcome accorded other religions of the East. Throughout this period religion in the Roman world was in an exceedingly fluid state. The allegorizing of Homer to remove the offensiveness of the grosser elements in his pictures of the lives of the gods had not met with complete success. Although Plato had attempted to set theism on a more solid foundation than the old Greek polytheism had given it, the net result of the philosophical currents which he had set in motion was to cut the ground from under the traditional religions and cast the people spiritually adrift. Some drifted into a sophisticated skepticism, others sought refuge in moral philosophies, but the rank and file welcomed any new religion that challenged their faith and offered promise of moral guidance and spiritual security. To these the high ethical monotheism was bound to have an appeal. This religious hunger was not confined to the lower strata of society. A surprising number of highborn women were to be found among the Jewish proselytes. In a similar way Christianity was soon to find a welcome even among the patrician women of Rome.

The Place of Proselytes in Judaism

That the lot of the proselyte was not always a happy one, however, is evident from the later rule that a proselyte was not to be reminded of his pagan origins. Such a law would hardly have been necessary if the acceptance of proselytes into the full life of the Jewish communities had not met with resistance. Of course, proselytes were not always innocent of causing such antagonism. Robert Pfeiffer cites a passage in the Jerusalem Talmud (*Qiddushin* 65b) which classified proselytes for unworthy motives: "love proselytes" were those who embraced Judaism in order to marry into a Jewish family; "proselytes for a place at the king's table" were seeking political or social advantage; "lion proselytes" acted out of fear or compulsion.[66] The latter type hardly obtained in the time with which we are concerned.

On the other hand, some proselytes made significant contributions to their newly espoused faith and many became highly esteemed. Aquila

[66] Pfeiffer, *History of New Testament Times,* p. 190 n.

is perhaps the outstanding example. A second century (A.D.) convert to Judaism, he produced a Greek translation of the Hebrew Bible which very quickly replaced the Septuagint in the synagogues of the Greek speaking Jews. His work was said to have been extremely literal; its main interest for us lies in the situation which occasioned it. The Septuagint, as we have already noted, was the Bible of the early Christians. As the conflict between the Jews and Christians increased, the Jews welcomed Aquila's translation as a replacement for the Septuagint which they promptly rejected though it, too, had been the product of Jewish translators.[67]

Requirements to Become a Proselyte

Three things were theoretically required of one who would become a proselyte: 1) circumcision; 2) baptism; 3) the offering of a sacrifice at the Temple. For obvious reasons the last could not be required in the Diaspora. But since the only practical effect of this deficiency was to prevent the proselyte from participation in a sacrificial meal should he go to Jerusalem, and the deficiency could at such a time be made up, it was not a live issue. G. F. Moore therefore questions that it should even be classified as a requirement:

The offering of a sacrifice is, thus, not one of the conditions of becoming a proselyte, but only a condition precedent to the exercise of one of the rights which belong to him as a proselyte, namely, participation in a sacrificial meal. As soon as he was circumcised and baptized, he was in full standing in the religious community, having all the legal rights and powers and being subject to all the obligations of the Jew by birth. He had "entered into the covenant."[68]

The argument between Rabbi Eleazer and Rabbi Joshua concerning the relative merits of baptism and circumcision is sometimes taken as evidence that circumcision was not always regarded as necessary to make a proselyte. Eleazer, who was an adherent of the stricter school of Shammai, contended that circumcision alone was sufficient to constitute a proselyte while Joshua in opposition contended that baptism

[67] Cf. Graetz, *History of the Jews,* II, 385–87.
[68] Moore, *Judaism,* I, 332.

alone would suffice.[69] This must be regarded, however, as a theoretical argument and can hardly indicate an actual difference in earlier practice. Nor does the appealing story, told by Josephus of Izates, king of Adiabene, on the Tiber, indicate a relaxing of the rule of circumcision.[70] According to the story Izates was persuaded toward Judaism by a Jewish merchant, Ananias by name, who nevertheless advised against circumcision. Later, one Eleazer arrived from Galilee and persuaded the king that he was violating the very Law which he so much admired in declining to be circumcised. Whereupon he "retired to another room, and sent for a surgeon, and did what was commanded to do." Ananias' argument against Izates' circumcision, however, does not indicate the existence of a practice of receiving proselytes without it. He, rather, was fearful of the consequences for the king—and perhaps for himself as well—of such an act should it become known in the kingdom.

If there had been in Diaspora Judaism any serious tendency to relax the requirement of circumcision, it is difficult to understand the violent controversy which Paul had over the question of circumcising gentile Christian converts, a controversy which occasioned his letter to the Galatians. Furthermore, it appears from the extant evidence that the majority of proselytes were women. This is understandable if circumcision was generally required of men.

God-Fearers

Many were strongly attracted to Judaism, who were unwilling to undergo the painful and often dangerous operation of circumcision. These, sometimes called God-fearers (from Acts 10:2, *passim*), attended the synagogue and followed the so-called Noachian Laws.[71] As important as these people were to the spread of Christianity,

---

[69] See Foakes Jackson and Lake, *The Beginnings of Christianity,* V, 78–79 where the original quotation from a baraita, *Yebamot,* 46a, is given and evaluated. For the opposite conclusion from this same argument see Graetz, *History of the Jews,* 384–85. Epictetus is perhaps not a good authority on Jewish practices but it is interesting that in his reference to proselytes to Judaism he refers only to baptism and seems to know nothing of circumcision. For Epictetus baptism serves as the characteristic rite by which one becomes a Jew. See his *Discourses,* ii, chap. 10.

[70] Josephus, *Ant.,* XX, chap. 2.

[71] *Sanhedrin,* 56 a, "Rabbi Johanan said: 'Seven laws are binding on the descendants of Noah (Gentiles): establishment of courts of justice; blasphemy

too much has often been made of their position in the synagogues. Terms applied to them such as God-fearers or proselytes of the gate— especially the latter—cannot be taken in any technical sense. Any pious person whether Jew, proselyte, or faithful gentile could be called a God-fearer. That this phrase was used of such gentiles is apparent, but it did not indicate any status or official recognition. .

The significance for Judaism of such gentile admirers of Judaism is better indicated by Juvenal's bitter description of the way Judaism attracted gentile followers the burden of which is that the father goes so far as to worship only the clouds and the divinity of heaven, abstains from eating pork, and observes the sabbath; but the son goes farther and, having submitted to circumcision, flouts the laws of Rome in favor of the laws of Moses. The father, Juvenal said, was to blame by observing the sabbath.[72] Undoubtedly many proselytes came into Judaism in this way. Josephus, writing in Rome, describes the influence of Judaism on the gentiles in somewhat exaggerated terms, to be sure, but he must have had considerable basis in fact for saying that

the multitude of mankind itself have had a great inclination of long time to follow our religious observances; for there is not any city of the Grecians, nor of any of the barbarians, nor any nation whatsoever, whither our custom of resting on the seventh day hath not come, and by which our fasts and lighting up lamps, and many of our prohibitions as to our food, are not observed . . . as God himself pervades all the world, so hath our law passed through all the world also. . . . For though we should not be able to understand the excellency of our own laws, yet would the great multitude of those that desire to imitate them, justify us in greatly valuing ourselves upon them.[73]

---

prohibition; prohibition of the worship of other gods, of murder, of incest and adultery, of theft and robbery, and of eating the flesh of a living animal before it dies.' " (Newman, *The Talmudic Anthology*, p. 303.). The obedience of these laws, which tradition says were revealed to Noah, would bring salvation to the gentile, according to Jewish teaching. They have frequently been compared to the "apostolic decrees" in Acts 15:28–29. Possibly they were in the mind of Paul when he wrote Romans 1:19–32, especially verse 32.

[72] *Satirae*, 14, 96. See M. S. Enslin, *Christian Beginnings*, pp. 97–98. Also Foakes Jackson and Lake, *The Beginnings of Christianity*, I, 167 and V, 88–89.

[73] *Against Apion*, II, 39. Josephus also quotes Strabo as saying "that Egypt . . . and a great number of other nations imitate their (the Jews) way of living." *Ant.*, XIV, 7, 2 (Whiston's translation). Cf. Plutarch, *Superstition*,

The phrase, "those that desire to imitate them," may not altogether refer to the gentiles on the fringe of the synagogue, but may point to the syncretistic cults which modeled themselves after the pattern of the synagogue but omitted circumcision and other such distinctly Jewish practices.[74] The rise of such movements in an age so characterized by religious syncretism as the first century A.D. should not surprise us.

The importance for the spread of Christianity of these groups of gentiles, enamored of Judaism but unwilling to take the final steps of circumcision, renouncing all their family and social ties, and binding themselves to share the uncertain fortunes of the Jews, is not difficult to see. When Paul came preaching the good news of the fulfillment of the hope which they had learned from their Jewish teachers and declared that the old legal requirements for membership in the Messianic age, i.e., circumcision,[75] had been set aside by Christ, his message found a ready response among many of the pious, God-fearing gentiles (Cf. Eph. 2:11-18). Soon Judaism came to look on Christianity as another and more dangerous syncretistic cult—more dangerous because it drew to itself not only these pious gentiles but also many faithful Jews as well.

Pharisaical Judaism

We have come now to the point where we may profitably summarize this survey of Pharisaical Judaism and add some general observations concerning the place of the Pharisees in the Jewish Commonwealth.

✴ The Pharisees, as we have seen, were the legitimate heirs of the pietism that arose in the Exile and eventuated in the Hasidim who

---

where he classes sabbath-keeping among the superstitions of the Greeks which he deplores.

[74] On the evidence for the existence of such cults see Foakes Jackson and Lake, *The Beginnings of Christianity*, V, 88–96.

[75] Failure to share in the Messianic age did not necessarily mean they were completely lost; they might still share in the World-to-come. "The righteous among the Gentiles will have a share in the World-to-Come." *Yalhut Shimeoni, Prophets*, Section 296, quoted from Newman, *The Talmudic Anthology*, p. 302. See Foakes Jackson and Lake, *The Beginnings of Christianity*, I, 165–66. However, Jewish thought on such matters was by no means uniform or consistent. It is all too easy to discover a system of thought here that did not actually exist. Also Moore, *Judaism*, I, 108.

figured so prominently in the Maccabean revolt. Their history is inexorably bound up with both the study of the Torah and the development of the Oral Law which became the foundation of the Talmudic
and Midrashic literature. Representing as they did the urban middle
class rather than the wealthy aristocrats, they became the popular,
dominant party in Judaism. They were heirs, too, of the Sopherim,
Ezra and his successors, and thus their leaders early became the official
teachers and interpreters of the Torah. Both the Sages, who produced
the Wisdom Literature, and the Apocalyptists arose from their sphere
of influence. The synagogues were essentially their institution. Although
the Diaspora understandably displayed the influence of its environment
and was, in consequence, less strict and exclusive, it came within the
orbit of Pharisaical Judaism.

The Place of the Pharisees in   Our actual knowledge of
Judaism   the structure and divisions
                                       within Judaism in the New
Testament period, unfortunately, is considerably less than we could
wish, as Professor Enslin reminds us.[76] It is easy for a modern student
to ascribe to the Pharisees a homogeneity which they did not possess.
That there were differences among them on quite basic levels is evident, for example, in the well-known running dispute between the
schools of Hillel and Shammai. We have noted one aspect of this dispute over the different theories of interpretation between Akiba and
Ishmael. Evidence for other wide divergences of ideas and points of
view are not wanting.

It may be going too far to call them a sect; certainly in our modern
sense the term is inappropriate. The word party—or movement—is
safer. The fact that, after the Fall of Jerusalem (70 A.D.) the Sadducees
disappeared and similarly the Zealots after the disastrous rebellion of
Bar Cochba (132–135 A.D.), and that a virile and widespread Judaism
survived, thanks to the Pharisees, indicates how broad and representative the movement was. That it could embrace such opposites as the
Wisdom writers on the one hand and the Apocalypticists on the other,

[76] Enslin, *Christian Beginnings,* p. 111.

the extreme literalists hanging on every word and letter of the Torah, and the allegorists of Alexandria, should occasion no surprise. Indeed such an individual as Paul could reflect the influence of all of these opposites!

From the moment the prophetic movement appeared in Israel such a development of parties and further divisions within parties was inevitable. When the emphasis shifted from the nation as a corporate unit with the king at its head for good or ill, as is the picture in the books of Samuel and Kings, to the importance of faithfulness and piety of the individual Israelite, the foundation for Pharisaism was laid. From the Exile on, therefore, as we have seen, the pious applied themselves to the Law in order to become a part of the righteous remnant in the end of time when God should bring to final fulfillment His promise to Abraham. Nor was the doctrine of the remnant, so important to the party divisions of Judaism, purely theoretical. Whether in Isaiah's formulation (cf. 1:25 f., 7:3 and 8:16 *passim*) or that of later prophets such as Zechariah (cf. 13:8–9 where the proportion of the faithful to the rest of Israel is attempted) the doctrine was an expression of the observable difference between the pious faithful whose trust and obedience to God distinguished them from the rest. Such, in brief, is the story of the Pharisees as it emerges from our historical survey.

Josephus on the Jewish "Sects"   Thus far we have taken little notice of the distinctive ideas of the Pharisees other than their passionate devotion to the Torah and their industry in its interpretation and application reflected in the growth of the Oral Law. For these ideas it will be helpful to compare the Pharisees at certain salient points with other movements within Judaism.

Our most extensive source of information on the Pharisees, in fact on the several parties and movements in Judaism in the New Testament period, is Josephus. In two extended passages and in several shorter scattered references throughout his writings, he describes the "philosophical sects," as he chooses to call them, as consisting of three principal ones, the Pharisees, Sadducees, and Essenes. To this he adds a "fourth philosophy" in one account.[77] Elsewhere he also mentions the Zealots who probably are to be associated with the "fourth philosophy."

Josephus is not, however, to be taken uncritically. In the first place, he manifestly used terms and descriptions which would not only be meaningful to his Graeco-Roman readers but would place Judaism and Jewish history in the most favorable light possible. When he described, for example, the Pharisees as "of kin to the sect of the Stoics," he sheds a great deal more light on his purpose and method than on the Pharisees.[78] Secondly, his own standing and relationship to Judaism would account for some of his bias of which the reader should be aware. Born of a priestly family, Josephus was something of an adventurer. He tells us that he tried all three of the sects he describes and apparently concluded by remaining with the Pharisees. His estimates of them, nevertheless, are not always either consistent or complimentary.[79] Perhaps the inevitable criticism of his role in the Jerusalem siege may have had something to do with this. The Pharisee manifested, on the other hand, enough inconsistencies to warrant much of this criticism, but taking these cautions into account, we would be immeasurably impoverished without the writings of Josephus.

The Pharisees   As we have already observed, the character of

[77] The earliest of these is in *Wars*, II, chap. 8. Curiously the bulk of the chapter is devoted to the Essenes though Josephus himself appears to have been a Pharisee. The second extended reference is in *Ant.*, XVIII, chap. 1. Here his treatment is more balanced. Although he proposes to describe the three philosophies he concludes with a description of the "fourth philosophy." Other references are: Josephus, *Wars*, I, 5; *Ant.*, XIII, 5, 9; 10, 6; 15, 5; XVII, 2, 4; *Life*, 2; 38; 39. On the Zealots see *Wars*, II, 8, 1; IV, 3, 9.

[78] Josephus, *Life*, 2. His appropriation of the name Flavius in recognition of his indebtedness to the Flavian Emperors, Vespasian and Titus, indicates something of his pro-Roman bias.

[79] See Josephus, *Ant.*, XVII, 2, 4: "A cunning sect they were, and soon elevated to a pitch of open fighting and doing mischief." (Whiston's translation). (Cf. *Ant.*, XVIII, 1, 3, where he speaks of "their entire virtuous conduct.") It is worthy of note that, although in principle the Pharisees were pacifists and generally stood aloof from political involvements, in their relations with Herod in this passage, in their bloody vengeance for her husband's atrocities in the reign of Alexandra, and the almost tyrannical power they exercised in her reign, they demonstrated how conveniently they could forget principles.

Pharisaism takes its rise from the attachment of the Pharisees to the Law. Josephus says they were "most skillful in exact explication" thereof. It has also been noted that they had "many observances by succession from their fathers, which are not written in the law of Moses." From this preoccupation with Scripture and tradition arose several other characteristic beliefs.

Josephus rather strangely emphasizes fate as the distinguishing doctrine among the three "philosophies." That they used such a term is very doubtful. This term is his concession to his gentile readers. It is clear that the Pharisees saw in the course of history the hand of divine Providence working toward a blessed period of peace and prosperity for Israel. Yet their insistence on human responsibility led them to hold these opposites in a rather precarious balance. God has determined human dispositions which, whether good or evil, ultimately accomplish His purpose. Man is at some points, nevertheless, free and fully responsible. His actions are "liable to fate" but are not so caused. This doctrine of the Divine control of history is of particular interest because of Paul's struggle with it in Romans, chapters 9–11.

The New Testament both confirms and corrects Josephus in describing the Pharisaical emphasis on the after-life. Probably Josephus' ambiguous description of souls passing over "into other bodies" may be taken as an attempt to make the doctrine of physical resurrection intelligible to the gentile mind. It is noteworthy that on this point he contrasts the Pharisees and the Essenes. At any rate, it is instructive to compare Josephus here with I Corinthians, chapter 15.[80] The New Testament makes it clear that the resurrection was one of the basic bones-of-contention between the Pharisees and the Sadducees. The Pharisaical pattern of rewards and punishments in the after-life reflects strong apocalyptic influence.

In addition to these main characteristics, Josephus ascribes to the Pharisees several other interesting traits. They "are friendly to one another, and are for the exercise of concord and regard for the pub-

---

[80] It should be noted in this connection that there is a profound difference between the notion of a resurrection and that of immortality. The latter is an inherent quality of the soul which becomes manifest upon its release from the prison of the body. The resurrection, on the other hand, results from an act of God at the end of the age.

lic." This recalls Paul's frequent admonitions concerning the Christians' duty to love one another and responsibility before the world (cf. Romans 13:1–10). They sometimes claimed special foreknowledge by Divine inspiration. Their predictions apparently occasionally went awry. They espoused a simple way of life, particularly in their diet. As is apparent from their voluminous and meticulous interpretations of Scripture, they were highly intellectual and, as Josephus claims, "ardent followers of reason." Though reason, from their point of view, was something quite different from the Greek philosophical use of the term. For them it was a way of mining from Divinely-given Scriptures the truths contained therein, rather than the deduction of universal ideas from observing the natural order.

The great popular influence of the Pharisees to which Josephus testifies has already been noted. Though this was sometimes abused, for the most part it was a vital creative religious influence. They controlled religious customs to such an extent that even where the Sadducees were in control they found it expedient to follow the directions of the Pharisees. For the most part the Pharisaism that appears to us in these ancient writings was a lay movement, yet Josephus mentions several members of the party who were priests.

Although Edersheim's elaborate picture of the Pharisees as a highly organized sect with rules of membership very much like those of the Essenes may be overdrawn, we should distinguish between the active minority, (Josephus in *Ant.*, XVII, 2, 4 numbers them at 6,000.) usually called the *Haberim* (Associates) and the far larger number of their followers and sympathizers.[81] It is within the inner circle that Paul unquestionably belongs.

The Sadducees   The New Testament and Josephus unite in picturing the Sadducees by contrasting them with the Pharisees. They recognized only the Written Law. Whether this means that they rejected the Prophets as well or only the Oral Law is not clear. The Torah itself

[81] Edersheim, *The Life and Times of Jesus the Messiah*, I, 311–12. Edersheim's evidence, as his references indicate, is drawn from the Talmud. Also Finkelstein, *Pharisees*, II, 573. Cf. the caution in Enslin, *Christian Beginnings*, pp. 109–10.

cannot have had the profound meaning and application for them it had for the Pharisees. Hence they saw no need to interpret and elaborate it as did the latter. Most prominent among the differences between them, of course, was on the resurrection. The Sadducees believed that "souls die with the bodies." Retribution, in consequence, is confined to the fortunes, good or ill, in this life. In terms of Josephus' favorite basis of comparison, they denied the existence of fate and "suppose that God is not concerned in our doing or not doing what is evil." Man is therefore a free agent to do good or evil as he chooses. Josephus adds that they are not friendly to one another but behave toward one another in a barbarous fashion. Further, they were confined to a few wealthy nobles and were "able to persuade none but the rich." This last indicates not only their place in Jewish society but also conforms to their pro-Roman political bias, for which they were so unpopular with the Jewish populace in general.

The Essenes   It is evident that, although Josephus was not a member, he had the greatest admiration for the Essenes. Perhaps his emphasis on this monastic sect was due to the affinity it had for the ascetic strain so well known in Greek thought. Since the Essenes lie somewhat outside the range of our concern and their beliefs have been brought into prominence by the recent discussions of the Dead Sea scrolls, we need only note a few general characteristics.[82] In all probability they originated with the Hasidim as an extreme wing of the piety which produced Pharisaism.[83] Their extreme asceticism, their celibacy (except for one branch which married for purposes of procreation only), their doctrines concerning the evil and transiency of matter, their belief that pleasure is evil, and their doctrine of immortality, show remarkable similarities to Greek ideas. If Josephus is to be believed, they rejected in fact the Pharisaical idea of the resurrection in favor of an essentially

[82] For a valuable comparison of the new information on the Essenes from the Scrolls with that from the classical sources see Frank M. Cross Jr., *The Ancient Library of Qumran and Modern Biblical Studies* (Garden City, New York: Doubleday & Company, Inc., 1958), pp. 52–79. As yet there is little or no evidence for any direct influence of the Essenes on Paul. See footnotes 41 and 46 in chap. VIII.

[83] See Finkelstein, *Pharisees*, II, 573; Graetz, *History of the Jews*, II, 16–17.

Greek theory of immortality of the soul. In terms of Josephus' favorite criterion, they were thorough-going fatalists in contrast to the milder position of the Pharisees and the rejection of fate altogether by the Sadducees. Like the Pharisees they were preoccupied with the study of the Scriptures, but on the other hand they substituted their own sacrifices for those of the Temple.

The Zealots   The "Fourth Philosophy," according to Josephus, was in beliefs and religious practice like the Pharisees except for their attachment "to liberty." Enslin calls them "the Home Rule Party."[84] It seems evident that they are to be identified with the Zealots in the time of the great revolt led by John of Gischala in 66 A.D. They were in reality the spiritual heirs of the Maccabees as W. R. Farmer has ably demonstrated.[85] Their main objective seems to have been to wrest Palestine from foreign control, claiming that their only ruler was God.

The "Sects" and the Hope of   Each of these groups stood
Israel   in a particular relationship to the hope of Israel, and it will be helpful for their understanding to compare their aims.

The Sadducees in control of the high priesthood and standing in a closer political relationship to the Roman overlords seem to have had little stomach for eschatological aspirations. They were the conservatives, concerned largely to preserve the *status quo*. The Pharisees, on the contrary, were deeply interested in the deliverance of Israel and sought to promote a righteousness worthy of the "new age." A later rabbinic saying may well reflect their thinking on the matter: "If Israel would properly observe a single Sabbath, the Son of David would come immediately."[86] The Essene movement appears to have been simply a more extreme version of this same concern. The Zealots, on the other hand, were more impatient. More Messianic in the strict sense of the word they sought by force of arms to return the rule of

---

[84] Enslin, *Christian Beginnings*, p. 126.

[85] W. R. Farmer, *Maccabees, Zealots and Josephus* (New York: Columbia University Press, 1956), esp. ch. VIII, 175–204.

[86] *Shemot Rabbah*, 25, 16. Quoted from Newman, *The Talmudic Anthology*, p. 396.

Palestine to the Jews and to realize the ancient dream of a restored monarchy brought back with the returning Exiles (cf. Haggai 2:23). Thus they would bring to reality the long awaited Golden Age of Israel; the Divine Promise to Abraham would at last be fulfilled.

An Appraisal   In modern speech the word Pharisee is synonymous with hypocrite. As a result of this unfortunate usage, which stems from the sharp denunciations of Pharisees in the Gospels, a very distorted idea of Pharisaism has arisen. In the Gospels it is not theoretical Pharisaism that is condemned, but that element within the movement which, like similar elements in every other religious movement, fell pitifully short of its pretensions and profession. An ancient Baraita classified the Pharisees in seven categories:

1) Shoulder Pharisees—they wear their good deeds ostentatiously on their shoulders.

2) Wait-a-little Pharisee—wait until I have done the good deed awaiting me.

3) Bruised Pharisee—who runs into a wall to avoid looking at a woman (cf. Matthew 5:28).

4) Pestle Pharisee—who walks with his head down like a pestle in a mortar.

5) Ever-reckoning Pharisee—let me know what good I may do to counteract my neglect.

6) God-fearing Pharisee—like Job.

7) God-loving Pharisee—like Abraham.[87]

It is apparent that Pharisees themselves were quite as aware as were Jesus and the early Christians of the shortcomings of their own party.

The effective vital force in Judaism came from the Pharisees. Although they remained aloof for the most part from politics and opposed armed resistance to Roman rule, they were in close touch with the people and earnestly sought to provide a progressive, intellectual religious leadership.[88]

This is the heritage of Paul and a noble heritage it is. The marks of

---

[87] Singer, *The Jewish Encyclopedia*, IX, 665. Cf. Moore, *Judaism*, I, 35–36, for an appreciation of the true spirit of Pharisaism.

[88] Moore, *Judaism*, I, 77.

this heritage remain on every page of his letters. If this chapter seems overlong and has ranged over a wide area it has sought thereby to comprehend something of the meaning of Paul's significant boast, "as to the law a Pharisee" (Philippians 3:5). To do so is to take the first and most important step toward understanding him.

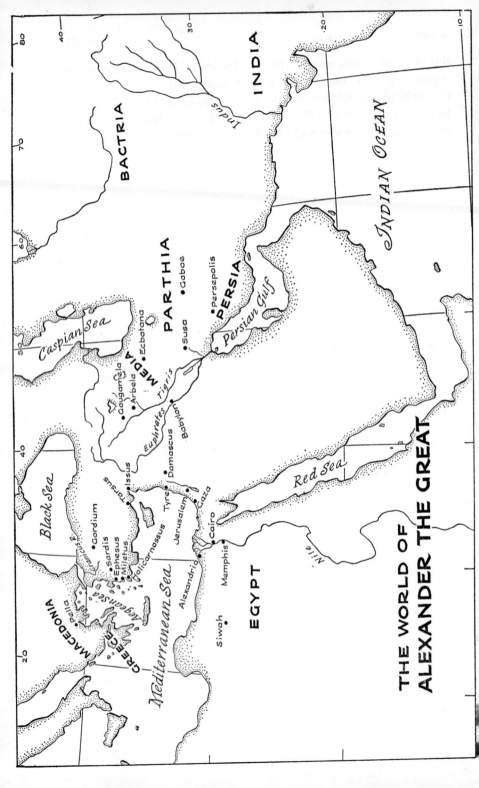

THE WORLD OF
ALEXANDER THE GREAT

4 GReeks seek wisdom...

For Jews demand signs and Greeks seek wisdom.
(I Corinthians 1:22)

If Paul was a Pharisee by birth and training, he nevertheless belonged as a Diaspora Jew to a far larger world. From the standpoint of interpreting his letters, therefore, our task in this chapter is to describe the life and religious environment of that part of the Mediterranean world known as the Levant, more particularly, Asia Minor and the Aegean area. The latter, including Ionia (in Acts called Asia, its Roman provincial name), Macedonia and Greece (or Achaea as it was known in Roman times), was predominantly the location of Paul's ministry. Most, if not all, of his letters either originated here or were addressed to churches located in this area. We must now turn to this complex Mediterranean East.

"Greeks seek wisdom." In so short a phrase Paul comprehended the character of Greek culture. Philosophy, the love of wisdom, was the Greek's gift to the world, but it was not to Athens nor to the Greek peninsula that Paul referred in using the word Greek. Though in this instance he was writing to Corinth, one of the ancient and most important of the Greek cities, he was using the term in the general way he always used it to refer to the culture of the world he knew. He was a Roman citizen, but he never used the word "Roman" in a cultural sense. He speaks of barbarians, as Greeks would, meaning the peoples who remained unassimilated in the dominant Hellenistic culture, and therefore, from the Greek point of view, were backward and inferior. Our interest in the Roman Empire, in consequence, is secondary and concerned mostly with the ways in which Rome affected the Levant in the course of extending its Empire to include the East. We have to do, then, primarily with that amalgam of Greek and oriental cultures which, for convenience, it is customary to call Hellenistic. The term, while not altogether a happy one, is used to distinguish this latter culture—the result of widespread Greek influence throughout the East—from the older Hellenic culture of classical Greece.

Among the empire builders of history Alexander the Great and Augustus Caesar stand out above all the rest. The world of Paul was the legacy of these two men, for the culture of the Levant was the legacy of the former and its political structure the work of the latter. Their stories will help us understand this part of Paul's background.

Alexander and the Rise of Hellenism

The Age of Pericles, the golden age of Greece, had ended in the internecine strife of the Peloponnesian Wars. In the period that followed, Greece bequeathed the world her greatest and most lasting gifts. In the succession of Socrates, Plato and Aristotle, Greek philosophy came to full flower. Thereby it was assured for all time a place of first magnitude in the world of thought. In this same period occurred a series of events that forever changed the map of the world and prepared it for the form it was to take as the eastern end of the Roman Empire.

Taking advantage of the weakness and division of the Greek city states after the Peloponnesian Wars, Philip II, of Macedon, brought the Greeks under his rule and, except for Sparta, brought to them a unity before unknown in their history. It was the end of the era of the city states. Ironically this barbarian—for so they regarded the Macedonians even though ethnically they were Greeks—not only was the first to solve the problem of Greek unity but to set in motion the events which brought the vengeance against Persia for which they had lusted since the days of Marathon and Thermopylae, and even more, the end of the ever present Persian threat of invasion.

The Conquests of Alexander   In 336 B.C. Philip was murdered, leaving Alexander to make good his claim to the Macedonian throne. In a few bold strokes

Alexander established himself as King of Macedonia, quelled uprisings in Thrace, and confirmed Macedonian leadership in Greece. Within two years he was ready to begin the adventure which was to make him the most fabled conqueror in history.

Crossing the Hellespont in 334 B.C., Alexander won his first engagement with the Persian armies led by the Greek mercenary, Memnon, at Granicus River. Moving south along the Ionian coast, he set the Greek cities of Asia Minor free, settling old scores between the Greeks and the Persians. Later at Issus, in the Cilician area east of Tarsus, Alexander for the first time encountered Darius III. When the battle turned against him, Darius fled, leaving his family and possessions in the hands of Alexander. The march of conquest now turned south to include Tyre, Gaza, and Egypt.

After establishing his rule in Palestine and Egypt and founding the city of Alexandria in the Egyptian Delta, Alexander turned back north to continue his march toward the heart of the Persian Empire.

At Gaugamela in the upper Tigris valley, as Plutarch is at pains to point out,[1] Alexander and Darius met for the decisive battle. Defeated, Darius again fled and again Alexander declined to pursue. Not until after he had marched on Babylon, Susa, and Persepolis did he turn north toward Ecbatana to take up the pursuit of Darius. Turning east near the southern end of the Caspian Sea, he came upon the body of the murdered Darius. The Persian Empire ended and with it an age was closed. History was moving into a new era.

A wide circuit through India brought Alexander, so he believed, near the Great Ocean and the eastern extremity of the world. The refusal of his troops to go any farther prevented him from discovering his geographical error. He would have made an equally astonishing discovery had he succeeded in carrying out his resolution to sail from the Persian Gulf around Africa and enter the Mediterranean through the Straits of Gibraltar![2] Returning to Mesopotamia through southern Persia, Alexander contracted a fever and died in June of 323 B.C. His empire in a sense died with him. Yet in a dozen short years he had cut so deeply across old boundaries and through established institutions as

[1] Plutarch, *Alexander*, XXXI, 3.
[2] Plutarch, *Alexander*, LXVIII, 1.

to leave the old world beyond recovery. He had bridged the Hellespont; and across that bridge Paul was one day to move to plant Christianity firmly in the Western world.

The Successors The story of the break-up of Alexander's empire and the struggles which eventuated in the Hellenistic kingdoms which Rome found upon her invasions of the East need occupy us only briefly. The untimely death of Alexander left his empire without any provision for a successor. Almost immediately a struggle for power arose among his generals (known as the *Diadochi,* Successors) which resulted in cutting the empire into pieces and finally in the murder of Roxane, Alexander's Iranian wife, and the son whom she bore Alexander after his death.

In Central Asia Minor some semblance of order appeared after the battle of Ipsus (301 B.C.) succeeded in eliminating Antigonus whose wars were calculated to regain the whole empire for himself. The Seleucid dynasty in Syria and the Ptolemaic dynasty in Egypt remained established until Roman times. The establishment of a stable dynasty in Macedonia was brought about by an event which will have importance for us because of its connection with the vexing question of the destination of one of Paul's letters.

In 279 B.C. a horde of Celtic peoples migrating from Gaul invaded both the Greek peninsula and Asia Minor. The Macedonian King was killed, and the invaders penetrated deeply into Greece before the last of them were beaten back by Antigonus Gonatas. The popularity accruing to Antigonus because of his role in defeating the Galatians resulted in establishing his dynasty in Macedonia. These three dynasties persisted until one by one their territories were taken over and reorganized into provinces by Rome. The Galatians, as they became known, finally settled in an area in northern Asia Minor west of Cappadocia which remained the kingdom of Galatia until it was combined with a strip of territory to the south to become the Roman province of Galatia. The struggle between Syria and Egypt over the control of Palestine which ended with the independence of the latter under the Maccabees has been described in the previous chapter.

The Greeks under Alexander and his successors had succeeded in doing what the Persians under Darius and Xerxes had failed to do.

They had successfully crossed the Hellespont and bridged the East and West. The two great power blocs threatening each other across the Aegean Sea were dissolved into the smaller and more closely related competing units of the new Hellenistic world. Thus the whole aspect of both political and cultural affairs in the Levant was changed. With Alexander oriental despotism came to an end except as elements of it appeared in the rule of the Successors.

Characteristics of the Hellenistic World   Exactly what Alexander had in mind when he started on the road of conquest is difficult to guess. His father, Philip II, had entertained the ambition to invade Persian territory—doubtless to avenge the ancient Persian invasions—to free the Greek cities of Ionia, and to remove the Persian threat. Surely the realization of his father's ambition was an element in Alexander's thought, but there was more to it than that. The sizeable company of observers, scientific and historical, which he took with him, reveal Alexander's expedition as much more of an adventure than a mere campaign of vengeance or conquest. The idealistic dream of one world uniting barbarian and Greek, which is sometimes attributed to him, is probably reading too much into the story. We must remember he was a pupil of Aristotle—his most illustrious. And from Aristotle he learned only to despise all barbarian cultural attainments. Plutarch wrote:

For Alexander did not follow Aristotle's advice to treat the Greeks as if he were their leader and other peoples as if he were their master [despot].[3]

Certainly one of his motives was a profound curiosity, as though he would test Aristotle's teachings by actual observation. Probably, too —and this shows itself clearly in some of his successors—he was possessed of a "missionary" zeal for the spread of Greek culture and learning. The impression left by Plutarch's account, at any rate, is that Alexander's ambitions enlarged and changed as one achievement after

[3] *On the Fortune of Alexander*, 329. Reprinted by permission of the publishers and The Loeb Classical Library from Plutarch, *Moralia*, trans. Frank Cole Babbitt (Cambridge, Mass.: Harvard University Press, 1936), IV, 397.

another crowned his ventures. His estrangement from Aristotle in later years and his adoption of the dress and manners of the oriental court indicate a growing appreciation of Persian culture. The famous episode of the marriages of his Macedonian generals to Persian women at Susa represents some attempt to weld Eastern and Western peoples into a new cosmopolitan civilization.

Whatever may have been his purposes, the effect of Alexander's conquests was to turn the stream of history into a new direction that was to leave its impress on events for centuries. The immediate effect was to spread a veneer of Greek culture throughout the East. This was to be seen mostly in and around the numerous Greek cities and colonies which he left in his wake. Plutarch wrote, perhaps rather too enthusiastically:

> But Alexander established more than seventy cities among savage tribes and sowed all Asia with magistracies, and thus overcame its uncivilized and brutish manner of living.[4]

Contacts between the Greeks and Eastern peoples had been occurring in a limited way for generations, particularly in matters of religion.[5] Several foreign deities had been naturalized and became established elements in Greek religion. On the other hand, a Greek traveling abroad would feel it quite proper to pay homage to the gods in the cities he visited. Furthermore, foreign residents in the Greek cities brought their deities with them.[6]

In other ways also the Greeks were not in complete ignorance of Eastern cultures. The Ionian cities on the west coast of Asia Minor knew painfully well the strength of Persian military conquests. Trade and commerce which had for many years been on the increase brought many contacts both by sea and land. The Greeks and Phoenicians found themselves in competition on the Mediterranean and the well developed Persian system of roads brought overland traffic from the

---

[4] *Ibid.*, 328, p. 395.

[5] For a good summary of the religious situation in Greece before Alexander see A. D. Nock, *Conversion* (Oxford: Clarendon Press, 1933), ch. II, 18-32. Also Pfeiffer, *History of New Testament Times*, pp. 127-33.

[6] A. D. Nock, *Conversion*, p. 20.

far east. Natural curiosity as well as commerce had taken Greeks on adventurous journeys in the East. Herodotus is a classical example of this, and the fascinating digressions in his *Histories* provide a picture of the interest and fascination which the East held for the Greek.

The Greek's heart, nevertheless, remained in his home city. To be sure, Greek colonies, particularly in the West, had been established as early as the eighth century B.C., but for the most part the Greek away from home, like Homer's Odysseus, longed to return to his own.

With Alexander these contacts received tremendous impetus and assumed a new character. World citizenship (*Oikoumene*) began to replace the older, narrower loyalties to the city states of Greece. The economic straits at home, and new opportunities for wealth, adventure and status abroad stimulated migrations of the Greeks to the numerous colonies of the East. Oriental peoples in their turn were swept into the stream of Hellenism.

Under the rule of "the Great King" of Persia the various nations which went to make up the old Empire had undergone little assimilation. So long as the regularly assessed taxes were collected, the trade routes open, and her borders secure, Persia was content to allow her possessions a large measure of autonomy, and in matters of religion virtually complete freedom. Under Persia the Jews, for example, were entirely free to practice unmolested their exclusive monotheism. As their essential identities were discovered, local gods were given the names of Olympian deities. Usually this resulted in little or no change in the character of the worship or beliefs involved. In the Greek settlements throughout the East Greek art and architecture became the models for widespread imitation.

The bridge over the Hellespont erected by Alexander, however, carried traffic in both directions. As the gods of the East were renamed after Greek divinities, so the renamed gods made their way into Greece to be worshiped along with the native ones. Luke's comment in Acts 17:21 is characteristic:

Now all the Athenians and the foreigners who lived there spent their time in nothing except telling or hearing something new.

Nor did philosophy escape oriental influence. The great age of Plato was over and very little of the profundities of Greek metaphysical speculation found its way into the Hellenistic world. Meanwhile astrology and moralistic ideas of the East became more and more popular. It is significant that Stoicism, the most popular and influential school of philosophy in this period—one which was to find great favor in high circles in Imperial Rome—was founded by Zeno, a Semite from Cyprus, who came to Athens to study and then remained to teach.

Economically the new world was one of increasing prosperity. The already good system of roads was expanded. Vastly increased trade brought new contacts and new knowledge, and hence, new wants which in turn created new markets. Thus, international travel became easier and more common. A world in which Paul could dream of carrying his Gospel to the whole world was rapidly developing.

One of the most obvious effects of Hellenism, and one most important for our purposes, was the spread of the Greek tongue. Throughout the Levant Greek became the common language of communication as well as literature. Naturally it underwent changes. Local dialects tended to melt into a common tongue which was further modified by idioms of other languages of the peoples who adopted it. The result was what we know as koine (Greek: common) which is the language of Paul and of the New Testament. The appearance of the Hebrew Scriptures in koine (the Septuagint) in the second and first centuries B.C. indicates how widely it had been adopted. Throughout the Hellenistic world an itinerant philosopher or a Christian missionary would thus encounter little difficulty with the language barrier.[7] As time went on even the Latin world was invaded by koine Greek. It is said that the first real Greek grammar was written in the time of Pompey by

---

[7] The picture of the Hellenization of the Levant, however, can be easily overdrawn. What is said here applies mainly to the urban areas and the upper classes. In the rural areas and among the lower class the old native religions, languages and cultures often stubbornly resisted assimilation. On this William M. Ramsay wrote: "The efforts of Rome to naturalize Western culture in Asia Minor were more successful than those of the Greek kings had been; but still they worked at best very slowly. The evidence of inscriptions tends to show that the Phrygian language was used in rural parts of the country during the second and even the third century. In some remote and rustic districts it persisted even until the fourth century, as Celtic did in parts of North Galatia." William Ramsay, *St. Paul the Traveller and the Roman Citizen*, reprinted from the Third Edition, 1897 (Grand Rapids, Michigan: Baker Book House, 1960), p. 132.

Dionysius Thrax for the purpose of teaching Greek to his Roman pupils.[8] That Paul wrote his letter to the Roman Christians in Greek is significant of more than his disinclination to write Latin.[9]

As the world grew larger the individual grew smaller and less significant. As loyalties to the smaller social units of the city-states gave way to the new cosmopolitan spirit the individual found himself adrift on a vast sea of humanity. The new world was too vast and heterogeneous to command the kind of loyalty in which, in the smaller communities of earlier times, the individual had found his meaning and significance. The new problems thus created called forth important and far-reaching changes in philosophy and religion. These we shall survey later in this chapter.

Many of these changes were brought about naturally by the enthusiasm for things Greek generated by the presence of the Greek colonies in the East. That there was also conscious effort on the part of Greeks to bring about such changes is evident. The Greek went forth under the firm conviction that he represented all that was worthy of being called civilization. The very word, barbarian, by which he described all other peoples expressed this attitude. It was the peculiar intransigence of the Jews that probably occasioned the outrageously violent methods of Antiochus Epiphanes in his attempt to convert the Jews to Hellenism. For other peoples, whose religious scruples did not prevent them from adding another god or so to their devotional list, or who did not mind renaming their own deities according to their apparent Greek counterparts, such methods were unnecessary. The motives and attitudes of the purveyors of Greek culture elsewhere were not nevertheless basically different from those of Antiochus toward the Jews.

Weaknesses of Hellenism   In spite of the many advances made by the Hellenism of the Diadochi, however, it manifested certain fatal defects which finally brought it to an end and placed the Levant within the Roman Empire.

---

[8] Max Miller, *Lectures on the Science of Language* (New York: Charles Scribner's, 1862), pp. 100–101.
[9] See "Paul's Languages" in chap. 5.

One of these defects was the continuous struggle for power among the various dynasties of Alexander's Successors. The failure of the *Oikoumene,* the one world, to become a reality was in no small measure due to the reappearance of the ancient rivalry, so characteristic of the Greek city-states, in the new world. The drain on the resources of wealth and manpower of the countries involved, the periodic disruption of commerce, the inevitable destruction in the wars, and the increasing unrest and dissatisfaction of the people created a situation into which Rome found itself increasingly and inexorably drawn.

A second and perhaps even more disastrous weakness was the failure of the Greeks and their oriental subjects to form any kind of enduring amalgam. In Egypt, for example, the lot of the native population was little better than serfdom. The regimentation and heavy taxation imposed on the Egyptians by their Greek overlords were bound to create an explosive unrest as they watched the Greeks live in wealth and ease at their expense. Owing to abuses and misrule and the persistent influence of their own religions and cultures, the Oriental's initial enthusiasm for things Greek began to wane. The result was a ground-swell of resistance to the Greek rulers and a return to oriental kings. The Maccabean Revolt and the disappearance of the Hellenistic party represented by such men as Jason and Menelaus are typical. At the same time that Judas Maccabaeus was struggling with the armies of Antiochus Epiphanes to regain possession of the Temple for faithful Jews, Antiochus himself was in Mesopotamia attempting to salvage the east end of his kingdom—an attempt that was foredoomed to failure. The Euphrates became the eastern boundary of the Hellenistic world. Years later, just prior to the arrival of Herod the Great to make good with the help of Roman armies his claim to the throne in Jerusalem, the Parthians under Pacorus actually overran Palestine and enthroned Antigonus in Jerusalem.

The situation was hardly less volatile in Asia Minor. Among the Orientals of Asia Minor, we hear of increasing discontent and occasional revolts led by descendants of the ancient Persian nobility which had thrived there in the days before Alexander the Great. Finally, the ambitious designs of Mithridates VI of Pontus carried him into Greece where Sulla defeated him. Later his interference with the Roman inheritance of Bithynia brought first Lucullus and then Pompey to end his rebellion and place his kingdom under the aegis of Rome.

It must be remembered that Greek settlements in the East were largely limited to cities which they either built or occupied in the course of their conquests. As a result Hellenistic influence beyond those cities was comparatively slight. Outside the Hellenistic cities native uprisings consequently found a ready following among the populace. Thus the veneer of Hellenistic culture in the Near East was revealed to be thin indeed. All too often the rapacity of the Greeks was to blame.

Asia Minor remained, even in Roman times, largely Oriental except in the great cities and along the main trade routes. Yet the Roman settlement brought a stability which advanced the Hellenizing processes in a way that the Greek rulers had been unable to do. It is noteworthy that Paul in his missionary journeys both in Asia Minor and Greece followed the trade routes through the main cities and avoided the by-paths into the more backward and more Oriental hinterland. In this regard Paul must be reckoned among the influences from the East which migrated into the West over Alexander's bridge across the Hellespont, but Paul's journeys took place in a Roman world. We must now turn to the story of the way in which the Roman world came to be.

Augustus and the Roman Empire

From the days that Rome, having won its independence from the Etruscan kings, had extended its control until it included the entire Italian peninsula, it was inevitable that Rome should come into conflict with the Greeks and therefore be drawn into the East. The ephemeral victories of the Greek adventurer Pyrrhus, who invaded Italy early in the third century before Christ, although of no consequence in themselves, mark the beginning of the conflict of Rome with Greek armies and indicate how easily the Romans could become involved in war with the Greeks. The defeat of Pyrrhus brought the old Greek cities on the Italian peninsula under Roman control. The acquisition of Sicily, as a result of the first Punic War (264–241), extended the Roman power to the important Greek city of Syracuse.

Roman Expansion in the East   In 217 B.C. a peace conference seeking to end war
among the Greek Leagues was held at Naupactus. Agelaus, an Aetolian,
pleaded for Greek unity, pointing prophetically to rapid extension of
Roman power as "clouds gathering in the West" which were threatening to settle on Greece. Actually, those "clouds" had already crossed
the Adriatic Sea. Several years before, an affair over the raiding of
Greek cities on the Italian mainland by Illyrian pirates brought Roman
armies into Illyria. Attempts by Philip V of Macedon to expel the
Romans from Illyria resulted in the first and, indirectly, the second
Macedonian Wars. Rome was now irrevocably involved in the affairs
of Greece itself. In the meantime trouble was brewing in the East
which was soon to draw Rome across the Aegean Sea into Asia Minor.
Antiochus the Great (III), the Syrian Ruler who wrested Palestine
from the Ptolemies of Egypt,[10] was attempting a series of conquests
designed to recover for himself as much as possible of Alexander's
empire. These conquests brought him through Asia Minor, Thrace,
and, having established his headquarters at Ephesus, into Macedonia
itself. Antiochus' attempted invasion of Greece was too much for
Rome. He was beaten at Thermopylae, and later in the battle of
Magnesia (189), was driven from Asia Minor as well. Rome now had
a grip on an important part of the Hellenistic world. In many ways
it was a very uncomfortable one—difficult to maintain and dangerous
to let go—but the Greeks had not yet learned the value of unity.
Quarreling factions, each one for his particular cause, had their representatives in Rome to appeal for help.

Eventually Macedonia and Greece were made Roman provinces.
The events which led to the annexation of Macedonia began when
Eumenes II of Pergamum warned Rome that Perseus, son of Philip
V of Macedon, had rallied an anti-Roman faction and was preparing
for war. Rome entered the Third Macedonian War, and in 168 B.C.
Aemitius Paullus defeated Perseus at Pydna. Macedonia was thereupon
divided into four republics, and a number of hostages were taken to
Rome. Because of an abortive rebellion in 148 B.C. the republics were
disbanded and Macedonia became a Roman province. Two years later

---

[10] See "Ezra and the Scribes" in chap. 3.

following a quarrel between Sparta and the Achean League, the Roman Consul Lucius Mummius marched on Corinth, the head of the League. The city was razed and its people sold into slavery. Not until a century later, after Julius Caesar settled some of his veterans there, did Corinth begin to rebuild. Long before Paul entered the city to found a Christian Church, Corinth had won back its commercial importance and much of its old prominence as the leading city of Greece. In the meantime Greece remained under the supervision of the Macedonian Proconsul until, shortly after the resettling of Corinth, it was made into a separate province known as Achea (c. 42 B.C.).

Although Roman armies had pursued Antiochus III to Magnesia near Ephesus, not until Attalus III of Pergamum died in 133, having bequeathed his kingdom to Rome, was Roman territory extended into Asia Minor. After a brief struggle with an uprising, inspired chiefly by oriental resistance to Western rule, Rome annexed the western part of Asia Minor, including ancient Greek Ionia, as the Roman province of Asia. In the references in the New Testament to Asia it is this province which is intended.

To stop the depredations of pirates and brigands on eastern shipping and the trade routes to the East a second province, that of Cilicia in southeast Asia Minor, was annexed before the end of the century. Thus Tarsus, Paul's home city and principal city of Cilicia, became a part of the Roman World.

We have already mentioned the revolt of Mithridates of Pontus. In 66 B.C. Pompey finally vanquished him and added Pontus to Roman territory. In the meantime Nicomedes III of Bithynia, following the example of Attalus of Pergamum willed his kingdom to Rome; upon his death in 74 B.C. it became a province. After the defeat of Mithridates the western part of Pontus was added to the Province of Bithynia. Armenia and Galatia became client-kingdoms under Rome. Pompey then proceeded to Syria, which became a province, and in 63 B.C. took Jerusalem, making all of Palestine Roman territory subject to the supervision of the governor of Syria. John Hyrcanus II became a client-ruler in Jerusalem although his minister, the Idumean, Antipater, wielded the actual power. Roman rule now extended to the Euphrates.

Effects of Roman Invasion   Piece by piece the Hellen-
                                       istic world thus came under
Roman control. With the exception of Egypt and Mesopotamia, which
remained under oriental rule, virtually all of the territory of Alexander's successors came into Roman possession during the Republic.
Roman occupation, while it put an end to the constant power struggles
and petty wars which plagued the East, was not an unmixed blessing.
The taxes in the provinces were farmed out to native publicans whose
extortions were not always successfully resisted by the governors. Indeed, the governors themselves in their short tenure of office were
sometimes not above reproach and frequently managed to enrich themselves handsomely. Moneylenders exacted such exorbitant interest that
in one instance, so Plutarch tells us, although the principal had been
twice repaid, yet the outrageous interest left the balance six times the
amount of the original loan![11] Perhaps worse was the systematic looting
of the country by the armies of the rival generals in their struggle for
power during the civil wars. All of these abuses ravaged the economy
of Greece and Asia Minor and many years were required for even
partial recovery. For a time it appeared that the Greek World had
been rescued from the ravages of warring rulers only to be devoured by
the power-struggles of ambitious Romans.

One major change was needed to bring about the world of Paul:
the founding of the empire by Augustus Caesar. The haphazard growth
of Roman imperialism allowed no proper adjustments of governmental
structure for effective administration of Rome's sprawling territory.
The futility of trying to rule the world with a city government, added
to the declining influence of a decadent aristocracy and other demoralizing influences in the once proud city, worked to collapse the Republic.

Octavian Becomes Augustus   The story of the civil wars
                                    and the rise of Octavian to
power is familiar and need occupy us only briefly. Attempted reforms,
such as those of the Gracchi and Drusus, failed to placate popular unrest in Italy which erupted in the Social War of 90–88 B.C. Sulla and
Pompey were successful in putting down the rebellion. As a result of

[11] *Lucullus*, XX, 4.

this and his victory in the first Mithridatic War two years later, Sulla amassed sufficient prestige and forces to take over the reins of government as dictator. Sulla's reforms, including his remodeled senate proved ephemeral; turmoil and popular unrest continued to increase. Two of Sulla's young lieutenants, Pompey and Crassus, began the series of events which led to the end of the Republic. They served as consuls in 70 B.C. and, in spite of mutual jealousy, joined with Julius Caesar, consul for 59 B.C., to form the First Triumvirate. The arrangement was never intended to last. Each was simply awaiting an opportunity to supersede the others.

Crassus conveniently removed himself from competition by provoking a war with the Parthians in which his armies were slaughtered and he was beheaded. The struggle between Pompey and Caesar came to a head with Caesar's famous crossing of the Rubicon. The enmity behind the devious political maneuvers of Caesar and Pompey had now come into the open. At Pharsalus Pompey's armies were routed, and he fled to Egypt where he was murdered. Having pursued him to Egypt, Caesar continued on into Syria and Asia Minor where he quelled an uprising by Pharnaces of Pontus. Caesar returned to Rome and dictatorship, which ended with his assassination on the Ides of March, 44 B.C.

Instead of restoring the Republic, the assassination of Caesar plunged Rome into renewed chaos and revealed the alarming weakness of the City's entire political structure. In his brief tenure Caesar had instituted a number of reforms which helped to alleviate some of the more pressing immediate problems. Many of these were retained and his further plans were carried out by Mark Antony.

One of his acts, while not new, has especial interest for us. To the many soldiers he had recruited in the provinces as well as to others —sometimes whole communities—who had been valuable to him in his campaigns Caesar extended Roman citizenship. Pompey had done some of this before him and Antony later. It became more and more a standard practice until, in the early part of the third century A.D., something like universal enfranchisement was proclaimed by Caracalla. Roman citizenship, a prized possession originally limited to the City itself, had been extended to include virtually the Italian peninsula at the beginning of the first century B.C. The action of these Roman generals served not only to placate the natural resentment of the provinces against being ruled by a distant city as mere subjects without any political status, but also created a nucleus of loyal citizens distributed among the provinces whose presence helped greatly to strengthen Roman rule and political unity. This extension of citizenship to provincials will concern us again in the discussion of Paul's claim to be a Roman citizen.

One other act of Caesar's should be noted in passing. In consequence of assistance he received from Jewish forces while he was in Egypt, he granted special recognition to the Jews, including the guarantee of respect for their religious scruples and traditions, exemption from military service, and the right to collect the Temple tribute.[12] With the exception of a few instances such as Caligula's mad attempt to place his image in the Temple, this policy was continued by Augustus and the early emperors. Until the time of Nero Christians seem to have been regarded as a Jewish sect and therefore enjoyed similar privileges. Thus Paul enjoyed the double advantage of Jewish privilege and Roman citizenship.

During the chaos that followed the assassination of Caesar, Mark Antony armed with Caesar's papers which contained, among other things, proposals for further legislation to be brought before the Senate asserted his leadership as consul. With the help of Lepidus, Caesar's deputy, who appeared in the city at the head of a Legion, he restored order. Caesar's will in which he named his great-nephew Octavian as his adopted son and heir was read. A short time later Octavian arrived in Rome to claim his inheritance. At first he seemed little threat to Antony, but while the latter was in Cisalpine Gaul, Octavian was elected consul and managed to accumulate power enough to force his attention upon Antony and Lepidus, who were jockeying for power. The result was the Second Triumvirate. While Lepidus guarded things at Rome, Antony and Octavian pursued the assassins, Brutus and Cassius, to Philippi, where they were defeated and committed suicide. Later Lepidus was squeezed out of the Triumvirate; Antony went east to become involved in his well-known affair with Cleopatra; and Oc-

---

[12] Josephus cites a series of documents to this effect in *Ant.*, XIV, chap. 10.

tavian built up his own strength in Rome. The term of the Triumvirate expired and in the "Donations of Alexandria" Antony proposed to give half the Empire to Cleopatra. Octavian took this occasion to arouse Rome to action and declared war. At Actium on the western shore of Greece the forces met. When the battle turned against Antony, Cleopatra fled with her navy and Antony followed. Octavian pursued them to Egypt where they committed suicide. Octavian returned to Rome, reorganized the constitution, nominally at least, restored the Republic and the rule of the Senate, and was promptly given the title of Augustus. In actual fact Augustus, with the armies and treasury at his command, held the power of an Emperor. In being thus restored the Republic was at an end, and the sprawling territories of provinces and client-kingdoms became the Roman Empire. Egypt was annexed; Macedonia and Achaia became senatorial provinces with capitals at Thessalonica and Corinth. In Asia Minor, where the provinces of Asia, Bithynia and Cilicia were already established, further reorganization took place. When the death of the Galatian king Amyntas in 25 B.C. left the territory without a ruler, Augustus created the Province of Galatia including in it, along with the original kingdom of Galatia, in the north, territories to the south as far as the borders of Pamphilia such as Pisidia and part of Lycaonia.[13] In 17 A.D. Tiberius annexed Cappadocia. Thus the Levant took the shape which Paul knew as a Christian missionary.

After Augustus   When in 14 A.D. Augustus died, he was succeeded by his stepson Tiberius whose efficient though autocratic rule made much progress in stabilizing both the political and economic conditions in the Empire. On the death of Tiberius in 37 A.D. Gaius, Augustus' great grandson, more commonly known by his nickname Caligula ("Little Boots"), became Emperor. His successor, Claudius, later branded him as insane. Whether he was or not, he is remembered in religious history

---

[13] Anticipating later discussion of the location of the Galatian churches, it may be worthwhile to note here that this arrangement of the Province of Galatia was not as radical an alteration of geography as it may appear because Amyntas had already held under his kingship considerable territory south of old Galatia including territory which went to make up the Province.

for his unsuccessful attempt to place his statue in the Temple in Jerusalem.

Gaius' highhanded methods in dealing with the Senate got him assassinated in 41 A.D.; whereupon the Praetorian Guard presented his uncle, Claudius, to the Senate as his successor. Claudius was said to have been something of a pedant. *The Pumpkinification of Claudius,* a satire attributed to Seneca, pictured him as a palsied man with a speech impediment whose head was constantly shaking and who dragged his lame right leg as he walked. The picture is undoubtedly overdrawn but there must have been some truth in it.[14] Claudius was, nevertheless, a capable administrator. One event of particular interest to us is his expulsion of Jews from Rome which brought Prisca and Aquila to Corinth. Paul met them there and lived and worked with them during his stay in that city.[15]

Though his critics were merciless and have left a distorted picture of him, Claudius was a vastly superior ruler to his stepson and successor, the infamous play-boy, Nero. The latter, who came to power at the death of Claudius in 54 A.D., had been tutored by the famous Roman stoic, Seneca[16] whose brother, Gallio, came to Corinth as proconsul at the end of Paul's sojourn there.

During the first part of Nero's reign, Seneca was the virtual ruler and things went well. When, however, he was shoved aside in favor of Tigellinus, affairs at Rome degenerated. The profligacy for which Nero is notorious became finally too much for the Senate and he was ordered to commit suicide. Nero is remembered in Christian history for his attempt to implicate the Christians in the burning of Rome and the pogroms which followed, and for the fact that he was the Caesar to whom Paul appealed during his trial under Festus (Acts 25:11–12). As the story of Paul ends in the reign of Nero, we may at this point conclude this survey of the political background to his life and work.

---

[14] *Apocolocyntosis Divi Claudia,* 5.

[15] Suetonius, *Claudius,* 25. Acts 18:1–4.

[16] A fictitious tradition relates Paul and Seneca by a series of correspondence which persuaded St. Jerome to include Seneca among the pious in his *Lives of Illustrious Men,* XII. For a translation of these letters see, M. R. James, *The Apocryphal New Testament* (Oxford, Clarendon Press, 1955), pp. 480–84. Seneca, having been implicated in a plot against the life of Nero, was ordered to commit suicide in 65 A.D.

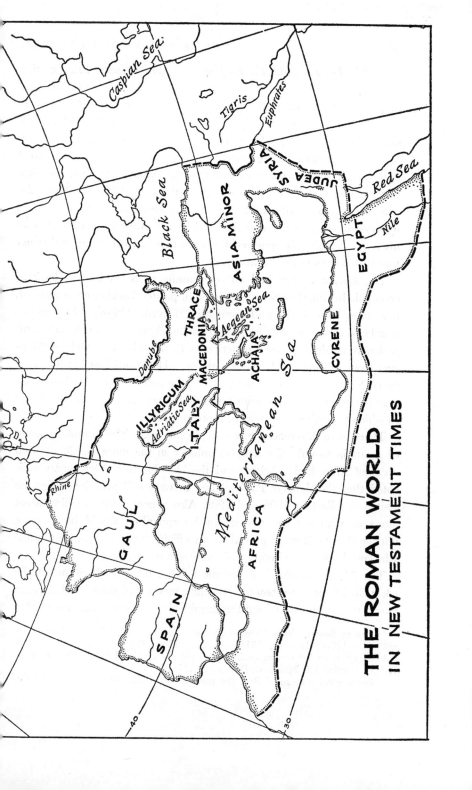

THE ROMAN WORLD
IN NEW TESTAMENT TIMES

The Levant under the Empire   The Roman Empire thus took shape and in turn shaped the East. After Actium (31 B.C.) the Eastern world began to experience the peace which it desperately needed. The Hellenistic search for *Oikoumene* which began with Alexander found its answer in the *Pax Romana* of Augustus. In many ways these two men were opposites. Alexander was a man of amazing physical stamina. Augustus was plagued with illness which at times threatened his life. Alexander conquered great territories, but whether he could have organized them will never be known. He never lived to try. Augustus found most of his territories already acquired but gave them an organizational structure destined to last for centuries.

The Levant at last had an opportunity to begin its way back to economic health. The Sea was cleared of pirates. Roads were improved, new ones were built, and commerce thrived. Although by modern standards it was often still perilous enough, travel was made safer and easier. Regarding his own experiences Paul could still speak of "dangers from robbers" and "danger at sea" (II Corinthians 11:26). Professor Samuel Dill has written: "Until the appearance of railways and steamboats, it may be doubted whether there was any age in history in which travelling was easier or more general."[17]

There were differences, of course, in the areas. The mountain passes of Anatolia would offer dangers unlikely in the more highly civilized areas of Macedonia, Achea, and the like. Professor Deissmann indicated that the dangers Paul alluded to were still prevalent when he visited the East in 1906 and 1909. Also a poor man traveling afoot alone or with one or two unarmed companions would be in more danger than a Roman official in an official post or a wealthy noble who could afford the luxury and safety of a private post.[18]

The Mediterranean had become a Roman sea and around it the early Christians were soon to carry their message of salvation. Churches would spring up throughout the Empire. In this work Paul was to play

[17] *Roman Society from Nero to Marcus Aurelius*, 2nd. ed. (London: Macmillan and Co., Limited, 1911), p. 205. The following two pages in this volume offer an interesting and helpful picture of travel in the first century Roman Empire. Cf. Epictetus, *Discourses*, III, 13.

[18] For a vivid picture of Paul the traveller see Deissmann, *Paul*, pp. 63–65.

a decisive role. The people to whom Paul and his fellow laborers addressed their message were diverse. As the people of Galatia or Macedonia, or Achaia listened, each of them would understand Paul in the light of his own culture and background. Even in the Diaspora synagogues the cultural assimilation of the Jews would affect their reaction to Paul's Gospel.[19] Among the gentiles the diverse cultures were a major factor. Among the Jews, however far from Palestinian Judaism they may have been, Paul found a broad base of common ground. In speaking to gentiles, except for those who as "God-fearers" had come under the influence of the synagogue, he could assume none of the common tenets of religion so familiar to him as a Jew. Even the "God-fearers" would find their thinking colored by their pagan background. That Paul used many terms of common coinage among the pagan religions of his time is well known. It has been said, on the basis of this, that his own theology was a mixture of pagan ideas and primitive Christianity. If we are to understand Paul and the problems that occasioned his letters, if we are to assess his own religious beliefs, it is important that we understand something of the nature of the religions and philosophies which Paul encountered in the Levant. A survey of a few of the more prevalent and important tendencies in philosophy and religion, particularly the mystery cults, will help us.

Philosophies and Religious Needs

The foregoing sketch of the political history of the Graeco-Roman world of Paul has been necessary because neither religious nor philosophical ideas grow in a vacuum. They are intimately related to the experiences, problems, and circumstances of the people. Our survey of the ideas and beliefs prevalent in Paul's world must be read against the background of its history and circumstance.

Changes in the Religious   The *Pax Romana* as we
Situation   have seen brought into the
                                   chaotic East an order hitherto unknown, but for the majority it was still far from the Golden Age. Greece, which had been nearly denuded of both wealth and pop-

[19] Sir William Ramsay believes this to be the cause of Paul's greater success among the Jews in central Asia Minor. *St. Paul The Traveller*, pp. 141–44.

ulation, had a long way to go to reach prosperity. Asia Minor was in somewhat better circumstances, but at least two factors made for a continuing unrest that profoundly affected its religious life. In the first place, the new prosperity came primarily to the Hellenistic upper classes and in the urban areas. Although the Romans were more successful than the Greek Successors had been in securing and advancing Hellenistic culture, the breach between the West and the Orientals was far from healed. The well-known Jewish Rebellion (66–70), which led to the fall of Jerusalem and the destruction of the Temple by Titus, is but an extreme example of the resistance which the Roman rule encountered in the Levant. Border skirmishes continued. Slavery was widespread, and many of the lower classes staggered under the load of impossible debts or eked out a drab existence in abject poverty. A number of allusions in Paul's letters let us know that it was among these lower classes that he worked. One of the most self-revealing of his personal letters was written to a slave owner of Asia Minor in behalf of his run-away slave (Philemon). In a letter to the Corinthian Christians (I Corinthians 7:21) he wrote: "Were you a slave when called? Never mind. But if you can gain your freedom, avail yourself of the opportunity." Earlier in the same letter (1:26) his words: "not many of you were wise according to worldly standards, not many were powerful, not many were of noble birth," picture for us the lower classes from among whom for the most part Christianity drew its early adherents.

The second factor which had a profound effect on the religions of the Levant was the break up of the remnants of old social structures which cast the individual adrift in an even larger sea of humanity than had the spread of Hellenistic society under Alexander's successors. The new mobility of society and the realignment of territories in Roman provinces left multitudes without the social roots which make for security, status and traditional morality. State religions became meaningless under the hammers both of political changes and of philosophical skepticism. Emperor worship, which attempted to supply the social cohesion lost in the decline of the civic gods, was an Eastern import. Augustus allowed his genius to be worshiped in the Eastern provinces, and, as were his successors, he was deified on his death by the Senate. Before the end of the first century the worship of the Emperor, actually little more than a political exercise, became a major problem for the Christians, but during Paul's lifetime Christianity was regarded as a Jewish sect and consequently enjoyed legal immunity. Emperor worship, however, did little toward meeting the real religious needs of the people.

As the individual found his world growing larger his concerns grew narrower. His loyalty was no longer commanded by a meaningful group. His quest now was for something that could give his life meaning, something to which he could belong, and within which he could find status. The new order in the larger scene was often not reflected in a corresponding order on the more personal level. There seemed to be no reason or stability in the course life often took. The individual felt himself to be at the mercy of the caprice of Fortune (Tyche) which, deified, became an object of worship.

Philosophy Becomes Science   It is not difficult to see how such changes would bring an end to the classical philosophies of such thinkers as Plato and Aristotle. The Academy and the Peripatetic School founded by these two men continued, but the thinking of their successors took quite different directions. With the passing of the independent Greek city-state the attempts to comprehend all experience in one grand, meaningful whole gave way to more modest and specialized efforts. The world had become too large.

In Alexandria in Egypt, where a comparatively stable environment was favorable, science and literary studies flourished and produced truly astonishing achievements. Following the lead of Aristotle and the stimulus of Alexander's followers, particularly the sponsorship of the Ptolemies, the librarians and scholars of Alexandria in the third century before Christ made phenomenal progress in science and mathematics. The vast library assembled there led to the development of highly scientific literary scholarship. It should be remembered that it was under the shadow of the great Alexandrian Museum that the Septuagint was produced, such books of Jewish wisdom as the Wisdom of Solomon were written, and especially in the work of Philo the allegorical method of interpreting Jewish Scriptures was developed.[20] Undoubtedly Philo was guided in the development of this method by a similar method ap-

[20] See "The Oral Law and Jewish Literature" in chap. 3 for the importance of these influences on Paul.

plied to Homer, the "Bible" of classical Greek religion, in order to make Homer's gods palatable to more refined Greek sensibilities.

In the establishment of a standard text of Homer and similar literary studies, the Alexandrian scholars became the founders of the sciences of textual criticism and philology. These achievements, together with the later important influence of such men as Clement of Alexandria and Origen, make Alexandria a city of major importance in Christian history.

Cynicism and Skepticism   Elsewhere philosophy turned to an almost exclusive pre-occupation with ethics. Except insofar as Plato's ideas were later incorporated into Stoicism or appeared in Philo, the academy had little influence on the world of Paul. The ideas most prevalent in his world go back by an independent route to an older pupil of Socrates, Antisthenes. He and his more famous pupil, Diogenes[21] founded a school which became known as the Cynics. Through its principal idea that the only good in life is virtue and therefore that the ideal mode of life is to be indifferent to all external circumstances and to concentrate on the cultivation of one's private virtue, it became the ancestor of stoicism.

Diogenes and his followers abandoned the conventional methods of teaching in the schools, took to a life of begging, and addressed their teaching to the common man. The ragged lecturer in the forum or on the street corners, a familiar sight in Paul's world and one which he copied on occasion, went back to the practice of Diogenes. Bion of Borysthenes, it is said, refined the harangue of these mendicant philosophers into the popular diatribe. The diatribe, which exerted a wide influence on later literature, notably on such authors as Horace, Juvenal, Philo, and Plutarch, had a considerable effect on Paul. Among the characteristics of this form of speech found in Paul's writings are: the rhetorical question, the dialogue, the oral style, the substitution of a loose structure moving by a chain of association for the more formal logical outline.

Important for us principally because of its damaging effect on the

----

[21] Diogenes was supposed to have gone through the streets with a lantern searching for an honest man.

old state religions, skepticism began with Pyrrho, one of Alexander's soldiers, and came to prominence through his disciple, Timon. Its main contribution was an epistemological skepticism which challenged the possibility of any established knowledge. Arguments for one system of philosophy or another are therefore fruitless. The influence of this skepticism, surprisingly enough, continued through the Academy. Together with the fact that political changes had made the state religions relatively meaningless for the masses, skepticism was an important factor in the disappearance of the old religions as a practical force in the lives of the people. It was therefore not the gods of Olympus or of old Rome, though their names were sometimes appropriated, but the gods of a different kind that Paul encountered in his travels. These gods had been carried into the Roman World on the flood tide of the Mysteries for which skepticism helped to prepare the way.

The Epicureans   The two philosophical schools of importance in the world of Paul were the Epicureans and the Stoics. Of these the Stoics were by far the more popular and influential.[22]

Epicurus, himself, was a highminded thinker who lived and taught in the latter part of the fourth and early years of the third century B.C. His primary concern was with personal tranquility. For him the basic good was pleasure, but because many pleasures are transient and leave painful after-effects, the pleasures of the mind are the true values. The quiet, retiring life with constant friends seems to have been his ideal. In some ways it was a doctrine of escape in quest of peace of mind. Later Epicureanism frequently degenerated into an outright hedonistic quest for sensate pleasure and the familiar maxim to "eat, drink, and be merry" became their motto.[23] While not actually denying the existence of the gods, Epicurus held that they remained quite aloof from the affairs of the world, hence his teaching became a kind of practical atheism. Many of the people of the war-weary and confused Levant were hardly in a position to follow or benefit from such a philosophy.

---

[22] In treating these philosophies we need not be concerned with the more technical and metaphysical aspects which were subordinate to the ethics at all events.

[23] For a Stoic criticism of the Epicureans see Epictetus, *Discourses*, II, 20.

The Stoics   Stoicism was more sensitive
                                          to the prevailing moods and
wielded an influence far beyond its own circle of adherents. Such influence, of course, is a two-way street and Stoicism was modified in
turn by many influences from the popular religions of the day. Zeno,
the founder, was born of Phoenician parentage in the latter part of the
fourth century B.C. in Citium on the Island of Cyprus. Though the
name, Stoics, was derived from the porch (Stoa) in Athens where Zeno
taught, the leadership of the school seems to have remained largely
Syrian.[24]

Like Epicurus, Zeno was a materialist, though his concept of God
was quite different. Far from positing dispassionate gods, who because
of their detachment from human affairs, were irrelevant, Stoicism
identified God with nature as the reason or providence that guides and
determines it. The result was a kind of materialistic pantheism. In the
Stoic view history runs in cycles which have been predetermined. The
world will be destroyed by fire only to be renewed and to repeat its
cycles endlessly.[25] Man's duty, therefore, is to submit his will to the
divine will of nature. This being in his power is his freedom. All aspects of his life are governed by fate and to oppose fate is not to alter
the course of life but only to lose the happiness and virtue of being in
harmony with the will of God.

Following the Cynics, Zeno made virtue the *summum bonum*. In
this instance virtue is the dispassionate submission to the laws of nature,

[24] Some of the outstanding names connected with Stoicism are Cleanthes
and Chrysippus, successors of Zeno, and Athenadorus, who maintained a
school at Tarsus about the time of the birth of Paul. Seneca, Epictetus and,
later, Marcus Aurelius were prominent among Roman Stoics.

[25] Seneca sought to console a friend with this description of the end of the
age: "And when the time shall come for the world to be blotted out in order
that it may begin its life anew, these things will destroy themselves by their
own power, and stars will clash with stars, and all the fiery matter of the world
that now shines in orderly array will blaze up in a common conflagration. Then
also the souls of the blest, who have partaken of immortality, when it shall seem
best to God to create the universe anew—we, too, amid the falling universe,
shall be added as a tiny fraction to this mighty destruction, and we, shall be
changed again into our former elements." *De Consolatione Ad Marciam*,
XXVI, 6. Reprinted by permission of the publishers and The Loeb Classical
Library from, Seneca, *Moral Essays*, trans. John W. Basore, rev. (Cambridge,
Mass.: Harvard University Press, 1951), II, 95–97.

the refusal to be perturbed by the course of external circumstance.[26] Perhaps the real heart of Stoicism is found in Epictetus' words: "Ask not that events should happen as you will, but let your will be that events should happen as they do, and you shall have peace."[27]

In later Stoicism the materialistic emphasis was much weakened and the movement took on far more the character of a religion. Although God was still thought of quite pantheistically as the soul of nature, Providence was referred to with a warmth of genuine piety. Since God pervades all things, every man possesses a spark of the divine. All men are therefore in reality brothers whatever may be the differences in their external circumstances.

There was in Stoicism an admirable courage but it was born more of stubborn endurance than hope. The Stoic would hardly say with Paul:

For this slight momentary affliction is preparing for us an eternal weight of glory beyond all comparison, because we look not to the things that are seen but to the things that are unseen; for the things that are seen are transient, but the things that are unseen are eternal (II Corinthians 4:17–18).[28]

It was the unyielding will before "the slings and arrows of outrageous fortune." Doubtless many, lost in the vastness of a troubled and capricious world, found in this faith a source of strength, but many more found it too strong a medicine and turned elsewhere for their salvation.

[26] Epictetus began his manual with the words: "Of all existing things some are in our power, and others are not in our power. In our power are thoughts, impulse, will to get and will to avoid, and in a word, everything which is our own doing. . . . Things in our power are by nature free, unhindered, untrammelled . . . if you think that only your own belongs to you, and that what is another's is indeed another's, no one will ever put compulsion or hindrance on you . . . no harm can touch you." *Manual*, I. Cf. Epictetus, *Discourses*, I, 1. Quoted from Whitney J. Oates, ed., *The Stoic and Epicurean Philosophers,* Copyright, 1940, by Random House, Inc. By arrangement with the Oxford University Press. (New York: Random House, 1940), p. 468.

[27] Epictetus, *Manual*, 8. *Ibid.*, p. 470.

[28] Compare this with Epictetus' admiring description of Agrippinus: "I must die, must I? If at once, then I am dying: if soon, I dine now, as it is time for dinner, and afterwards when the time comes I will die. And die how? As befits one who gives back what is not his own." *Discourses*, I, 1. *Ibid.*, p. 226.

Stoicism and Paul   Stoicism is of particular interest not only because of its prevalence in the time of Paul, but also more directly because a number of striking similarities between the writings of Paul and those of the Stoics have sometimes led to the conclusion that Stoicism had considerable influence upon him.[29] The question derives particular relevance from the fact that Tarsus, his native city, was the seat of an important school of Stoicism which would provide a source for such an influence.

That similarities exist can easily be seen by anyone who, after reading Paul, will take the trouble to read Stoic authors such as Seneca or Epictetus. Both make use of the diatribe; both are fond of illustrations drawn from athletics, war and the like; both continually exhort the reader to endurance; both are deeply concerned with ethics; both place duty to God above all else; both draw sharp contrasts between the spiritual and the physical; they have a sizeable number of terms in common.

For an example of one of these similarities we may compare the words of Epictetus:

Do you want to compete in the pentathlon or in wrestling? . . . Do you suppose that if you do this you can live as you do now—eat and drink as you do now, indulge desire and discontent as before? Nay, you must sit up late, work hard, abandon your own people . . . in a word, you must choose between the position of a philosopher and that of a mere outsider.[31]

with those of Paul:

Do you not know that in a race all the runners compete, but only one receives the prize? So run that you may obtain it. Every athlete exercises self-

[29] Much has been written on this problem. Cf. S. J. Case, *The Evolution of Early Christianity* (Chicago: The University of Chicago Press, 1923), Ch. VIII; William Morgan, *Religion and Theology of Paul* (Edinburgh: T. & T. Clark, 1917); Carl Clemen, *Primitive Christianity and Its Non-Jewish Elements*, trans. Robert G. Nisbet (Edinburgh: T. & T. Clark, 1912); T. R. Glover, *Paul of Tarsus* (New York: George H. Doran Company, 1925), especially pp. 19–23.

[30] It would take but a little alteration, for example, of Cleanthes' *Hymn to Zeus* to make it suitable for Christian usage!

[31] *Manual*, 29, Oates, *The Stoic and Epicurean Philosophers*, p. 476. Cf. *Discourses*, III, 24 with Rom. 13:12, II Cor. 10:4 and I Thess. 5:8.

control in all things. They do it to receive a perishable wreath, but we an imperishable (I Corinthians 9:24-25).

The Stoics could hold up Socrates as an authority and example in a manner reminiscent of Paul's treatment of Christ.[32] The contrasts between them which exist at these same points are, nevertheless, even more impressive. These contrasts stem mainly from the difference in the meaning of God. For Paul God is the personal Deity of the Old Testament and Judaism; for the Stoics He is the impersonal Law, the "soul" of the world by which all things are determined.[33] Providence in Paul's view is the loving care of God for His people; for the Stoic it is Fate which for good or ill has determined from time immemorial the course of all events. Paul's was a religion of revelation in which religious knowledge comes from God's self-disclosure, while the Stoic derived his knowledge from reason based on empirical observation. Before Paul stretched the exhilarating hope of the restoration of all things in the New Age to be ushered in by Christ, while the Stoic with courageous resignation faced the end of his brief existence in inevitable death.[34] In contrast to Paul who admonished his readers to "bear one another's burdens" (Galatians 6:2) and argued that "if one member suffers, all suffer together" (I Corinthians 12:26), the Stoic maintained an inward detachment from the suffering of his fellows. Epictetus advised:

When you see a man shedding tears in sorrow for a child abroad or dead . . . do not hesitate to sympathize with him so far as words go, and if it so chance, even to groan with him; but take heed that you do not also groan in your inner being.[35]

[32] Cf. Epictetus, *Discourses*, III, 12 with Gal. 6:2; Rom. 13:14; *Discourses*, I, 4, 9, II, 2, IV, 1, 5; *Manual*, 51; Seneca, *Epistulae*, LXX, 9, with Phil. 2:5-9.

[33] Seneca, *De Vita Beata*, VIII, 4.

[34] It is perhaps not quite fair to suggest that Stoicism had no notion of immortality at all. Opinions differed on the matter. At any rate, the idea was an addendum and formed no real part of Stoic philosophy, nor did it provide anything like the Christian hope of the Kingdom of God in the new age. Cf. Marcus Aurelius, *Meditations*, VII, 32; VIII, 58. Cf. Epictetus, *Discourses*, I, 27; II, 1, 6; Seneca, *Epistulae*, LXXXII.

[35] *Manual*, 16. Oates, *The Stoic and Epicurean Philosophers*, p. 472. Cf. *Discourses*, III, 24.

There was nothing, therefore, in Stoicism that made for social cohesion or satisfied the longing of people to "belong" to a social unit. Each person must, according to the Stoics, remain in an impassive, isolated detachment to preserve his virtue and tranquility. It was a self-centered philosophy which stood at the opposite pole to Paul's grand concept of the Church, the unity of believers in the body of Christ.

A Jew and a Stoic listening to Paul would each find much that sounded familiar, but there would be a vast difference between their understanding of him. The language of the diatribe as well as the terminology of Stoicism had been spread far and wide by itinerant lecturers, and was repeated and given common currency by those who heard them. It would be a wonder indeed if in his messages Paul had not made use of the language and rhetoric which lay ready to hand. Probably he was often unaware of the source of the terms he used. Paul's

traditions are those of orthodox Judaism; he conceived himself to be an orthodox Jew. But an open mind in such a world receives impressions from many sources, and he could not use Greek speech unreflectively. It was bound to tell upon him and it did. He met the Greek spirit in Tarsus, city of athletes, rhetoricians, and Stoics; and the very fact that his scriptures were in Greek secured the influence of that spirit; he was to be a man of all the world. But meanwhile he was a young Jew and orthodox.[36]

The Mystery Religions

As the old civic religions lost the allegiance of the populace their worship became little more than patriotic exercises. In their place Stoicism, for those whose temperament it suited, became a genuine religion, but the rank and file found their dispositions unequal to its demands. Into the vacuum thus created flowed a number of religions whose promise corresponded far closer to the religious needs of the masses. Because membership in these cults was obtained through initiation by certain secret rites, they are called Mystery Religions. Since a number of remarkable, if superficial, resemblances to Paul's letters in terminology, doctrines and rites have long been noted, it is important that we understand these religions. Unquestionably many of Paul's

[36] T. R. Glover, *Paul of Tarsus* (New York: Harper & Bros., 1925), p. 23.

listeners—and converts, for that matter—were not only familiar with them but were members of one or more of them. A number of factors converged to make them exceedingly popular in the Graeco-Roman world and for several centuries in the Christian era.

The Appeal of the Mysteries   Firstly, they offered the initiate a sense of belonging and consequently a sense of importance. The little world of his own community in which the individual had once found his meaning and identity, and to which he gave his loyalty had long since been swallowed up in the expanding Hellenism. The Roman Empire which fostered and reinforced it was too abstract and too vast at best to replace it. In the Levant, furthermore, Rome was often resented by the lower classes as a foreign invader. In such a world the common man found himself unimportant, unnoticed and insignificant, but in the brotherhood of his Mystery cult the individual discovered the meaning of his life in a fellowship of those who not only shared his beliefs and experiences but who also claimed a unique and intimate relationship with their deity. It was this latter relationship which gave the brotherhood its importance. The devotee looked condescendingly upon the uninitiated around him and gloried in the fact that he was not as they; he was possessed of divinity and belonged to a sacred fraternity.

Secondly, the Mysteries proffered a secret knowledge of divine affairs based on the most religiously satisfying dogmas of divine revelation rather than on the tentative foundations of philosophical reason. The belief that he had thus been taken into the confidence of the gods gave the initiate both a sense of importance and a feeling of security which no amount of logic of the philosophers could supply.

Thirdly, the initiate found in the Mysteries a guarantee of immortality and a purification from sin which answered his deepest longing. Both of these matters were left largely untouched by the philosophers. Stoicism, as we have seen, refused to take the question of immortality seriously, but deemed it far more important to learn to die courageously. As to sin the Stoic could only exhort his listeners to will to act virtuously. But it was precisely the question of the will that was at issue. The devotee would understand very well Paul's meaning when he wrote: "I see in my members another law at war with the law of my mind and making me captive to the law of sin which dwells in my members" (Romans 7:23).

When, therefore, the Mysteries extended the promise of a rebirth by which the individual would partake of divinity, be freed from his evil self, and survive in a blessed immortality after death, they found a ready response among the thousands of guilt-ridden, hopeless, and insecure throughout the Empire.[37] The Mysteries often went even farther by offering protection from the misfortunes and ills of everyday life. Formulae were provided for invoking the appropriate gods who, like patron saints, watched over the faithful while engaged in the activity within their particular province.[38] Thus both the caprices of Fortune and the decrees of Fate could be circumvented by means of divine aid.

Finally, the emotional satisfaction provided by colorful pageantry, awesome mystery, ecstatic rites, and elaborately vested clergy wielded a profound influence upon many who turned from the dull repetition of public ceremonies addressed to gods no longer believable—thanks to the skeptics—and the arid lecture halls of the philosophers to find release and renewal in the Mysteries. Crude and vulgar as the Mystery rites often were, they could elicit a response from the multitudes who found the dispassionate contemplation of life by the Stoics quite beyond them. The majority of the people knew religion in tangible and emotional terms. The language of the Mysteries was one they could understand. To such the Mysteries could speak and be heard as the philosophers could not.

The Role and Character of the Mysteries

The study of the religious situation in the early Roman Empire is exceedingly complicated and difficult. The information provided by classical writers is scattered and fragmentary, and archaeological finds of recent years indicate it is not always dependable. Among the authors who have survived to our day there were not many spokesmen for the common man. More serious is the fact that the initiatory rites were secret, hence they

[37] Cf. Paul's vivid description of the gentiles in Romans 1:18–2:16.
[38] For archaeological evidence of this see Adolf Deissmann, *Light from the Ancient East* (London: Hodder and Stoughton, Ltd., 1927) esp. pp. 139–40, 154, 179–80, 254–65, 302–306, *passim*.

were not preserved except in veiled hints and vague generalities.[39] Furthermore, the religions, with the notable exception of Judaism and Christianity, were not exclusive, so that an ardent devotee to better insure his soul's well-being and future might seek initiation in as many as he could afford. The result was that a borrowing and cross-fertilization took place which affected the whole religious atmosphere of the ancient world. Even philosophy was not exempt from syncretism, as it is known. Astrology and magic were early introduced into the welter of dogmas and ideas. Any attempt at a systematic description of these religions must therefore inevitably result in a more or less distorted picture.

For our purposes it will only be necessary to observe a few of the main characteristics of the more prominent religions that were current in the world of Paul. In general the Mysteries took their rise from the myths of the ancient Eastern fertility cults based on the rhythm of the seasons. The many genealogical details and variations of these myths reflect the religious history of the cultures in which they originated and their migration, conquests, and assimilations. By personifying the death of vegetation in winter in the form of their hero-gods, the primitive peoples attempted to explain the seasons in a drama involving the death of a consort or child who is finally restored to life by the faithful search of the divine wife or mother. Usually an appeal to the gods brought about the restoration of the lost loved one and so brought about the revival of life in the Spring. In the cultic rituals the worshippers reenacted the story in order that by sympathetic identification they might aid in the successful rejuvenation of nature, and the security of another harvest, by the restoration of the dead hero. The agricultural concerns were left behind in time and larger questions about life and death were raised. The myths took on deeper meaning. The resuscitated hero was elevated to a god and therefore became immortal. (A devotee of the Mysteries would interpret Paul's words concerning Jesus, "desig-

[39] Apuleius in his *Metamorphosis*, XI, describes the initiation of his hero into the cult of Isis but at the point where the secret rites enter the story he lapses, with an appropriate apology, into generalization. Cf. the similar reticence of Herodotus with respect to the Egyptian mysteries, *Histories*, II, 47, *passim*. Plutarch, while relating in detail the myth of Isis and Osiris and adding a lengthy commentary, carefully avoids the matter of the secret rites although he broadly hints that he knows them.

nated Son of God in power according to the Spirit of holiness by his resurrection from the dead," (Romans 1:4) in a far different light from our understanding of their meaning.) The worshipper now sought by means of secret rites to identify himself with the experiences of the resurrected god and thereby assure his own immortality. Food and drink came now to represent not the successful harvest but communion in the divine life of the immortal gods.

The Eleusinian Rites   Several of these cults flourished in Greece in classical times. The Eleusinian rites,[40] which some scholars believe came originally from Egypt, dramatized the story of how Demeter, the corn goddess, searched sorrowfully for her daughter Persephone whom Pluto, the god of the nether world, abducted to be his queen. When the barren soil refused to yield the harvest and starvation threatened mankind, Zeus intervened and forced Pluto to return Demeter's beloved daughter. Unfortunately Persephone had eaten a pomegranate seed while in the world of the dead and having partaken of the food of the underworld Persephone must return to Pluto for a part of each year. Both goddesses were installed finally among the deities of Olympus. The rites at Eleusis reenacted the mourning of Demeter and the return of Persephone.

Dionysus and Orphism   Wilder and less attractive were the orgies that celebrated the mysteries of Dionysus. The cult appears to have come into Greece from Phrygia or Thrace. Dionysus, most widely recognized as the god of the vine, and therefore of wine, was slain by Titans. His heart was salvaged by Zeus and enshrined. In some versions he was either reassembled or reborn by means of his heart. The many variations of this myth and the story of the travels of Dionysus over the world indicate the vicissitudes of the cult and the resistance it encountered from the various people among whom it was introduced.[41] Women seem to have been particularly addicted to the worship of

[40] The name derives from the shrine at Eleusis near Athens where the rites were celebrated. Cf. Herodotus, *Histories*, VIII, 63.

[41] Euripides, *Bacchanals* is based on the futile resistance to the introduction of these frenzied rites by Pentheus of Thebes.

Dionysus.[42] With flaming torches and beating timbrels they danced over the hills to the music of flutes. In the ecstasy induced by excitement and wine they supposed themselves to be possessed by the god. As a gory climax they tore a live goat limb from limb and devoured its quivering flesh raw.

Whether Orpheus was ever a real person, his name is associated with a reform of the Dionysiac rites which modified the ecstatic worship and developed in time an impressive theology. Later Orphism, associated with the Pythagoreans, taught that the body is "the prison house of the soul" and is reincarnated in an endless, dreary cycle of existences unless by renunciation of the world and rites of purification it finds escape from the body and union with God. In Orphism there developed a strong sense of sin and guilt from which the soul must be delivered, and, somewhat inconsistently, a doctrine of rewards and punishments in the after life clearly reflected in the Christian *Apocalypse of Peter* (c. 135 A.D.). How influential this system became can be seen from the fact that the mystic side of Plato's thought may be traced back to the intellectual side of Orphism. The ecstatic frenzy of the Bacchic-Orphic rites throws considerable light on the abuses at the Lord's Supper in I Corinthians 11:17–34 and the problem of spiritual gifts in chapters 12–14.

The Myth of the Great Mother

From the East came several similar religions which gained considerable popularity in the Graeco-Roman world and therefore form a part of the milieu of Paul. From Asia Minor Cybele, the Great Mother, was brought to Rome during the Second Punic War on the advice of the Sybilline Oracle. During the Republic, participation in these rites was frowned upon, although the religion was tolerated out of gratitude for its supposed deliverance of Rome from Hannibal. With the coming of the Empire, however, the cult gained in favor, and its rites were widespread.[43]

According to one version of the myth, Attis, the god of vegetation

---

[42] *Ibid.*

[43] Cybele was the "Artemis (Diana, A. V.) of the Ephesians" over whom the riot recorded in Acts 19:23–41 occurred.

and consort of Cybele, Mother Earth, went mad and, emasculating himself under a pine tree, bled to death. The rituals which began on the twenty-second day of March were designed to assist in his restoration to life. The ghastly nature of these rites makes it easy to understand the repugnance which the conservative Romans had felt toward them. After a season of preparation a pine tree was cut and placed in the shrine. Churned into a state of wild frenzy by the Phrygian music, the devotees slashed themselves with sharp instruments to offer their blood as a sacrifice. Finally, as a climax to the day, appropriately known as the Day of Blood, the novices emasculated themselves in imitation of Attis. After a day of joy following the night in which the resurrection of Attis had been proclaimed, and an obviously needed day of rest, the image of Cybele was taken to the river and cleansed.

Isis, Osiris, and Serapis   Among the prominent Mysteries of the Roman World was that of Isis and Osiris from Egypt. The myth, as might be expected, reflects the Egyptian dependence on the Nile. According to Plutarch's account of the story, Osiris, the ideal Pharaoh of Egypt, was tricked by his brother Tryphon into lying down in a coffin which was promptly closed, secured, and thrown into the Nile. Floating out to sea, the coffin was finally washed ashore at Byblos on the Phoenician coast. In the meantime Isis, his sister-wife, who in her grief had been going from place to place in search of him, learned that the coffin was at Byblos and recovered it but later, while she was away, Tryphon came upon it, removed the body of Osiris, tore it into fourteen pieces, and scattered them all over Egypt. Isis then traveled from place to place celebrating funerals wherever she found a part of the dismembered corpse and leaving a trail of shrines called "Tombs of Osiris."

Later the gods reassembled the body and Osiris emerged as the god of the underworld. The emphasis in the popular rites reenacting the myth of Osiris appears to have been on the funeral celebrations which accorded with the elaborate Egyptian practices and were supposed to accomplish the immortality of the deceased.

At the beginning of the Hellenistic period Ptolemy I, probably to Hellenize the cult, reorganized the worship of Osiris by introducing the god Serapis. Isis and Serapis, each with impressive rituals became among the most popular and refined Mysteries in the Graeco-Roman world.

Syrian Religions and Mithraism   There is no need to go into the less important Syrian religions such as Tammiz-Adoniz and Atargatis-Hadad. Their mythologies and rites were not significantly different from the ones we have already noted.

Mithraism, by far the most elaborate and elevated of the Mystery religions, did not attain any importance outside its native culture until long after the time of Paul.[44] That it existed in Asia Minor is evident not only from the well-known reference to the devotion of the Cilician pirates to Mithra by Plutarch,[45] but from the name Mithridates, born by kings of Pontus and Parthia.[46] The fact that these devotees were enemies of Rome indicates that the late arrival of Mithraism in the Empire may have been due in part to its involvement in the old antagonism between the orientals and the West.[47]

The Influence and Secret Rites   The public ceremonies and
of the Mysteries   festivals associated with the
                                     Mysteries spread their influence far beyond the inner circle of the Initiates.[48] Probably fragments of the secret rites leaked out. At least their general nature, along with the myths and their interpretations were well known, and their terminology was in common currency. Such words in Paul's letters as mystery, knowledge, wisdom, mature, soul, transformed, light, mind, and contrast between spirit and flesh, natural and spiritual, and the like have back of them Greek words that were technical terms among the Mystery cults.

[44] See Franz Cumont, *The Oriental Religions in Roman Paganism* (Chicago: The Open Court Publishing Company, 1911). Reprinted in paperback (New York: Dover Publications, 1956), p. 140. Also Machen, *The Origin of Paul's Religion,* p. 236; H. A. A. Kennedy, *St. Paul and the Mystery Religions,* (London: Hodder and Stoughton Ltd., 1913), pp. 114–15.
[45] *Pompey,* XXIV, 5.
[46] See "Weaknesses of Hellenism" in this chapter.
[47] Nero's initiation into Mithraism by visiting Magi indicates the novelty of the religion in Roman society and the beginning of the change of relations that brought Mithraism into the West.
[48] In the case of Isis there was a daily liturgy in which the temple was opened with singing and the deity was clothed and fed.

Detached from their native culture the Mysteries changed their character. The references to the fertility of nature were interpreted symbolically. Borrowing from philosophy as well as from each other, they became religions of redemption concerned with the mastery of Destiny and with achieving immortality. Whether or not they had used secret rites in their earlier forms, such rites became their most attractive feature. Some of the main elements of these secret rites can be learned from the veiled references that have come down to us. Sir James Frazer finds in the *Hymn to Demeter* "significant hints" of the initiatory rites of the Eleusinian mysteries.[49] Plutarch betrays something of the mystic rites of Isis and Osiris in Egypt in his statement: "I pass over the chopping of wood, the rending of linen, and the libations that are offered for the reason that many of their secret rites are involved therein."[50] But for the rites in the later period the most important evidence is the well known passage in Apuleius' *Metamorphosis*. After recounting the ceremonies of purification, being given "charge of certain secret things unlawful to be uttered," and after a period of fasting, Lucius was taken to the most secret and sacred place of the temple:

Thou wouldest peradventure demand, thou studious reader, what was said and done there: verily I would tell thee if it were lawful for me to tell, thou wouldest know if it were convenient for thee to hear; but both thy ears and my tongue should incur the like pain of rash curiosity. Howbeit I will not long torment thy mind, which peradventure is somewhat religious and given some devotion; listen therefore, and believe it to be true. Thou shalt understand that I approached near unto hell, even to the gates of Proserpine, and after that I was ravished throughout all the elements, I returned to my proper place: about midnight I saw the sun brightly shine, I saw likewise the gods celestial and the gods infernal, before whom I presented myself and worshipped them. Behold now have I told thee, which although thou hast heard, yet it is necessary that thou conceal it; wherefore this only will I tell, which may be declared without offence for the understanding of the profane.[51]

[49] Frazer, *The Golden Bough*, abridged ed. (New York: The Macmillan Company, 1960), pp. 456–62.

[50] *Isis and Osiris*, 359, *Plutarch's Moralia*, Loeb Classical Library, V, 53. This essay is a good example of the theology which a symbolic treatment of the myths and rituals could yield.

[51] Apuleius, *Metamorphosis* XI, 23. Reprinted by permission of the publishers and the Loeb Classical Library, trans. W. Adlington, rev. S. Gaselee (Cambridge, Mass.: Harvard University Press, (1922), pp. 579–81.

The next day he appeared in vestments and attended a feast in his honor. From this description it appears that the initiate in some manner dramatically reenacted the story of Isis and Osiris journeying into the abode of the dead and arriving finally at the celestial home of the sun.[52] He received a secret formula—probably the password to the celestial regions and hence the key to immortality. An ancient Egyptian text reads: "As truly as Osiris lives shall he live; as truly as Osiris is not dead, shall he not die; as truly as Osiris is not annihilated, shall he not be annihilated."[53] Cf. I Corinthians 15:17–18; John 14:19.

According to Clement of Alexandria the password of the Eleusinian Mysteries was: "I have fasted, I have drunk the cup; I have received from the box; having done, I put it into the basket, and out of the basket into the chest."[54] Hippolytus, in reference to the same cult, speaks of "an ear of corn in silence reaped."[55] The corn is a probable reference to the harvest granted by Demeter, the corn goddess, upon receiving Persephone back from the nether world. Now it has become a sacred object which, along with the contents of the basket referred to by Clement, was symbolic of the rebirth of the initiate into immortality. Paul uses a strikingly similar figure in reference to the resurrection:

You foolish man! What you sow does not come to life unless it dies. And what you sow is not the body which is to be, but a bare kernel, perhaps of wheat or of some other grain. But God gives it a body as he has chosen, and to each kind of seed its own body. . . . So is it with the resurrection of the dead. What is sown is perishable, what is raised is imperishable. It is sown in dishonor, it is raised in glory. It is sown in weakness, it is raised in power. It is sown a physical body, it is raised a spiritual body. If there is a physical body, there is also a spiritual body (I Corinthians 15:36–38 . . . 42–44).

That a sacramental meal lies back of the cup in Clement's reference is confirmed by Firmicus Maternus whose words with reference to the Cybele-Attis cult

show clearly that there was a genuine parallelism between the Christian rite

[52] Cf. Herodotus, *Histories*, II, 170.
[53] Quoted from Kennedy, *St. Paul and the Mystery Religions.*
[54] Clement, *Exhortation to the Heathen*, II, 15.
[55] Hippolytus, *Refutation of All Heresies*, V, 3.

and the pagan. Both were believed to communicate divine life to the devotee and assure him of salvation. Maternus concluded his invective against the pagan rite with the appeal, "It is another food that gives salvation and life. Seek the bread of Christ and the cup of Christ!" Apparently, therefore, the sacred meal in the Cybele-Attis cult was a genuine sacrament that enabled the devotee to absorb the divine life in a realistic manner.[56]

The sacral meals of these cults have been compared to the seriousness with which Paul regarded the Lord's Supper: "The cup of blessing which we bless, is it not a participation in the blood of Christ? The bread which we break, is it not a participation in the body of Christ?" (I Corinthians 10:16; cf. 11:17–34.) But two important differences are immediately apparent: The Lord's Supper is not secret, and it is not an initiatory rite.

To summarize, the secret initiations of the Mysteries included participation in a sacred Passion Play, a sacred meal, the bestowal of a password and certain esoteric knowledge, and the display of symbolic objects. In preparation for these rites the novice was purified by lustrations and fasting. Tertullian compares these lustrations with Christian baptism: "we recognise here also the zeal of the devil rivalling the things of God, while we find him, too, practising baptism in his subjects."[57] Paul, however, carries the meaning of baptism farther than a ritual cleansing and refers it to the believer's identification with the death and resurrection of Jesus (Romans 6:3–11). That which in the Mysteries was a preparation for initiation became in Paul the initiation itself, if we can call it that.[58] It was not a secret rite but it did mark the entrance of the believer into the Church. In the identification of the believer with the Passion of Jesus, Paul comes as close as he does anywhere to the ideas in the Mystery initiations. On first reading Paul seems to parallel the esoteric "knowledge" claimed by the Mysteries:

Yet among the mature we do impart wisdom . . . we impart a secret and

[56] Harold R. Willoughby, *Pagan Regeneration* (Chicago: The University of Chicago Press, Copyright 1929 by the University of Chicago), p. 135. The similarity of these cults at other points allows such inference from one to the other.
[57] Tertullian *On Baptism*, V.
[58] On the other hand Paul still regarded baptism as a purification. Cf. I Cor. 6:11.

hidden wisdom of God, which God decreed before the ages for our glorification (I Corinthians 2:6–7).

But it is not this knowledge, as is clear from the context, that either
makes the believer mature or is necessary to his salvation. The "trans-
formation" of the initiate into an immortal being likewise recalls the
"mystery" which Paul discloses to the Corinthians: "we shall all be
changed" (I Corinthians 15:51). Here we come upon a clue, however,
to one of the fundamental differences between Paul and the Mysteries.
The context of this statement places it unmistakably in the framework
of Jewish eschatology. In a later chapter we shall examine the whole
orientation of Paul's thought. Such an examination is fundamental to
an understanding of his actual relation to pagan ideas.

As the various Mysteries spread over the Graeco-Roman world and
became the popular religions of the day, filling in the void left by the
waning of the old civic cults, they met one another; ideas were ex-
changed; their several deities were identified with one another, and the
great age of religious syncretism arose. The old gods of Mt. Olympus
and the Roman Palatine appeared again, in name at least, in the new
dress of cultic divinities.[59] Concepts and theories were borrowed from
the philosophies. High ethical ideals were mingled with practices of
unspeakable crudity.

But in this syncretism there was a noticeable trend away from polytheism. The various gods began to be considered either simply as different names for the same deity or as subordinate daemons. Aided by the
influence of Diaspora Judaism, the pantheism of the Stoics, and the
worship, fostered by astrology, of the universal, ineffable god manifested
in the sun, the movement toward monotheism served to prepare the
minds of men for the message of the Christian preachers as Hellenistic
influence on culture and language and the political unity of the Empire
prepared the world for their travels.

Astrology and Magic   In the melange of religions,
                                     astrology and magic played

---

[59] Cf. Acts 14:11–13 where Paul and Barnabas were taken to be Zeus and
Hermes. These cannot have been the classical Greek gods, but their names
had been applied to the local deities. Cf. William M. Ramsay, *The Church in
the Roman Empire* (New York: G. P. Putnam's Sons, 1893), p. 58.

significant roles. Astrologers argued from the demonstrable effects of
the sun on the seasons, the moon on the tides, and similar phenomena
to the theory that all life is controlled by the stars which, in their view,
are either gods or at least incorporate divinities. The constancy and
precise mathematical orderliness of the heavenly bodies impressed the
observers with a sense of inflexible destiny. Believing that when the
heavenly bodies assume the exact positions of a former time the same
events will be repeated, the astrologers reinforced the fatalism of the
Stoics. Centuries of observation of the heavens enabled the Babylonians
to amass an impressive and sound body of astronomical data along with
much of gross superstition. From the orbiting planets came the cyclical
concept of eternity. The Elysian field in which reposed the souls of the
blessed departed were moved from beneath the earth to a region beyond the stars, while the wicked dead were still imprisoned beneath the
earth. In his discussion of the nature of the resurrection Paul makes use
of astral language (I Corinthians 15:40–41), although a reader addicted to astrology would get an idea different from Paul's intended
meaning. The idea that the human soul becomes imprisoned in a physical body after descending through the spheres of the seven planets
from its eternal abode in "outer space" was taken up in Gnosticism.
Great dependence was placed on the astrologer's art of divination.

But divination would be useless if the decrees of the stars were really
and finally inexorable. Actually a person had two recourses to outwit
his destiny. One of them was the Mysteries by which, having enlisted
the power of the gods beyond the stars, he was regenerated into an
immortal being. By this means his well-being in the after-life was assured. But for the more immediate contingencies magic became the
popular answer. Through magic the gods could be adjured or cajoled,
and fate altered. Magic books abounded which contained formulae
guaranteed to effect the needed cure or protection. Modern archaeology has turned up numerous papyrus fragments of such material in
Egypt.[60] The formulae consisted principally in naming as many gods
as possible and piling on phrase after phrase from sacred literature. In
one such papyrus occur numerous Old Testament names and references and a reference to Jesus as the God of the Hebrews.

[60] For some examples see Deissmann, *Light from the Ancient East*, pp. 255–
63.

It is not difficult to understand the impression an episode such as that told in the nineteenth chapter of Acts would make on a mind steeped in such lore. Here were healings effected with the use of only one name! Understandable, too, is the burning of the costly collection of magic books after the discomfiture of seven Jewish exorcists who attempted using the name of Jesus in their profession (Acts 19:13–19).

Gnosticism   One important result of the syncretism of the time was the rise of a pattern of ideas commonly known as Gnosticism. It would be more accurate to use the term as an adjective rather than a noun since it must cover a wide variety of tendencies rather ill defined and certainly not organized into a distinctive system. The term comes from the Greek word for knowledge and refers to the claim of secret, divinely-revealed knowledge which possessed saving power. From the Mysteries these gnostic movements borrowed the idea of secret formulae which would afford their souls' safe passage in the great journey after death past the seven planets to the divine abode from whence they had come. The latter notion they borrowed from Chaldean astrology. From Orphism came the dualism of the evil material world and the incorruptible spirit. From Orphism, also, came the asceticism characteristic of many of them. It was undoubtedly against such a movement in the Colossian Church that Paul was writing (Colossians 2:8–23). If many gnostics went to the extremes of asceticism, others, on the basis of the same sharp distinction between the material and the spiritual, surprisingly swung to the opposite extreme of libertinism. The soul, they apparently reasoned, is incorruptible and the material body, being essentially evil, is beyond redemption, therefore there can be no harm in allowing the body to surfeit itself in sensual pleasure. Thus evil will destroy itself.[61] There is some reason to suppose that the self-styled "spirituals" in Galatia (Galatians 6:1) were under the influence of this type of gnostic antinomianism (cf. Galatians 5:13–6:5).[62] In

[61] So the gnostic libertines would understand Paul's order to the Corinthians: "You are to deliver this man to Satan for the destruction of the flesh, that his spirit may be saved in the day of the Lord Jesus" (I Cor. 5:5). Again, however the Jewish eschatology must be noticed in Paul's thinking.

[62] On the composition of the Galatian errorists see James Hardy Ropes, *The*

time gnostic syncretism included Christianity and as a result the Church was rocked by controversy the last echoes of which did not die out for centuries. Already in Paul's day the clouds of that storm were beginning to move across the sky.

Paul and the Religions of the Levant   If the development of philosophy into science, psychology, ethics and the like seems familiar to modern minds, the cacophony of voices from the many religions jostling one another in the ancient world sounds equally strange. Miracle workers and moral preachers, such as Apollonius of Tyana, wandering from place to place easily gathered curious and eager crowds. To many, Paul's voice was simply another among the many voices crying their religious wares in the market places of the Levant. The decline of the old civic religions had left no vacuum. There were many religions preaching ideas of every sort. If Paul on occasion expressed ideas similar to theirs, we cannot infer that he had abandoned Judaism in favor of Stoicism or the Mysteries, or that he attempted to graft pagan branches on the Judeo-Christian stalk. The language of religion and philosophy was common currency; Paul must use it if he was to be understood. If he was misunderstood in the process, it was a risk that he had to take.

It can be shown that the ideas and language which seem to bring Paul closest to Hellenism can be traced more directly to Judaism.[63] It is possible, too, that paganism occasionally borrowed from Paul. Certainly it borrowed from Judaism. Furthermore, similarity of ideas does not necessarily mean borrowing in either direction, still less the work of the devil as some of the Church Fathers charged.[64] Man's spiritual needs change very little. That they come to expression in similar ways in different religions is not surprising.[65]

What is more important, from the clamor of religious voices of that ancient world an insight can be gained into the profound needs of

---

Singular Problem of the Epistle to the Galatians (Cambridge, Mass.: Harvard University Press, 1929).

[63] See Kennedy, *St. Paul and the Mystery Religions.*

[64] For instance, Tertullian, *On Baptism,* V; Justin Martyr, *First Apology,* LXVI.

[65] Cf. Frazier, *The Golden Bough,* pp. 415–16.

those upon whose shoulders the weight of bewilderment and guilt rested as an intolerable burden while they cast about from one cult to another seeking deliverance. Paul voiced their cry in his words: "Wretched man that I am! Who will deliver me from this body of death?" (Romans 7:24), and set himself to carry his answer across the Empire: "Thanks be to God through Jesus Christ our Lord!"

my manner of life . . .

*My manner of life from my youth,
spent from the beginning among my own nation and
at Jerusalem, is known
by all the Jews.* (Acts 26:4)

5 a citizen of no mean city...

I am a Jew, from Tarsus in Cilicia, a citizen of no mean city. (Acts 21:39)

In early Christianity there was nothing comparable to our modern interest in biography. There was no Plutarch in the Early Church to supply us with a lengthy account of the "Parallel Lives" of Peter and Paul. What was recorded in the New Testament and later in the writings of the Apostolic Fathers had for them basic and immediate religious value. Consequently, they did not anticipate many questions we naturally ask. When in Christianity, during the later centuries some such interests did begin to appear, the result was a luxuriant growth of fanciful tales which only here and there show signs of genuine historical reminiscence. The first question then in a study of the life of Paul, is: What are the sources?

Sources for the Life of Paul

It is a striking fact that, although Paul was the "thirteenth Apostle" and stood in a somewhat oblique relationship to the original church at Jerusalem, we have material concerning a larger part of his life than that of anyone else in the New Testament. The material comes from the Book of Acts and Paul's own letters. Considerably more than half of Acts, the second longest book in the New Testament, is devoted to the activities of Paul. In the letters we are fortunate to have a number of most important autobiographical sketches. By a careful, critical comparison of these with the story of Paul in Acts a fairly clear outline of his life emerges.

Comparison of the Sources   There are serious difficulties,
                                 nevertheless, in the way of
the biographer of Paul. Some of these lie in the character and purpose
of the Book of Acts. Surprising as it may seem, there is nothing in Acts
to suggest that Paul ever wrote any letters. Acts is much less help,
therefore, than we could wish in determining the date and place of
writing of Paul's letters. The fact has often been commented upon that
Acts reflects very little of the characteristic thought of Paul.

Even more disconcerting, at a few points it is difficult to correlate
the data of Acts with that of the letters. The most familiar and
thorniest of such problems is the Jerusalem Council described in the
fifteenth chapter of Acts and second chapter of Galatians. Although
an occasional scholar has tried to solve the problem by making these
two separate events, it appears likely that the same event is being
described in both instances.

In II Corinthians (11:23–25) Paul refers to "far more imprisonments" and to having been shipwrecked three times. But Acts, except
for the night in the Philippian jail, mentions no imprisonments nor
shipwrecks until after Paul's final journey to Jerusalem which would
be too late to coincide with the Corinthian letter. Although Luke is
careful to date the birth and ministry of Jesus and John the Baptist in
the customary literary fashion by the governors and the Emperor (Luke
2:2; 3:23), by the mention of Gallio at Corinth he only incidentally
helps us in the chronology of Paul. An inscription discovered at Delphi
has enabled archaeologists to fix the date of Gallio's consulship (50–51
A.D.),[1] but this leaves the chronology of Paul far from solved. Luke
supplies the age of Jesus at the beginning of his ministry but drops not
one hint of the age of Paul.

Far more disappointing is the way in which the author of Acts as he
ends his book with Paul staying two years under house arrest in Rome
leaves the story hanging. That he may have intended, as some scholars
believe, to write a third volume in which the outcome of Paul's trial
would be given, is no help to us now.[2]

---

[1] A full discussion of the inscription and its significance for Pauline chronology will be found in Deissmann, *Paul*, Appendix I, 261–86.
[2] Cf. Ramsay, *St. Paul the Traveller*, p. 23.

The letters of Paul, on the other hand, while supplying firsthand information contain only incidental allusions to the events and facts of Paul's life. As they are in no order they do not supply a chronological key. What Paul found useful in meeting the needs of the churches to which he was writing determined what he put in his letters.

There is a remarkable number of correspondences between Acts and Paul's letters, nevertheless, and—what is more important—a number of points at which they supplement each other. The story of Paul's escape in Acts 9:25 and told again by Paul in II Corinthians 11:33 is a good instance of the correspondences. The differences in the two versions of the episode are exactly what one might expect from two independent sources. The word for basket in the two accounts is different: in one it is a basket woven of reeds; in the other it is a rope hamper. We learn from Acts that the Jews instigated the affair, but only Paul tells us that it was the governor under Nabatean king Aretas who actually alerted the guard against him.[3]

One valuable instance of the way in which Paul's letters and Acts supplement each other may be worth citing. We know from the Corinthian letters that Paul had come to Corinth (I Corinthians 2:1; 3:5; 15:1), established a church, and after he had left, Apollos had assumed the leadership. Sometime during correspondence, some of which originated in Ephesus (I Corinthians 16:8), he had revisited the church and at one time was writing from Macedonia (II Corinthians 2:12; 9:2-4) after having come from Troas. Where he went when he left Corinth is not clear, nor do we know anything of Apollos except that he was more eloquent than Paul, and that his followers by challenging Paul's authority, were creating dissension in the church. Also Paul was urging that a collection be taken for the Jerusalem church which if necessary he would help deliver. It is not always easy to realize how automatically we read the information from Acts into our understanding of the circumstances of the Corinthian correspondence. It is from Acts (18:24-28) that we learn that Apollos was an Alexandrian who came first to Ephesus, and after being tutored by Priscilla and Aquila, moved to Corinth. It is Acts likewise which informs us that Paul, after staying in Corinth for eighteen months, went to Ephesus

---

[3] Cf. I Thess. 2:2 with Acts 16:12-40.

and later, having visited Jerusalem and Antioch, went from Ephesus to Troas and on to Macedonia. Although Acts tells of Paul's determination to go to Jerusalem, it is from the Corinthian letters that we learn that the collection for the Jerusalem Christians was his motive.[4] We are indebted to Acts, furthermore, for our knowledge of the outcome of Paul's projected visit to Jerusalem.

Use of the Sources   It is beyond our scope to enter into the wilderness of hypotheses concerning the book of Acts. Its date and whether it was written by a companion of Paul are questions the answers to which rest largely on external and extra-Biblical evidence[5] and are not of great concern for us.

It is important to make some observations, however, concerning the value of Acts as a source for the study of Paul. As in the use of any source, the purposes of the author need to be kept in mind.[6] Even though Paul dominates Acts, the book was not written as a study of Paul but as a story of the establishment of the Church in the Empire. The phrase "in Jerusalem and in all Judea and Samaria and to the end of the earth" (Acts 1:8) serves as a kind of table of contents. The way in which the over-all plan of Acts answers the test of the validity of the Christian movement proposed in Gamaliel's advice to the Sanhedrin is remarkable:

[4] The collection is incidentally mentioned in Paul's defense before Felix (Acts 24:17). Luke refers to it as though he assumed the reader already knew it! Of course Paul also mentions the contribution for the Jerusalem saints in Romans 15:25–28.

[5] The so-called "we sections" in Acts, in which the narrative is related in the first person plural, and the references to "Luke the beloved physician," (Col. 4:14; also II Tim. 4:11) comprise the New Testament basis for the theory that Acts was written by Paul's companion, Luke. Cf. Adolf von Harnack, *The Acts of the Apostles,* trans. J. R. Wilkinson (New York: G. P. Putnam's Sons, 1909). For recent arguments in the same direction see, Goodspeed, *Paul,* note 1, on ch. XVI, 235–36. W. L. Knox, *The Acts of the Apostles* (London: Cambridge University Press, 1948), esp. ch. I, 1–12. The literature is extensive and scholars are sharply divided on this and related questions.

[6] A convenient summary of various theories of the purposes of Acts is found in C. S. C. Williams, *A Commentary on the Acts of the Apostles,* Harper's New Testament Commentaries (New York, Harper & Bros., 1957), pp. 15–18.

So in the present case I tell you, keep away from these men and let them alone; for if this plan or this undertaking is of men, it will fail; but if it is of God, you will not be able to over-throw them. You might even be found opposing God! (Acts 5:38–39).

A number of interests manifest themselves throughout the book and it is unlikely that any one purpose accounts for its writing. Its irenic spirit ignores the sharp differences which arose between Peter and Paul; indeed the whole controversy in the Church over the question of the circumcision of gentile believers is reduced to little more than two peaceable deliberations at Jerusalem (Acts 11:2–18; 15:6–29). In a number of instances the narrative gives way to the briefest editorial summaries. Christians are mentioned in cities such as Tyre and Ptolemais on the Palestinian coast, and Puteoli and Rome in Italy, with no explanation except the mention of Phoenicia in Acts 11:19, as to how they were evangelized.

If any one purpose dominates the writing of Acts, it is to illustrate by a series of representative episodes the way in which, under the guidance of the Holy Spirit, Christianity expanded from a Jewish community in Jerusalem to a world Church with communities of faithful as far as Rome itself. By Gamaliel's test the Faith is vindicated. In the several encounters with Roman authorities the Church has shown itself innocent of any subversion.[7] Christianity is the true continuity of God's redemptive activity in the world which has been manifested of old in Israel's history. Luke's puzzling silence on important matters in the history of the primitive Church and in the story of Paul can be understood, in part at least, as being outside his purposes and interests.

The purposes of Paul's autobiographical material, on the other hand, are dictated by the circumstances of the letters in which they are found; and the material must be evaluated from that standpoint. That none of the sources for the study of Paul was written for purposes that exactly coincide with ours needs to be kept in mind. This fact helps to qualify the inferences we make to fill in the gaps in our knowledge of Paul. It also helps us to understand why problems exist which must remain beyond solution concerning his itinerary and letters. We are in

[7] Acts 25:8.

remarkably good circumstance in this study, nevertheless, especially because we have access through Paul's own letters to his mind in a way
not possible in the study of other personalities of the New Testament.
Furthermore, the judgment of scholarship has come in more recent
times to a greater appreciation than was the case a generation or so
ago of the historical reliability of Acts.[8] The appropriateness of the incidental references and allusions in Acts to the circumstances of Paul's
world have been made increasingly evident by historical and archaeological study.[9] With the cautions offered here we may use Acts with
confidence in charting his life and work.

Tarsus, Paul's Native City

There is something fitting—almost prophetic—in the fact that
the "apostle to the Gentiles" should be born of strictly Jewish parents,
yet in such a proud, gentile city as Tarsus.

The City   With characteristic Tarsian
                               pride Paul identified himself
to the tribune in Jerusalem: "I am a Jew, from Tarsus in Cilicia, a
citizen of no mean city." Located on the maritime plain just south of
the famous and important Cilician Gates through the Taurus mountains, Tarsus was the principal city of Cilicia.[10] The Cydnus River, the
pride of the city, flowed through its center. Strabo described the Cydnus as a cold, swift stream which for that reason possessed certain healing qualities; although, according to Plutarch, Alexander the Great

8 Cf. Martin Dibelius and Werner G. Kümmel. *Paul*, trans. Frank Clarke
(Philadelphia: The Westminster Press, 1957), pp. 9–13. John Knox, however,
is followed by several scholars in making a lower estimate of the historical
value of Acts. See *Chapters in a Life of Paul* (New York: Abingdon Press,
1950), esp. pp. 21–43. Also John Knox, *Marcion and the New Testament*
(Chicago: University of Chicago Press, 1942). Cf. Henry J. Cadbury, *The
Making of Luke-Acts* (New York: The Macmillan Company, 1927); Martin
Dibelius, *Studies in the Acts of the Apostles*, Heinrich Greeven, ed., trans.,
Mary Ling and Paul Schubert (New York: Charles Scribner's Sons, 1956).

9 On this two books are especially worthy of mention: Ramsay, *St. Paul the
Traveller* and Henry J. Cadbury, *The Book of Acts in History* (New York,
Harper & Bros., 1955).

10 For an extensive, historical study of Tarsus and its significance as the
birthplace of Paul, see William M. Ramsay, *The Cities of St. Paul*, reprinted
from 1907 ed. (Grand Rapids, Michigan: Baker Book House, 1960), pp. 85–
244.

found it to produce the opposite effect when following a swim, he contracted a nearly fatal illness.[11] Just below the city the Cydnus flowed into a lake known as Rhegma (formed by a widening of the river and so taking its name from the word meaning break or rent) which in turn was connected to the Mediterranean by the lower Cydnus. According to Strabo the Rhegma provided the harbor and naval base for Tarsus.[12] The commercial importance of Tarsus is evident from its strategic location between the Cilician Gates and the Sea.

In several ways Tarsus was a meeting place between the East and West. Geographically it was essentially eastern and had been a part of the Persian empire. Later, under the Seleucids, it was associated with Syria and shared with the latter both Hellenistic and oriental characteristics. Greek colonies had reached as far as Cilicia centuries earlier and therefore the founders of Tarsus may have been Greek.[13] Its role as a commercial city and seaport brought it into continual contact with eastern and western influences. Two different traditions of the founding of Tarsus are given by Strabo: according to one the founder was Sardanapalus[14] (often identified with Ashurbanipal, the last great ruler of Assyria). According to the other the Argives (Greeks), accompanying Triptolemus in search of the goddess Io, had founded the city.[15] Whatever their historical value these traditions represent the dual character of Tarsus as oriental and Greek. For its loyalty in Roman times Tarsus was rewarded by Antony by being made a free city (i.e., self-governing)—a status which was confirmed by Augustus when he became Emperor.

The Jewish population of Tarsus probably dates back to the Seleucids. Josephus describes the settlements of Jews in the cities of Syria by Seleucus Nicator I and later, after he had wrested Palestine from Egypt in 198 B.C., by Antiochus the Great.[16] The settlements by Anti-

[11] Strabo, *Geography*, 14.5, 12. Plutarch, *Alexander*, XIX, 1. It was at Tarsus, also, that Cleopatra and Mark Antony held their famous meeting to which she came sailing up the Cydnus in her incredibly lavish galley. *Antony*, XXVI.
[12] Strabo, *Geography*, 14.5, 10.
[13] Ramsay, *The Cities of St. Paul*, pp. 116–21.
[14] Strabo, *Geography*, 14.5.9.
[15] *Ibid.*, 14.5.12; 16.2.5.
[16] See "The Diaspora in Asia Minor" in Chap. 3.

ochus included the cities of Lydia and Phrygia.[17] We may safely assume
that the same period saw Jews colonized in Tarsus. Professor Ramsay
has found reason to believe that Tarsus was reorganized about 171
B.C. under Antiochus Epiphanes and that a sizeable colony of Jews was
settled there at that time and continued to play a significant part in its
life thereafter.[18]

The University   Important for the study of
                                    Paul is the fact that Tarsus
claimed some eminence as a university city. Strabo is our source of information here:

> The people at Tarsus have devoted themselves so eagerly, not only to
> philosophy, but also to the whole round of education in general, that they
> have surpassed Athens, Alexandria, or any other place that can be named
> where there have been schools and lectures of philosophers. But it is so
> different from other cities that there the men who are fond of learning are
> all natives, and foreigners are not inclined to sojourn there; neither do these
> natives stay there, but they complete their education abroad; and when they
> have completed it they are pleased to live abroad, and but few go back
> home.[19]

It is sometimes said on the authority of Strabo's statement that Tarsus
was one of the three great university centers of the ancient world,[20]
but this is not what Strabo says. It is rather the people of Tarsus who
have excelled those of Athens and Alexandria in their eager patronage
of their own school.

That Paul, a loyal Pharisee reared in a Pharisaical home, would
attend the university is unthinkable. But with the native interest in the
university surrounding him, Paul could hardly escape its influence.
Many times he must have heard some fledgling philosopher in the
marketplaces or on the streets practicing his new found skill in rhetoric.

---

[17] Josephus, *Ant.* XII, 3.

[18] Ramsay, *The Cities of St. Paul*, pp. 59–186.

[19] *Geography*, 14.5.13. Reprinted by permission of the publishers and the
Loeb Classical Library from Strabo, *Geography*, trans. H. L. Jones (Cambridge,
Mass.: Harvard University Press, 1950), VI, 347.

[20] Ramsay admits to this error in Hastings Bible Dictionary but corrects it
in his *Cities of St. Paul*. See p. 232 f. and note.

Arguments and discussions among the citizens could not escape his attention. Probably in Tarsus more than anywhere else the indirect influence of a university was felt by the inhabitants who for one reason or another formed no part of its life. When, according to Acts 17:18, the Athenian philosophers referred to Paul by the slang word which is translated "babbler," they used a term which literally meant "one who picks or gleans seeds of learning." Perhaps Paul did not deserve this instance of the philosophers' scorn, but there was a grain of truth in it. In his letters, as we have seen, he clearly shows a knowledge of terms and ideas in the philosophies of his time. He had gleaned these "seeds of learning" first of all in Tarsus.

⚹ The Tarsus school may not have been a great university, but it had some eminent teachers. Strabo lists them for us: Two men bore the name of Athenodorus. The second of these, the son of Sandon, known as Cananites and a companion of Strabo himself,[21] was the tutor and later the advisor of Augustus. In his later years he retired from Roman political life to his native Tarsus to reform the corrupt political machine of Boethus and his friends which was plaguing the city. We can see something of the seamy side of Tarsian life in Strabo's story of these reforms. At first Athenodorus attempted to reform the Boethus crowd by persuasion. But when, after the appearance of a vulgar bit of verse addressed to him on a wall of the city, an unspeakably crude prank proved too much even for a Stoic, he exercised the authority of his commission from Augustus, sent the lot of them into exile, and assumed the reins of government himself.[22] This occurred about the time of Paul's birth.

Athenodorus Cananites was succeeded by Nestor, the tutor of Marcellus, the nephew of Augustus. But for his untimely death, Marcellus

[21] Strabo, *Geography*, 16.4.21.

[22] Strabo, *Geography*, 14.5.14. Philostratus tells how Apollonius of Tyana was so repelled by the insolence and love of luxury he found in Tarsus, where the lazy populace sat along the banks of the Cydnus River like water-fowl, that, taking his teacher with him, he moved to nearby Aegae. *The Life of Apollonius*, I, 7. Dio Chrysostom in his thirty-third and thirty-fourth *Discourses*, which were delivered in Tarsus in the early second century, probably exaggerates the conditions which he set himself to criticise, but the picture he paints of the sensuality of Tarsian life suggests that a considerable part of Paul's knowledge of gentile moral degradation may have come from his observations as a boy in Tarsus.

should have succeeded his uncle as Emperor of Rome. Unlike the
earlier philosophers of Tarsus, Nestor was a follower of the Academy
founded by Plato. Among the Tarsian philosophers Strabo also mentions Antipater, Archedemus, and an earlier Nestor, all of whom, like
the two Athenodoruses, were Stoics.

Such was the city of Paul's birth and childhood. Better known than
its location and lack of natural attractiveness would seem to warrant,
Tarsus made its influence felt across the ancient world through its
sons who went from its halls to teach emperors and princes. Its influence was felt, too, by a young Jewish lad in whom, as in Tarsus, the
East and West met and in whom, with far-reaching results, the philosopher met the Pharisee. In the judgment of the succeeding centuries it
is to this Jewish lad rather than the philosophers that Tarsus owes its
place in history.

Paul's Family Background

From the steps of the Antonian Tower, opposite the Temple
in Jerusalem, Paul addressed the mob from which he had just been
rescued. Speaking in Aramaic, he began: "I am a Jew, born at Tarsus
in Cilicia, but brought up in this city at the feet of Gamaliel, educated
according to the strict manner of the law of our fathers, being zealous
for God as you all are this day" (Acts 22:3). These words summarize
virtually all the external facts we have concerning the early life of
Paul.[23]

In view of the patriotic pride with which, according to Acts (21:39),
he referred to Tarsus as his native city, it is curious that Paul nowhere in his letters mentions his native city. But for Acts, we might
conclude from Paul's passionate insistence on his authentic Hebrew

[23] On the date of Paul's birth estimates vary from approximately the beginning
of our era to about 15 A.D. The only clue is in the account of the stoning of
Stephen, Acts 7:58, where he is referred to as a "young man." We have no
exact idea of the date of this episode, nor is the term "young man" (Greek:
neanias) definite. It can mean a man anywhere from 24 to 40 years of age.
Goodspeed, however, points out that in Luke's writing the term is more restricted, and apparently means a youth between 18 and 25 years of age. *Paul*,
ch. II, n. 2, pp. 224–25. The word "ambassador" in Philemon 9 is a conjectural substitute for the word aged, but neither the word nor the date of
Philemon is certain. The verse, therefore, is of little help in estimating the
age of Paul.

background in such passages as II Corinthians 11:22 and Philippians 3:5 that he was born in Jerusalem, or at least, Palestine. The phrase "and again I returned to Damascus" in Galatians 1:17 might suggest that he had originated there.[24] As it is, these references furnish an incidental confirmation of Acts that can hardly have been contrived. Paul's reference to his return to Damascus, for instance, assumes the reader's knowledge that it was in that region that God had been pleased to reveal his Son to him. It is just such knowledge that Acts supplies; yet Luke can hardly have inferred his information from the passages in Galatians, but must have obtained it from an independent source.

It is sometimes argued from Paul's statement that he "was still not known by sight to the churches of Christ in Judea" (Galatians 1:22) that before the fifteen-day visit with Peter (Cephas, verse 18) he had never been in Jerusalem.[25] But this leaves the following verse unexplained, in which it is clear that it was just these churches that Paul had persecuted. In fact the references in I Corinthians 15:9 and Philippians 3:6 presuppose the kind of information with which we are provided in Acts 8:3 and 9:1-2. Therefore, as brief and summary as is the information in Acts, it is of basic importance for the life of Paul.

The Gischala Tradition   The problem of Paul's origin is complicated by a tradition preserved in Jerome's *Lives of Illustrious Men:*

> Paul, formerly called Saul, an apostle outside the number of the twelve apostles, was of the tribe of Benjamin and the town of Gascalis in Judea.[26] When this was taken by the Romans he removed with his parents to Tarsus in Cilicia.[27]

[24] John Knox does, in fact, suggest that Paul had moved from Tarsus to Damascus and resided there at the time of his conversion. *Chapters in a Life of Paul,* pp. 36-37. But his exegesis of this Galatian passage is not as certain and necessary as his argument assumes. The difficulties in this new variation of a much older theory were anticipated by Machen and Weiss. See following footnote.

[25] Cf. Machen, *The Origin of Paul's Religion,* pp. 48-52; Johannes Weiss, *Earliest Christianity,* F. C. Grant, ed. English translation (New York: Harper & Bros., Torchbook edition, 1959), I, 186 n.; Dibelius, *Paul,* p. 47.

[26] Jerome obviously means the Gischala in northern Galilee.

[27] Chap. V. Trans. by E. C. Richardson, *The Nicene and Post-Nicene*

The tradition is in obvious conflict with Acts. However, in his *Commentary on Philemon,* Jerome recounts the same tradition more cautiously but in greater detail.[28] Here it is Paul's parents who moved from Gischala to Tarsus when the province was devastated by the Romans and the Jews scattered over the world. The context shows that the tradition was, in part, an attempt to explain Paul's orthodox Hebrew background (cf. II Corinthians 11:22 and Philippians 3:5). In spite of the difficulty of reconciling this statement with Palestinian history, a number of scholars are inclined to see in it a genuine reminiscence that Paul's family had migrated to Tarsus from Galilee. It is frequently assumed that they were taken captive to Tarsus by Pompey in 63 B.C. and were later freed. Such an assumption partially solves the historical problem and offers one explanation of Paul's Roman citizenship. But, for obvious chronological reasons, it cannot have been his parents who were brought from Gischala by Pompey; thus this theory removes Paul at least one more generation from Galilee than does Jerome's.

Professor Ramsay, however, rejects the whole Gischala tradition in favor of his theory that Paul's ancestors were settled in Tarsus about 171 B.C. as part of a Jewish colony by Antiochus IV (Epiphanes). According to Ramsay Paul was born into an old established Tarsian family.[29]

Paul, a Citizen of Tarsus?

Two questions make the problem of Paul's family important. His emphatic claim to be a "Hebrew born of Hebrews" (Philippians 3:5; II Corinthians 11:22) is apparently a reference to the distinction between the stricter adherents of the Palestinian Pharisaical tradition on the one hand and the broader, more philosophical Judaism found in the Diaspora, notably in Alexandria, on the other. Such a distinction seems to be intended in Acts 6:1.[30] If this distinction

---

Fathers, Second Series (New York: The Christian Literature Company, 1892), III, 362. Jerome's *Lives* is a kind of Who's Who of Early Christian writers.

[28] Jerome, *Ad Philemonem,* 23.

[29] Ramsay, *The Cities of St. Paul,* pp. 169–86. Edgar J. Goodspeed follows him in this theory; see *Paul,* p. 3.

[30] The terms Hebrew and Hellenist are commonly understood to refer to the Aramaic versus the Greek-speaking Jews: the language is an index to their

is valid, then Paul's family, it is argued, must have had closer connections with Palestinian Judaism than would be likely for an established
Tarsian family. That Jerome's Gischala tradition attempted to provide
such connections we have already seen. But the distinction between the
Hellenists and the Hebrews may not indicate as much about religious
attitudes as is often assumed. To assume that Judaism in such places
as Tarsus necessarily manifested the accommodations to Greek thought
that were characteristic of Judaism in Alexandria is unwarranted. In
several ways Alexandrian Judaism appears to have been unique. Normal communications between the Diaspora Synagogues and Jerusalem
were sufficient to encourage a vigorous orthodoxy in places such as
Tarsus. Indeed it is not unheard of in religion to find an outlying
community even more passionately conservative than the "mother
church."

The second question concerns Paul's claim according to Acts 21:39
to be a citizen of Tarsus. If the family had arrived in Tarsus within
one or two generations of Paul, their Tarsian citizenship would be unlikely, since citizenship was a jealously guarded privilege and rarely
possessed by any but the old families. A more serious objection to Paul's
Tarsian citizenship is the fact that citizenship in a Hellenistic city
would involve the faithful Jew in an impossible relationship with
paganism. Some scholars dismiss the claim of Tarsian citizenship,
therefore, as carelessness on Luke's part.[31] Professor Ramsay, however,
offers an elaborate argument to show that a Jewish tribe existed in
Tarsus through which the member families held citizenship in the city.
Paul's family, he concludes, belonged to this tribe.[32] The Gischala tradition is obviously incompatible with such a theory and explains why
Professor Ramsay rejects it. The difficulties in his theory need not oc-

---

general religious disposition as well as to their connection with Palestinian or
Diaspora Judaism. Cf. Machen, *Origin of Paul's Religion*, pp. 46–47. But see
Foakes Jackson and Lake, *The Beginnings of Christianity*, V, 59–74.

[31] For instance, A. D. Nock, *St. Paul* (New York: Harper & Bros., 1937),
p. 22 n. Cadbury, *The Book of Acts in History*, p. 85, note 35.

[32] *Cities of St. Paul*, pp. 176–80, 185. Cf. Goodspeed, *Paul*, p. 6; Pfeiffer,
History of New Testament Times, pp. 180–81; Lietzmann, *The Beginnings of
the Christian Church*, p. 78. For a different view of the position of the Jews
in Hellenistic cities, see Foakes Jackson and Lake, *Beginnings of Christianity*,
V, 290–92 and also Cadbury, *The Book of Acts in History*, pp. 80–81 and notes.

cupy us here, except to say that his case, while plausible, cannot be proved. Whether Acts 21:39 means Paul was an actual citizen of Tarsus or simply a native must remain an open question until the status of the Jews in Hellenistic cities can be determined more accurately.

Born a Roman Citizen

There was nothing in the ancient world comparable to modern national citizenship. Citizenship as it was conceived in ancient society resided in the cities. Roman citizenship, therefore, meant being a citizen of the city of Rome. In republican days it involved certain popular voting rights in the city for those close enough to be present at the elections. Under the Empire when the popular vote became relatively meaningless and finally disappeared, the advantages of social and legal status together with certain protections continued it as a highly prized possession. Roman citizenship, with the disappearance of popular elections—in which those who resided any distance from Rome could not participate anyway—and the rapid increase of those around the Empire who by one means or another had come into possession of citizenship, did begin, however, to take on some of the aspects of national citizenship.

We have already noted in the course of Roman expansion the beginning of the practice of bestowing Roman citizenship on favored peoples.[33] During Paul's lifetime this continued at an increasing rate until it became the subject of satire. In the famous satire ascribed to Seneca, *The Pumpkinification of Claudius,* Mercury is discussing with Clotho, one of the three fates, the question of how long to continue the thread of Claudius' life, and suggested that it be ended immediately.

Clotho replied: "Upon my word, I did wish to give him another hour or two, until he should make Roman citizens of the half dozen who are still outsiders. (He made up his mind, you know, to see the whole world in the toga, Greeks, Gauls, Spaniards, Britons, and all.) But since it is your pleasure to leave a few foreigners for seed, and since you command me, so be it."[34]

[33] See "Octavian Becomes Augustus" in Chapter 4.
[34] *Apocolocyntosis,* 3. Reprinted by permission of the publishers and the Loeb Classical Library from Seneca, *Apocolocyntosis,* trans. W. H. D. Rouse (Cambridge, Mass.: Harvard University Press, 1939), p. 373.

Unquestionably this picture is an exaggeration, but to have point it must have been based on a well-known attitude of Claudius toward the spread of the franchise. Along with certain social and economic advantages, the citizen had legal rights which in Paul's case were important. A citizen, for instance, could not be punished without fair trial, and he had the right of appeal to the court of the Emperor.[35] These legal rights may not have always been observed, and Paul, for reasons of his own, may not have availed himself of them. He mentions having been beaten with rods three times (II Corinthians 11:25), and it was not until after the magistrates in Philippi had summarily released him that Paul demanded the more respectful treatment due a citizen (Acts 16:35–39).

Paul, himself, was freeborn, that is, he inherited Roman citizenship from his father. How his father obtained the franchise is impossible to know. It is usual to suppose that Pompey may have brought Paul's ancestors from Galilee into Tarsus as slaves and that they became citizens upon being manumitted. Certainly this was one way of obtaining citizenship.[36] Some plausibility is given the theory by Jerome's tradition that Paul's family came to Tarsus from Gischala. If Professor Ramsay is correct, on the other hand, and if Paul stems from one of the old families of Tarsus, the manumission theory is impossible. Several of the ways in which Roman citizenship was obtained, such as through military service, may be regarded as unlikely in Paul's case. As likely a theory as any is that the family had received the franchise

[35] Two good discussions of Paul's Roman citizenship will be found in, Cadbury, *The Book of Acts in History*, pp. 65–82 and Ramsay, *The Cities of St. Paul*, pp. 205–14 (cf. pp. 269–70). Cicero describes the privileges of citizenship, the violation of which by Verres he cited as an unspeakable crime: "To bind a Roman citizen is a crime, to flog him is an abomination, to slay him is almost an act of murder: to crucify him is—what? There is no fitting word that can possibly describe so horrible a deed." *In C. Verrem*, II, v, 66. Reprinted by permission of the publishers and the Loeb Classical Library from Cicero, *The Verrine Orations*, trans. H. G. Greenwood (Cambridge, Mass.: Harvard University Press, 1953), II, 655–57.

[36] Apparently Lysias had acquired it in this way by purchasing his own manumission. Citizenship was also obtained through bribery, of course, but it is doubtful that one who had obtained citizenship in that manner would dare to boast of it. Cicero tells how Pompey granted citizenship to a certain Theophanes for writing a record of Pompey's achievements. *Pro Archais*, 10. This whole oration is an interesting commentary on the ways of obtaining citizenship.

for some notable service rendered the state. In this connection Professor Cadbury refers to

> . . . a set of decrees awarding citizenship and other privileges to a certain naval captain of Octavian, Seleucus of Rhosus in Syria, or rather on the border of Cilicia and Syria. It is a copy of a decree recorded on a stele at the Capital in Rome but it provides that it should be copied in the public records not only at Rhosus, the citizen's home, but also at the neighboring metropolis of Tarsus, at Antioch and elsewhere. The date of the award is 41 B.C., perhaps no earlier than the acquisition of citizenship by the Apostles' forebears. In which case they and Seleucus of Rhosus would have appeared on the same Tarsus list.[37]

Paul's Languages

Paul was a Tarsian, a Roman citizen and a Benjamite. We are indebted to Acts for our knowledge of the first two identifications. Although no mention of it occurs in Acts, he spoke with pride of being a Benjamite in his letters to the Philippians (3:5) and to the Romans (11:1). These designations raise the question of language. As a native of Tarsus, a Hellenistic city, at least in all contacts outside his immediate environment he would use Greek. His letters provide first hand evidence of this fact. Greek was his native tongue. Paul's Greek, however, was not the polished, literary language of the self-conscious rhetorician; it was rather the simple, graphic language of everyday life. Yet it is not the colorless, stumbling style of the ignorant or poorly educated that meets us in Paul's letters. Together with the semiticisms that come to him mainly from the Septuagint, whose Greek is heavily influenced by the Hebrew which lies back of it, there is an energy and power in Paul's style that reflect not so much formal training as a strong and highly original mind.[38]

That Paul could use Hebrew seems evident from the fact that he studied under Gamaliel. Even though that broadminded Rabbi was said to have taken an unusual interest in Greek writings, it is most

---

[37] Cadbury, *The Book of Acts in History*, p. 73.

[38] On the literary character of Paul's writings see Nock, *St. Paul*, pp. 233–39 and Weiss, *Earliest Christianity*, II, 399–421. The importance of the Greek language for Paul's career is indicated by Cicero's remark that almost all nations speak Greek, while Latin is a local language. *Pro Archias*, 10. On the characteristics of Paul's style see "Characteristics of Paul's Letters" in Chap. 8.

unlikely that he would depart from the established custom of teaching the Torah in Hebrew. As his consistent use of it shows, Paul was brought up on the Septuagint, but that fact does not warrant the conclusion that he was not also required to learn Hebrew in the synagogue school, especially if his parents were consciously planning for his career as a teacher of the Jewish Law.[39]

His familiarity with Aramaic (the common language of Palestinian Judaism and closely related to Hebrew) is attested both by the account of his speech from the steps of the Antonian Tower (Acts 21:40; 22:2) and probably by his reference to himself as a "Hebrew born of Hebrews" (Philippians 3:5). Aramaic is regularly called Hebrew by the New Testament writers. When Paul called himself a "Hebrew," however, he was referring to more than the fact that his family used Aramaic in the home; he was saying that his traditional sympathies had been on the side of the narrower Palestinian Pharisaism which steadfastly resisted the encroachment of Greek ideas.

Latin, too, must have been spoken by Paul. It was required of Roman citizens.[40] Suetonius records that Claudius withdrew the rights of citizenship from a prominent Greek because of his ignorance of Latin.[41] Of course the action itself proves that there were citizens who could not speak Latin. Presumably the obscure Jewish Tarsian so far removed from Rome might never have been challenged. But it is inconceivable that Paul would have dared to appeal to the Emperor as he did if he were not able to speak Latin. It would have meant the loss of his citizenship and consequently the loss of his case.

Saul, also Called Paul

Paul's triple relationship to Hellenism, Rome, and Judaism is also reflected in his name. It is a curious fact that we do not know his

[39] On the relation of the Septuagint to the Hebrew Scriptures in Jewish practice, see chapter 3, note 27 and "Homogeneity of Judaism." A tabular analysis of Paul's use of the Old Testament in either direct or tacit quotations is found in Fernand Prat, *The Theology of Saint Paul* (Westminster, Md.: The Newman Press, 1946, I, 411–14). (Reprinted in Thomas S. Kepler, *Contemporary Thinking about Paul* (New York: Abingdon-Cokesbury Press, 1950), 197–200.

[40] Cf. Ramsay, *St. Paul the Traveller*, p. 225 and *The Cities of St. Paul*, p. 214. See also Cadbury, *The Book of Acts in History*, p. 68.

[41] *Claudius*, 16, 2.

full name either as a Jew or a Roman. From Acts we learn that his
Jewish name was Saul. Because he was a Benjamite, it is usually assumed that he was named for the Benjamite hero and first king of
Israel, Saul, son of Kish. It is equally possible that he was named for
a more immediate ancestor, perhaps his own father.[42] In its full form,
Paul's Jewish (Aramaic) name would include a patronymic connected
to his own name by the word *bar* (in Hebrew, *ben*). Peter's original
name for example, was Simon bar Jona (Matthew 16:17). Due to the
Palestinian background of the Gospels we know that the name of the
father of the obscure James, listed among Jesus' disciples, was Al-
phaeus, whereas we have no clue whatever to Paul's father's name. Of
Paul's parentage we only know that his father was an Aramaic speaking
Pharisee, a resident of Tarsus, and a Roman citizen.

As a Roman citizen, of course, Paul had a full Roman name. This
included three names: a praenomen, nomen, and cognomen. The
praenomen was the individual's personal name; the nomen designated
the clan, the largest unit in Roman society; and the cognomen represented the family. Paul (*Paulos* in the Greek New Testament) could be
used either as a praenomen or cognomen, and there is no way of telling which it was in the case of the Apostle except that in such instances
the cognomen was most commonly used for the single name. Because
there was a limited number of praenomina, they were often indicated
by the initial as in M. Tullius Cicero.

In the Greek world it was common for those who acquired Roman
citizenship, having taken the praenomen and nomen of the one through
whom they obtained it, to retain their Greek name as their cognomen.
It is interesting, therefore, to observe that Paul is a Latin rather than a
Greek name. Of course such a person could retain his old name as an
alternate name which could be included by the reverse of the form in
Acts 13:9: "Saul, who is also called Paul." The knowledge of Paul's
full Roman name would likely provide some clue as to how or when
the franchise came into the family. For instance, Professor Ramsay suggests "if we had any lists of Tarsian citizens during the first two centuries of the Empire, we should probably find in them more than one

[42] Cf. Luke 1:59–61. The name means "asked for" and has suggested to
some that he was the oldest child and was the answer to anxious prayers. Cf.
I Sam. 1:9–20.

family bearing the name Pompeius," which would mean that these families had received Roman citizenship from Pompey during his Cilician campaign.[43] If Paul's citizenship was acquired in this way, his name would be G. (Gnaeus) Pompeius Paulus, who is also called Saul. That Paul uses only one name and that Acts omits his patronymic altogether reflects, in part, the Hellenistic background. The Greeks used only one name. The name Paul, meaning "very small," hardly justifies picturing him as a little man, for it was given to him in infancy. It is sometimes suggested that the similarity in sound between Saul and Paul prompted its choice. Jerome is responsible for the old idea that Paul took his Roman name after Sergius Paulus of Cyprus (Acts 13:7).[44] This assumption is not only reckless exegesis, but it is impossible to reconcile with the fact that he was born a citizen. That Paul invariably used his Roman name in his letters is perhaps significant of Paul's pride of Roman citizenship. But for Acts we would not know of his Jewish name. The significance of this fact is heightened when we observe that he almost invariably referred to Peter as Cephas, the Aramaic form of the Greek name Peter.[45]

Paul's Early Training

The early influences and training which Paul experienced can only be reconstructed from our meager knowledge of Jewish practices in his time. Being reared in an orthodox Pharisaical home he was certain, from the earliest impressions of infancy, to have his thinking molded by the strict regimen and strict heritage of Judaism. Constantly he would be reminded that he was a son of Abraham.

Religious Training   Among his earliest recollections would be the festivals of the Jewish calendars. From each of these he would learn a story of

---

[43] *The Cities of St. Paul,* p. 206. This section, XVIII, pp. 205–14, provides a very helpful discussion of Roman names in connection with the New Testament, especially that of Paul. See also Cadbury, *The Book of Acts in History,* pp. 69–71.

[44] Jerome, *Lives of Illustrious Men,* chap. V.

[45] Of the five possible exceptions in Gal. 2:7–14 (four of these read "Peter" in the AV), three are textual variants which indicate that the other two (which appear in the RSV) may also be the result of scribal assimilations to Acts.

Israel's duty to God and of God's providential acts in Israel's history. With each passing year these lessons would be etched more indelibly in his impressionable mind. He would at a very early age learn to help search the house for the least fragment of leavened bread before the Feast of the Passover (cf. I Corinthians 5:7-8). As the family gathered around the table to eat the Passover feast he would ask the traditional questions, and he would hear with increasing comprehension each year the story of God's mighty act through Moses in delivering the children of Israel from Egyptian slavery.

As a child Paul would go with his mother to the synagogue. In oriental modesty her head would be veiled. Years later Paul was to require this same covering of the women in his church in Corinth (I Corinthians 11:5-16). Perhaps he heard his father in his turn read the lessons from the Law and the Prophets; perhaps his father also recited the prayers on occasion. In after years, as he remembered the solemn responses of the congregation he had so often heard, he admonished the Corinthians to pray intelligibly so that the people would know when to say the "Amen" (I Corinthians 14:16).

His father would be Paul's first teacher. As a faithful Jew he would follow the admonition of Deuteronomy 6:7 in handing on to his children the great traditions of his people so that before he entered the synagogue school he was familiar with the stories of the Pentateuch, God's promise to Abraham, and His covenant with his people.

An ancient rabbinic saying concerning the ages of man begins: "At five years of age the study of Scripture; at ten, the study of Mishna; at thirteen, subject to the commandments; at fifteen, the study of Talmud."[46] Some such program must have been Paul's experience. At the synagogue school he would begin his formal education based on the Torah and, later, the Oral Law. He learned to read and write. Undoubtedly he learned Hebrew here also, but, as his letters show, it was the Greek Bible that became most familiar to him. When he wished to appeal to a passage of Scripture it was usually from the Septuagint that he quoted.

Judaism was justly proud of its schools. Josephus in his answer to

[46] *Pirke Aboth*, V, Goldin, *The Living Talmud*, p. 222.

the calumnies of Apion wrote: "Our principal care of all is this, to educate our children well."[47] A Talmudic saying runs, "A town without schools will not be guarded by the Lord."[48] According to another passage in the Talmud, Joshua ben Gamla (High Priest c. 64 A.D.) instituted schools in the villages throughout Palestine and later, because the older boys if they chose would simply walk out of the school, he "ordained that children should be brought to school at the age of six or seven."[49] It is not unlikely that such schools for small children existed in the wealthier communities much earlier and that Paul began his formal schooling in his sixth or seventh year.

Learning a Trade As another aspect of his education, Paul was taught the tentmaker's trade (Acts 18:3).[50] It was likely the family trade and Paul learned it from his father; for it was the father's duty, along with his responsibility to give his son an education, to give him a trade. Far from being incompatible with his preparation to be a teacher of the Torah, it was until a much later time the accepted practice for rabbis to work at a trade so that they might not seem to be making material profit from teaching the Torah. According to a tradition assigned to Hillel, "He that puts the words of Torah to personal profit removes his life from the world."[51] Rabban Gamaliel II (second century) is quoted as saying: "Splendid is the study of Torah when combined with a worldly occupation, for toil in them both puts sin out of mind; but study (Torah) which is not combined with work falls into neglect in the end and becomes the cause of sin."[52] Although Paul did not ad-

---

[47] *Against Apion*, I, 12. (Whiston's translation).

[48] *Y. Hagigah*, 1. Newman, *The Talmudic Anthology*, p. 417.

[49] *Baba Batra*, 24. Newman, *The Talmudic Anthology*. On ancient Jewish education and the synagogue schools see J. F. Moore, *Judaism*, I, pp. 308–22 and *The Jewish Encyclopedia*, X, 42–44.

[50] The word tentmaker (*skenopoios*) is usually associated with the coarse goats hair cloth for which Tarsus was famous. The term, however, can refer to leather work. See Foakes Jackson and Lake, *The Beginnings of Christianity*, IV, 223.

[51] *Pirke Aboth*, IV, Goldin, *The Living Talmud*, p. 160. In a number of instances the names of the ancient rabbis indicate their trade. See *The Jewish Encyclopedia*, X, 294–95.

[52] *Pirke Aboth*, II, Goldin, *The Living Talmud*, pp. 80–81. Cf. Eph. 4:28. The story is told of R. Gamaliel II who, after a serious difference with R.

vocate self-support for other apostles (I Corinthians 9:7–11), he could
boast of his own practice: "For you remember our labor and toil,
brethren; we worked night and day that we might not burden any of
you while we preached to you the gospel of God" (I Thessalonians
2:9).[53] That he did not derive all his support from his own labor,
however, is evident from his words in II Corinthians: "I robbed other
churches by accepting support from them in order to serve you" (11:8).

Paul's Family

That Paul learned a trade does not imply that the family was
poor. The likelihood is that his father, a Roman citizen, was fairly
well-to-do.[54] The fact that he sent his son to Jerusalem to study tends
to confirm this. It has sometimes been suggested that Felix knew of
Paul's family wealth and for that reason detained Paul in the Caesar-
ean prison hoping "that money would be given him" (Acts 24:26). But
the question arises: why, if he came from a family of means, did Paul
have to work to support himself and depend on contributions from
poverty-stricken churches? (Cf. Philippians 4:10–16.) There are several possibilities: He may have been a younger brother, in which case
his share of the estate might have long since been exhausted; the resources of a prominent family may have proved insufficient to maintain
such a person as Paul in his extended travels around the world and out
of touch with the family business; or, as Professor Ramsay suggests, he
may have been disinherited.[55]

Joshua, resolved to pay a call on the latter. He was surprised to discover that
R. Joshua was a smith and in humble circumstances. R. Joshua's acid retort
was, "Woe to the generation of which thou art the leader; woe to the ship of
which thou art the captain; for thou didst never show interest in the affairs
of the scholars, nor in the manner of their livelihood." *Berakot,* 27. Newman,
The Talmudic Anthology, p. 471.

[53] Cf. Acts 18:3; 20:34; I Cor. 4:12; 9:6, 15–18.

[54] Dio Chrysostom, in his thirty-fourth *Discourse,* (23), strongly implies
that Tarsus was a timocracy at the time of his visit (at the beginning of the
second century). If this was true in Paul's day, and it is assumed that he was
a citizen of Tarsus, he must have belonged to a family of means. But, to
confuse matters, Dio further says in the same paragraph that linen workers
were arbitrarily forbidden citizenship in the city. Would this apply to Paul as
a tentmaker?

[55] *St. Paul the Traveller,* pp. 34–37. Some weight is given this theory by

Except that he had a sister whose son rendered him invaluable service by warning him of a plot against his life (Acts 23:16–22) we have no further knowledge of Paul's family. The presence of Paul's nephew in Jerusalem has led to the supposition that his sister and her husband lived there and that when as a lad he came to study under Gamaliel, he had stayed with her. This can be no more than conjecture. Paul's nephew would by this time be old enough to be in Jerusalem by himself. The same word, *neanias* (young man) is used to describe the nephew that was used on Paul himself in the story of the stoning of Stephen (Acts 7:58).

There is a tender note in Paul's greeting to Rufus in Romans 16:13. To that greeting he adds: "also his mother and mine." Had he lost his mother in infancy and found in this wonderful Ephesian matron the maternal devotion he had never known as a child? Or, as a Christian Apostle, was he separated from his own family by a gulf far wider than the distance that separated Corinth from Tarsus? We can never know, but it may be that here and in his familiar admonition to fathers not to "provoke your children, lest they become discouraged" (Colossians 3:21), we have fleeting glimpses into his own childhood. Certainly he never forgot the experiences that brought him to manhood, for he frequently exhorted his Christians to grow into spiritual maturity (cf. I Corinthians 14:20), and referred to himself as an example: "When I became a man, I gave up childish ways" (I Corinthians 13:11).

As Paul, from the perspective of his work as a Christian apostle, looked back upon his own origins and the course of his life, he saw in it all the providential hand of God. A unique sense of calling and purpose possessed him. In Jeremiah's words he saw the meaning of his own life:

Now the word of the Lord came to me saying, "Before I formed you in the womb I knew you, and before you were born I consecrated you; I appointed you a prophet to the nations" (Jeremiah 1:4–5; cf. Isaiah 49:5).

When Paul's apostleship was called into question in the crisis in

---

Paul's words: "I have learned the secret of facing plenty and hunger, abundance and want" (Philippians 4:12).

the Galatian Churches, he bared the inner meaning of his birth and
early life:

But . . . he who had set me apart before I was born, and had called me
through his grace, was pleased to reveal his Son to me, in order that I
might preach him among the Gentiles . . . (Galatians 1:15–16).

6 at the feet of Gamaliel...

*I am a Jew, born at Tarsus in Cilicia, but brought up
in this city at the feet of Gamaliel, educated
according to the strict manner of the law of
our fathers, being zealous for God as you all are this
day. (Acts 22:3)*

Paul first appears on the pages of the New Testament in Jerusalem as a collaborator in the stoning of Stephen. He had now grown to manhood and the part he played in the persecution of the Church shows him possessed of a religious zeal bordering on fanaticism. His own letters confirm this impression: "as to zeal a persecutor of the church, as to righteousness under the law blameless" (Philippians 3:6). These early years in Jerusalem were undoubtedly among the most important in Paul's life. The attempt to reconstruct this period makes us realize how incomplete our knowledge of Paul is. Yet we are not without a few glimpses which we may profitably examine.

Paul's Personal Traits

In a well-known passage in the *Acts of Paul and Thecla*, written about 160 A.D.,[1] Paul is described as a small, bald-headed man with crooked legs but healthy body, a long nose and eyebrows that met. The

[1] *Paul and Thecla* is the best known and best preserved part of a larger work, *The Acts of Paul*, which is not complete in any extant manuscript. This work is one of a number of pseudo-Acts that began to make their appearance in the second and following centuries. See Alexander Roberts and James Donaldson, eds., *The Ante-Nicene Fathers* (Buffalo: The Christian Literature Company, 1886), VIII, 487 and James, *The Apocryphal New Testament*, pp. 270–99.

appearance of his face alternated between that of an ordinary man and that of an angel. Written nearly a century after the death of Paul, this description sounds like a popular Roman caricature of a Semite. Several of the items in the description, in fact, could have been inferred from his own letters. The idea that he was small may have been an inference from his Latin name, and in II Corinthians 10:10 his generally unattractive appearance is certainly implied: "For they say, 'His letters are weighty and strong, but his bodily presence is weak, and his speech of no account.' " That he sometimes appeared with the face of an angel may have been mistakenly inferred from his statement that the Galatians had received him "as an angel of God" (Galatians 4:14).

His Personality   It is surprising, nevertheless, to find such an unflattering description of Paul in a book obviously written to enhance his prestige.[2] *The Acts of Paul* is of course fiction. The presbyter who wrote it is said to have been deposed for the forgery.[3] But some scholars find reason to believe that the legend of Thecla has back of it an historic person. Professor Ramsay has gone so far as to offer an elaborate argument to show that the work in its present form developed from a first century document containing genuine historical reminiscences.[4] Although his theory has not found much favor among scholars, it does point to the possibility that the story may contain some very early tradition, perhaps existing within the lifetime of those who could still remember Paul. Elsewhere Professor Ramsay expresses the belief that the description of Paul, because of its uncomplimentary character, is such an early tradition.[5] If so, it may represent more than mere reckless inferences from Paul's letters.

Whatever may be the value of this apocryphal description of Paul, the modern reader of the New Testament may draw his own inferences. Although II Corinthians 10:10 implies that Paul did not present a commanding appearance, he was not devoid of personal magnetism.

[2] For good character studies of Paul see Deissmann, *Paul,* Ch. III, 55–81 and Knox, *Chapters in a Life of Paul,* Ch. VI, 89–107.
[3] Tertullian, *On Baptism,* XVII.
[4] See Ramsay, *The Church in the Roman Empire,* pp. 375–428.
[5] *Ibid.,* pp. 31–32. Cf. Deissmann, *Paul,* p. 55.

The responses he elicited seem to have been either strongly positive or negative. Galatians 4:14–15 and I Thessalonians 1:9 indicate the warmth with which Paul was received on his initial visit to these places. His hyperbolic statement that if possible the Galatians would have given him their eyes is testimony to their amazing response to his first impression. From the devoted Philippians he received active support that followed him in his travels and finally to prison (Philippians 4:10–18). Even in Corinth, where he met some of his bitterest opposition, he had loyal supporters who, because of their partisan support, were known as those "of Paul" (I Corinthians 1:12). His capacity to love his churches and his co-workers, which shines especially in the many greetings of his letters, found a deep response.[6] Prisca and Aquila, who he said, "risked their necks for my life" (Romans 16:4), furnish an example of the almost fanatic personal loyalty Paul enjoyed.

Yet he suffered equally bitter opposition. In writing to the Philippians Paul complained that there were some who "proclaim Christ out of partisanship, not sincerely but thinking to afflict me in my imprisonment" (Philippians 1:17). His enemies dropped dark hints of his dishonesty and ulterior motives (II Corinthians 12:16; I Thessalonians 2:3–6). Probably there was a personal as well as a doctrinal element in the antagonism of those to whom Paul once sarcastically referred as "superlative apostles" (II Corinthians 11:5). His reaction to these opponents was vitriolic; he called them dogs, evil-workers, false apostles, deceitful workmen, servants of Satan (II Corinthians 11:13–15; Philippians 3:2). To one who would preach a gospel contrary to his, Paul uttered the terrible words: "let him be accursed" (Galatians 1:8–9), and he wished that those who sought to impose the requirement of circumcision upon the Galatians "would mutilate themselves" (Galatians 5:12). One who evoked from those he encountered such extremes of devotion and hate can hardly have presented an unimpressive appearance.

The extremes of reaction to Paul in a sense reflect the extremes of moods within his own soul. Looking back on a crisis in the church at Corinth he wrote: "For even when we came into Macedonia, our

---

[6] Cf. Rom. 16:3–15; I Cor. 16:17–19; Phil. 1:3–4, 24–26; Col. 4:10–15; I Thess. 3:1–3, 6; Philemon 1.

bodies had no rest but we were afflicted at every turn—fighting without and fear within. But God, who comforts the downcast, comforted us by the coming of Titus" (II Corinthians 7:5–6).[7] Yet a letter written from his prison cell to his beloved Philippians echoes a boundless joy. During the Corinthian crisis his anger was such that he refrained from visiting them to settle the matter in person (II Corinthians 13:10). When the storm was over his generous forgiveness was even greater: "Our mouth is open to you, Corinthians; our heart is wide . . . widen your hearts also" (II Corinthians 6:11–13); "Any one whom you forgive, I also forgive" (II Corinthians 2:10). The same Paul who could boast: "Are they servants of Christ? I am a better one" (II Corinthians 11:23) could also say under oath: "I could wish that I myself were accursed and cut off from Christ for the sake of my brethren, my kinsmen by race" (Romans 9:3). With effort he held a check on his tempestuous spirit:

We are afflicted in every way, but not crushed; perplexed, but not driven to despair; persecuted, but not forsaken; struck down, but not destroyed (II Corinthians 4:8–9).

Such a stormy spirit as Paul's cannot hide successfully behind an unattractive and unimpressive physique. We would do well to remember that the charge that "his bodily presence is weak" was made by his enemies and must not be taken too seriously. Paul, himself, did not believe it. "Let such people understand that what we say by letter when absent, we do when present" (II Corinthians 10:11). In bitter irony Paul quotes his enemies earlier in this same chapter: "I who am humble (i.e., deferring servilely to others) when face to face with you, but bold to you when I am away!" and threatens in the next sentence to show them that he can be bold when face to face. It was not Paul's letters that got him beaten, imprisoned, and stoned. A man who became a storm center wherever he went and yet commanded such undying devotion from his co-workers and followers cannot have been an anemic, colorless personality.

[7] Some interpreters believe that II Cor. 1:8–10 refers to Paul's despair during the same crisis rather than any physical danger that threatened him in Ephesus. Cf. II Cor. 2:4.

Our evidence for Paul's appearance has been drawn from letters written in his later years; but a man's temperament is his lifelong possession. Gamaliel's young student from Tarsus may not have been statuesque or handsome, but there was that about him which commanded people's attention. They could worship him as a god (Acts 14:11–13) or drag him and his companion into court crying, "these men who have turned the world upside down have come here also" (Acts 17:6), but they did not ignore him. Throughout his life people responded to Paul in love or hate.

In his features and dress Paul was characteristically oriental. This is evident from the fact that the tribune who rescued Paul from the mob in Jerusalem could mistake him for an Egyptian Jew who had recently eluded arrest. The Egyptian had assembled a mob on the Mount of Olives, promising them that at his command the walls of Jerusalem would collapse and that they could then invade the city to start a revolt against the Romans. The procurator Felix learned of the affair and scattered the mob, but the Egyptian escaped.[8] When Paul was dragged from the Temple and mobbed in the street, the tribune thought he had his man and was amazed to learn that Paul was a Roman citizen.

His "Thorn in the Flesh"   Two passages in his letters have often been interpreted to indicate that Paul suffered from a chronic disease.[9] In Galatians 4:13 he reminded the Galatians that "It was because of a bodily ailment that I preached the gospel to you at first." That the ailment referred to in Galatians was chronic has often been inferred from Paul's familiar reference in II Corinthians 12:7 to his "thorn in the flesh."[10] His frequent reference to afflictions and suffering lend support to the theory of a chronic illness.

Centuries of debate have been engendered by these two brief pas-

---

[8] Josephus, *Ant.*, XX, 8; *Wars*, II, 13.

[9] For a good brief summary of the theories concerning Paul's "thorn in the flesh" see James Hastings, ed., *A Dictionary of the Bible* (New York: Charles Scribner's Sons, 1911), III, 700–701.

[10] Some interpreters have regarded the "thorn in the flesh" as a moral temptation of some sort; others have contended that the phrase refers to a personal opponent. These theories have not found much favor among modern scholars.

sages. Among the diagnoses of Paul's malady that have been made three are sufficiently plausible to justify our attention. Epilepsy has suggested itself because of the revolting nature of Paul's illness while he was with the Galatians. He reminded the Galatians (4:14) of their magnanimity in refusing to be repelled or to despise him. The word here translated "despise" (Greek: *exptuo*) means literally to spit out and is supposed to refer to a superstitious act of spitting performed by a witness to an attack of epilepsy. The disease was well known in ancient times and often regarded as a peculiarly divine visitation. Advocates of the epileptic theory also point to Paul's numerous visions, presumably a characteristic of epileptics, especially the fact that Paul himself relates his "thorn in the flesh" to his visions and revelations.

One of the motives back of the theory that Paul was an epileptic is to account for his conversion experience.[11] The theory, however, considerably outruns the evidence. An epileptic attack does not usually produce the kind of change and life-long influence that followed Paul's experience on the Damascus Road. Elsewhere his references to visions offer no evidence that would associate them with epileptic seizure. The argument actually hinges on the word "despise" in Galatians 4:14, but this word was also commonly used in the ordinary sense of showing disgust or revulsion without reference to a particular cause. If Paul were an epileptic, he suffered seizures from early childhood and the disease belongs to a description of his early years. It seems improbable, however, that he would have regarded an affliction from which he had suffered from childhood as something given him to keep him "from being too elated" over his later religious experiences (II Corinthians 12:7).

The last sentence in Paul's reference in Galatians 4:13–15 to illness turns the evidence in another direction: "For I bear you witness that, if possible, you would have plucked out your eyes and given them to me." Was it eye trouble, after being blinded on the Damascus Road, that plagued him through the years? Advocates of this theory point to the final paragraph of Galatians as evidence of failing eyesight:

[11] For a more recent restatement of this theory and its connection with Paul's conversion see Joseph Klausner, *From Jesus to Paul*, trans. William F. Stinespring (New York: The Macmillan Company, 1943), pp. 326–30, 442.

"See with what large letters I am writing to you with my own hand" (6:11). The evidence is meager. The statement that the Galatians would have given Paul their eyes may be no more than an hyperbole to emphasize, as the entire passage is intended to do, the radical change that had taken place in the attitude of the Galatians toward Paul. Paul's large handwriting at the end of Galatians, which is sometimes regarded as evidence of poor eyesight, is for emphasis. His words can no longer convey his emotions. He wrests the pen from the hand of his amanuensis and with bold strokes accents his final words. The difference in handwriting will be evident to the Galatians. In modern writing the conclusion of the letter would be underlined. The argument for eye trouble as Paul's "thorn in the flesh" rests entirely on a literal construction of Galatians 4:15.

Professor Ramsay has offered persuasive arguments for another hypothesis which has much to commend it.[12] Paul, according to this theory, contracted malaria at Pamphylia on his first missionary journey. This explains why Paul and his companions turned inland and made their way to the highlands of Antioch in Pisidia. In the cooler, drier climate of this mountainous region Paul would find relief. Modern observations of the climate and the incidence of malaria in that region lend support to the malaria theory. The stabbing pains that accompany the recurring attacks of the disease suit very well the description a "thorn in the flesh."

The malaria theory has the advantage of taking seriously the words: "it was because of a bodily ailment that I preached the gospel to you at first." Neither epilepsy nor eye trouble would be likely to cause Paul to travel into Galatia or remain there to establish churches. The argument assumes, of course, that the Galatians to whom Paul addressed his letter were the churches in southern Asia Minor which he had founded on his first missionary journey.[13] One difficulty in the way of a theory that Paul's malady was either eye trouble or malaria is that neither of these illnesses would be likely to cause the Galatians to "scorn or despise" him. Any theory concerning Paul's "thorn in the

[12] Ramsay, *The Church in the Roman Empire,* pp. 59–68.
[13] On the question of the location of the Galatian churches, see "The North vs. the South Galatian Hypotheses" in chap. 7.

flesh," therefore, can be no more than guesswork. Even when ancient maladies are described in detail, diagnoses are hazardous enough, but the meager evidence in Paul's case leaves the modern student with little enough for a good guess.

Neither of these last two maladies would be observable in the young student of Gamaliel in Jerusalem. Although Paul has often been thought of as sickly because of his two references to his illness, anyone who reads and considers the almost incredible list of the hardships and punishments he endured is bound to conclude that Paul actually possessed a most remarkable physical constitution. Whatever was his "thorn in the flesh," it did not undermine his basic health.

Paul's afflictions and sufferings were not illnesses but persecutions and hardships. In later years his appearance must have borne the evidence of these afflictions. His clothing covered the mass of scars from the beatings he received from Roman lictors and scourgings from the synagogues, but the pain left its indelible marks on his face. There were lines also on his face from "the daily pressure" of his "anxiety for all the churches" (II Corinthians 11:28). Probably, too, there were scars on his face from the stoning at Lystra. With an authority uniquely his he closed his letter to the Galatians (6:17): "Henceforth let no man trouble me; for I bear on my body the marks of Jesus." But those marks and the experiences that caused them were still far in the future for the small Jewish lad as he made his way from Tarsus to Jerusalem to begin his studies under Gamaliel.

Paul and Gamaliel

If we may take the ancient rabbinic saying cited in the last chapter[14] to reflect the custom in Paul's time, he may have been about fifteen or sixteen years of age when he arrived in Jerusalem to study under Gamaliel. The Greek word *anatrepho* which is translated by the phrase "brought up" in Acts 22:3, if taken literally, would mean that Paul was with Gamaliel as a mere infant. The same word occurs in Acts 7:20 in reference to the first three months of Moses' infancy. But such a meaning of the word in the relation of Paul and Gamaliel is

[14] See p. 136.

impossible. Metaphorically, the term also means to be educated. Used in this way it, nevertheless, implies youthfulness. Paul's basic and form-ative training was had "at the feet of Gamaliel." Josephus, who was perhaps a generation later than Paul, tells us that he was sixteen when he decided to investigate the sects in Judaism.[15] If we assume that Paul was about the same age when he went to Jerusalem and we accept the latest suggested date for his birth, about 10 or 15 A.D., he would arrive in Jerusalem between 25 and 30 A.D. This means that he was studying in Gamaliel's school at the time of the crucifixion of Jesus.

The Teacher   In spite of his fame, con-crete, reliable information about Gamaliel is surprisingly meager. The tradition which does exist has to be taken with caution because of the confusion which easily arises between Gamaliel I (he is called the elder in the tradition) and his grandson, Gamaliel II.[16] It is often said that Gamaliel was a *Nasi,* i.e., a president of the Sanhedrin during the last years before Jeru-salem was taken by Titus. Since it is clear from reliable sources that the high priest always presided over the Jerusalem Sanhedrin, this statement is reading back into the earlier period a practice that only began with Johanan ben Zakkai's Sanhedrin at Jamnia.[17] Gamaliel II was for a time the president of the latter organization.

Although tradition treats Gamaliel as one among the greatest of the rabbis and the first to be honored with the title Rabban, sayings at-tributed to him are extremely rare. One well-known saying of his is not very profound: "Provide thyself with a teacher, and eschew doubt-ful matters, and tithe not overmuch by guesswork."[18] Probably his greatest contribution was the establishing of his grandfather's reputa-tion and place in rabbinic tradition—*Beth Hillel* it was called. The legend of the dispute at Jamnia between the schools of Hillel and Shammai symbolized his success. A voice (*Bath Kol*) from heaven an-nounced that: "The dicta of both the schools of Hillel and Shammai

[15] Josephus *Life,* 2.
[16] Schürer, *The Jewish People in the Time of Jesus Christ,* Part II, I, 364-65 and notes.
[17] *Ibid.,* pp. 180–81.
[18] Goldin, *The Living Talmud,* p. 72.

are words of the living God, but that of the school of Hillel is the norm."[19]

Like his grandfather, Gamaliel instituted a number of humane interpretations of otherwise burdensome laws. He is also said to have shown a broadminded interest in Greek. In other matters of ritual purity and religious duty, however, he was said to be very strict.[20]

All in all, it appears that his greatness lies not so much in his own scholarship or originality as in his organizing and disseminating the tradition of his grandfather. The picture of him presented in Acts 5:34-39 is of a practical diplomat who dreaded violence. He was in no way compromising Judaism; yet as a result of this passage in Acts Christian fancy years later placed him among the secret believers.[21] That Gamaliel was an ardent champion of the Law appears from a Talmudic passage which singled out the peculiar virtues of twelve great rabbis. Of Gamaliel the passage said, "With R. Gamaliel respect for the Torah, purity and abstemiousness ended."[22]

The Pupil   As a disciple of Gamaliel, Paul would participate in two types of instruction. The first would be the monotonous repetition involved in committing the Oral Torah to memory (cf. Isaiah 28:10). The second would be asking questions and taking part in the discussion of the meaning of obscure and minute details of the Law. The teachers regarded this discussion as a part of their own continuing education. A Talmudic riddle asks, "Why is Torah like a piece of wood?" The answer is: "As a small piece of wood kindles the log, so a minor scholar sharpens the mind of the greater."[23] In the intricate and involved exegesis displayed in his letters, Paul shows how his own mind was "sharpened" by the exercises in Gamaliel's school.

[19] *Y. Berakot,* 3 b. Newman, *The Talmudic Anthology,* p. 524.
[20] *The Universal Jewish Encyclopedia,* IV, 506.
[21] *Clementine Recognitions,* I, 65–66. According to this tradition Gamaliel's Christianity was kept secret, on the advice of the Apostles, to allow him to continue in the Sanhedrin in order to protect the interests of the Christians in just such actions as this one in Acts. In his speech in I, 66, he swore by a solemn oath that he would not allow the Jewish authorities to lay hands on the Church.
[22] *M. Sotah,* 49; *Y. Sotah,* 9, 4. Newman, *The Talmudic Anthology,* p. 469.
[23] *Taanit,* 7, *Ibid.,* p. 464.

Some scholars have questioned the statement that Paul studied under Gamaliel.[24] Usually this objection is coupled with the assertion that he was never in Jerusalem until after his conversion. One reason for questioning Paul's connection with Gamaliel is the difficulty of reconciling Paul's violent persecution of the church with Gamaliel's benign spirit. Such arguments have little force. That Gamaliel abhorred violence and, like his grandfather, benevolently longed to bring the gentiles near the Law did not prevent him from being a loyal supporter of the Law's exclusive claims. Paul's enthusiasm for the Law manifested itself differently; he was of a different temperament from Gamaliel. Furthermore, teachers are not always successful in effecting much change in the basic temperament of their students. It is asking too much of Gamaliel to insist that Paul as his pupil should have shown such a moderate attitude as Gamaliel did in Acts 5:34–39. Nor should Paul's failure to quote typical sayings from the Oral Torah surprise us. His relation to Christ provided him a new basis for interpreting the Scriptures and entirely replaced the Oral Tradition. The sayings of Jesus replaced those of the Fathers of Judaism.

More serious is the objection that Paul misrepresents rabbinic thought in statements such as: "If you break the law, your circumcision becomes uncircumcision" (Romans 2:25), and in the implication that the demands of the Law are all or nothing in nature.[25] Judaism was not without a doctrine of the mercy and forgiveness of God.[26] But the difficulty is not solved by denying Paul's contact with Gamaliel. To suppose that Paul's interpretation of the "all or nothing" demands of the Law was due to his ignorance of rabbinic teaching is to deny his

[24] Cf. Knox, *Chapters in a Life of Paul*, pp. 34–40, for a recent restatement of this position. For opposite view see Machen, *The Origin of Paul's Religion*, pp. 47–52. Joseph Klausner finds in references in the Talmud to an unnamed impudent pupil of Gamaliel oblique references to Paul. These are for him impelling evidence that Paul studied under Gamaliel. *From Jesus to Paul*, pp. 309–311. Also Johannes Munck, *Paul and the Salvation of Mankind*, trans. Frank Clarke (Richmond, Virginia: John Knox Press, 1959), pp. 80–81.

[25] Cf. Galatians 3:10 and 5:3. The Epistle of James (2:10) puts it even more baldly: "For whoever keeps the whole law but fails in one point has become guilty of all of it." Cf. Nock, *St. Paul*, pp. 29–33.

[26] "Of the seven things which were created before the creation of the world, the Torah is first and repentance the second." *Pesahim*, 54b. Newman, *The Talmudic Anthology*, p. 494.

own insistent claim to be a Jew at all. Judaism's teaching on the obligations of the Law and the mercy of God would be familiar enough to any boy reared in a faithful Jewish home, and acquainted, as Paul certainly was, with the Scriptures.

We must seek the origin of Paul's idea elsewhere. To begin with, in the passages in question his concern is polemical. He is seeking to prove that the Law as a means of salvation is inadequate by reducing the rabbinic doctrines concerning the Law to a logical absurdity. Paul bases his argument on the text from Deuteronomy 27:26, "Cursed be every one who does not abide by all things written in the book of the law, and do them" (Galatians 3:10).[27] With characteristic rabbinic reasoning Paul defends his proposition that "all who rely on works of the law are under a curse" (Galatians 3:10). He is not assigning this all or nothing theory of the Law to Jewish teaching; he is rather attempting to show that Judaism, to be consistent in depending on the Law, would have to adopt such a theory. These arguments do not display Paul's ignorance or distortion of Judaism, but rather his skill in using the Rabbis' methods, premises, and Scriptures against them.

Paul the Persecutor

Older writers on the life of Paul have usually presumed that, in the interval between his studies under Gamaliel and the stoning of Stephen, Paul had returned to Tarsus, or perhaps traveled elsewhere in search of further education. Two considerations have motivated this assumption. The first consideration is the time at which Paul arrived in Jerusalem to study. Traditionally the date of his birth has been placed at approximately the beginning of our era. This would bring him to Jerusalem about 15 to 18 A.D. The stoning of Stephen cannot have been much before 31 A.D. which leaves a considerable span of time to be accounted for.

If, however, the later date, 10–15 A.D., for Paul's birth more recently suggested by Professor Goodspeed is assumed, his arrival in Jerusalem

---

[27] This is a free quotation of the Septuagint, but the essential words and sense of the latter are retained. It may be significant of Paul's method as well as his attitude toward the Septuagint that the Greek translation of this verse serves the purpose of his argument somewhat better than the Hebrew original would have.

would be about 25 or 30 A.D. and the problem disappears. In favor of the later dates is the tradition that during the last decade before the destruction of Jerusalem in 70 A.D. Gamaliel was the President of the Sanhedrin. That Gamaliel was actually the head of that judicial body, as we have seen, is very unlikely, but the tradition may reflect the fact that he was prominent in its affairs at that time. Acts 5:34–39 tends to confirm this assumption. On this reckoning the traditional dates for Paul would be too early for Gamaliel. The later dates for Paul's birth and arrival in Jerusalem, therefore, seem the more likely, and there are no intervening years to account for between his study under Gamaliel and his persecution of the Church.

Did Paul See Jesus?   The second consideration
                             has to do with the question:
Did Paul ever see Jesus? At first reading two passages seem to say that he had. In I Corinthians 9:1 he wrote: "Am I not free? Am I not an apostle? Have I not seen Jesus our Lord?" But this verse is an obvious allusion to his experience on the Damascus Road (cf. I Corinthians 15:8).

Commentators have offered a number of interpretations of the other passage: "From now on, therefore, we regard no one from a human point of view; even though we once regarded Christ from a human point of view, we regard him thus no longer" (II Corinthians 5:16). That this verse refers to the earthly appearance of Jesus is clear, but the indefinite pronoun in the following sentence suggests that Paul is using the pronoun "we" rhetorically. If to regard Christ is to be a disciple as the verse seems to imply, Paul cannot intend to include himself but is describing the change in the understanding of Jesus which took place in the minds of the disciples after the crucifixion and resurrection. As a result of the resurrection, therefore, believers also regard one another in a different light. The meaning of the verse is at any rate too uncertain to use as evidence that Paul had seen the earthly Jesus.

Several scholars have on other grounds argued Paul's knowledge of Jesus. One argument points out that his opposition to the Christian movement would be made all the more understandable if he had seen the Galilean Teacher who so ill-fitted Paul's majestic picture of the coming Messiah. The emphasis on the humility of the incarnation in Philippians 2:5–11 adds weight to this argument. That Paul recognized Jesus on the Damascus Road requires, according to Professor Ramsay,[28] that Paul, like the other Apostles, had seen him in the flesh. Luke, however, offers some difficulty to this argument, because, in all three accounts of Paul's conversion in Acts, Paul asks, "who are you, Lord?" But the point must not be pressed; for according to the Gospel by the same author, the companions on the road to Emmaus and the eleven in Jerusalem also failed to recognize Jesus when he appeared to them.

Perhaps the most telling argument against the theory that he had seen Jesus is Paul's silence. If he had seen Jesus, would not he have used that fact against those who challenged his apostleship? The weakness in this reasoning is that, if the criterion for the apostolate in Acts 1:21 is taken seriously, what counted was being a disciple. If Paul saw Jesus it was not as a disciple but as a contemptuous onlooker. In defending his apostleship he would find no advantage in disclosing such a fact. As his words in I Corinthians 15:9, "For I am the least of the apostles, unfit to be called an apostle, because I persecuted the church of God" show Paul was not proud of his persecution of the followers of Jesus. His silence actually indicates little either way. Like many other questions that arise in the study of Paul, this question has no satisfactory answer.

That Paul could have been in Jerusalem during the crucifixion without seeing Jesus is not only possible but also likely. With the normal population of the city swelled by thousands of Passover pilgrims the trial and the execution of a Galilean accused of inciting a revolt would not be witnessed by more than a fragment of the people. There is a subtle hint in the words of Acts 26:26: "I am persuaded that none of these things has escaped his notice, for this was not done in a corner" that, as Luke understood it, Paul knew about the crucifixion at the time. But his attitude toward Jesus, if he heard of him, was undoubt-

[28] Cf. W. M. Ramsay, "Did Paul See Jesus?" from, *The Teaching of Paul in Terms of the Present Day* (London: Hodder and Stoughton, Ltd., 1913), pp. 21–30. Reprinted in Kepler, *Contemporary Thinking about Paul*, pp. 122–27; Johannes Weiss, *Earliest Christianity*, I, 188; Klausner, *From Jesus to Paul*, pp. 312–16.

edly the same as that which Gamaliel is said, in Acts 5:35–37, to have taken toward Judas and Theudas.

Was Paul ever Married? In the account of Paul's persecution, in Acts 26:9–12, the words, "I cast my vote against them" seem to imply that he was a member of the Sanhedrin at the time. Paul's membership in that high court is made virtually impossible by Luke, however, when, in the story of the stoning of Stephen (Acts 7:54–8:1), he describes Paul as a "young man" and assigns him such a minor part in the episode. The Greek word translated "vote" in Acts 26:10 is capable of a figurative use which probably is intended in this instance.[29]

The problem of Paul's relation to the Sanhedrin bears on another question regarding his life: Was Paul ever married? According to Talmudic tradition, he would have to be the head of a family in order to be a member of that body, but we know from I Corinthians 7:7 that Paul was not married at the time he was writing that letter. As has often been suggested, he may have been a widower; but his description of his unmarried status as a gift (*charisma*) from God makes that possibility unlikely. Since his membership in the Sanhedrin is very doubtful, there is little to suggest that Paul was married.[30] His marital status remains, then, as another unknown item in his vital statistics.

The Persecution According to Acts The occasion for Paul's persecution of the Church, according to Acts, was the persistence of Jesus' followers after the crucifixion in preaching in his

---

[29] See Foakes Jackson and Lake, *Beginnings of Christianity*, IV, 317.

[30] But see Dibelius, *Paul*, pp. 35–36. The picture of Paul as an enthusiastic advocate of celibacy in apocryphal writings such as the *Acts of Paul* may have this much basis in fact, that it is based on a firm tradition that he was never married. Cf. Weinel, *St. Paul*, p. 179; W. Wrede, *Paul*, trans. Edward Lummis (London: Philip Green, 1907), p. 26. For a good statement of the argument that Paul was married see F. W. Farrar, *The Life and Work of St. Paul* (New York: E. P. Dutton and Company, 1885), pp. 44–46. In addition to the above arguments Farrar urges the high regard in which marriage was held in Judaism. It was, he contends, virtually a moral obligation. A further interesting point is his suggestion that "unmarried" (*agamois*) in I Corinthians 7:8 probably means widower (the Greek word is indefinite); hence Paul is referring to himself as a widower, but it is hard to believe that Paul would express the wish that a married man be widowed! (see vs. 7).

name. Although the first mention of Saul's role in the persecution follows the martyrdom of Stephen, Luke may not intend to say that Paul's
persecution of the Church began with or was caused by Stephen's martyrdom. Perhaps Paul is included among "those from Cilicia" in Acts
6:9 along with others, including some from the synagogue of the
Freedmen, whose disputations with Stephen led to his death.[31]

The subject of the disputations is not given, but the reader knows
from the previous chapters (Acts 2:23, 36; 3:15–18; 4:10–11;
5:28–31) that it was the charge that in crucifying Jesus the Jews had
killed the Messiah. Unable to withstand the logic of Stephen, the disputants haled him before the Sanhedrin on the trumped-up charge
of blasphemy against the Temple and the Law. Stephen cleverly countered the charge by a lengthy recital of Israel's history which showed
that God's revelation had always met with just such a resistance from
Israel as the Jews were now offering to the preaching of Jesus. The
recital ended with a reference to Solomon's Temple followed by a
quotation from Isaiah 66:1–2, the burden of which is that God does
not dwell in buildings. This point tended to confirm the charge against
Stephen, and his concluding remarks so infuriated the members of the
Sanhedrin that they dragged him outside the city and stoned him.

Paul's role in the stoning apparently was confined to guarding the
garments and giving his approval. Luke dates the outbreak of the
persecution from Stephen's martyrdom. Although from Acts 8:1 it
appears that Paul was not the only persecutor, verse 3 gives him a
prominent role. (See Acts 9:31). We may infer from Galatians 1:22
that his part in the persecution was not as great as Luke seems to
imply. Paul's part in the affair reached its climax in his proposed expedition against any of "the Way" he might find in Damascus.[32] On
this journey Paul's career as a persecutor came to an abrupt end.

Such in brief is Luke's account of the external facts, but from Paul's
letters we can learn something of his own feelings about his role as a
persecutor. An understanding of Paul the persecutor is important be-

---

[31] *Ibid,* p. 82. Weiss, *Earliest Christianity,* I, 165–66.

[32] Some scholars question that the Sanhedrin had the authority to issue
"letters" such as those given to Paul (Acts 9:2). Cf. Knox, *Chapters in a
Life of Paul,* p. 39. For a different view see Foakes Jackson and Lake, *Beginnings of Christianity,* IV, 99.

cause of its bearing on the nature and meaning of his conversion. From such matters as his attitude toward the Jews and toward the persecution he suffered at their hands, and his interpretation of his conversion we can glean some insight into Paul's reasons for persecuting the Church.[33]

The Persecution According to Paul

In retrospect Paul reflected with profound remorse on his persecution of the Church as something that made him uniquely culpable and unprepared for Christ's appearance to him (I Corinthians 15:9).[34] But nothing in this passage suggests what his motives had been. Although his two other references to his persecution of the Church (Galatians 1:13–14, 23; Philippians 3:6) are made for the specific purpose of demonstrating his former zeal for and loyalty to the Law, they undoubtedly contain a key to his motives in the persecution. In both instances Paul was confronting challenges of his teaching made by legalistic Jewish Christians, and his point is that his rejection of Jewish legalism did not stem either from ignorance of the meaning of the Law or from an heretical background but was the result of the revelation of Christ to him. The point of his argument rests on the fact that his persecutions were in some way a defense of the Law and therefore proved both his zeal for the Law and his thoroughly orthodox relation to it.

We must ask, however, what it was in the nascent Christian community that Paul saw as a threat to the Law. The question is particularly relevant if we consider, as is customary, that it was Paul himself who later as a Christian apostle brought into the open the implicit opposition of Christianity to Jewish legalism. The charge of blasphemy against the Temple, which in Acts is the reason for Stephen's martyrdom, is never mentioned in Paul's letters; in fact, there is nothing in the letters to warrant the usual inference from the story in Acts of Paul's presence at the stoning of Stephen that that episode occasioned his persecution of the Church.

[33] Cf. Dibelius, *Paul*, p. 51; Foakes Jackson and Lake, *Beginnings of Christianity*, V, 212–18; B. W. Bacon, *The Story of St. Paul* (Boston: Houghton, Mifflin and Company, 1904), pp. 55–57.
[34] Cf. I Tim. 1:13.

Pharisees were not traditionally persecutors and harbored among their number many of widely divergent opinions.[35] For Paul to turn persecutor, then, meant that he saw in the growing movement of the followers of Jesus something that struck at the very tap root of the Law. That he persistently associated both his mission to the gentiles and his abrogation of circumcision with the revelation afforded him at his conversion must mean that the content of his revelation on the Damascus Road included a radical and authoritative change of mind on these two points.[36] Now, to a Pharisee there could be nothing objectionable in a mission to the gentiles per se; for proselyting, as we have seen, had long been an accepted and widespread activity of the Pharisees.[37] We are left with the almost unavoidable conclusion that the Church's mission to the gentiles had already shown certain peculiar aspects which were inimical to the Law.

Did these aspects include waiving circumcision? From Paul's interpretation of his conversion in Galatians we may infer that they did. So Luke understood the matter. In a series of vignettes, in the early chapters of Acts, he pictures the first steps of Christianity outside Jerusalem. Philip in Samaria, Peter at the house of Cornelius in Caesarea, and the conversion of the Greeks in Antioch illustrate the way in which the missionaries approached the gentiles and ignored the requirement of circumcision for their converts. We may suppose that some of the more conservative members of the movement had misgivings about such a departure—misgivings that were later to crystallize into organized opposition and create a major problem for Paul.[38] But there is no need to divide the primitive Christian community from the beginning into two parties over the question of circumcision.[39]

[35] Cf. Klausner, *From Jesus to Paul,* p. 313.
[36] The clearest statement of this association is in Galatians 1:11–2:9. The whole issue over the Law in Galatians actually revolves around the question of the necessity of circumcision. To continue the requirement of circumcision was a violation of the gospel which Paul had received by revelation, i.e., at his conversion. Cf. Carl von Weizsäcker, *The Apostolic Age,* trans. James Millar, 2nd ed. rev. (London: Williams and Norgate, 1894), pp. 89–90.
[37] "Proselytes and God-Fearers" in chap. 3.
[38] On the opposition to Paul see George S. Duncan, *St. Paul's Ephesian Ministry* (New York: Charles Scribner's Sons, 1930), chaps. XVIII, XIX, 253–281.
[39] We shall have occasion in the succeeding chapters to refer to a theory

Probably the neglect of circumcision at first was without any theoretical basis and simply resulted from the enthusiasm of those of "the Way" who, knowing that in Jesus the Messiah had come, were hurriedly spreading the Good News in preparation for the end of the present evil age. Peter justified his baptism of Cornelius, for example, by his vision which concluded with the words, "What God has cleansed, you must not call common" (Acts 10:9–16). But later, in Antioch, he was not prepared to stand by the logical consequences of his action (Galatians 2:11–16). How much of this disregard of the obligation of the Law for gentiles was explicit in the Church as Paul the Pharisee knew it we cannot tell, but at any rate Paul quickly saw that the logical implications of what he heard from the believers would carry the movement altogether outside the Law. What these followers of Jesus were preaching in the synagogues threatened the very foundation of Judaism.

We may surmise that something of this nature was the subject of the debates between Stephen and his opponents in Acts 6:9–10. If Paul were one of the Cilicians, he would thus have ample opportunity to study the significance of the movement, at least as Stephen represented it.[40] The mission of the Apostles was, from the beginning, something

---

still influential in interpreting Paul that divides the Christian community virtually from the beginning into two opposing parties: The Hebrews, who dominated the Jerusalem Church; and the Hellenists, whose stronghold was Antioch. The theory goes back to F. C. Baur of the University of Tübingen and is a part of a system of Pauline interpretation known as the "Tübingen School." While many of the theories on which this system rests have long been disproved and abandoned, the picture of conflict between Paul and the Hellenists on the one hand and the Jewish Christianity in Jerusalem on the other hand, still colors much of the writing on Paul. The picture is based on the references in Acts to the Hellenists who, because they were from the Diaspora and influenced by Greek culture and ideas are supposed to have been more liberal and less attached to the Law and the Temple, but this is a misreading of Acts. It was the Hellenists with whom Stephen disputed and who probably were responsible for his death. They also were the disputants with Paul in Acts 9:29. They seem to have been the narrowest group of all! See Munck, *Paul and the Salvation of Mankind,* chap. III, 69–86. But see Cadbury, "The Hellenists" in Foakes Jackson and Lake, *The Beginnings of Christianity,* V, 59–74, where the Hellenists are said to be Greeks and not Jews at all. For a critical study of the history of Pauline research see Albert Schweitzer, *Paul and his Interpreters,* trans. W. Montgomery (New York: The Macmillan Company, 1951).

[40] Cf. Weiss, *Earliest Christianity,* I, 165–66. Luke appears to be justified, on this reasoning, in relating Stephen and Paul to the rise of the persecution.

different from the Pharisaical interest in making proselytes.

That the mission of the Apostles was messianic, i.e:. based on the belief that in Jesus the Messiah had come, goes without saying. Conceivably if Paul had been able to accept the Messiahship of Jesus, he would have accepted the setting aside of circumcision. The fact that these two propositions are in his later thinking so closely related lends support to such an assumption.[41] That Paul, like other Pharisees of his time, ardently awaited the coming of Israel's Deliverer shines through all his letters. But it is equally clear that Jesus not only did not fulfill the pre-Christian Paul's messianic expectations but also actually represented an affront to the Law.

The core of Paul's former opposition to the preaching of Jesus appears in I Corinthians 1:23: "We preach Christ crucified, a stumblingblock to Jews." The force of this statement will be clearer if we remember that Christ is the Greek translation of the Hebrew word messiah. Paul's emphasis is almost defiant: "We preach that the Messiah was crucified!" (Cf. I Corinthians 1:18; 2:2; II Corinthians 13:4; Philippians 2:8.) Paul understood the Jewish objection to Jesus because it had been his own. That God's Deliverer should suffer defeat at the hands of Israel's oppressor was, as Gamaliel's logic in Acts 5:38 shows, naturally unthinkable. But the failure of a messianic movement would not, in itself, constitute a threat to the Law. The blasphemy in the Christians' claims for Jesus was that they persisted in claiming him to be the Messiah after he had been crucified. Paul explains in Galatians 3:13 why this claim is blasphemous by quoting from Deuteronomy 21:23 the words, "Cursed be every one who hangs on a tree." The whole passage runs:

"And if a man has committed a crime punishable by death and he is put to death, and you hang him on a tree, his body shall not remain all night upon the tree, but you shall bury him the same day, for a hanged man is

---

That Stephen's blasphemy against the Temple was a trumped-up charge (Acts 6:13–14) may reflect Luke's awareness that the real issue arose out of the disputes rather than the stoning. His treatment of the whole episode is understandable if it is assumed that, writing from a later perspective, he did not know what the disputes were about.

[41] Cf. Klausner, *From Jesus to Paul*, pp. 320–22.

accursed by God; you shall not defile your land which the Lord your God gives you for an inheritance" (Deuteronomy 21:22-23).

The violent persecutions of the Church arose, then, not simply because of the apparently ridiculous claim that a humble Galilean who had been executed by the Roman authorities was nevertheless the Messiah, but because of the blasphemy in the claim that one who was manifestly "accursed by God" was yet the "Righteous One." Such a claim indeed threatened the whole structure of Judaism; it contradicted the provisions of the Law itself.[42] Paul in his pre-Christian days saw what apparently the followers of Jesus had not seen so clearly: that to accept the *crucified* Jesus as the Christ was to make God counter His own Law and thus bring it to an end. This Paul the Persecutor could not do. So he set himself, with no qualms of conscience whatever, to remove the outrage from Israel. Significantly, Paul's most important and most original contributions in later years to Christian theology had as their starting point the "stumbling-block" of the cross.[43] The "stumbling-stone" for Paul the Persecutor became a "corner-stone" for Paul the Christian (Romans 9:32-33).

In theory at least Paul could not object to the resurrection. As a Pharisee he was an ardent believer in it, but he could not believe that God would raise from the dead one who had been accursed. If Paul were to accept the believers' claim that Jesus had been resurrected, his whole theology would collapse. That is exactly what happened to him on the Damascus Road.

Paul's Conversion

The word conversion when used to refer to Paul's experience on the Damascus Road is somewhat misleading. The change that took place in Paul was neither a change from one religion to another nor from a life of irreligion and sin to a life of faith. Paul would be the first to protest such implications. Yet the experience did produce a drastic change in Paul—a change which we must understand if we are to understand him.

[42] Cf. Maurice Goguel, *The Birth of Christianity*, trans. H. C. Snape (New York: The Macmillan Company, 1954), p. 211.
[43] See "Jesus Died and Rose Again" in chap. 9.

In studying Paul's conversion we must keep two things in mind: First, it is basic to all of Paul's thinking as a follower of Christ that he still regarded himself as moving within the true continuity of Israel. His faith was the faith of Abraham. Far from abandoning the religion of his fathers he had found in Christ its true fulfillment (cf. Romans 9:3–5). Even the Law had not been wrong; it had been superseded. Second, as deeply as he regretted his persecution of the Church and as futile as was his righteousness under the Law, Paul never disparaged his former religious motives. "As to righteousness under the law blameless" (Philippians 3:6), he boasted. He still served the same God with the same zeal, but it had been a zeal blinded by ignorance; now it was enlightened. Before the Damascus Road he had stood exactly where he saw unbelieving Israel still standing when, in Romans 10:2, he wrote "I bear them witness that they have a zeal for God, but it is not enlightened."

Pre-conditions The study of Paul's conversion usually begins by a survey of the factors that led to it.[44] Among the physical factors are the blazing desert sun beating mercilessly on the head of the restless traveler who was in too much of a hurry to make the customary pause during the heat of the day; the glittering desert sands playing tricks upon Paul's weary eyes coupled with an overwhelming weariness from the impossible strain of his frantic persecutions; and perhaps a thunder storm and an awesome bolt of lightning, or one of his ever-recurring epileptic seizures. The psychological description of Paul's conversion usually begins with Romans 7:7–25. Paul the Pharisee, reared from childhood in a passionately religious atmosphere, controlled by an absolute devotion to the Law, but whose keen intellect and uncompromising sincerity would not admit the casuistry by which others had made peace with the Law's demands, was driven to fanatical extremes by his quest for peace with God. His persecutions were the overt expression of his inner conflict. The stoning of Stephen produced the crisis. Still haunted by the glowing face of Stephen and his dying words: "Behold, I see the heavens opened, and the Son of man standing at the right

[44] One of the best descriptions of the pre-conditions of Paul's conversion is in B. W. Bacon, *The Story of St. Paul,* pp. 52–67.

hand of God," Paul set out for Damascus. The week of traveling gave him time to reflect. His faith in the Law as the way of salvation, corroded by doubts and assailed by the stubborn witness even to death of the followers of Jesus, began to crumble. At last he gave in. Before his tortured mind came a vision of Jesus calling him to discipleship; he obeyed.

Whatever value such reconstructions may have in helping us to understand Paul's experience, they must be recognized as modern interpretations. Neither Luke nor Paul would think in such terms. Some such factors may well have played a part in his conversion, but they do not explain Paul. That we seek to understand his conversion as he interpreted it is far more important. Only so can we see how that experience affected—indeed controlled—his life and thought.[45]

The Conversion According to Acts   Concerned with the providential growth of the Church, Acts tells the story as the miraculous end of the great persecution which was accomplished by a vision that converted the arch-enemy to a most effective ally (cf. 9:31). Except for the fact that the experience occurred "at midday" (22:6; 26:13) and near Damascus with the journey nearly completed (9:3; 22:6), nothing in Acts suggests the physical factors that are supposed to have contributed to Paul's vision. The story occurs three times in Acts. In chapter 9:1–22 it is a part of the main narrative; in chapter 22:3–21 and chapter 26:9–18 it is incorporated in Paul's speeches.

Luke, who elsewhere has shown a tendency to give Old Testament form to certain important episodes, tells the story of Paul's vision in the literary framework of Daniel 10:7–12. The variations in the three accounts are for the most part of no significance. In chapter 9, for example, Paul's companions heard the voice yet saw no one, but in chapter 22 they saw the light but did not hear the voice; in chapter 9 Paul was blind for three days, but in chapter 22 his sight was restored upon arriving in Damascus; in chapter 26 all of the men fell to the ground,

[45] For a technical criticism of psychological theories concerning the background of Paul's conversion, see Munck, *Paul and the Salvation of Mankind,* chap. I, 11–35.

but the other two accounts mention only that Paul did so. There is a marked tendency toward compression in the successive accounts. The part of Ananias in the first account occupies more than half of the narrative; in the second account it is considerably abbreviated and in chapter 26 omitted altogether.

The one variation of significance is in Paul's commission to preach to the gentiles. In the first two accounts the commission is relayed through Ananias and, although the gentiles are placed foremost, the "sons of Israel" (9:15) are included (in 22:15 it is "all men"), but in chapter 26 Paul receives his commission *to the gentiles* directly from Jesus. Although this difference may be no more than the result of compression, Professor Kirsopp Lake has found in it evidence of different sources which Luke used.[46] Since this problem bears on a question with which we shall be concerned later it will be worthwhile to take note of it.

That chapter 26 coincides more closely with Paul's emphasis in Galatians 1:11–17 that he did not receive his gospel from men suggests that it came from a source closer to Paul than the other two accounts, which appear to reflect the tendency of the Jerusalem Church to subordinate Paul to its authority. The difficulty is that, in the first place, the mediation of Ananias in Damascus would not place Paul under obligation to the Jerusalem Apostles, which is the bone of contention in Galatians; in the second place, chapter 9 makes it clear that the commission was from the Lord and that Ananias was only relaying to Paul what in a vision the Lord had given him. Here, as elsewhere, Luke shows little concern for the issues over which Paul and his opponents contended so sharply.

According to Acts the conversion of Paul had three important meanings: 1) With the removal of the arch-persecutor the harassment of the Church, which was impeding its growth, ended. 2) Paul became a believer. 3) Paul was appointed to be a "witness" (only once, in Acts 14:4, is Paul called an Apostle by Luke) for Jesus, especially to the gentiles. In connection with this last meaning we may note one

[46] "The Conversion of Paul and the Events immediately following it," Foakes Jackson and Lake, *The Beginnings of Christianity*, V, 188–91, for a criticism of Professor Lake's theory see Munck, *Paul and the Salvation of Mankind*, pp. 16–20.

dominant difference in point of view between Luke and Paul. Not only in the story of Paul's conversion but also throughout the narrative of his missionary work, according to Acts, Paul's ministry includes the Jews. He regularly begins his work in each new city with the synagogue, and only when his message is rejected by them, does he turn to the gentiles. The pattern of appealing to the Jews first and then to the gentiles is further reinforced by having Paul begin his preaching in Jerusalem (Acts 9:28–29; 26:20. In 22:17–22, however, he was apparently sent immediately out of Jerusalem). In his treatment of the story of Paul, Luke is simply following the scheme in Acts 1:8 which governs the arrangement of the entire work.

The Conversion According to Paul   Paul gives his own version of the "revelation," as he prefers to call it, in three passages. The most important and most complete is in Galatians 1:11–17; the other two, each of which adds an important interpretation, are in I Corinthians 15:8–10 and Philippians 3:5–16. Beside these, a few passages make incidental reference to the experience. Among the more important of these references are I Corinthians 9:1; (possibly II Corinthians 4:6); and Romans 1:1–5. Since for understanding his letters the most important aspect of Paul's conversion is the meaning it held for him, we must now study these passages for his own description of the experience.

In Paul's references to his conversion there is no suggestion of a psychological conditioning, or for that matter, preparation of any kind. The revelation was a sudden, unexpected incursion into a life already dedicated to doing the will of God as he understood it. The passage in Romans 7:7–25 which is often used to picture Paul's pre-Christian struggles with the Law is not autobiographical, but as the context shows is a description of the current struggles of the Christian life intended to show the purpose of the Law. To argue otherwise is to make the deliverance in the climactic verses (24–25) refer to Paul's conversion, whereas it clearly points to the eschatological future.

From his words, "as to righteousness under the law blameless" (Philippians 3:6b) it is clear that Paul was conscious of no personal failure with respect to the Law. The struggle in Romans 7 is the same as the one which he describes in Philippians 3:12: "Not that I have already obtained this or am already perfect; but I press on to make it my own, because Christ Jesus has made me his own." For Paul the failure of the Law was not his failure to keep it, but its failure to produce the right kind of righteousness (Philippians 3:9).[47]

If Paul's conversion had been a radical volte-face resulting from an unendurable inner torment, we would expect the typical radical rejection of his previous faith characteristic of such "converts." But Paul is at pains to show that he has not abandoned Judaism. He does not condemn the Law. It has been misused by being made a means for establishing one's own righteousness (Romans 10:3-5). But we cannot say "that the law is sin" (Romans 7:7); rather it "was our custodian until Christ came" (Galatians 3:24).

It is significant of Paul's own understanding of his experience that, in his most explicit reference to it, he regards it as a prophetic call like that of Jeremiah and Deutero-Isaiah. A clear understanding of the nature of Paul's conversion is of basic importance because that experience controls his own concept of his mission and his interpretation of the Christian Faith. To misunderstand Paul here is to throw his whole treatment of the Law and its place in God's program of redemption out of perspective.

Paul's pre-Christian life is by no means irrelevant, however, for not only his training in Judaism but also his acquaintance with the Christian movement provided material for the content of his experience of conversion and the framework within which it occurred. It is possible, of course, that Paul was unconsciously influenced more than he ever realized or admitted by his contests with the followers of Jesus. Perhaps, too, those contests had shaken the subconscious foundations of his confidence in the Law.[48] But his own interpretation of the experience and his subsequent thought reflect only a sudden divine intervention—a revelation from God.

The most prominent feature of Paul's allusions to his conversion is

---

[47] Interpreters of Paul often lose sight of the fact that the Law for a Pharisee included the Oral Law, the casuistry which brought the Law within reach of human performance. This fact explains why Paul could boast as he did of his achievements under the Law (Phil. 3:6).

[48] Cf. Weiss, *Earliest Christianity*, I, 189.

the resurrection. In I Corinthians 15:8–10 he deliberately lists his experience as the final appearance of Jesus after the resurrection. The subject of this chapter is the Christian's resurrection, and the whole discussion is based on what he had preached to the Corinthians on his initial visit:

> For I delivered to you as of first importance what I also received, that Christ died for our sins in accordance with the scriptures, that he was buried, that he was raised on the third day in accordance with the scriptures, and that he appeared to Cephas, then to the twelve. Then he appeared to more than five hundred brethren at one time, most of whom are still alive, though some have fallen asleep. Then he appeared to James, then to all the apostles (I Corinthians 15:3–7).

To be sure, it was what he had received, (i.e., the "tradition" of the Apostles); but his addition, "Last of all, as to one untimely born, he appeared also to me" (verse 8) shows that he himself was a part of that tradition. In reality, therefore, the discussion in this chapter rests on Paul's own experience. As he reminded the Corinthians earlier in the letter (9:1), he had "seen Jesus our Lord."

Paul is at pains here to make it clear that his experience was of a piece with that of the other Apostles to whom the Risen Lord had made his appearances. Professor John Knox rightly points out that Paul distinguished this experience from his many later "visions and revelations."[49] Paul's conversion has sometimes been compared to Stephen's vision (Acts 7:55–56) at the end of his speech; but even under the formal similarities in Acts the differences are pronounced: in contrast to Stephen's vision, Luke is discreetly vague about what Paul saw. For Paul there is neither an opening of heaven nor a glimpse of the ascended Jesus. For reassurance against his coming martyrdom Stephen's is a vision of heaven to one who already believed; Paul's is a light and a voice which accosted him, an enemy of the believers, in the way. The difference seems deliberate. In I Corinthians 15:8 Paul tells us that the experience was not a vision but an appearance of the Risen Lord.

The effect of that experience was to reverse the thinking which had

---

[49] Knox, *Chapters in a Life of Paul*, p. 121.

provided Paul's reasons for opposing Christianity. For Paul the resurrection of Jesus was now a fact. The claim of Jesus' followers was true:
Jesus is the Messiah. He has become "the first fruits" of the believers'
resurrection. On this foundation Paul rebuilt his theology. That is
why he wrote in Romans 1:4 the strange statement: "designated Son
of God . . . by his resurrection from the dead." Not that Jesus was
not the Son of God until the resurrection but that the resurrection
defined him as such is the point. This was Paul's experience and, therefore, the order of his thinking.

We shall come in a later chapter to examine the way in which this
experience shaped Paul's thinking about the crucifixion which had
been for him the "stumbling-block."[50] We need only note here that the
resurrection proved to Paul that Jesus was the Christ in spite of the
fact that he had "become a curse" by being crucified. This could only
mean that the Law in some way had been superseded.

Now Paul also accepted the mission to the gentiles, including the
waiving of circumcision, to which he had so strenuously objected. Characteristically, he thought out the connection between his revelation and
the mission to the gentiles in a way that made that mission a logical
necessity. Because the Church had not arrived at a logical and consistent position regarding its relation to the gentiles, Paul found himself
in bitter controversy with certain conservative elements within it.

Another prominent feature in Paul's descriptions of his conversion
is its relation to his apostleship. The importance of this matter is evident from the fact that a major part of two of his letters is concerned
with it. So important was the issue that we will need to examine it in
some detail.

It will help us to understand the controversy over Paul's position
and authority as an Apostle if we observe that the word apostle is used
in at least three ways in the New Testament.[51] In a few instances
apostle has the simple meaning of a messenger without any indication
of status or authority. This meaning is found, for example, in II Co-

[50] See chap. 9.
[51] For a study of the term apostle see Ernest DeWitt Burton, *The Epistle
to the Galatians, The International Critical Commentary* (New York: Charles
Scribner's Sons, 1920), Detached Notes I, 363–84. Also Weiss, *Earliest Christianity,* I, 46–48.

rinthians 8:23 and Philippians 2:25 where the distinction between the simple and the more technical uses of the term is preserved in English by translating the Greek with the word messenger. The other two uses of the term involve specific offices in the work and life of the Church. Apostles are official emissaries commissioned to proclaim the gospel and instruct the churches. Perhaps still another use was beginning in the lists of church officers in I Corinthians 12:28–29 and in Ephesians 2:20; 3:5; 4:11. In its most restricted use, however, the term refers to the original disciples of Jesus whose number, having been reduced by the defection and suicide of Judas, had been restored to the significant number of twelve by the election of Matthias (Acts 1:15–26). Acts employs the word almost exclusively in this restricted sense. The picture in Acts is of an Apostolic College which sat in Jerusalem as the governing body of the Church. That the picture is idealized appears in the fact that Peter, who had been the leader, left Jerusalem according to chapter 12, verses 17 and 19, and James, the Lord's brother, was in charge according to both Acts 15 and Galatians 2 (cf. Acts 21:18 and Galatians 2:12).

Paul distinguishes between the Apostles of Christ and apostles of men (Galatians 1:1). Apostles of Christ had received their commission directly from him, but apostles of men were subordinate missionaries commissioned by the Church to extend its work. Paul's kinsmen in Romans 16:7 belong in this group. The church officers he mentions in his letters may also be included here. Acts appears to place Paul and Barnabas in this category in the only place in that book where the term is applied to Paul (Acts 14:4; cf. 13:1–3). Luke apparently sided with the Jerusalem authorities on the status of Paul. Probably the "superlative apostles" in II Corinthians 11:5 and 12:11 belong in this category as does Apollos according to I Corinthians 4:9. That Paul, who elsewhere repeatedly calls himself an Apostle of Christ, rather surprisingly equates himself with Apollos in the same sense in this last passage indicates only how loosely the term as such could be used.[52] Yet the distinction between the apostles of men and Apostles of Christ is valid. It was not the term but the source of the authority which it

---

[52] Paul also relates himself to Barnabas in the same way in I Corinthians 9:6. Cf. Acts 14:4. But in Acts 9:27 Barnabas is distinguished from the Apostles.

represented which was the subject of Paul's controversy over his apostleship. If he had been made an apostle by the Church, then he was responsible to it, especially to the Jerusalem Apostles for what he taught, but if he, like them, had received his commission directly from Jesus he became a primary authority.

The issue turned on being a witness to the resurrection. As Luke understood them the conditions of apostleship are detailed in Acts 1:21-22. Paul's argument was that the condition *sine qua non* of apostleship in the restricted sense was to have seen the Risen Lord, since being a witness to the resurrection was the real function of the Apostles (Acts 1:22; 4:33; 10:41). His experience was the same as theirs; therefore, in the restricted sense of the word he was an Apostle.

Paul himself paid little attention to the Twelve. For him they did not occupy a place of any such peculiar importance as they do in Acts. Only once, in I Corinthians 15:5, does he even mention the Twelve.[53] Significantly, he includes them in a list which includes "all the apostles." That there were other Apostles of Christ, i.e., Apostles who had seen the resurrected Lord, appears also in Luke's Gospel (24:33-48), but in Acts they lacked the special designation which constituted the Twelve. In Paul's view, however, the Twelve were merely the governing body of the Jerusalem Church. The fact that the composition of the Twelve underwent some changes—Matthias replaced Judas, and probably James the brother of Jesus had replaced James Zebedee after Herod Agrippa executed the latter (Acts 12:1-2; Gal. 1:19)—lends weight to Paul's view. With the departure of Peter from Jerusalem, James seems to have succeeded to the chairmanship of the Twelve. They were therefore simply the "first among equals" of the Apostles of Christ. It may be that Paul's references to "those who were of repute" (Galatians 2:2, 6) indicates the Twelve, but verse 9 implies an even narrower reference to James, Cephas, and John. (Does this point back to Peter, James, and John, the "inner circle" of the disciples in the Gospels?)

Paul was contending, not for a place among the Twelve, but among the Apostles of Christ, all of whom in his view bore the teaching au-

---

[53] A doubtful textual variant reads "eleven." But see Weiss, *Earliest Christianity*, I, 24, and note.

thority bestowed upon them by their witness to the resurrection of Jesus and their commission received from him. Somewhat inconsistent with his general view, then, is Luke's description of Paul's commission *by Jesus* to be such a witness (Acts 9:15–16; 22:15; 26:16). Paul's basic argument for his position was that he had been a witness to the resurrection exactly as had the other Apostles; and since for him the Twelve held no basic advantage over other Apostles of Christ, he held an authority equal to theirs. When this argument is kept in mind, the strange order of the list of Jesus' appearances in I Corinthians 15:5–8 becomes meaningful. Three persons are mentioned individually: Cephas (Peter), James, and Paul. Cephas and James are the two Apostles with whom Paul visited on his first trip to Jerusalem after his conversion. As he does here and in Galatians (1:18; 2:7–14) the only other time Paul mentions Cephas in connection with the Apostles in Corinthians (9:5) he singles him out from the rest. This was by no means to deny Peter's apostleship, but in some way to place him in a special category within the Apostolate. Peter had, like Paul, experienced an appearance of Jesus to him individually. Furthermore, he was commissioned in a special way "with the gospel to the circumcised," just as Paul had been "for the Gentiles" (Galatians 2:8; but Cf. Acts 15:7).

The list in I Corinthians 15:5–8 relates Cephas to "the Twelve" in a way parallel with that of James to "all the apostles." The two groups are separated by the mention of a company of "more than five hundred brethren." It would be hard to find a more effective way of demolishing the exclusive claims for the Twelve than this arrangement of the list of appearances. The mention of James in connection with "all the apostles" is interesting because he apparently was not a follower of Jesus until after the resurrection.[54] Jerome has preserved a quotation from *The Gospel According to the Hebrews* which tells how Jesus appeared to James, who had sworn not to eat until he saw Jesus' resurrection, and broke and blessed bread with him.[55] Early tradition, aware of the parallel between James and Paul, both of whom came to the

---

[54] On James, the Lord's brother, see James Hardy Ropes, *The Epistle of St. James, International Critical Commentary*, pp. 62–74.
[55] Jerome, *Lives of Illustrious Men*, II.

apostolate from outside the circle of the original disciples of Jesus, accorded James a similar individual experience of the resurrection. If James, who belonged with "all the apostles" rather than the Twelve, could supersede Peter in the leadership of the Jerusalem Church itself, surely Paul, who had seen the Lord, deserved to be recognized as an Apostle of Christ and his authority duly recognized.

Finally, Paul mentions himself along with the others as a witness to the resurrection. It is noteworthy that he describes himself as "the least of the apostles, unfit to be called an apostle," not because of any difference in his relation to the resurrection, but because he "persecuted the church of God."

"As to one untimely born," so Paul describes his conversion experience. The word "untimely" does not refer to the lateness of Jesus' appearance to him. The term itself means a premature birth. Paul had come to the resurrection experience without the preparation of being a disciple of Jesus.[56] Neither he nor James qualified under the terms set forth in Acts 1:21–22 for a place among the Twelve. Yet James had succeeded to Peter's leadership in Jerusalem and Paul became the Apostle of Christ to the gentiles. That this passage in I Corinthians is not involved in the controversy over Paul's authority or "gospel" makes it all the more significant. This is the natural pattern of his thought about the Apostles of Christ and his place among them.

The first two chapters of Galatians, where the issue of Paul's authority is paramount, are usually interpreted to mean that Paul claimed to be independent of the tradition of the Church. But he cannot have meant this, for twice in I Corinthians, for example, he explicitly cites the tradition which he had received. Both in Damascus and later during his fifteen days with Peter, unquestionably Paul had learned the tradition which he taught his churches. The issue was the interpretation of the tradition, especially in regard to the mission to the gentiles. Paul's argument, as Galatians 1:10 shows, is that no other man is an arbiter of his interpretation. He is responsible directly to Christ.

In these chapters Paul is writing to show, by his movements after

[56] It almost seems as if Paul was deliberately exerting himself to compensate for this deficiency and for having persecuted the Church: "I worked harder than any of them."

his conversion, that neither was he made an Apostle by the Jerusalem authorities, nor was he subject to them, but like the prophets of old he had been chosen from birth for the ministry in which he is engaged, and he was commissioned Apostle to the gentiles by Christ. He had no need to please men, for he was a slave of Christ and, unlike the apostles of men, responsible only to Him. His authority on matters of doctrine, therefore, was as great as that of the Jerusalem Apostles. Those "reputed to be pillars" had recognized this; let the Galatians recognize it too!

The deeply personal, religious meaning of the experience Paul relates in Philippians 3:5-16. For Paul the experience was not merely an event in the past but a continuing present reality. Whatever he had gained in his old life under the Law he continued to regard as loss, for the sake of a new kind of righteousness based on faith in Christ. He still pursued the knowledge and power of the risen Christ; he still sought to share Christ's sufferings in order that, as on the Damascus Road he had been seized by Christ, he might seize the resurrection. His entire life was now dedicated to pursuing "the goal for the prize of the upward call of God in Christ Jesus."

In one great event Paul was changed from a persecutor to a believer; from an expositor of the Jewish Law to a Christian teacher; from an emissary of the Sanhedrin to the Apostle of Christ to the gentiles. That event holds a profound significance for us, too, because it produced the author of one fourth of the New Testament.

After Damascus

Three passages in Acts and two in Paul's letters afford us glimpses into the period between his conversion and the time when he set out toward the west on his great missionary enterprise. The passages in Acts (9:18-30; 22:16-21; 26:19-20) in each case follow as a conclusion to the narratives of Paul's conversion. Even more than in the story of the conversion itself, the increasing compression in the succeeding accounts is obvious.

In the first and fullest of the three accounts, Acts 9:18-30, Luke's characteristic editorial generalizations are evident. Leaving aside the editorial summaries, the following items emerge: Paul is baptized by

Ananias; he begins preaching in the neighborhood of Damascus; after some time (the time here is significantly indefinite), because of a plot against his life by the Jews, he escapes over the wall of the city and returns to Jerusalem where Barnabas introduces him to the Apostles; because of a plot against his life by the Hellenists in Jerusalem he is hurried off to Tarsus.

The second account, in Acts 22:16–21, simply mentions Paul's baptism by Ananias, his return to Jerusalem, and replaces the story of the plot of the Hellenists with his vision in the Temple warning him to flee the city.[57] That the account of the vision allows Luke to point out the understandable reaction of the Jewish authorities in Jerusalem to Paul's conversion suggests that this story, too, incorporates an editorial summation. In Acts 26:19–20, the whole matter is reduced to the briefest possible generalization. Ananias and Paul's baptism have been left out altogether and only the sequence of Damascus and Jerusalem remains. But the reader of course knows these things from the previous accounts, so Luke is content to leave the matter with a reiteration of his favorite motif: the gospel is preached first to the Jews and then to the gentiles (cf. Rom. 1:16).

Paul refers incidentally in two of his letters to the events of this period. In the course of his argument with the Galatians (1:11–24) that he was not dependent on men, meaning the Jerusalem Apostles, for his interpretation of the gospel, Paul outlines the salient facts concerning his movements after his conversion. The point at issue is his authority for setting aside in his mission to the gentiles such requirements of the Law as circumcision. What he writes, is therefore only that which is germane to his argument.

With some differences and the addition of some details, the general pattern of the account in Acts, which includes a period of time spent in the vicinity of Damascus, an escape over the wall of the city, a trip to Jerusalem and his return to Cilicia, appears also in the Galatians account. That Paul did not immediately seek counsel from "flesh and blood" does not rule out the account in Acts of his baptism by Ananias.

---

[57] Professor Ramsay believes that Luke in this account has omitted Paul's first visit to Jerusalem, and identifies the Jerusalem visit here with Paul's second visit. *St. Paul the Traveller*, pp. 62–64.

The verb translated "confer" means to consult, or to take one into counsel, and by no means excludes all contact with other Christians. That Paul was baptized is obvious from the way he writes of it, for instance, in Romans 6:3–11; and there is no good reason for doubting that Ananias did it.

In the Region of Damascus That Paul went immediately[58] into Arabia we are told only in this passage. Undoubtedly Arabia here refers to the Nabatean Kingdom of Aretas IV which included much of the Transjordan area from the Negeb north. Where in Arabia he went and why have been the subjects of much conjecture. Some have supposed that he retreated to Mt. Sinai, or at least to some secluded area, to think through the significance of his revelation. But it is at least equally possible that he began to preach in the Nabatean Kingdom, which might help to explain why King Aretas wanted his arrest. How long he remained in Arabia we are not told; but he did return to Damascus and obviously began proclaiming the gospel there.

That Paul preached in Damascus is not only stated in Acts but is evident from the fact that he lists his own account of his escape from Damascus (II Corinthians 11:30 ff.) among the hardships he had endured in his missionary work. The story of his escape raises some historical problems. What authority did Aretas have in Damascus? For about a century the city had been Roman territory; but because Roman coins found in Damascus show a gap in dates from 34 A.D. for a period of about 30 years, it is usually assumed that Aretas had resumed control during that time.[59] But the action may have been extra-legal. In such an outpost of the Empire as Damascus the risk involved in an abduction would not be great. That Acts assigns the plot against Paul to Jews suggests that they may have been in collusion with the Nabataeans.[60]

---

[58] For some reason the adverb "immediately" is omitted in the RSV. It actually modifies the whole clause, i.e., he went immediately into Arabia rather than first consulting "flesh and blood" or going to the Jerusalem Apostles.

[59] See Cadbury *The Book of Acts in History,* pp. 19–21, for a good treatment of questions raised by this story.

[60] But cf. Foakes Jackson and Lake, *The Beginnings of Christianity,* V, 193–94.

The First Visit to Jerusalem   In Galatians 1:18 Paul gives
a more definite period of
time for his stay in the region of Damascus than the "many days" of
Acts 9:23. But it is not clear whether he means he went to Jerusalem
three years after his conversion or after his return from Arabia, although the former is more likely. Paul's purpose in going to Jerusalem
was to interview Peter. The word translated "visit" in this verse has
the more serious meaning of inquiring or investigating, and indicates
that Paul did not intend to remain aloof from the Jerusalem Apostles.
He was anxious for their approbation so long as he did not have to
surrender his authority to interpret the gospel, especially as to its requirements for the gentiles. The fact that he returned again to Jerusalem fourteen years later to compare his gospel to the gentiles lest he
"should be running or had run in vain" (Galatians 2:2) indicates his
deep concern to remain in fellowship with Jerusalem.

For fifteen days he remained with Peter, undoubtedly receiving much
of the tradition which he later handed on to his churches (cf. I Corinthians 11:23; 15:3). Certainly he had known from the claims of those
he had persecuted the main facts concerning Jesus—perhaps Ananias
had been of help to him in this regard. But the numerous echoes of
Jesus' teaching which his letters contain require a more definite source
of knowledge than these contacts would have provided.[61]

That the meeting was not to receive from the Twelve his commission as an Apostle he proves by the fact that beside Peter he became
acquainted with none of the other Apostles except James, the Lord's
brother. This fact was so important to his argument that he took an
oath on it. We need not suppose from this statement that he had not
seen anyone else in the Jerusalem Church. He is speaking here specifically of the Apostles, and, furthermore, the word translated "saw" in
1:19 implies more than a casual meeting.

That the meeting with Peter (and James) was attended with some
secrecy is understandable. With an appropriate sense of the dramatic
Luke depicts the fear and suspicion with which the converted persecutor was regarded in Jerusalem by the story of Barnabas' interven-

[61] Cf. Morton Scott Enslin, *The Ethics of Paul* (New York: Harper & Bros.,
1930), p. 112.

tion in his behalf (Acts 9:26–27). When the fifteen days were complete Paul, still unacquainted with the Judean churches, left for "the regions of Syria and Cilicia."

Thus ends Paul's own account of his movements after his conversion. Too much must not be read into this passage. That at the end of his meeting with Peter he was still unknown by sight to the Judean churches does not preclude his former residence in Jerusalem or his persecution of the Church there. Obviously, the statement is meant to be general or else Paul is made to contradict himself.[62] Such examples of Paul's way of writing as the afterthought in I Corinthians 1:14–16, by which he qualified his statement that he had baptized none of the Corinthians except Crispus and Gaius, should caution us against demanding too much from Paul's general statements. Paul has left no hint in Galatians of the episode he relates in II Corinthians 11:32–33 which forced him to leave Damascus. Yet, as Acts indicates, the story of his escape over the wall of Damascus must belong here.

Such observations make the argument less convincing that the reference in Galatians 2:1 to a "second visit" to Jerusalem, which was the occasion of the Jerusalem Council usually identified with that in Acts 15:2–29, necessarily excludes the earlier "famine visit" in Acts 11:30 and 12:25.[63] Paul refrains from saying that this was his second visit, and a brief visit intervening between Galatians 1:18 and 2:1 would not affect in any way Paul's argument in this passage. The point of the first visit is that he spent his time only with Peter and James and then only after three years in the region of Damascus. On the visit in 2:1 the point is that when he laid his gospel before "those of repute" they obviously did not disapprove of it because they did not compel his Greek companion, Titus, to be circumcised.

---

[62] It is hard to believe that he could have stayed fifteen days with Peter without his presence being known and some of the believers in Jerusalem having at least a glimpse of him. That "the churches of Christ in Judea" included Jerusalem, as is often assumed, is not clear. Acts 1:8 definitely distinguishes between Jerusalem and Judea.

[63] Cf. Weiss, *Earliest Christianity*, I, 200 n; Machen, *The Origin of Paul's Religion*, pp. 84–86. For opposite view see Goodspeed, *Paul* note 3 on Ch. IV, p. 226; Knox, *Chapters in a Life of Paul*, p. 69; Kirsopp Lake, *The Earlier Epistles of St. Paul* (London: Rivingtons, 1911), pp. 274–93. The matter is important because it bears on a question with which we shall be concerned in the next chapter.

In our quest for information on the period between Paul's conversion and his great missionary journeys we must keep in mind the limits and purposes of our sources. It is very tempting to endeavor to squeeze more information from them than they can actually supply. Not all of the differences between the narratives in Acts and Galatians are necessarily contradictions, but simply dovetailing the various items together may lead to an even more inaccurate picture. As the voluminous amount of material proposing a variety of solutions to these questions indicates, parts of the puzzle are missing and we will do well to leave some of these questions open.[64]

The Return to Cilicia

Both Galatians and Acts leave Paul in Cilicia, his homeland. If his visit to Jerusalem, mentioned in Galatians 2:1, is the same as that in Acts 15:2, it came shortly after his first journey with Barnabas into Asia Minor and therefore not long after his recall from Tarsus to Antioch. This means that he spent several years in the area of Tarsus. These are sometimes called his "silent years." How many they were is not easy to estimate. Much depends on whether or not we interpret the fourteen years in Galatians 2:1 to include the three years in 1:18.[65] Either interpretation is grammatically possible, but it seems more natural to begin the fourteen years from the end of the first Jerusalem visit.

The years spent in Cilicia have occasioned much speculation. Presumably he spent the time in missionary work; for we can hardly imagine a man of Paul's zeal and sense of mission remaining silent for any length of time.[66] Some scholars, who hold that Galatians was written to churches in north-central Asia Minor, suppose that Paul established those churches during this time. Not infrequently the hardships and persecutions listed in II Corinthians 11:23–27 have been placed in this period.

[64] Cf. The timely caveat in Chester Warren Quimby, *Paul for Everyone* (New York: The Macmillan Company, 1946), pp. 28–33.

[65] It is frequently pointed out that the phrases can be translated: in the fourteenth year, and in the third year, counting the terminal fractions of a year as years. Thus the total lapse of time in these phrases, if one includes the other, could be as little as thirteen years or if they are consecutive, as much as seventeen years.

[66] But cf. Ramsay, *St. Paul the Traveller*, pp. 46, 85–86.

If we are to judge by the impression left by his letters, Paul's work in the Cilician area left little to show for it in comparison with the comparable period of his Aegean ministry. With the possible exception of Galatians we have no letters from Paul written to churches in this area. The only hint of such churches is in the mention of Syria and Cilicia in Acts 15:23 and the statement that Paul and Silas "went through Syria and Cilicia, strengthening the churches" (Acts 15:41). In spite of the many conjectures, Paul's years in his homeland remain silent.

We may note in passing an hypothesis advanced by Professor John Knox which virtually eliminates the silent years.[67] By bringing forward the date of the Jerusalem Council (Galatians 2 and Acts 15) to a time after Paul's initial stay in Corinth, Professor Knox makes the "fourteen years" include the greater part of Paul's Aegean ministry. On this theory Paul's stay in Cilicia would be quite brief. We will have occasion to refer to this theory again in the next chapter.

To Antioch   Whatever their number, whatever their achievements, the silent years came to an end when Barnabas came to Tarsus to take Paul back with him to Antioch. In the capital of Syria had sprung up a strong and aggressive church which was well suited to launch Paul on his mission as the apostle to the gentiles.

The Paul who, with Barnabas, set out from Tarsus for Antioch was a very different person from the young lad who years before had left the same city to study under Gamaliel. Many things had happened to change him, as is true in any life, but the great change in him was wrought by the revelation on the Damascus Road. It was a miracle of grace, and the churches welcomed the rumor that "He who once persecuted us is now preaching the faith he once tried to destroy" (Galatians 1:23). The full power of that miracle was yet to be felt. Neither Barnabas nor Paul could have suspected what forces were being set in motion as they set out for Antioch.

---

[67] *Chapters in a Life of Paul*, Part 2, 47–88. A condensation of these chapters appears in Kepler, *Contemporary Thinking about Paul*, pp. 161–69.

THE WORLD OF ST. PAUL

7 set apart for me Barnabas and Saul...

While they were worshiping the Lord and fasting, the
Holy Spirit said, "Set apart for
me Barnabas and Saul for the work to
which I have called them." (Acts 13:2)

The description of Paul's missionary activity in Acts follows the pattern of three journeys westward, each of which is separated by a return to Jerusalem and Antioch. These journeys, therefore, furnish a natural pattern for treating the main period of Paul's life. In part the pattern is justified, but it can easily lead to some misconceptions. To begin with, the impression that Paul is on tour in Asia Minor, Macedonia, and Greece while retaining his residence in Jerusalem is, to a considerable degree, an accidental result of the purpose of Acts to picture the progress of Christianity across the Empire from its starting point in Jerusalem. That Paul played an exceedingly important part in that process explains his prominence in the book and the way he is related to the church in Jerusalem.

From Paul's letters, however, a different picture emerges. He never speaks of Jerusalem as home, or of his trips there as though they were returns to his base of operations. Even his final trip to Jerusalem with the contributions from his Aegean churches was a necessary interruption which he had at first hoped to avoid (cf. I Corinthians 16:3–4 with Romans 15:25). The difference is not necessarily one of fact but of point of view.[1] For Luke Jerusalem is the Mother Church and his

[1] For a different inference from this contrast see Knox, *Chapters in a Life of Paul*, pp. 40–42.

story is oriented to that center, but Paul would naturally think of Tarsus, not Jerusalem, as his home. Paul had gone to Jerusalem to study under Gamaliel, but after his conversion he had eventually returned to his Cilician homeland. Paul had great reverence for the Jerusalem Church and was deeply concerned to remain in fellowship and good standing with it. But his home was with his churches; his journey was a constant westward movement.

Even in Acts Paul is more closely connected with Antioch than Jerusalem. He came with Barnabas directly from Tarsus to Antioch. The first journey began and ended with Antioch, and the Jerusalem Council, in Acts 15, represented a separate trip. The second journey likewise began at Antioch; while the description of the return, which separated it from the third journey, does not actually mention Jerusalem, but only says that when "he had landed at Caesarea, he went up and greeted the church, and then went down to Antioch" (Acts 18:22). The "church" in this statement is obviously in Jerusalem, but the emphasis falls on his arrival in Antioch. After he had spent some time there, it was from Antioch again that he set out for Ephesus.

Paul's relations with Jerusalem are more indirect. The coming of Agabus from Jerusalem to Antioch occasioned the relief mission in Acts 11:29-30. The trip to Jerusalem for the Council was the result of the coming to Antioch of "some men" from Judea and the trouble they aroused. If Paul had a "home base" it was Antioch, not Jerusalem.

Except for the brief mention of his visit there in Acts 18:22-23, furthermore, Paul's connections with Antioch are confined to the period of his work in eastern Asia Minor. When compared with Paul's allusions to his travels in his other letters, we gain a similar impression from Galatians 1:21 and 2:11. We should probably regard Paul's relations with Antioch, therefore, as a part of his work in Syria and Cilicia, and assume that they became less significant as he moved westward.[2]

In this study we shall not be concerned primarily with the "journeys," but shall study Paul's work from the standpoint of the geographical areas in which he founded churches and to which he wrote

---

[2] Cf. Nock, *St. Paul*, p. 118.

letters, following his movements only where they are necessary to the
continuity of the study and the significance and meaning of his letters.

Antioch of Syria

Located some seventeen miles or more up the Orontes River
from the seacoast, Antioch was a city of both commercial and political
importance. Strabo rates it as little less in power and size than Alexandria in Egypt.[3] Josephus calls it "the third city in the habitable
earth."[4] It was the capital of the Syrian kingdom under the Seleucids,
and later, under Rome, it was the residence of the governor. We have
already seen that Seleucus Nicator, the founder of the city, had planted
a Jewish colony there.[5] Its population, made up of Oriental, Greek,
and Roman elements, included a large settlement of Jews. The fickle-
ness of Antioch's turbulent population is indicated by its stormy history;
yet its culture was a source of justifiable pride.[6] Four or five miles
above Antioch was Daphne whose grove, famous for its beauty and
equally infamous for the sensual worship of its temple to Apollo and
Artemis, added to the reputation of Antioch.[7] It was Daphne which
Juvenal had in mind when, lamenting the demoralizing influence of
the influx of Orientals into Rome, he made the famous remark that
the Orontes had flowed into the Tiber.

Into Antioch came some believers, who had been driven from Jerusalem by the persecution, preaching the gospel of Jesus. They met with
singular success and a thriving church resulted. Upon learning of this
development, the Jerusalem Church sent Barnabas to inspect and encourage the new work.[8] Barnabas remained in Antioch as the leader
of the church. The church in Antioch is noteworthy in several respects:
In the first place, it was apparently here that the gospel was first addressed directly to gentiles (Acts 11:20).[9] The "men of Cyprus and

[3] Strabo, *Geography*, 16, 2, 5.
[4] Josephus, *Wars*, II, 4.
[5] "In Asia Minor," in chap. 3.
[6] Cicero speaks fondly of Archias, a Greek poet and native of Antioch, as
one of his teachers. *Pro Archias*, 3.
[7] Strabo, *Geography*, 16, 2, 6.
[8] Goguel believes, however, that Barnabas, who was also a Cypriot, was one
of the founders of the church in Antioch. *The Birth of Christianity*, pp. 182–83.
[9] There is some uncertainty in the text as to this term but gentiles is prob-

Cyrene" who did this seem to have arrived in Antioch after the first group from Jerusalem, and it is implied that their success among the gentiles largely accounted for the church's rapid growth.

In the second place, the name "Christian" for the followers of Jesus originated in Antioch (Acts 11:26). It was more than likely a term of derision. Luke speaks of it as though it was familiar and yet the word only occurs twice elsewhere in the New Testament (Acts 26:28; I Peter 4:16). In both instances the context is concerned with trials under Roman authorities and may indicate that it was a rather common nickname used by outsiders to distinguish the followers of Jesus from normative Judaism. Not until much later was the word Christian accepted as a self-designation by the Church.[10] We may wonder if back of this sentence in Acts is a story of the believers' first encounter with the scorn of skeptical pagan attitude toward their gospel.

In the third place, at Antioch the Church made its first contact with a great center in the cosmopolitan Graeco-Roman world. Thus the Church, which had started and developed in an essentially Jewish milieu, was forced in Antioch to face squarely the issue of the relation of the gentile converts to the Law, and consequently, the relation of the Church to Judaism. Antioch, with its large and important Jewish population in an urban gentile setting, formed an excellent laboratory in which the Church could work out its missionary program to the world. In spite of his interest in Jerusalem as the Mother-Church and the authoritative center of Christianity, Luke significantly places Antioch as the base for the great missionary enterprise in Asia Minor and Greece in which Paul became the leading figure.

To this thriving young church, which was growing not only in numbers but in breadth of vision, Barnabas returned from Tarsus with Paul. For a year they worked together while the seed of a daring new idea for the missionary enterprise grew in their minds. During this time, according to Acts 11:29–30, the famine occurred which occasioned the generous relief mission sent to Jerusalem by the church at Antioch.[11]

---

ably correct. See Foakes Jackson and Lake, *The Beginnings of Christianity,* III, 106–107, and IV, 128.

[10] Cf. Cadbury, "Names for Christians in Acts," Foakes Jackson and Lake, *The Beginnings of Christianity,* V, 383–86.

[11] This famine "in the days of Claudius" is usually dated 46 A.D.

The role of Paul in this mission and its connection with the visit to Jerusalem which he describes in Galatians 2:1 will concern us a little later in the chapter.

The Province of Galatia

In one of the decisive moments in the history of Christianity —indeed, of the world—the church in Antioch, impelled by a deep sense of the leadership of the Holy Spirit, solemnly consecrated Barnabas and Paul (Acts still calls him Saul) for a definite program of invading the Graeco-Roman world with the gospel. Taking with them John-Mark, the young cousin of Barnabas, they set out for Cyprus, Barnabas' homeland. By the subtle means of the order of their names, Luke indicates that until they reached the mainland of Asia Minor Barnabas was in charge.[12] It may be that Luke's change from Paul's Hebrew name to his Roman name in Acts 13:9 is also intended to indicate the change of leadership and that Cyprus was Barnabas' territory. This implication in Acts accords with the impression left by his letters: that Paul's mission began in Asia Minor.

Pisidian Antioch   The city in which Paul began his work in Asia Minor is in Acts called Pisidian Antioch (i.e., the Antioch near Pisidia. Some texts read, Antioch of Pisidia, as in the RSV).[13] Strabo refers to it as "Antioch toward Pisidia" because of its proximity to the Pisidian border, but it was actually in Phrygia.[14] Not until a time much later than Paul was it included in Pisidian territory.

Professor Ramsay believes this city was founded by Seleucus Nicator I and, like a number of his other foundations such as Antioch of Syria,

---

[12] Cf. Ramsay, *Paul the Traveller,* pp. 83–85. At Lystra, however, Luke reverts temporarily to the original order, Barnabas and Paul, but this may be for literary effect since it occurs in the story of how Barnabas and Paul were taken to be Zeus and Hermes. Zeus, the chief god, would be named first.

[13] In the following pages I have made considerable use of the excellent, extensive discussion of the cities of the Galatian province which Paul visited, in Ramsay, *The Cities of St. Paul,* pp. 247–419. In this book Professor Ramsay has placed the students of Paul heavily in his debt. On the name Pisidian Antioch see also Ramsay, *St. Paul the Traveller,* p. 91 and Foakes Jackson and Lake, *The Beginnings of Christianity,* III, 119 n.

[14] Strabo, *Geography,* 12, 3, 31; 12, 6, 4.

was named for his father.[15] It formed a garrison on the important road from Syria which connected at Apameia with the great road from Ephesus to the Euphrates.[16] Situated on a plateau of some 3,500 feet elevation, Antioch in Paul's time was the seat of Roman administration for the southern part of the province of Galatia. Strabo indicates that it was settled by Greeks from Magnesium (brought there, according to Ramsay, by Seleucus) and had in his day a colony of Romans.[17] In view of its administrative importance, the city probably contained a sizeable proportion of Romans when Paul entered it to found a church.

When the Seleucids were driven from Asia Minor in 190 B.C., Rome made Antioch a free city, and it later came under the rule of Amyntas, the client-king who willed it to Rome.[18] Upon his death it became a part of the province of Galatia.[19] Like many foundations of the Seleucids, Antioch had an old and important settlement of Jews. Luke calls particular attention to proselytes in this city (Acts 13:43) and leaves the impression that they became the nucleus of the church there.[20] Undoubtedly such proselytes and devout gentiles formed an important part of the core of most, if not all, of Paul's churches. Although in Acts Luke does not again mention proselytes—yet refers several times to the devout and those who fear God—we should probably not understand that Antioch was in this respect unique. In keeping with his usual method of writing Luke here introduces an element which the reader is expected to take for granted in the following narratives. What is noteworthy in the story is that not all of the gentile followers of the synagogue went over to Paul's side. The "devout women" in verse 50 were probably Roman women of influence, either proselytes or "God-fearers," who found Paul's message little to their taste and persuaded the city fathers (their husbands?) to expel the apostles.

In this area the Jewish influence implied in Acts is not surprising.[21]

[15] Ramsay, *The Cities of St. Paul*, p. 252.
[16] *Ibid.* On the route of the road from Ephesus to the East see Strabo, *Geography*, 14, 2, 29.
[17] *Ibid.*, 12, 8, 14.
[18] *Ibid.*, 12, 6, 3–4.
[19] See "Octavian Becomes Augustus" in chap. 4.
[20] See "Proselytes and God-Fearers" in chap. 3.
[21] See "The Diaspora" in chapter 3.

But Paul also encountered, as the story of his experience in Lystra shows, strong and important pagan religions. Strabo speaks in several places of the worship of *Men* who had a temple and priesthood near Antioch.[22] According to Professor Ramsay *Men* was not a moon god, as is often stated following the ancient Greek descriptions, but was "the Anatolian supreme god, the impersonation of their entire conception of the Divine nature and power."[23]

As we should expect, the worship of Cybele, the Mother goddess, was prominent in Antioch.[24] Professor Ramsay cites coins of the city which bore her image and indicates that she had been combined with Artemis, the goddess, in essential respects similar to Cybele, who had been brought to Antioch by the Magnesian Greek settlers.

There seems to have been a decided contrast between the culture of the city itself and that of the surrounding country.[25] For the most part the latter remained Anatolian, unaffected by the Graeco-Roman influence of the city. Writing some forty or fifty years before Paul's journey into southern Galatia, Strabo says of the Pamphylians who, with the Pisidians to the north of them, inhabited the Taurus mountains, that they "do not wholly abstain from the business of piracy, nor yet do they allow the peoples on their borders to live in peace." And of their neighbors, the Pisidians, he writes that they "are divided into separate tribes governed by tyrants, like the Cilicians, and are trained in piracy."[26]

Paul and Barnabas crossed over the Taurus Mountains through these regions on their way from Perga to Antioch (Acts 13:14). According to Acts 13:13 John-Mark left them at Perga. Was it for fear of the robber-infested mountains that he refused to accompany them farther? Similar conditions met Paul and Barnabas as they crossed through the hills south of the Sultan Dagh on their way to Iconium.[27] Paul's

[22] Strabo, *Geography*, 12, 3, 31; 12, 8, 14; 12, 8, 20.

[23] *The Cities of St. Paul*, pp. 285–87.

[24] *Ibid.*, pp. 287–90. On the character of Cybele worship see my "The Myth of the Great Mother" in chap. 4.

[25] Ramsay, *The Cities of St. Paul*, pp. 260–62.

[26] Strabo, *Geography*, 12, 7, 2–3. Loeb Classical Library, V, 481. See "Roman Expansion in the East" in chap. 4.

[27] On Paul's route from Antioch to Iconium see Ramsay, *The Church in the Roman Empire*, pp. 27–35.

words, which more than likely refer to his travels by land and sea in this area, thus take on vivid meaning: "in danger from rivers, danger from robbers . . . danger in the wilderness, danger at sea . . . through many a sleepless night, in hunger and thirst, often without food, in cold and exposure" (II Corinthians 11:26–27).

Iconium   The second city Paul visited
                                 in the province of Galatia
was of a different character and history from Pisidian Antioch. Strabo mentions Iconium (modern Konia) only in passing as a town which had been held by Polemon in a prosperous territory.[28] Polemon as a client-king had received the area from Antony in 39 B.C., and it later became a part of the Galatian kingdom which Amyntas bequeathed to Rome.[29] Professor Ramsay comments on the similarities between Iconium and Damascus, not only as to their respective topographical situations but as to their antiquity.[30] The origins of Iconium are lost in antiquity. After Alexander the Great the city came under Hellenistic influence; its legends and religion took on Hellenistic form. The native religion, of course, was a form of the worship of Cybele.

Professor Ramsay is at pains to show that although Iconium was in the Roman period joined to Lycaonian territory for administrative purposes, it had been and would continue to think of itself as a Phrygian city. Acts 14:6 where Luke describes Paul and Barnabas crossing the border into Lycaonia in going from Iconium to Lystra and Derbe provides an illustration of the accuracy of the local color.[31] Unlike Pisidian Antioch Iconium was not a Roman colony and, therefore, retained its Greek form of city government. This popular form of government would be less quickly influenced by Paul's enemies, which, Professor Ramsay believes, is why Paul could remain so long in the

[28] Strabo, *Geography*, 12, 6, 1.
[29] *The Cities of St. Paul*, pp. 358–59. Also *The Church in the Roman Empire*, p. 41. The chapter on "Localities of the First Journey," pp. 16–58, is a valuable study of these south Galatian cities.
[30] *The Cities of St. Paul*, pp. 317–26. The very interesting analysis by Professor Ramsay of the legend of King Nannakos and the Flood is valuable for the light it sheds on the character of pre-Grecian Anatolia, the influence of which was still felt underneath the Hellenistic culture in Paul's day.
[31] *Ibid.*, pp. 352–53 and note. Cf. *The Church in the Roman Empire*, pp. 37–45.

city after he began to encounter opposition (Acts 14:2–3).[32] Iconium is interesting for the fact that in this city, one of the oldest in the world, Christian tradition has remained continuous into modern times. Although Acts describes the work of Paul and Barnabas in Iconium in a brief, general way, it appears to have been the effective center of Christian influence in South Galatia and therefore the most important of the missions of Paul in this area.[33]

Lystra and Derbe

To the south of Iconium along the edge of the Lycaonian plain in the foothills of the Taurus mountains were located Lystra and Derbe, two cities to which when they were threatened with stoning in Iconium, Paul and Barnabas fled (Acts 14:6). Little is known of these cities for they do not seem to have held any importance for ancient writers. Strabo mentions Derbe in passing as the capital of the tyrant Antipater Derbetes.[34]

The location of Lystra was not known in modern times until it was discovered by Professor Sterrett in 1885 to be about a mile northwest of modern Khatyn-Serai.[35] The few coins of Lystra that have been found and an inscription concerning a statue of Concord, which Lystra had presented to Pisidian Antioch, indicate that Lystra was a Roman colony and reflect the pride which the city took in that fact.[36] Yet the Hellenic character of the coins and the story in Acts point to the conclusion that Roman influence was weaker here than in Antioch. The mention of the native Lycaonian language in Acts 14:11 suggests that Hellenistic culture, too, was less entrenched here than in the cities which Paul had previously visited.

The stoning which Paul had escaped in Iconium found him in Lystra. The supposition that many of the trials enumerated in II Corinthians 11:24–27 occurred in Galatian territory is strengthened by the inclusion of a reference to this event: "once I was stoned." Ironically, shortly before, because Paul had healed a lame man, the

---

[32] Ramsay, *The Cities of St. Paul*, p. 371.

[33] *Ibid.*, pp. 370–71, 374.

[34] Strabo, *Geography*, 12, 6, 3.

[35] Ramsay, *The Cities of St. Paul*, pp. 411. Also *The Church in the Roman Empire*, pp. 49–50.

[36] Ramsay, *The Cities of St. Paul*, pp. 412–17.

people of Lystra were ready to worship Paul and Barnabas as gods. In connection with this incident commentators have often drawn attention to the Phrygian legend of the visit of Zeus and Hermes to an old couple, Philemon and Baucis.[37] Perhaps the legend was known in Lystra and was responsible for the reaction to the apostles. According to the story, out of a thousand homes to which the gods had sought entrance only the old couple had the good grace to show them hospitality and, in consequence, they alone were saved from the ensuing flood. The people of Lystra were determined not to repeat the mistake!

The deities called Zeus and Hermes were, however, Greek in little more than name. One of the effects of the veneer of Hellenism in the East was the partial assimilation of local gods to Greek divinities.[38] Except for his speech in Athens (Acts 17:22–31) Paul's speech on this occasion is significantly different from those attributed to him in Acts. Appropriate for a pagan audience, it voices the typical Jewish opposition to pagan idolatry and calls on the hearers to turn to the one living God. That God "did not leave himself without witness" (Acts 14:17; cf. Acts 17:24–25), but can be known from his providence and creation, is characteristic of Paul's thought concerning the heathen and is stated in a significantly similar way in Romans 1:19–20. The gentiles whom Paul was addressing in Lystra, unlike those in Pisidian Antioch, had not come under the influence of Judaism. That there were Jews in Lystra, however, appears in Acts 16:1 where Timothy is described as the son of a Jewess married to a Greek. Since no synagogue is mentioned, either here or in Derbe, we may suppose Jewish influence in these cities to be comparatively slight.

Fortunately the stoning at Lystra, which Jews from Antioch and Iconium had instigated, had not accomplished its purpose. The next day Paul and Barnabas made their way to Derbe. The site of ancient Derbe is not certain, but is supposed to be near modern Zosta. It was a frontier Roman fortress, from which an Imperial Road ran to Pisidian Antioch.[39] Very little is told us of the mission in Derbe except that they "made many disciples" there.

[37] Ovid, *Metamorphosis*, VIII, 615–720.
[38] See "Characteristics of the Hellenistic World" in chap. 4.
[39] Ramsay, *The Cities of St. Paul*, 396–99.

From these two cities Paul gained two valuable companions. Timothy, who was his most faithful helper in his Aegean ministry, came from Lystra, and Gaius, who accompanied him on his final voyage to Jerusalem (Acts 20:4) was from Derbe.[40] That Paul circumcised Timothy in Lystra when he invited Timothy to join his company (Acts 16:3) is surprising in the light of what he later wrote about circumcision in Galatians. It may be that this action lies behind the puzzling words in Galatians 5:11, "But if I, brethren, still preach circumcision, why am I still persecuted?" Professor Nock has suggested that since Timothy was born to a Jewish mother, Paul regarded him as a Jew and therefore one who ought to have been circumcised.[41] The logic of Paul's action in that case would fit his words in I Corinthians 7:18: "Was any one at the time of his call already circumcised? Let him not seek to remove the marks of circumcision." However, Timothy may not have been circumcised at all. In Colossians, although he included Timothy's name in the opening salutation (1:1), he omits it in the list of "the only men of the circumcision among my fellow workers" (4:11).

In the briefest possible summary Luke describes how Paul and Barnabas retraced their steps through Lystra, Iconium, and Antioch to Perga, and set sail for Antioch of Syria. After the story of the Jerusalem Council and the separation of Paul and Barnabas in Acts 15, Luke again, in the most general way, summarizes Paul's return to South Galatia, this time through Syria and Cilicia. The narrative begins again with Paul's vision at Troas. The Galatian ministry is over. This does not mean that Paul either abandoned his supervision of or his concern for these churches. Whether he visited them again (cf. Acts 18:23) and whether his letter to the Galatians was written to them are questions to which we must now turn.

The North vs. the South	Before leaving this part of
Galatian Hypotheses	our study we must consider
	two important questions

---

[40] Perhaps a textual error in Acts 19:29 is responsible for identifying the Gaius there, along with Aristarchus, as a Macedonian. If so, he, like Timothy, had followed Paul in the mission to the West. Cf. Foakes Jackson and Lake, *The Beginnings of Christianity*, IV, 248.

[41] Nock, *St. Paul*, p. 108.

that arise in connection with the Galatian Churches. The first of these is: Did Paul write his letter to the Galatians to the churches in Pisidian Antioch, Iconium, Lystra, and Derbe in the Roman province of Galatia, or had he founded churches in the area of the old kingdom of Galatia to which his letter was addressed?[42]

Traditionally the destination of the letter to the Galatians has been regarded as the old region of North Galatia. Toward the end of the eighteenth century the traditional assumption began to be challenged by the so-called South Galatian hypothesis. The new theory did not make much head-way until the end of the nineteenth century when it found a powerful champion in the learned historian and archaeologist Sir William M. Ramsay. Since that time scholarship has been sharply divided on the question. Any list of the exponents of either theory must contain an imposing number of outstanding New Testament scholars. Among the more recent scholars, however, there appears to be a trend toward the South Galatian position.

The problem is essentially whether Paul in Galatians 1:2 and 3:1 is using the word Galatia (and Galatians) in its ethnic sense or in its Roman meaning. The exponents of the traditional view argue that the natural meaning of Galatians is ethnic and that the peoples of the southern territory of the Roman province would have been insulted to be called Galatians.[43] This argument raises the objection that Paul, whose itinerary otherwise was confined to the important cities and urban areas of the Empire, would hardly have gone into the backward country of old Galatia. To meet this objection proponents of North Galatia have contended that the North Galatian cities did come under Roman and Hellenistic influence. Archaeological evidence, furthermore, is cited to show that the cultural gap between North and South

[42] For the historical background of this question see "The Successors" in chap. 4.

[43] One of the best analyses of the various arguments on both sides of this problem is in Burton, *The Epistle to the Galatians*, pp. xxi–liii. Also Enslin, *Christian Beginnings*, pp. 224–26; A. C. McNeile, *An Introduction to the Study of the New Testament*, 2nd ed., rev. C. S. C. Williams (Oxford: Clarendon Press, 1953), pp. 143–49; Lake, *The Earlier Epistles of St. Paul*, pp. 254–55. Professor Ramsay's extensive arguments for the South Galatian theory are scattered throughout his writings, but see esp. *St. Paul the Traveller*, pp. 8–9, 130–151, *passim*. Also *The Church in the Roman Empire*, pp. 97–111.

Galatia was not great.[44] But if the cultural differences between North and South Galatia were so small why should the peoples of the southern territory be so insulted when called Galatians? The cities in question had reason to be proud of their status in the Roman administration of the Province and could hardly object to being identified by the name of their province. Also, it would be difficult to find a single term other than the word Galatians by which Paul could address the churches in all of these cities of South Galatia.

The strongest point in the argument over the term itself is that where the terms are unambiguous Paul's geographical references always accord with Roman usage. But this point is not decisive because in several instances the terms can be taken either in their older, popular sense, or as Roman provinces. Galatia itself is an example. The question, therefore, must be decided on other grounds.

A second question arises, however, if we are to assume that Galatia refers to the northern territory. When were these churches founded? We have already seen that Luke has not given us the complete story of Paul's travels, or the foundation of all the churches with which he was concerned. It is possible, therefore, that it lay outside the purpose of Acts to relate the foundation of the churches of North Galatia. Or perhaps Paul may have founded them during the "silent years."[45]

A great part of the discussion of these hypotheses has concerned two phrases in Acts which the North Galatianists contend indicate that Paul traveled through North Galatia. They are the words, "the region of Phrygia and Galatia" in 16:6 and "the region of Galatia and Phrygia" in 18:23. In both instances the question is whether "Galatia" and "Phrygia" are adjectives modifying the word "region" and refer to the same territory (i.e., South Galatia) or are nouns and refer to the old kingdoms. The problem is further complicated by the fact that the two passages in the Greek are not exactly parallel in grammar and word order, so that a decision regarding one does not automatically apply to the other. If Luke means to indicate the old kingdoms, the

[44] The argument that Lystra and Derbe were backward cities comparable to North Galatia is countered by the statement that Paul only fled to them for safety until the officials of Iconium could cool off or until a change of magistrates would allow him to return.
[45] See "The Return to Cilicia" in chap. 6.

order of the terms indicates that he traversed the two territories in opposite directions on the journeys described in Acts 16:6 and 18:23. The phrases, unfortunately, are unusual, and the elaborate grammatical arguments offered by proponents of both sides have not led to any definite conclusions.

But to show that Paul did go through at least part of North Galatia is not to say that he founded churches there. Although Luke records Paul's preaching in Athens, for example, he is careful not to say that Paul founded a church. The proponents of the North Galatian hypothesis usually suppose, on the basis of Paul's words in Galatians 4:13, "You know it was because of a bodily ailment that I preached the gospel to you at first," that Paul became ill on his journey through old Galatia and established the churches in question while he was recuperating. But Professor Ramsay turns this passage to good account in supporting the South Galatian theory by supposing that Paul fell victim to malaria in Pamphylia on his first journey and sought relief in the higher altitude of Pisidian Antioch.[46] The theory is attractive but not decisive.

Two pieces of supporting evidence which tend to increase the probability of the South Galatian theory are worth noticing. One is the fact that Paul mentions Barnabas in Galatians (2:9, 13) as though the Galatians knew him. Since Barnabas was with Paul only on the first journey which took them through the cities of South Galatia, the letter must have been addressed to them. The other piece of evidence concerns Paul's companions on his last journey to Jerusalem. In I Corinthians 16:1–4 Paul indicates that the Galatian churches are sharing in the "contribution for the saints" in Jerusalem and the contributions are to be accompanied by representatives from the donating churches. (Cf. II Corinthians 8:16–24; 9:4.) In Acts 20:4 Luke lists the companions of Paul as he left for his final visit to Jerusalem. The significance of this list for the South Galatian theory is that it includes Gaius of Derbe and Timothy of Lystra but no one from North Galatia.[47] Apparently they are the delegates accompanying the Galatian gift. We may safely assume that Galatia in I Corinthians 16:1 and in

[46] See "His 'Thorn in the Flesh' " in chap. 6.

[47] Professor Carl von Weizsäcker offers this as one of the decisive arguments for the South Galatian theory. *The Apostolic Age*, pp. 271–72.

Galatians 1:2 refers to the same territory, which therefore must be South Galatia.

None of these arguments is conclusive, but the probabilities seem to be in favor of the South Galatian theory. Part of the difficulty here, as in several of the problems we have encountered, is the nature of our sources. What was clear enough to the first readers of Galatians, time has obscured from us. As for Acts, we are probably again attempting to squeeze more information from the book than its author put in it.

The character and purpose of Acts does, however, provide one significant clue to the answer. The journey from Lystra to Troas, Acts 16:4–8, is described in the briefest summary, and only two facts are singled out for mention: That Paul and his company were prevented by the Holy Spirit from preaching in Asia and that later they were similarly prevented from entering Bithynia. Luke is explaining why Paul in his westward movement did not work in Bithynia at all but crossed the Aegean Sea to establish churches in Macedonia and Greece before coming to Ephesus in Asia. Since Luke's purpose is to picture the progress of Christianity across the Empire, he confines his story to the founding of significant churches. If Paul had founded churches in North Galatia important enough to occasion such a letter as Galatians, it is hard to believe, especially in light of the attention he gives to the churches in South Galatia, that Luke would not have noticed them. Even if Luke were dependent on a source for this·part of his story, the difficulty is only pushed back one step.

To the natural question why did the North Galatian theory arise so early and become so universally assumed by the ancient interpreters of Paul, Professor Ramsay answers that in the reorganization of the provinces of Asia Minor in the second century a great part of Lycaonia, including the cities Paul visited, was separated from Galatia so that the term Galatians could no longer apply. The succeeding generations interpreted Paul's references to Galatia in the light of the geographical facts of their own time.[48]

The Jerusalem Council   The second question that arises in connection with Paul's work in Galatia is the relation of Paul's visits to Jerusalem as

[48] *The Church in the Roman Empire*, p. 111.

listed in Galatians 1:18 and 2:1 on the one hand, and in Acts 9:26, 11:27–30, and 15:2 on the other hand. This is one of the most difficult problems in the study of the life of Paul and it is especially important because some of the proposed answers radically affect the chronology of his life.

The crux of the problem is the relation of the Jerusalem Council described in Acts 15:1–29 to the meeting Paul describes in Galatians 2:1–10. There are two facets to the problem: 1) The differences in the two accounts raise the question as to whether they are the same event. 2) How can the two visits of Paul to Jerusalem in Galatians be correlated with the three visits listed in Acts? The following comparison will help us to see the differences between the meeting in Acts and that in Galatians:

Acts 15:1–29	*Galatians 2:1–10*
1) Paul went to Jerusalem from Antioch of Syria.	No indication is given as to where Paul was when he left for Jerusalem.
2) Debate with men from Judea over circumcision caused the appointment of Paul and Barnabas to go to Jerusalem with the question.	Paul went to Jerusalem "by revelation" to lay before those of repute his gospel to the gentiles.
3) Paul was accompanied by Barnabas and "some others."	Paul was accompanied by Barnabas *and Titus* (a gentile).
4) The delegation met with "the Church and the apostles and the elders."	Paul met privately with "those who were of repute."
5) Peter and James are the only ones in the Jerusalem Church specifically named.	John is mentioned by name along with Peter and James.
6) Some believers of the Pharisean party in the meeting insist on circumcision and the Law.	False brethren slipped in to "bring us into bondage."

7) A demand was made to circum-   Titus was not required to be cir-
   cise "them" (to whom does   cumcised.
   "them" refer?) but it did not
   carry.

8) God had chosen that the gen-   Peter was entrusted with the gospel
   tiles hear the gospel from Peter.   to the circumcised.

9) A letter including the "Apostolic   Paul and Barnabas are to go to the
   Decrees" was dispatched by Judas   gentiles and "remember the poor."
   and Silas.

The differences in this list are not all mutually exclusive. Numbers
1, 3, 5, 6, and 7 may supplement one another. The real contrast in the
two accounts appears in numbers 2, 4, 8, and 9. The last of these
present the most serious problem. The motivation for the visit to Jerusalem in number 2 is partly a matter of point of view and Paul's
"revelation" may have been the source of the decision of the Church
at Antioch which appointed him and Barnabas to go to Jerusalem.
Perhaps Luke's inexact language in number 4 accounts for the inclusion of the church in the meeting in Acts. Luke does not explicitly
mention the church, in fact, except in the welcome (verse 4). "All
the assembly" in verse 12, however, seems to imply the whole church.
(But cf. verse 6.) To argue from this difference in the two accounts
that Luke was guilty of an essential inaccuracy or that these were two
different events requires a more strained interpretation than to reconcile them. Such differences are not uncommon between a first-hand
and a second-hand report of an event.

That Peter began the gentile mission is not improbable. We have
already observed reasons for believing that gentiles were being evangelized before Paul's conversion.[49] Peter more than likely took part
in that activity. Also, the division of labor in Galatians 2:7–8 may have
been a later arrangement; it no more restricted Peter from preaching
at all to gentiles than it did Paul from preaching to Jews (cf. Romans
1:16; I Corinthians 9:20–23).

The one serious difference, then, between the accounts of the council
in Acts and Galatians is the letter containing the so-called Apostolic

---

[49] "The Persecution according to Paul" in chap. 6.

Decrees. We should note, however, that these decrees are a problem within Acts itself. In Acts 21:25 James tells Paul of these decrees as though Paul had not known of them before. For this reason and because it seems certain that had Paul known of the decrees he would have referred to them in Galatians, a number of scholars have assumed that they were drawn up and circulated sometime after the Council.[50] This one difference in the two accounts, at any rate, is not enough to indicate that they refer to two different events.

In order to determine whether the similarities between the two accounts are sufficient to show that they concern the same event, we may summarize them as follows:

1) Each meeting was held in Jerusalem some time after Paul's conversion and return to Syria and Cilicia.

2) In each instance Paul and Barnabas went to Jerusalem in the company of at least one other person.

3) Peter and James were principals in each meeting.

4) The issue was the necessity of circumcision for gentile converts.

5) Concerned to be in accord with Jerusalem, Paul represented the validity of his position according to both accounts by presenting his gospel to the Jerusalem leaders.

6) Both accounts imply that the issue is being debated by that assembly for the first time.

7) In both accounts, the Apostles approved Paul's gospel and position.

The fact that the same principals are involved and reach agreement on the same issue makes it highly improbable that there were two such meetings.[51] It is possible, of course, that there was a private conference of Paul and Barnabas with Peter and James and a later meeting involving the whole Jerusalem Church, when fresh opposition broke out. There is little, however, in the accounts themselves to justify such a conclusion. Therefore, unless there is other evidence to the contrary, it seems probable that Acts 15:1–29 and Galatians 2:1–10 refer to the same event.

[50] On the problem of the decrees see Weizsäcker, *The Apostolic Age*, pp. 199–216; Foakes Jackson and Lake, *The Beginnings of Christianity*, V, 204–12; Machen, *The Origin of Paul's Religion*, pp. 87–97.

[51] For opposite view see Ramsay, *St. Paul the Traveller*, pp. 55–64.

If we equate the meeting described in Acts 15 with that in Galatians 2, we are confronted with the question of Paul's silence regarding his visit to Jerusalem described in Acts 11:27–30 and 12:25. This facet of the problem of the Jerusalem Council has led to several theories which are important enough to notice here.

One solution is to deny the connection between Galatians 2 and Acts 15 and instead to identify the meeting Paul describes in Galatians with the visit in Acts 11:27–30. Acts 15, then, describes a subsequent conference involving the whole Jerusalem Church, which may have occurred after Galatians was written. The theory has several attractive features. First, in Galatians 2:12, Paul indicates that those who came to Antioch from Jerusalem to disturb the Jewish-gentile relations arrived after his meeting with the Apostles. If the meeting in Acts 15 came after the one in Galatians 2, these men would be the same as those in Acts 15:1. Second, the motive for the visit to Jerusalem in Acts 11:27–30 was to bring relief for the victims of the famine. In Galatians 2:10 Paul's words, "only they would have us remember the poor, which very thing I was eager to do" seems to imply a similar motive for his visit. Third, it not only eliminates the intermediate visit which Paul failed to mention, but it eases the discrepancy between Paul's claim to have gone up "by revelation" (Galatians 2:2) and Luke's statement that Paul and Barnabas "were appointed to go up to Jerusalem" by the Antioch Church (Acts 15:2).[52] The "revelation" in Galatians 2:2, on this view, refers to Agabus' prophecy in Acts 11:28, while the appointment of Paul and Barnabas as delegates refers to the later meeting.

In the minds of a number of scholars, these advantages do not surmount the difficulty of explaining how, after the issue of circumcision for gentile Christians had been settled in a private conference with the Apostles, it could be raised again in an open meeting in which those same Apostles played the principal role. Together with the reasons which we have observed for identifying Galatians 2 with Acts 15 this

[52] On this theory see Ramsay, *St. Paul the Traveller;* also Machen, *The Origin of Paul's Religion,* pp. 78–100. A valuable summary of this problem is found in Foakes Jackson and Lake, *The Beginnings of Christianity,* V, 199–204. See also Enslin, *Christian Beginnings,* pp. 226–30; Weizsäcker, *The Apostolic Age,* pp. 104–10 and 199–204.

difficulty weighs heavily against such a solution of the problem.

A more radical solution maintains that Acts 11:27–30 and 15:2–29 are two versions of the same event.[53] The theory rests on an analysis of sources which Luke used in writing this part of Acts and the assumption of a strong competition for leadership between Antioch and Jerusalem.

According to the Antioch version of the story Paul's visit to Jerusalem was to bring famine relief; according to the Jerusalem version it was to appeal to the authority of the Jerusalem Church to settle the dispute over circumcision. That each of these accounts of Paul's visit to Jerusalem is followed by a story of Paul's journey through South Galatia (Acts 13 and 14 and 15:36–16:6) and that the second of these journeys is given only in a brief summary lends force to this theory. If Acts 11:27–30 and 15:2–29 refer to the same visit, then 15:36–16:6 is also a repetition of chapters 13 and 14 and Paul toured South Galatia only once.

Professor Weizsäcker subjects Acts to an even more radical treatment to arrive at much the same position. This he accomplishes by eliminating the famine altogether as an occasion for Paul's visit and by moving the story of the Council in Acts 15, in which he believes Luke used Galatians 2:1–10 as a source, back to a position before Paul's journey into Galatia. In either form the theory that reduced the two visits in Acts 11 and 15 to the second visit in Galatians depends on the Tübingen hypothesis of a basic conflict between Paul and the Jerusalem Apostles and the "tendency" in Luke, by radically rewriting his material, to obscure that conflict.[54] The difficulty is that according to both Galatians and Acts Paul and the Jerusalem Apostles were in essential agreement, and that the conflict arose when certain believers (Paul calls them "false brethren") insisted on circumcision for the gentile Christians. Such a radical treatment of Acts, in the light of its evident historical value elsewhere and the lack of more definite evidence, hardly seems warranted.

More recently Professor Knox, by rearranging the material in Acts,

[53] Perhaps the best statement of this theory, advanced by E. Schwartz, is by M. S. Enslin in his treatment of the problem cited in *Christian Beginnings,* pp. 226–30.

[54] On the Tübingen hypothesis see chapter 6, note 39.

has made a similar attempt to solve the problem of the relation between Acts and Galatians.[55] He begins by observing that Paul in his letters mentions only three visits to Jerusalem after his conversion, i.e., "after three years" (Galatians 1:18), "after fourteen years" (Galatians 2:1), and the proposed visit with the collection for the Jerusalem Christians (Romans 15:25 *passim*), while Acts, by adding a famine visit in 11:27–30 and a trip to Jerusalem and Antioch from Ephesus in 18:21–19:1, brings the number of visits to five. Two of the visits in Acts, he concludes, must be doublets, but instead of equating Acts 11:27–30 with Acts 15:2–29, he places the Council in Acts 15 during Paul's visit to Jerusalem in Acts 18:21–19:1. Since, on this theory, both of these passages refer to the same event described in Galatians 2:1–10, a considerable part of Paul's Aegean ministry as well as his Galatian ministry took place during the fourteen years prior to the Jerusalem Council. The visit in Acts 11:27–30 was created by Luke to find a place for the relief visit which was actually Paul's last journey to Jerusalem. It is, therefore, a doublet of the journey in Acts 20:3–21:17.

The strength of this theory is that, beside solving the problem of the relation of the visits in Acts with those in Paul's letters, it supplies a motive, strangely omitted by Luke, for the trip to Jerusalem in Acts 18:21–19:1 and explains Luke's omission of the motive for Paul's final journey to Jerusalem. On this view, Luke did not recognize the collection for the Jerusalem Christians as a "peace offering" which had been required of Paul at the Jerusalem Council and placed it instead before the Council at the time of the famine in the reign of Herod Agrippa. He was, consequently, left without a motive for Paul's final visit.

Of the last two theories we have surveyed the one by Professor Knox, because it attempts a broader solution of the problems of the relation of Acts to Paul's letters and the chronology of Acts, is the more attractive. We should note, however, that this theory also assumes the Tübingen hypothesis of the conflict between Paul and Jerusalem, and that both theories depend on interpretations that unnecessarily sharpen the differences between Acts and Paul's letters.

[55] See *Chapters in a Life of Paul*, part 2, 47–48. See "The Return to Cilicia" in chap. 6

A much simpler solution leaves the famine relief sent by the Antioch Church where it is in Acts but assumes that Luke was mistaken in saying that Paul accompanied Barnabas in taking it to Jerusalem.[56] As we noted in chapter 6, however, Paul in Galatians may not have intended to list all his visits to Jerusalem, but mentioned only those which were relevant to his argument. If this is true, one of the major problems of the relation between Acts and Galatians which these theories seek to solve disappears.

The number and complexity of the theories indicate the difficulty of this problem. While the solution we choose will affect our chronology of Paul's life, more serious for our purposes is its influence on the interpretation of his letters. If the solution of the problems of the Jerusalem Council includes the assumption of a basic conflict between Paul and the Jerusalem Apostles, as the Tübingen school maintained, Paul was preaching "a different gospel" and the charge that he was responsible for changing what was simply a Jewish messianic sect into a new, essentially gentile religion is sustained. Such a conclusion decidedly alters our understanding of the whole pattern of Paul's thought.

The chronological problems do not in themselves affect the interpretation of Paul so seriously. Details concerning the sequence of events and the like are more important to a study of the history of the Primitive Church and only affect our study in a secondary way. This is not to say that a knowledge of Paul's life and experiences is unimportant, but that, assuming that we understand his background, environment, and experiences, we can afford to leave some of the intricate problems concerning the external facts of Paul's life undecided.

In evaluating these proposed solutions to the question of the relation of Acts to Galatians we must again recall the nature of our sources. Luke's reference to the famine in Acts 11:28, for example, raises an interesting chronological problem. This famine must be the same as the one mentioned by Josephus, who dates it after the death of Herod Agrippa and during the procuratorship of Fadus and Tiberius Alexander (45–46 A.D.).[57] But Luke places the reference to the famine

---

[56] Cf. Goodspeed, *Paul,* p. 35 and note, pp. 226–27.
[57] Josephus, *Ant.* XX, 2, 5 and 5, 2. On this and related matters in the

204 MY MANNER OF LIFE

before his story of Agrippa's persecution of the church and subsequent death, which would date it between 41 and 43 B.C. Clearly the famine story in 11:28 belongs after the events told in 12:1-24. Luke has placed it at the end of chapter 11 because of its connection with the story of the church at Antioch.[58]

❧ The problem is significant because it shows that Luke is not primarily interested in chronology, but allows the topical organization of his material to disrupt the chronological order. We should, therefore, allow considerable latitude in interpreting such references to time as the words "in these days" in Acts 11:27 and "about that time," in 12:1. Luke was not so much concerned with the order of events or the lapses of time as with the way they served to develop his themes. / Transposing the order of events in Acts to conform to Paul's letters as the theories we have surveyed attempt to do does not, then, do the violence to Luke's purpose and meaning that we might suppose.[59]

Whatever may be our decision on the location of the Galatian churches and the problems of the Jerusalem Council, Paul's work in Galatia is of major importance both for the history of early Christianity and the New Testament because from it came the charter of freedom and definition of Christianity as a universal Faith—the letter to the Galatians.

The Province of Macedonia

Prevented from entering the provinces of Asia and Bithynia on their westward movement from Galatia, Paul and his companions arrived in Troas. At Troas Paul stood on the threshold of the most productive and important period in his life—his Aegean ministry. In a vision Paul saw "a man of Macedonia" calling him to "come over to

---

chronology of Acts see Foakes Jackson and Lake, *The Beginnings of Christianity*, V, 445-74.

[58] Perhaps Luke intended the famine relief journey to come at the end of chapter 12 and was only anticipating it in 11:30, which would explain the curious fact that in 12:25 a significant number of manuscripts read, "and Barnabas and Saul returned to Jerusalem when they had fulfilled their mission" (collecting the relief money?).

[59] For a significant application of the method of Form Criticism to the study of Luke's treatment of the Jerusalem Council see Dibelius, *Studies in the Acts of the Apostles*, pp. 93-101.

Macedonia and help us" (Acts 16:9–10). Because at this point the narrative changes from the third to the first person, Professor Ramsay suggests that the "man of Macedonia" was Luke whom Paul had met in Troas.[60] The appearance of the pronoun "we" here and in Acts 20:6 in connection with Macedonia and the fact that it is dropped again as Paul leaves Philippi strongly suggests that Luke (or the author of the "we source" which he used in writing Acts) was a resident of Philippi.

Philippi   In response to the vision Paul and his companions sailed via Samothrace to Neapolis (modern Kavalla), the port city of Philippi, and continued to Philippi. On the following Sabbath they met a group of Jewish and proselyte women at "the place of prayer" outside the city alongside the Gangites River. A prominent merchant woman from Thyatira named Lydia, apparently a Jewish proselyte, was converted and baptized and took them into her home. The generosity of this presumably wealthy woman anticipated the distinguishing characteristic of the Philippian Church in later years.

The city of Philippi, situated on a hill overlooking the coastal plains near the Thracian border, was anciently known as Crenides (fountains) because of the springs which fed the marshy lakes below it.[61] Philip of Macedon refounded the city and named it after himself. After Pydna (168 B.C.) Philippi became the capital of the most easterly of the four provincial districts into which Rome divided Macedonia. When these districts were dissolved the seat of government went to Thessalonica where it was in Paul's day. The territory of Philippi lay between the Nestos and Strymon Rivers. Although well-known for its gold mines, according to Strabo, it remained a small settlement until after it became the scene of the battle in which Antony and Octavian avenged the assassination of Julius Caesar by defeating Brutus and Cassius, when it was made a Roman colony.[62] The Jewish population of the

[60] *St. Paul the Traveller*, pp. 202–203.
[61] Strabo, *Geography*, VII, Fragment 34–42.
[62] "Octavian Becomes Augustus" in chap. 4. What Luke means in calling Philippi "the leading city of the district of Macedonia" (Acts 16:12) is not clear.

city was apparently very small. Luke implies that it was confined to a few women, some of whom were proselytes.

Although from Acts 16:12 it appears that Paul remained only a short time in Philippi, his letter to the Philippians indicates that in spite of continued and severe persecution (Philippians 1:28–30) a well-organized and strong church developed there (Philippians 1:1). The Philippian Church was remarkable for the constancy of its affection for Paul, which must have been a great source of comfort to him during the stormy period of his conflict with the churches in Corinth and Galatia. When the Philippian Christians learned of Paul's imprisonment they sent Epaphroditus to care for him; except for the brief warning against "evil workers" in 3:2–3, no words of bitterness or rebuke mar the warmth of his letter to the Philippians. Paul's appreciation of the faithful devotion of the Philippians shines forth from the closing words of his letter:

> Yet it was kind of you to share my trouble. And you Philippians yourselves know that in the beginning of the gospel, when I left Macedonia, no church entered into partnership with me in giving and receiving except you only; for even in Thessalonica you sent me help once and again. Not that I seek the gift; but I seek the fruit which increases to your credit. I have received full payment, and more; I am filled, having received from Epaphroditus the gifts you sent, a fragrant offering, a sacrifice acceptable and pleasing to God. And my God will supply every need of yours according to his riches in glory in Christ Jesus. To our God and Father be glory for ever and ever. Amen (Philippians 4:14–20).

Paul's days in Philippi were cut short by an encounter with the city authorities. A slave girl possessed of a "spirit of Python" (the phrase is frequently taken to mean that she was a ventriloquist) [63] was being exploited by her owners to satisfy the superstitious love of the pagan Philippians for soothsayers. Paul exorcised the spirit from the girl; and enraged by the financial loss, the owners arrested Paul and Silas. Why Paul did not plead his Roman citizenship until his release by the magistrates the next morning we cannot say. Here at Philippi occurred one of the three beatings by the Roman lictors and one of the "far more

[63] But see Foakes Jackson and Lake, *The Beginnings of Christianity*, IV, 192.

imprisonments" Paul lists in II Corinthians 11:23–25. An earthquake during the night resulted in the conversion of the jailer. The next day Paul and Silas were duly released and, being ordered from the city, they with Timothy made their way to Thessalonica. In a letter to the Thessalonian Church, probably written not long afterward, Paul reminded them of the experience that forced him to leave Philippi, comparing it with his similar difficulties in Thessalonica as proof of his sincerity (I Thessalonians 2:2). To encourage them to be patient under their trials Paul some time later reminded the Philippians of his own suffering (Philippians 1:30).

Thessalonica and Beroea

Being forced to leave Philippi, Paul and his companions next took up their work in the largest and most important city in Macedonia. Thessalonica (modern Salonika), the residence of the Macedonian governor, stood at the head of the Thermaean Gulf (now the Gulf of Salonika) and was an important station on the great Egnatian Way.[64] Its strategic location along one of the main routes of East-West communication made it a city of great commercial importance. According to Strabo the city was originally known as Therma and was refounded in 315 B.C. by Cassander, one of the Diadochi, who renamed it for his wife, the stepsister of Alexander the Great.[65] The Jewish population in Thessalonica was considerably larger than in Philippi. Luke takes particular notice of the synagogue in Thessalonica.

Paul's stay in Thessalonica was longer than in Philippi. Luke mentions his preaching in the synagogue on three Sabbaths (Acts 17:2), and in his letters to them Paul reminds the Thessalonians that in order not to burden them financially he had worked at his trade during his stay with them.

In addition to his own earnings the Philippians apparently had twice sent Paul money to help support him in his work in Thessalonica (Philippians 4:16).[66] That Paul sought employment at his trade and

[64] Strabo, *Geography,* VII 7, 4, VII, Fragment 10. Fragment 13 apparently misunderstands Strabo to mean that the Egnatian Way terminated at Thessalonica.

[65] Strabo, *Geography,* VII, 24.

[66] It is possible, of course, that this aid was sent on a later occasion.

that there were time and need for Philippian aid imply a stay in Thessalonica of considerably more than three weeks.[67]

The strategic importance of a church in the principal city of Macedonia is obvious and Paul emphasizes its importance in his letter: "For not only has the word of the Lord sounded forth from you in Macedonia and Achaia, but your faith in God has gone forth everywhere, so that we need not say anything" (I Thessalonians 1:8).

That the Thessalonian Church was predominantly gentile is clear from Paul's comment that the Thessalonians had "turned to God from idols" (I Thessalonians 1:9). Luke indicates that some Jews along with many God-fearing gentiles and "not a few of the leading women" "were persuaded" (Acts 17:4). There is a textual problem here. Manuscripts representing the so-called "Western Text" insert the word "and" between devout and Greeks indicating two different classes of converts. Professor Ramsay argues that this is the more accurate reading. Certainly Paul's reference to the Thessalonians as former idol worshippers would bear out the conclusion that many, if not most of them, had been pagans rather than attendants at the synagogue. The Thessalonian Church, then, was basically gentile and included people of some prominence in the city.

From II Corinthians 8:2 we learn that the Macedonians were extremely poor, but the problem of the idle who were living off the resources of others (I Thessalonians 4:11; II Thessalonians 3:6–12) suggests that Paul may have been referring more to the Philippians than to the Thessalonians. The remarkable endurance and faithfulness of the Macedonian Christians appear again in Thessalonica. Paul commends them in a striking passage:

For you, brethren, became imitators of the churches of God in Christ Jesus which are in Judea; for you suffered the same things from your own countrymen as they did from the Jews, who killed both the Lord Jesus and the prophets, and drove us out, and displease God and oppose all men by hindering us from speaking to the Gentiles that they may be saved (I Thessalonians 2:14–16a).

In contrast to his experience at Philippi, the storm that drove Paul

[67] Cf. Ramsay, *St. Paul the Traveller*, p. 228.

out of Thessalonica was raised by the Jews (Acts 17:5-9). The outcome of the riot which followed was that Jason, who had been host to Paul and his companions, was placed under bond to preserve the peace, and the apostles were hurried out of the city. The action against Jason placed Paul in an awkward position in relation to the Thessalonian Church. If it were a matter of risking his own life, Paul would not have hesitated to return, but he could not, in good conscience, place his host in further jeopardy. He had been outwitted by Satan.[68] How keenly he felt this he reveals in his words:

> But since we were bereft of you, brethren, for a short time, in person not in heart, we endeavored the more eagerly and with great desire to see you face to face; because we wanted to come to you—I, Paul, again and again— but Satan hindered us (I Thessalonians 2:17-18).

Traveling west along the Egnatian Way the apostles came to the city of Beroea (modern Verroia) which, as Strabo says, is situated in the foothills of Mt. Bermium.[69] Located in a fertile and prosperous area, it was a city of some size and prominence and contained, according to Acts, a Jewish population large enough to have a synagogue.

By the accident that we have no letter from Paul to Beroea and that Luke treats Paul's stay there in a very brief way, we know very little about the church at Beroea. As in Thessalonica, however, a number of gentile converts responded to Paul's message, but in contrast to the Thessalonian Jews those at Beroea "were more noble" and "received the word with all eagerness, examining the scriptures daily to see if these things were so" (Acts 17:11). The list, in Acts 20:4, of those who accompanied Paul on his final journey to Jerusalem includes Sopater of Beroea, indicating that the church there was among those of Macedonia whose generosity Paul held up to the Corinthians as a challenge for them to emulate (II Corinthians 8:1). We are warranted therefore in including the Beroean Church among the Macedonians Paul refers to in such passages as II Corinthians 11:9.

As the opposition Paul encountered in Thessalonica followed him to Beroea, Paul left, going by sea to Achaia. According to Acts his com-

---

[68] Cf. Ramsay, *St. Paul the Traveller,* pp. 230-31.
[69] Strabo, *Geography,* VII, Fragment 26.

panions, Silas and Timothy, remained in Beroea. But I Thessalonians
3:1–6 reads as though Timothy had accompanied Paul, and Paul had
sent him back to Thessalonica from Athens. In that case, the return
of Timothy to Paul in verse 6 would correspond with the coming of
Silas and Timothy in Acts 18:5 to join him in Corinth. This is simply
another of those incidental differences between Acts and Paul's letters
to be expected between a firsthand and secondhand account, and tends
to confirm rather than diminish the essential historical value of Acts.

The Province of Achaia

Paul's first stop in the great province of Achaia was at the
ancient and renowned city of Athens, the cradle of philosophy, honored
as the intellectual capital of the ancient world. Although Luke lists
a few converts at Athens, there is no evidence that Paul succeeded in
establishing a church there. Nor is the city involved in any of Paul's
correspondence. The one city in Achaia that is important to our interests, therefore, is Corinth to which Paul came next.

The City of Corinth   The ancient city of Corinth,
                                          often called the "City of
Two Seas" was the citadel of the Peloponnesus. Situated just south of
the Isthmus that joined the Peloponnesus to northern Achaia, during
the Peloponnesian Wars it provided a formidable barrier to invading
armies from the north. It later became the capital of the Achaian
League and the home of the Isthmian Games which, Strabo says, drew
large crowds.[70] Acrocorinthus, the fortified hill against which the city
was built, rose to a height of 2,000 feet above sea level. Crowning this
hill was a temple to Aphrodite in whose service were said to be one
thousand temple prostitutes.[71] Corinth controlled the seaports of Cen-
chrea on the Gulf of Saronia to the West and Lechaeum on the Gulf
of Corinth to the east. There was also a small seaport at the narrowest
point on the Isthmus, Schoenus, which fell under the control of Corinth.

Thus Corinth controlled the main link between the Aegean and the

[70] Strabo, *Geography*, VIII, 6, 20.
[71] *Ibid.*

Adriatic Seas, which actually means the control of nearly all the sea traffic between the Levant and the West. Cargoes were portaged and even ships were carried overland across the Isthmus by means of rollers rather than make the dreaded trip around the Malean Cape.[72] A canal across the Isthmus was planned several times and was actually attempted by Nero.[73]

Besides being important centers for Mediterranean commerce, the Corinthian seaports were favorite winter quarters for Mediterranean ships. The city was also famous for its metallurgy, dyeing, and porcelain industries. Corinthian bronze was well known and greatly prized around the Mediterranean world.[74]

But that which made Corinth into such a cosmopolitan center also had its effect on the city's moral and religious life. Famous for its licentious worship of Aphrodite, it had become virtually a symbol for immorality. Such popular sayings as, "Not for every man is the voyage to Corinth," to "Corinthianize," and the phrase "Corinthian girl" serve to indicate how, even among pagan peoples, the city was regarded.[75]

Such was the city which Lucius Mummius destroyed.[76] The new foundation which began with Julius Caesar and became under Augustus the seat of the proconsul was more Roman and more cosmopolitan. The worship of Aphrodite never reached the proportions it had assumed in the old Corinth; yet in its own way the new city earned a similar reputation and much of both the old glory and the old shame belonged also to the new city.

As a seat of the Roman provincial government Corinth was a characteristic mixture of Greek and Roman society, but many other peoples found their way to the city. A Jewish synagogue was founded whose numbers were swelled by the expulsion of Jews from Rome by Claudius (c. 48 A.D.?). Modern archaeology has uncovered a stone

---

[72] Strabo quotes the proverb: "When rounding Maleae forget about returning home." *Geography*, VIII, 6, 20.

[73] *Ibid.*, I, 3, 11: On Nero's attempt see Philostratus, *Apollonius of Tyana,* IV, 24.

[74] Strabo, *Geography*, VIII, 6, 23.

[75] Cf. *Ibid.*, VIII, 6, 20. Cf. Aristophanes, *Lysistrata*, 91.

[76] See "Roman Expansion in the East" in chap. 4.

bearing an inscription from over the door of a Corinthian synagogue dating roughly from this period. Perhaps Paul walked under this stone as he entered the synagogue to preach for the first time the gospel to the Corinthians.[77]

Paul's Work in Corinth   The prominence of the Co-
                                  rinthian Church is evident
not only in the way it dominates Paul's correspondence but also in the length of time he spent in Corinth. Luke tells us (Acts 18:11) that he "stayed a year and six months," considerably longer than he had stayed in any place since setting out on his missionary enterprise toward the West. Silas and Timothy, coming from Macedonia, rejoined him in Corinth (Acts 18:5). The good news from Thessalonica which Timothy bore, coupled with his own anxiety to see them (I Thessalonians 2:17–18; 3:6), prompted Paul to send them a letter which is our I Thessalonians.[78] Probably the action against Jason was still in force and effectively prevented Paul from returning to Thessalonica. Apparently the bearer of the letter returned with news of problems which called for a second letter, which is our II Thessalonians. Possibly Paul also wrote his letter to the Galatians at this time. From Corinth, too, on his last visit, he wrote his great letter to the Romans.

When the synagogue rejected his message, Paul moved to the home of Titius Justus next door, taking with him Crispus the ruler of the synagogue. In I Corinthians 1:14–16 Paul mentions Crispus along with Gaius and the household of Stephanas as the only ones in Corinth whom he had personally baptised. Luke indicates (Acts 18:10) that during Paul's stay in Corinth the church grew to considerable size. There are several indications that this was the largest and most significant of the churches Paul had founded. Paul's extreme anxiety when factions and petty rivalry threatened to tear the church apart, is, therefore, understandable.

Throughout his stay in Corinth, as he later boasted to the Corinthians, Paul maintained himself at his own expense. Part of this ex-

---

[77] Deissmann, *Light from the Ancient East,* pp. 16–17.

[78] Some scholars find reason for reversing the order of the Thessalonian letters in which case our II Thessalonians would belong here. See Weiss, *Earliest Christianity,* I, 289–92.

pense came to him from Macedonia. We learn from Acts 18:2–3 that Aquila and Priscilla,[79] originally from Pontus in Asia Minor, had recently come to Corinth because of the expulsion of the Jews from Rome by Claudius.[80] Since Aquila and Priscilla were tentmakers, Paul worked at his trade and made his home with them. The ties between Paul and this wonderful Jewish Christian couple became very strong. Several years later, just before Paul left the Aegean world for the last time, he referred to them as his "fellow workers in Christ Jesus, who risked their necks for my life" (Romans 16:3–4).

The Corinthian Church Because of the difficulties which Paul later encountered in Corinth, calling forth the most extensive correspondence we have from him, we have a better and more detailed picture of the Corinthian Church than any other of the early churches. The church included some Jews and undoubtedly a number of proselytes. Paul's letters presuppose a knowledge of Judaism which would require some previous experience with the synagogue, and in the reference to the Israelites in the wilderness as "our fathers" (I Corinthians 10:1–11) he implies Jewish readers. As the discussion of the problem of food offered to idols (I Corinthians 8:1–13; cf. 10:14) shows, a significant number of the members came into the church directly from paganism.

There were few wealthy or prominent people among the Christians in Corinth. Paul could write without fear of insulting: "Not many of you were wise according to worldly standards, not many were powerful, not many were of noble birth" (I Corinthians 1:26). A little later on he concluded a list of the grossest sort of immoralities with the words: "Such were some of you" (6:11). Certainly a substantial part of the Corinthian congregation was made up of slaves, for slavery was an important factor in the Roman life and economy.[81]

---

[79] Priscilla is the diminutive of Prisca. Paul calls her by the latter name (Rom. 16:3; I Cor. 16:19).

[80] Some scholars date the expulsion of the Jews as early as 41 A.D. Except for the fact that Luke's use of such terms as "recently" is very broad and must not be pressed, this date would be far too early for Paul's stay in Corinth. Other authorities, however, date the expulsion about 49 A.D. See Foakes Jackson and Lake, *The Beginnings of Christianity*, V, 459–60. Cf. George S. Duncan, *St. Paul's Ephesian Ministry*, p. 18.

[81] Cf. I Cor. 7:21 and "Changes in the Religious Situation" in chap. 4.

The problems in Corinth reveal a different type of people from the dependable, warmhearted Philippians.[82] Their childish pride in the new-found wisdom which they had acquired from Apollos, their petty bickering which broke them into competing factions, their selfish gluttony which showed itself at the Lord's Supper contrast most unfavorably with the endurance, generosity, and concern of the Macedonians for Paul's mission and the Christian cause. While some of the Corinthians were boasting of their spiritual gifts such as speaking in tongues, one of their members had created an intolerably immoral situation in the church. So far from living peaceably with one another, they were haling one another into pagan law courts.

Fickle, childish, quarrelsome, selfish, and lacking in an elementary moral sense, were the members of Paul's church in Corinth. The power of Paul's gospel was put to the test. If Christianity could triumph in Corinth, it could triumph anywhere in the Graeco-Roman world. To this situation Paul addressed the Corinthian letters, and in the light of this situation the great anxiety for Corinth, which those letters display, is understandable.

Some time during Paul's stay in Corinth, probably near the end, the Jews haled Paul before Gallio, the proconsul of Achaia (Acts 18:12-17). When the charges were stated, however, Gallio dismissed the case on the grounds that it did not involve matters of concern to Roman law. The importance of this episode is that it supplies us with one of our best clues to the chronology of Paul. While it is by no means exact and dates only a single point of time during which Paul was in Corinth, the event does allow us to reckon both backward and forward and arrive at an approximate chronology.

At the beginning of this century an inscription found at Delphi in which Gallio, Seneca's brother, is referred to as a proconsul of Achaia at the time, came to the attention of New Testament scholars.[83] It is a copy of a letter from Claudius and the chronological references in it date it approximately 52-53 A.D. Whether Gallio was beginning or ending his proconsulship we cannot tell. Nor do we know at what

---

[82] See "To Macedonia" in chap. 8.

[83] See Deissmann, *Paul*, Appendix I, 261-86. Also Foakes Jackson and Lake, *The Beginnings of Christianity*, V, 460-64.

period in his tenure or in Paul's stay in Corinth Paul was brought before him. These uncertainties allow a maximum latitude of approximately four years in dating Paul's arrival in Corinth. The wording in
Acts 18:12, however, sounds as though the arrival of Gallio as the new
governor had encouraged the Jews to take advantage of the change in
administrations to get rid of Paul. Therefore it seems likely that Paul
came to Corinth about 49 or 50 A.D. and was near the end of his stay
when Gallio arrived.[84]

According to Acts 18:18–19 Paul left Corinth for Syria. Taking
his friends and co-workers, Aquila and Priscilla, with him as far as
Ephesus, he continued on to Jerusalem and Antioch.[85] In the meantime,
a young Alexandrian Jewish Christian, Apollos, arrived in Ephesus
and after being instructed in "the way of God more accurately" by
Aquila and Priscilla, he made his way to Corinth. The work of Apollos
in Corinth, as the first four chapters of I Corinthians show, uninten-
tionally caused Paul considerable trouble. After spending some time in
Antioch and revisiting the Galatian churches, Paul returned to Ephesus
to begin a new phase of his work.

The Province of Asia

The western part of Asia Minor, including the countries of
Caria, Lydia, Mysia, and a large part of Phrygia, constituted the Ro-
man Province of Asia whose capital in Paul's time was Ephesus. During
the first century a number of important churches appeared in the lead-
ing cities of Asia. Revelation 1:11 lists seven, including Ephesus and
Laodicea, which were associated with Paul's ministry. Four churches of
Asia are mentioned in Paul's correspondence: Ephesus, Colossi, Lao-
dicea, and Hierapolis. Colossi and Hierapolis are not mentioned in
Revelation, which brings the number of churches in the Province of
Asia mentioned in the New Testament to nine. Professor Ramsay be-

[84] This assumes that Gallio's term of office was, as usual, one year. A two
year tenure was not unknown, however, and the inscription may refer to
Gallio's second year. This would make Paul's arrival in Corinth possibly as early
as 48 A.D.

[85] It is on this visit to Jerusalem that Professor Knox locates the Jerusalem
Council. See "The Jerusalem Council" in this chapter. Professor Weizsäcker,
however, omits this journey altogether, *The Apostolic Age*, pp. 248–50.

lieves that all of these churches were founded under Paul's influence.[86] Since it is clear from Colossians 1:3–8 that that church was founded by one of Paul's co-workers, Epaphras, we may assume that, apart from Ephesus, Paul's "fellow servants" established most if not all of these churches. Because only four of these churches are involved in Paul's letters, we will confine our attention to them.

The City of Ephesus   The capital of the Roman
                                        Province of Asia and un-
doubtedly the most important city in Asia Minor, Ephesus was situated only a short distance up the Cayster River from the western coast. About a mile east and somewhat north of the city was located the famous Temple to Artemis which added to the fame and importance of the city. According to Strabo the city was once situated around the temple site and was moved to its later location by one of the Diadochi, Lysimachus. The people, however, were reluctant to change to the new location. During a rainstorm Lysimachus flooded the old city to force them to move. He then renamed the city after his wife Arsinoe, but the city soon reverted to the old name.[87]

The mixed oriental and Greek character of Ephesus is seen in the stories told by Strabo of the foundation of the city. Ephesus, according to him, was founded and named by the Amazon women.[88] Until Androclus, the Athenian, expelled them and settled the city with Greeks, Ephesus was inhabited by Carians and Leleges of Asian stock. Later the fabled Croesus was said to have held the city.[89] Alexander the Great wrested it from Persian control and brought it again under Greek rule.

In spite of the fact that silt deposited by the Cayster River threatened the usefulness of the harbor—a condition which was aggravated by the mistake of engineers in building a breakwater at the mouth[90]— Ephesus ranked as the greatest commercial center of Asia[91] and was

---

[86] *St. Paul the Traveller*, p. 274.
[87] Strabo, *Geography*, XIV, 1, 21.
[88] Strabo, *Geography*, XI, 5, 4; XII, 3, 21.
[89] Strabo, *Geography*, XIV, 1, 21.
[90] *Ibid.*, XIV, 1, 24.
[91] Strabo, *Geography*, XII, 8, 15.

noted for its good wine.[92] One of the seven wonders of the ancient world, the Temple to Artemis (Diana, A. V.) was burned to the ground on the night of the birth of Alexander the Great, but was rebuilt in even greater splendor.[93]

The goddess Artemis is another evidence of the combined oriental and Greek character of the city. Although she bore a Greek name, Artemis was essentially a form of the Great Mother deity otherwise known as Cybele.[94] Demetrius the silversmith, who raised the riot as Paul was about to leave Ephesus (Acts 19:23–20:1), was probably an officer of the Temple and made silver statuettes of the goddess.[95]

The prominence and influence of Ephesus made it an ideal center for Paul's work in Asia. That he found disciples there who had been baptized by John's baptism raises the vexing question of the relationship between the followers of John the Baptist and the Christian movement. To suppose that these disciples were won by Priscilla and Aquila accords neither with the picture of them in Acts 18:26 nor with the fact that Priscilla and Aquila were companions of Paul. They would not have administered John's baptism. Significantly, according to Acts (19:8–10), Paul remained in Ephesus more than two years, nearly a year longer than he had been in Corinth. The events Luke records during Paul's stay in Ephesus are characteristic of his interests. Paul began preaching in the synagogue, but after three months Jewish resistance caused him to leave and for the remaining two years he utilized the lecture hall of Tyrannus.[96] The stories of the discomfiture of the Jewish exorcists and the burning of the books of magic (Acts 19:13–20) bring Paul into contact with the magic and superstition so popular in Ephesus.[97]

Paul's Ephesian Imprisonment? From his letters we can gain important additional infor-

---

[92] Strabo, *Geography,* XIV, 1, 15.
[93] Plutarch, *Alexander,* 3. Strabo, *Geography,* XIV, 1, 22.
[94] See "The Myth of the Great Mother" in chap. 4.
[95] Cf. Foakes Jackson and Lake, *The Beginnings of Christianity,* IV, 245–46.
[96] See Ramsay, *St. Paul the Traveller,* pp. 270–71. The Western text adds the words: "from the fifth to the tenth hour" meaning apparently that Paul used the hall after Tyrannus had finished for the day.
[97] See "Astrology and Magic" in chap. 4.

mation of Paul's experiences and accomplishments in Ephesus. In I Corinthians 16:8-9 he writes: "I will stay in Ephesus until Pentecost, for a wide door for effective work has opened to me, and there are many adversaries." The reference to "many adversaries" cannot refer to Demetrius and the riot at Ephesus because that event did not occur until after this letter was written and just before Paul left. Several other references indicate that Paul was in serious trouble in Ephesus: "For we do not want you to be ignorant, brethren, of the affliction we experienced in Asia . . . we felt that we had received the sentence of death"[98] (II Corinthians 1:8-9. Cf. 4:11). "What do I gain if, humanly speaking, I fought with wild beasts at Ephesus?" (I Corinthians 15:32). All of these passages point to experiences not mentioned in Acts. In II Corinthians 11:23 Paul speaks of "far more imprisonments," but up to the time of writing II Corinthians Acts has mentioned only the night in the Philippian jail. These considerations have led a number of scholars to the conclusion that Paul was imprisoned in Ephesus and narrowly escaped with his life.[99]

The reference to having fought with wild beasts in Ephesus raises problems. If it is taken literally it is strange that Paul escaped death. He may, of course, have been sentenced and reprieved at the last minute. There is a well-known legend that tells how, when Paul was condemned to the arena in Ephesus, the lion which was put in the arena against him refused to attack and lay down at his feet and licked him. Although of no historical value the story, which goes back at least to Hippolytus, does indicate that the Patristic writers tended to take the words in I Corinthians 15:32 literally.

But a second difficulty is that as a Roman citizen he would not be liable to such a condemnation. Some have supposed that Paul means

[98] Professor Goodspeed's argument that this is a figurative description of Paul's anguish over the Corinthian disaffection is to me not convincing. *Paul,* 129.

[99] On the Ephesian imprisonment and its relation to the prison letters see Duncan, *St. Paul's Ephesian Ministry,* pp. 59-161; Professor Duncan finds reason for believing that Paul was imprisoned three times in Asia (cf. pp. 140-43), twice in Ephesus and once elsewhere (perhaps Laodicea) see pp. 165-225, esp. 195-99. See also McNeile, *Introduction to the New Testament,* pp. 180-85; Donald W. Riddle and Harold H. Hutson, *New Testament Life and Literature* (Chicago: The University of Chicago Press, 1947), pp. 122-23; Dibelius, *Paul,* 81; Weiss, *Earliest Christianity,* I, 320-21.

that he was condemned to the arena but was saved at the last minute by pleading his citizenship which, as in Philippi, he had not done before. But this seems unlikely. Possibly his plea of citizenship was ignored. Cicero charged Verres, for example, with a similar violation of the rights of Roman citizenship by crucifying a man who repeatedly insisted that he was a citizen.[100]

To take Paul's words figuratively, however, is difficult.[101] He cannot have been referring to the riot because: 1) I Corinthians was written before that time;[102] 2) he was not present at the riot (Acts 19:30–31); 3) he does not elsewhere use such figures of his human opponents. To add to the mystery, in Romans 16:3 Paul refers to Prisca and Aquila, who were with him in Ephesus, as his "fellow workers in Christ Jesus, who risked their necks for my life." Clearly, Paul experienced a crisis in Ephesus that brought him close to death, and at the risk of their own lives, his two companions had rescued him.[103] That crisis would surely include a period of time in prison.

Letters from Ephesus   The importance of the Ephesian imprisonment is in its connection with the possible place of origin of the letters which Paul wrote while in prison.[104] Traditionally the writing of these letters has been assigned to his imprisonment in Rome because, according to the story in Acts, that imprisonment seemed the most likely place. On the assumption that all the prison letters originated in the same place, the reference in Philippians 1:13 to "the whole praetorian guard" (the body guard of the Emperor) and "Caesar's household" in 4:22 seems to confirm this judgment.[105] But there is archaeological evidence that

[100] Cicero, *In C Verres,* II, 5, 66.

[101] Weizsäcker insists that the statement must be taken literally; see *The Apostolic Age,* p. 385.

[102] Professor Weiss, however, does believe, because the words "in Ephesus" sound as though he was elsewhere and referring back to the city, that this part of I Corinthians was written after Chapter 16 from some other place in Asia. *Earliest Christianity,* I, 323.

[103] Romans 16:4 could, of course, refer to an unknown crisis in Corinth where Paul had met Prisca and Aquila; but when all is considered, the reference is almost certainly to a crisis in Ephesus.

[104] On the occasion for these letters see "The Letter to Philippi" in chap. 8 and "To the Lycus Valley" and "The Question of Ephesians" in chap. 9.

[105] Cf. Weiss, *Earliest Christianity,* I, 385.

both the Praetorian and "Caesar's household" were to be found in Ephesus.[106] Philippians, at least, could therefore have been written in Ephesus. Five communications or trips between Paul's prison and Philippi are indicated in the letter. If Paul was in Ephesus, which was a brief sail from Philippi, rather than in Rome, which was from Philippi more than seven hundred land miles and across the Adriatic Sea, these communications would be more understandable. In his description of Paul's last journey to Jerusalem, Luke makes it clear that this was Paul's farewell to the Aegean area, but in Philippians 2:24 Paul hopes soon to visit Philippi again. If he was writing from Ephesus, the verse fits well with what we know of Paul's plans and movements; if he wrote from Rome, it is difficult to understand.

In the next chapter we will see that there are reasons to believe that Romans 16:1–23 is a separate letter and was written from Corinth to Ephesus. If this is true, Andronicus and Junias (verse 7), Paul's fellow prisoners, were probably involved with him in the crisis in Ephesus. Colossians and Philemon, which are closely related and therefore almost certainly were written at the same time and place, may also have come from Ephesus.[107] That Onesimus, Philemon's run-away slave, would stop in Ephesus has sometimes been questioned. Rome would seem to provide a better opportunity for him to hide in the anonymity of the masses. Onesimus would likely go to Ephesus seeking opportunity to ship to Rome and may have been found by Paul in the meantime; or he may have gone deliberately to Ephesus to seek asylum at the Temple of Artemis.[108] Also Epaphras, the leader and founder of the Colossian Church, is mentioned in both letters, and, according to Philemon, is a fellow prisoner with Paul. That Epaphras would come to visit Paul and become imprisoned with him is much more likely in Ephesus than in Rome.

If Philemon and Colossians were written in Ephesus, the "letter from Laodicea" was written there also.[109] On the basis of these suppositions

[106] Cf. Deissmann, *Light from the Ancient East*, p. 238.

[107] The question of the letter to the Ephesians, its authenticity, and its relation to Ephesus will be dealt with in the next chapter. See "The Question of Ephesians" in chap. 8.

[108] On the right of asylum at this Temple see Foakes Jackson and Lake, *The Beginnings of Christianity*, V, 254.

[109] As we shall see in the next chapter some scholars believe that the

we may reconstruct the order of events as follows: Paul arrived in Ephesus from his trip to Jerusalem and Antioch and sometime later a crisis arose in which he was imprisoned. During his imprisonment he wrote Philippians, Philemon, Colossians, possibly Ephesians, and if it is a separate letter, Laodiceans.[110] Although these theories are attractive and several of them are probable, we cannot be certain about any of them.

When we come to the Corinthian correspondence we can be more definite. I Corinthians 16:8–9 makes it clear that Paul is writing that letter from Ephesus near the end of his stay. If we assume that I Corinthians is all one letter the words "I wrote to you in my letter" in 5:9 mean that there had been an earlier letter which also must have been written from Ephesus. In II Corinthians 12:14 and 13:1–2 Paul refers to his proposed visit as his third. Some time between the writing of I Corinthians and this passage Paul had paid a visit to Corinth. That he is still writing from Ephesus is evident from his words in II Corinthians 10:16: "So that we may preach the gospel in lands beyond you." We know from Romans 15:23–24 that Paul is referring to Rome and Spain, which could not be said to be beyond Corinth if Paul were writing later from Macedonia. (Cf. I Corinthians 16:5.) The visit to Corinth between these two letters, therefore, was from Ephesus.

References in the earlier part of II Corinthians to a "painful visit" (2:1–3) indicate that something happened to prevent Paul from completing his plans and to call forth the second letter. Some scholars doubt this intermediate visit from Ephesus on the grounds that it seems to be denied in II Corinthians 1:23: "It was to spare you that I refrained from coming to Corinth."[111] But we should note that two proposed visits are under discussion (verse 16) and Paul is accused of vacillating. Apparently he had altered his plan in I Corinthians 16:5–6, intending

---

Laodicean letter is Philemon. A few others identify it as Ephesians. See "The Letter to Philemon" in chap. 8.

[110] If the Jerusalem Council occurred during Paul's trip from Corinth to Antioch (Acts 18:18–19:1), Galatians was also written from Ephesus.

[111] Cf. Ramsay, St. Paul the Traveller, 274–75. Professor Ramsay places the "second visit" of 13:2 after Paul's arrival in Macedonia. Several older scholars placed it before the writing of I Corinthians.

instead to go to Macedonia by way of Corinth and then return to
Corinth for the winter. He had gotten as far as Corinth when something caused him to turn back to Ephesus.[112] At the time of writing
he had not returned to spend the winter in Corinth.

From this sketch of Paul's relations with Corinth it is clear that he
wrote three letters from Ephesus to Corinth. If we suppose that the
prison letters also originated here, Ephesus was the scene of Paul's
greatest period of correspondence. But in other ways, too, the capital
of Asia saw the greatest and most effective period of Paul's missionary
career.

By this time Paul had assembled a large number of helpers. To the
original group of Paul, Silas, and Timothy, which came into Macedonia were added others like Epaphras who carried the gospel into
outlying cities of Asia. Many of those listed in the greetings at the end
of his letters were leading workers in the local churches (cf. I Corinthians 12:28), some of whom made their homes available as meeting
places for the churches (cf. Philemon 2). Among the churches established in Asia by Paul's co-workers were those in three cities situated
near one another in a triangle in the Lycus Valley, which, because
they are involved in Paul's correspondence, call for brief notice.

Cities of the Lycus Valley   The first and most promi-
                                      nent of these three cities on
the Great Road from Ephesus to the Euphrates was Laodicea.[113] From
early Seleucid times it was an important fortification on the main
trade East-West route. Its wealth (cf. Revelation 3:15-18) came from
the fertility of its land and its famous black wool[114] and partly from
its commercial importance. Laodicea, and to a considerable extent the
entire area, was subject to earthquakes, a fact which affected the religion of the area.[115]

[112] Professor Duncan raises the question whether Paul may have gone directly
from Corinth to Troas on this trip. *St. Paul's Ephesian Ministry*, pp. 181–83.
[113] Strabo, *Geography*, XII, 8, 16.
[114] Strabo says that Poseidon (the god of earthquakes as well as the sea) is
worshiped in the region of Apameia because of the earthquakes there. The
same was undoubtedly true of the Laodicean territory which was not far west
of Apameia.
[115] *Ibid.*, XII, 8, 16–18.

Hierapolis, located a few miles northeast of Laodicea on a branch road, was particularly famous for its hot springs. The springs were apparently credited with medicinal properties and thus helped to bring wealth and renown to the area. The water from the springs was heavily laden with calcite which encrusted the banks. Strabo claims that people constructed fences by channeling the water into ditches whereupon it would change into stone.[116] The water of the Lycus River at Laodicea, to a lesser degree, had similar properties.

A nearby cave emitted a constant vapour so poisonous as to cause instant death to anyone entering it. The place was called a Plutonian because it was supposed to be an opening into the netherworld ruled by the god Pluto. Strabo tells how he threw into the cave some sparrows which immediately died.[117] The eunuch priests of Cybele, however, entered it without any apparent ill effects. Although Strabo wryly observes that they held their breath, they were presumed to be endowed with divine powers which enabled them to enter the cave of death unharmed. We need little imagination to see what effect such strange phenomena would have on the superstitious minds of the people of this area. When in Colossians (2:8, 18, 20) Paul warned the church against the "elemental spirits of the universe (cosmos)" and the "worship of angels,"[118] he was referring to the fearful worship of the divine powers who were believed to produce these phenomena. Out of the belief in such divine powers developed philosophic speculation of a gnostic character concerning beings which mediated between a transcendent deity and men.[119]

Colossae was situated on the Great Road a short distance east of Laodicea. It shared in the reputation and ideas that the unusual natural phenomena brought to Laodicea and Hierapolis. The water in the area contained alum and was peculiarly suited to the dyeing industry. Colossae derived a large revenue from "colosseni wool," a cloth famous for its unusual and beautiful purple color.[120] As the pic-

---

[116] Strabo, *Geography*, XIII, 4, 14.

[117] *Ibid.*

[118] On angel worship in Asia Minor see Ramsay, *The Church in the Roman Empire*, pp. 465–80 and note 1 on p. 480.

[119] See "Gnosticism" in chap. 4.

[120] Strabo, *Geography*, XII, 8, 16.

ture of Laodicea in Revelation 3:15–18 and the subsequent history of the churches in this area show, the position of these cities as centers of wealth and religious shrines presented peculiar problems. Undoubtedly the warning in the letter to the Colossians against the prevalent pagan influences of the area was what Paul wanted the Laodiceans to hear when he asked the Colossians to have the letter "read also in the church of the Laodiceans" (Colossians 4:16).

The Collection for the Saints of Jerusalem

Paul had written the Corinthians of his plan to remain in Ephesus until Pentecost and then to come to them by way of Macedonia. But when the crisis in Corinth caused him to change his plans he apparently went directly to Corinth where he met with such a rebuff that he returned to Ephesus and sent Titus to Corinth with a "severe letter" and instructions to meet him at Troas (II Corinthians 2:12; 7:6–8). The story of the riot instigated by Demetrius, the silversmith, just as Paul was leaving Ephesus is told by Luke to show that the success of Paul's mission was great enough by interfering with the worship of Artemis to affect the economy of the city.

Paul arrived in Troas only to find that Titus was not there as agreed. Anxious over the Corinthian crisis and alarmed at the delay of Titus, he left Troas for Macedonia. When Titus met him there with the welcome news that the trouble was over, Paul wrote the letter to Corinth which, because of its expressions of forgiveness and joy over the outcome, is usually referred to as the conciliatory letter. II Corinthians 9:1–5 is the last specific reference in Paul's letters to his movements.

Paul's plans for the future, however, are clear, and from Acts we can follow the story of how he carried them out. For some time he had been organizing a collection from his churches for the relief of the poor in the church of Jerusalem.[121] From Ephesus he had written the Corinthians of this plan as though the Corinthians were familiar with it (I Corinthians 16:1–4).

Unless his first letter had proposed it, which is improbable, he had

[121] On the organization of the collection see Duncan, *St. Paul's Ephesian Ministry*, Ch. XVII, 236–49.

apparently started the collection while still in Corinth.[122] The Galatian churches were included, as undoubtedly the Asian churches were. Because of their poverty Paul had not intended to include the Macedonians, but it is an index to their character that they insisted on taking part in the collection (II Corinthians 8:2-5). At the time of writing his last letter to Corinth, Paul was preparing to leave Macedonia with the collection and delegates assembled in the churches there. Apprehensive that the Corinthians might embarrass him by not being ready with a worthy offering, he was sending messengers ahead to prepare for his coming.

Paul's motive in this collection for Jerusalem has often been interpreted as a peace offering, which had been agreed upon at the Council (Galatians 2:10) and intended to heal the rift between him and the Jerusalem Church. Because it supposes that Paul would attempt to buy agreement on a basic religious principle and that Jerusalem might compromise such a principle for money, such an interpretation is unfair to both. Paul's request (Romans 15:31) that the Romans pray "that my service for Jerusalem may be acceptable to the saints," is usually supposed to reflect Paul's anxiety that the Jerusalem Church might still reject him and his uncircumcised gentile churches by rejecting the offering.[123] But if Galatians 2:10 represents an agreement with the Apostles concerning such an offering, why should Paul be anxious?

This interpretation rests on the outmoded Tübingen hypothesis of a basic conflict between Paul and Jerusalem. There is no warrant for questioning Paul's affirmation in Galatians (2:6-14) that he and the Apostles were in agreement. As evidence of their agreement Paul mentions that the only suggestion the Apostles offered concerning his work among the gentiles—that he remember the poor—was one with which he readily agreed, and one which obviously in no way affected

---

[122] This creates a serious difficulty for the theory of Professor Knox that the collection was started upon Paul's return to Ephesus from the Jerusalem Council (Acts 18:21-19:1) in response to the agreement he had reached with the Apostles there (Gal. 2:10). Cf. *Chapters in a Life of Paul*, pp. 53-58.

[123] It is possible to interpret this verse to mean to pray that the offering be adequate to the needs of Jerusalem and therefore an occasion for thanksgiving to God by the saints. Cf. the use of this same term translated "acceptable" in II Cor. 8:12.

the issues under discussion. Only in the principle of Christian concern
for the poor is Galatians 2:10 related to the collection for Jerusalem.

Paul's reason for the collection, first of all, was to meet the need in
Jerusalem, word of which must have reached him in Corinth. Perhaps
one purpose of his trip from Ephesus to Jerusalem and Antioch was to
investigate the extent of the need in Jerusalem. If this is true, we may
assume that on his return through Galatia to Ephesus he had enlisted
the support of the Galatian churches.

Yet Paul's motive for the collection ran deeper than a humanitarian
sympathy with the plight of the Jerusalem Christians. He explains the
meaning of his project in his letter to the Romans:

For Macedonia and Achaia have been pleased to make some contribution
for the poor among the saints at Jerusalem; they were pleased to do it, and
indeed they are in debt to them, for if the Gentiles have come to share in
their spiritual blessings, they ought also to be of service to them in material
blessings (Romans 15:26–27).

The spiritual blessings cannot be divorced from the material; the gentiles' share in the Church must come to expression in material terms.
The collection for Jerusalem was therefore a symbol of the unity of the
Church. By means of this concrete expression of Christian love the
Jerusalem Church would be made aware that the gentile churches belonged with them as members of the Body of Christ. The gentiles, too,
would realize their oneness with the Christians of Jerusalem. The collection was an expression of the truth of Paul's words, "If one member
suffers, all suffer together" (I Corinthians 12:26; cf. verses 12–26).

In one sense, however, Paul was seeking the approval of the Jerusalem Church. On his trip to Jerusalem in Galatians 2:2 Paul sought
and obtained agreement on his gospel to the gentiles, lest he was or
had been running in vain. Now he was presenting this evidence that
his gentile churches were an acceptable offering to God (Romans
15:16). His mission to the uncircumcised had been successful and
therefore justified. (Cf. II Corinthians 9:12–14.) But everything
hinged on whether Jerusalem would, by accepting the offering, acknowledge their oneness with the gentiles. Paul would not be wrong

if they refused; but the unity of the Church would be threatened. The Body of Christ cannot be sundered.[124]

From Acts 20:3 we learn that Paul went to Corinth as he had planned and remained there for three months. During this his last visit to Corinth Paul wrote his letter to the church in Rome. If Romans 16 is a separate letter written to the Ephesians, as a number of scholars believe, it was probably written at this time. Because of the discovery of a plot against his life, Paul returned to Macedonia rather than board ship for Syria as he had planned. Since the narrative in Acts changes again to the first person, Luke, or the author of his source, must have rejoined Paul's party. In Acts 20:4 Luke gives us a list of the delegates who accompanied Paul to Jerusalem. Although Luke does not tell us the outcome of Paul's trial in Rome, he makes it clear by means of the dramatic scene at the end of Paul's speech to the Ephesian elders at Miletus that Paul is leaving the Aegean world for the last time:

And they all wept and embraced Paul and kissed him, sorrowing most of all because of the word he had spoken, that they should see his face no more. And they brought him to the ship (Acts 20:36–38).

Paul's Appeal to Caesar

Luke intensifies the foreboding in Paul's speech at Miletus (Acts 20:18–35) by relating two warnings given to Paul as the party proceeds on the way to Jerusalem. During Paul's stopover at Tyre the disciples there warned him by the Spirit not to go to Jerusalem (21:4); and later at Caesarea Agabus (Cf. Acts 11:28) dramatically depicted the imprisonment that awaited Paul there.

Making their way overland Paul and his company arrived in Jerusalem from Caesarea and were welcomed by the church. Later James, who was now the head of the Jerusalem Church, and the elders listened appreciatively to Paul's report of the progress of the gospel among the gentiles. Apparently Paul's apprehension in Romans 15:31 was un-

---

[124] For a recent similar interpretation of the Jerusalem collection see Munck, *Paul and the Salvation of Mankind*, pp. 282–308. Professor Duncan's suggestion that Paul intended the collection to work toward the unity of the Church as the annual Temple Tax expressed the unity of the Jewish Commonwealth, deserves serious consideration. See *St. Paul's Ephesian Ministry*, chap. XVI, 229–35.

warranted; his service was "acceptable to the saints" at Jerusalem.

The difficulties that fulfilled the dire predictions of his imprisonment arose from another quarter. In the course of assisting four Jerusalem Christians in the completion of their vows, Paul went with them into the Temple to complete the arrangements.[125] Shortly afterward some Asian Jews, assuming that Trophimus, one of Paul's companions whom they recognized as an Ephesian gentile, was one of the men whom Paul had taken with him into the Temple, incited a riot from which Paul was rescued by the Roman tribune. For a gentile to enter the Temple area was punishable by death. Inscriptions in Greek and Latin at the portals warned all non-Jews that they would be responsible for their own death should they trespass on the sacred precincts. Modern archaeologists have discovered the stone bearing the Greek inscription which is now in the museum of Constantinople.[126]

The tribune, thinking that he had captured a fugitive Egyptian rebel, was surprised to find that Paul could speak Greek and allowed him to address the crowd. When the uproar began again, the tribune took Paul into the barracks and would have examined him by scourging, but Paul appealed once more to his rights as a Roman citizen. Instead, the tribune placed him before the Sanhedrin, and when the assembly broke into a violent dispute he once more rescued Paul. Luke makes it clear in this episode that the real plaintiffs were the Sadducees, the ruling party of the Jews. When Paul's nephew informed the tribune of a plot against his uncle's life the tribune sent Paul under heavy guard to Felix the Procurator at Caesarea.

The trial under Felix was inconclusive; and when Felix was succeeded by Festus, Paul was held over to be tried under the new procurator. Luke suggests that Felix was hoping to receive a bribe and, disappointed in this, deliberately held Paul over for Festus as a parting favor to the Jews. Presumably, he should have disposed of all the cases on the docket before quitting office.[127] The change of procurators is of

[125] Presumably the vow referred to was the Nazarite vow. Cf. Foakes Jackson and Lake, *The Beginnings of Christianity*, IV, 272–74.

[126] For a picture and translation of this inscription see Deissmann, *Light from the Ancient East*, pp. 79–80 and plate. Cf. Josephus, *Wars*, VI, 2, 4 and *Ant.* XII, 3, 4.

[127] On the legal aspects of Paul's arrest and trial see H. J. Cadbury, "Roman

interest because of its bearing on the chronology of Paul. The evidence, however, for the date on which Felix was deposed is contradictory and scholars have suggested dates ranging from 55 to 61 A.D. Probably a date somewhere between 57–59 A.D. is the most likely.[128]

A second plot to kill Paul in ambush was foiled when Festus refused the Jews' request for a transfer of the trial back to Jerusalem. At the first hearing before Festus the Jewish representatives again asked for a transfer of the trial to Jerusalem. When Festus asked Paul if he wished to make the change Paul replied, "I am standing before Caesar's tribunal, where I ought to be tried . . . I appeal to Caesar" (Acts 25:10–11).

The story of Paul's audience with Agrippa indicates that Festus was at a loss to state the charges to the Emperor, but having granted Paul's appeal he could not now set him free. With the voyage to Rome the narrative changes again to the first person plural, indicating that Luke, or the author of his source, was with Paul on the journey.[129] It is noteworthy that, in spite of the terrible fortnight during the storm at sea and the shipwreck, there is in the story of Paul's voyage to Rome none of the dark foreboding that characterized the account of his last journey to Jerusalem. Twice Paul is assured by visions that he will reach Rome. Luke is preparing the reader, apparently, for a favorable outcome at Rome.

At the end of his eventful voyage Paul landed at Puteoli in Italy and found Christians there with whom he spent a week. A group of Christians came as far as the Forum of Appius and the Three Taverns to meet Paul and accompanied him to Rome. The warmth of their greeting may be taken as an indication of the effect of Paul's letter written from Corinth to them. Paul had achieved his purpose of visit-

Law and the Trial of Paul" in Foakes Jackson and Lake, *The Beginnings of Christianity,* V, 297–338. Cf. Munck, *Paul and the Salvation of Mankind,* pp. 309–34.
   [128] Cf. Foakes Jackson and Lake, *The Beginnings of Christianity,* V, 464–67. Also James Hastings, ed., *A Dictionary of the Bible,* I, 417–19. This entire article (especially Part II) on "Chronology of the New Testament" by C. H. Turner is important for the study of Paul.
   [129] The classic study of Paul's voyage to Rome is that of James Smith, *The Voyage and Shipwreck of St. Paul* 3rd ed. (London: Longmans, Green, and Co., 1866). See also Ramsay, *St. Paul the Traveller,* 314–46.

ing Rome—largely at the expense of the Empire—yet he was still under arrest and awaited trial before Nero. The trial depended, however, on the appearance of his accusers. Since the journey to Rome was long and expensive, it would be natural for the Jewish authorities in Jerusalem to send a message to their counterparts in Rome asking them to represent the case against Paul. That is probably why Paul asked for a meeting with the local Jewish leaders. But he learned, apparently to his surprise, that they had received no word from Jerusalem. Jerusalem's case against Paul apparently had been abandoned. With the statement that "He lived there two whole years at his own expense, and welcomed all who came to him, preaching the kingdom of God and teaching about the Lord Jesus Christ quite openly and unhindered," the story of Paul in Acts comes to an end.

Luke's purpose in writing Acts was accomplished, but from our standpoint he has left the story in midair. What was the outcome of the trial? Did Paul achieve his ambition to go to Spain? What was the end of his life? On these questions the New Testament supplies no answer. The prison letters cannot be used to supplement the picture of Paul's Roman imprisonment with any certainty because, as we have seen, they may have come from an earlier Ephesian imprisonment.

Nor are the Pastoral Epistles, I and II Timothy and Titus, of any real help. Aside from the fact that most scholars do not regard them, in their present form at least, as from the hand of Paul, they furnish much less information than has often been supposed.[130] Neither I Timothy nor Titus suggests that they were written from Rome. So they do not furnish any answers to our questions. There is no mention or hint of Paul's plan to visit Spain. Only II Timothy 4:6–8 and 16–18 contain anything that relates to Paul's trial. Paul appears to be facing execution, but it is not clear that this is the trial for which he was sent from Caesarea to Rome. The reference in verse 16 to his first defense is probably not to a previous trial. But nothing in this chapter indicates the actual outcome. In II Corinthians 1:9, for example, Paul had faced apparent death before. If Philippians were written from Ephesus, Paul's words in 2:17, which are strikingly similar to those in

[130] On the problem of the Pastoral Epistles see "Paul and the Pastoral Epistles" in chap. 8.

II Timothy 4:6, furnish another example of impending death that did not materialize.

The earliest and most reliable statement of the fate of Paul, the so-called First Clement, which was written to Corinth from Rome probably about 95 A.D., after referring to the martyrdom of Peter, simply states that having "come to the extreme limits of the west" he was martyred "under the prefects."[131] This writing is near enough to the time of Paul to be of considerable value, but we cannot be certain what is meant by the limits of the west. That his ancient readers understood him to mean Spain is evident from the fact that the author of the Muratorian Fragment (c. 200 A.D.) repeats the tradition that Paul went from Rome to Spain. A fragment attributed to Hippolytus of about the same period relates that after preaching the gospel from Jerusalem to Illyricum (cf. Romans 15:19), Italy and Spain, Paul was beheaded under Nero at Rome. Although he does not mention Paul's mission to Spain, Tertullian refers to the martyrdom of Peter and Paul in Rome.[132]

Eusebius (c. 325 A.D.) appears to be the first to record the tradition that made use of II Timothy. According to this tradition Paul was released (II Timothy 4:17) to continue his preaching and, returning a second time to Rome in the latter period of Nero's reign, was imprisoned and (II Timothy 4:6-8) along with Peter was martyred there.[133] In confirmation of his statements, Eusebius cites two writers from the second and third centuries: Caius of Rome and Dionysius of Corinth. Jerome and others follow Eusebius in relating the tradition and in addition, probably using I Clement, imply that Paul did complete his mission to Spain.[134] The tradition which thus crystallized looks like the result of inferences drawn from a combination of II Timothy, I Clement, and possibly Romans 15:24. That Paul was martyred in Rome, however, persists throughout the tradition. Because it was so

---

[131] I Clement, 5:7.

[132] *Scorpiace*, 15. The association of the martyrdom of Paul with that of Peter may be only an inference from the fact that they follow one another in I Clement. Cf. Tertullian, *Apology*, 5.

[133] Eusebius, *Church History*, II, 22, 2-8 and 25, 5-8. Cf. his quotation from Origen, III, 1, 11-13.

[134] Jerome, *The Lives of Illustrious Men*, V.

early, is widely accepted, and is intrinsically probable, we may safely assume the tradition that Paul was beheaded under Nero to be correct. The theory that Paul returned from Spain to spend some time with his Aegean churches before going to Rome for his second visit and martyrdom is the result of more recent attempts to correlate the Pastoral Epistles with Acts and to fit the prison letters into his Roman imprisonment. Luke makes it clear in Acts 20:18–38 that Paul did not return to the Aegean area. Professor Kirsopp Lake has advanced the attractive suggestion that there was a statute of limitation of two years in cases such as Paul's, and that when his Jerusalem accusers neither came themselves nor requested the Roman Jews to represent them the case was dropped and Paul was released.[135] Luke seems to prepare his readers for such an outcome by the lack of foreboding which characterized the last journey to Jerusalem and the protest of ignorance of Paul's case by the Roman Jews (Acts 28:21). In spite of the lack of any clear evidence for the existence of such a law and one or two difficulties, this suggestion accords well with the tradition in I Clement and offers one of the most plausible explanations for the strange ending of Acts.

Whether Paul realized his mission to Spain or remained a prisoner in Rome to the end, he died under Nero, as Tertullian says, in a manner befitting his Roman citizenship. He died as he had lived: a "witness" to the resurrection of Jesus Christ and there could be for him no more appropriate final words than those of II Timothy 4:6–8:

> For I am already on the point of being sacrificed; the time of my departure has come. I have fought the good fight, I have finished the race, I have kept the faith. Henceforth there is laid up for me the crown of righteousness, which the Lord, the righteous judge, will award to me on that Day, and not only to me but also to all who have loved his appearing.

---

[135] Foakes Jackson and Lake, *The Beginnings of Christianity*, V, 325–36.

my messaGe . . .

And my speech and my message
were not in plausible words of wisdom, but in
demonstration of the
Spirit and power, that your faith might
not rest in the wisdom of
men but in the power of God. (I Corinthians 2:4–5)

8 his letters are weighty...

For they say, "His letters are weighty and strong, but
his bodily presence is weak, and
his speech is of no account." (II Corinthians 10:10)

In the study of Paul our interest naturally centers in
the collection of his letters which stands at the heart of our New
Testament. Since they were first collected and published for the use
of the Church they have been the foundation of the second half of the
New Testament. With the rest of this division of the New Testament
Paul's letters stand in a relation to the Gospels similar to that of the
prophets in the Old Testament to the Torah: they provide an authoritative interpretation of the Gospel.

We find it hard to agree, however, with Paul's words, "we write you
nothing but what you can read and understand" (II Corinthians 1:13).
That "his letters are weighty" we will agree, but their meanings are
often obscured from us by the mists of unknown circumstances and the
strangeness of Paul's world. Our study thus far has attempted to clear
away some of the mists that surround his world and to trace the
course of his life within that world. We must now turn to the letters
themselves to see if, by studying them against their background, they
cannot be made to yield some information about their circumstances
that will help us to understand them better.

Characteristics of Paul's Letters

At the close of the sixteenth chapter of Romans occur these
words: "I Tertius, the writer of this letter, greet you in the Lord."

235

Tertius was Paul's amanuensis, or secretary. Probably Paul dictated all of his letters to such a person. At the close of his letters, Paul would take the pen from his amanuensis and add greetings and closing words in his own handwriting.[1] In I Corinthians 16:21, Galatians 6:11, Colossians 4:18, Philemon 19, and II Thessalonians 3:17 he calls attention to this practice, and in the last instance he adds, "This is the mark in every letter of mine; it is the way I write." This reference to his way of guaranteeing the genuineness of his letters is interesting. A gentleman of means would wear a ring bearing his personal seal. When the finished letter was rolled up and tied with a string secured by hot wax, he would press his ring into the wax, leaving an image that marked the letter as genuine. Paul would probably have no such seal, but in anticipation of our modern personal signatures he marked his letters with his handwriting.

Oral Style   That Paul's letters were dictated accounts for their oral style.[2] How much influence the amanuensis exercised on the vocabulary and style of the letters in their final form is impossible to know; but it is likely that at least some of the variations in style and vocabulary that have caused scholars at times to question the genuineness of some of his letters are due to the different persons who took them down. As his greeting shows, Tertius was a Christian. Probably most if not all of those who took Paul's dictation were from among his companions rather than professional amanuenses. Such persons would take his words in notes as best they could, reconstruct the letter from their notes, and show it to Paul for his approval and the addition of his final words.

Yet there is a peculiar literary quality that shows itself consistently in his letters which proves that their style depends on Paul. The violent changes of mood are his, as are the digressions and the favorite phrases. The influence on the whole of the amanuensis on Paul's letters was undoubtedly minor. Yet the dictation itself has affected the style of Paul. In the passion of controversy or the joy of reconciliation his thoughts

---

[1] Cf. Deissmann, *Light from the Ancient East,* p. 166, note 7.

[2] On Paul's style and the literary characteristics of his letters see Weiss, *Earliest Christianity,* II, 399–421; Deissmann, *Light from the Ancient East,* pp. 233–42 *passim,* Deissmann, *Paul,* pp. 8–26, 75–76; Nock, *St. Paul,* pp. 233–37.

raced ahead of his words. We can, for example, almost see Paul pause to reflect as he corrects himself in I Corinthians 1:14–16. Occasionally, a sentence begun in one form ends in another (the grammatical term for this is *anacoluthon*). While many such breaks in the sentence structure are obscured in translation, the interruption of thought caused by verse 7 in II Corinthians 5:6–8 which requires Paul to repeat the opening clause in order to recover the sentence furnishes a good example. (Cf. Galatians 2:3–5, 6.) His digressions, so troublesome to the modern commentators, are also the result of his dictation. A phrase captures his mind and beguiles it down byways of thought from which he regains with difficulty the main road. (Cf. I Corinthians 2:1–3:1; 5:6–9.)

His Use of Previous Material Not infrequently the reader of Paul comes upon a passage that sounds familiar because it echoes a similar passage in another letter. To take a few examples at random, the words in II Corinthians 4:14, "knowing that he who raised the Lord Jesus will raise us also with Jesus and bring us with you into his presence" repeat the same thought expressed in I Thessalonians 4:14, "For since we believe that Jesus died and rose again, even so, through Jesus, God will bring with him those who have fallen asleep." Or we may compare Paul's analogy of the relation of believers as "the body of Christ" in Galatians 3:28, I Corinthians 6:15; 12:27, Romans 12:5, and Ephesians 5:30. In two of these passages, I Corinthians 12:28–30 and Romans 12:6–8 (cf. Ephesians 4:11), the analogy is carried further to depict the function of the various officers in the church. (Cf. Galatians 3:26–29 with Colossians 3:11.) Because he had undoubtedly discussed these matters with his churches in person, such passages must have sounded familiar also to the original readers of Paul's letters. In Philippians 3:1 he half apologized for thus repeating himself so often.

Another group of passages are of such lyric quality that they can hardly have been dictated on the spur of the moment. The famous Hymn to Love in I Corinthians 13, the passage on the incarnation, Philippians 2:6–11, which some scholars believe may have been an early Christian hymn, the excursus on wisdom, I Corinthians 2:6–16, and such passages as Romans 8:35–39; 11:33–36, II Corinthians

4:16–18, and Colossians 1:15–20 stand out from their contexts in the clearest contrast.

These remarkable passages are not the result of prosaic letter writing. In some of them we are reading the characteristic teaching of Paul which in true rabbinic fashion would shape itself into easily memorized and retained aphorisms and parallelisms. In others we read the thoughts of Paul which were formed in lyric phrases as, on his journeys from place to place, he trudged along the Roman roads, or stood on the tossing deck of an ancient ship.

Semitic and Hellenistic Influences on his Style

Paul wrote as he spoke in *Koine*, the common Greek of the Hellenistic world. Yet his was not the faltering language of the ignorant.[3] His vigorous mind formed the popular language of the day into a powerful and flexible vehicle of thought. In the language of Paul Semitisms mingle with the Hellenistic love of antitheses. The Semitisms are not those of one whose mother tongue was Aramaic, but much as a modern sermon might under the influence of the Authorized Version echo Elizabethan English, they probably came second-hand from the influence of the Septuagint. This influence can be seen not only in his vocabulary but also in Paul's fondness for parallelism and balanced phrases. Probably the prominence in Paul's writing of antithetical statements balanced against one another owes as much to the Judaic Wisdom literature, with its motif of the two ways (good-evil, light-darkness, life-death), as it does to Hellenistic rhetoric.

The popular Greek diatribe[4] had its share in shaping the style of Paul's letters. Chapters three and four of Galatians, for instance, present an interesting combination of the diatribe form, using the rhetorical question, with rabbinic argument and allegorical exegesis. (Cf. Romans 2–4, I Corinthians 9–10.)

The Literary Genre of the Letters

Part of the difficulty in understanding Paul's letters arises from the fact that

---

[3] See "Paul's Languages" in chap. 5.
[4] See "Cynicism and Skepticism" in chap. 4.

they are not essays or formal epistles but genuine letters. The formal epistle was in Paul's day a popular literary form. Like the essay the formal epistle addressed itself to the general public and was therefore self-explanatory. The genuine letter, on the other hand, is addressed to a particular situation. It contains allusions and makes references which are fully intelligible to the intended readers but which are lost to others who attempt to understand them out of context. No small part of the problem of understanding Paul lies in the difficulty of recovering the context of his letters.

Yet these letters are not, strictly speaking, private letters. As their character clearly shows they were written to be read before the congregation to which they were addressed. The second person plural, the allusions to various persons, and the greetings and salutations make them group communications. At the close of I Thessalonians (5:27), which may be the first of his letters, Paul explicitly orders that it "be read to all the brethren." And at the close of Colossians (4:16) he requests that "when this letter has been read among you, have it read also in the church of the Laodiceans; and see that you read also the letter from Laodicea."

The hortatory passages which are so familiar and important a part of Paul's letters sound like, and perhaps are, excerpts from Paul's homilies. There is too much self-conscious literature in these letters to classify them with purely private correspondence. They are pastoral letters, which belong somewhere between an encyclical and a private letter. Paul created his own literary genre. The writers who follow him in the latter part of the New Testament carried the form over into the encyclical letter. But the distinction remains. The encyclical letter and the literary epistle are more formal and depend much less for their understanding upon a knowledge of the circumstances to which they are addressed.

In their opening and closing Paul's letters followed the typical letter form. The opening was in the usual three parts: 1) The sender. 2) The person or persons addressed. 3) Greetings. Usually it closed with some form of good wishes and a farewell.[5] With the address written

[5] The date of the letter was sometimes included at the close. How helpful it

on the outside of the folded letter it was ready to be carried to its destination.[6] It may help us to visualize Paul's writings as actual letters if we arrange the opening and closing of Romans according to our modern form of letters.

> Paul, a servant of Jesus Christ
> (called to be an apostle)

All God's beloved
(who are called to be saints)
Rome, Italy.
Grace to you and peace from God our Father and the Lord Jesus Christ:
First, I thank my God through Jesus Christ for all of you . . .

In the lower left hand corner of the last page, according to our practice, the initials T/P would appear indicating that the letter had been dictated by Paul to Tertius. Above these initials would be a postscript written in the characteristically large letters of Paul's own handwriting. On the right opposite the initials would be Paul's signature.

The Means of Delivery   Paul's letters usually, if not always, were carried by one of his helpers. From II Corinthians 7:6–8 we may assume that Titus was the bearer of the "severe letter" to which Paul was referring, and from verses 17 and 18 of the following chapter we may conclude that he was also to be the bearer of this letter. Epaphroditus carried the letter to the Philippians home with him (Philippians 2:25). Tychicus and Onesimus delivered the letter to the Colossians (Colossians 4:7–9), and may have delivered Philemon at the same time. If the sixteenth chapter of Romans is a separate letter to Ephesus, Phoebe must have carried it with her as she sailed from Cenchreae. Ships were constantly plying from port to port around the Aegean Sea. As the references to the movements of his helpers show, Paul took full advantage of the fact that travel in the Aegean area was rapid and easy. But the letters to the Galatians and to the Romans, because they would involve a

---

would be if the dates of Paul's letters had been included! See the ancient letters in Deissmann, *Light from the Ancient East,* pp. 166–73 *passim.*

[6] Cf. *Ibid.,* p. 151 and note 3.

much greater distance, may have been sent by the kindness of a trader or shipmaster.[7]

Classifying the Letters   Paul's letters have been classified in several ways. In the New Testament itself the arrangement is approximately according to length, Romans, the longest letter, being first. The exceptions are that Ephesians is slightly longer than Galatians and the Pastoral Epistles, two of which are longer than the preceding II Thessalonians, come just before Philemon, the last and shortest letter. With some exceptions the rule of length seems to have been the general guiding principle in the earliest collections.[8] For purposes of study, however, Paul's letters have frequently been arranged according to their supposed chronological order. The difficulty is that in several instances the order is uncertain. Some scholars, for instance, place Galatians as the earliest while others place it near the time of writing of the severe letter to Corinth and the letter to the Romans. The question of the origin of one or all of the prison letters in Ephesus also raises a problem for the chronological scheme.[9] Others have professed to see a development in the thought of Paul by which the chronological order can at least partially be determined. Attempts to demonstrate such a development, however, have not been very successful.

If the character and background of the recipients are important for understanding the letters, the places to which Paul sent them appear to provide a better basis than chronology for classifying them for study. Obviously, such an arrangement will bring together letters that were separated by some distance in time. The Thessalonian letters,

---

[7] If Galatians was written, as some scholars believe, from Antioch of Syria, the distance would not be great. Perhaps Timothy carried it to the Galatian churches. On the delivery of letters see the interesting instructions for delivery on the letters shown in Deissmann, *Light from the Ancient East,* pp. 151, 169, 171, 180, 195, *passim.*

[8] For a good discussion of the order of Paul's letters in ancient collections see Knox, *Philemon among the Letters of Paul,* Ch. IV, 71–90. Cf. James Moffatt, *An Introduction to the Literature of the New Testament* (New York: Charles Scribner's Sons, 1911), pp. 16–17.

[9] On the order of the prison letters, assuming that they were from Ephesus, see Duncan, *St. Paul's Ephesian Ministry,* pp. 144–61.

for example, are often supposed to be the earliest of Paul's extant letters, while Philippians, if it were written in Rome, may have been his last. Both, however, were written to Macedonians and are in several ways more similar than are Philippians and Colossians, or II Corinthians and Romans, which from the standpoint of time were probably much closer together. In the following survey of the letters we shall arrange them according to the geographical area to which they were addressed.

To Galatia

The letter to the Galatian churches shares with Romans, to which it is in some ways quite similar, the distinction of being the most influential of Paul's letters. Its message of salvation by faith is the cornerstone of Christian theology. Yet Paul wrote it in the heat of a controversy over issues that disappeared long ago from the Christian scene.

When and where Galatians Was Written Antioch, Corinth, and Ephesus have each been chosen as possible places of origin for this letter. Part of the problem lies in the interpretation of Paul's statement, "you know it was because of a bodily ailment that I preached the gospel to you at first" (Galatians 4:13). The words translated "at first" (Greek: *to proteron*) regularly imply the former of two times, which would indicate that Paul must have visited the Galatian churches twice before he wrote the letter. Since the return from Derbe through Lystra, Iconium, and Antioch on his first trip in the Galatian Province would not likely be counted as a second visit, the letter would have to be written sometime after going through Galatia on his tour through Macedonia and Achaia. On this theory Corinth seems the most probable place of origin.

If the letter were addressed to churches in North Galatia, this interpretation of "at first," because Paul probably would not have been in North Galatia before his journey to Macedonia, would require the letter to be written after the trip to Jerusalem and Antioch of Syria recorded in Acts 18:22–19:1 and would probably have been written in Ephesus.[10] If we assume, with Professor Knox, that the Jerusalem Council occurred on this trip, even if it was addressed to South Galatia, Galatians must have been written during Paul's stay in Ephesus.

But the words translated "at first" do not always mean the former of two times. The same phrase is translated "before" in John 6:62 and cannot mean the first of two previous occasions. For this reason some scholars place the writing of Galatians in Antioch of Syria after the Jerusalem Council (Acts 15:2–29) and before Paul set out on the journey which brought him to Macedonia. The argument for such an early date is reinforced by a strict interpretation of Paul's words: "I am astonished that you are so quickly deserting him who called you" (Galatians 1:6). This would make Galatians the earliest of Paul's extant letters.[11] The words translated "so quickly," however, do not require such a literal construction. Professor Ramsay believes that Galatians was written in Antioch of Syria but not until Paul's visit there, recorded in Acts 18:22, on his way to Ephesus.[12] The arguments are indecisive; but when all is considered Paul's eighteen-months stay in Corinth seems the most likely time and place for the writing of Galatians.

The Problem in Galatia   On the basis of the reference to "certain men" who "came from James" to Antioch and raised an issue over the Jewish Christians eating with gentiles (Galatians 2:4, 12; cf. Acts 15:1) and the reference to "those who unsettle you" (Galatians 5:12; cf. 3:1; 4:17; 5:10; 6:12–13), it is usually supposed that certain emissaries were sent from the church in Jerusalem to Galatia to extend the authority of that church over Paul's churches. These Judaizers, as they are called, were attempting to require Paul's gentile Christians to conform to the Jewish Law in order to complete their salvation. We can

[10] But see "The Return to Cilicia" in chap. 6 and "The North vs. the South Galatian Hypotheses" in chap. 7 for the possibility that he had evangelized Galatia during the "silent years."

[11] Cf. Lake, *The Earlier Epistles of St. Paul*, pp. 301–02. Also pp. 265–66.

[12] *St. Paul the Traveller*, pp. 189–92.

recognize here again the influence of the Tübingen theory of a basic antagonism between Paul and the Jerusalem apostles.

Several scholars have found reason to question this interpretation of the problem.[13] That there was considerable communication between Jerusalem and Antioch of Syria is not surprising and is evident from Acts. But there is no evidence that any emissaries from Jerusalem followed Paul into his mission fields. If such a delegation had arrived in Galatia, Paul would surely have known who they were, but the words, "whoever he is," in Galatians 5:10 imply that he did not. The presence of local Jews in Paul's churches would be sufficient to cause the reaction toward legalism which is evident in the Galatian churches.

There is a hint in the phrase "every man who receives circumcision" (Galatians 5:3) that the enthusiasts for the Law in Galatia were not Jews at all but gentiles who, through the influence of the Septuagint which was now their Bible and perhaps the local synagague, thought Paul had not gone far enough and began adding to his teaching. That converted pagans of Asia Minor would do such a thing is altogether likely. With their background in the orgiastic rites of Cybele, they would view circumcision in much the same light as the emasculation practiced by their former priests.[14] This may be what is back of Paul's strange "wish that those who unsettle you would mutilate themselves" (Galatians 5:12). Apparently some of the advocates of circumcision cared to go no farther toward legalism (6:13; cf. 5:3). In keeping with the prevailing syncretism of the time, they would feel free to develop their religion according to their own inclinations beyond what they had learned from Paul.

In Galatians 1–2, Paul may not be defending himself, as is usually supposed, against actual interference from Jerusalem. Since the Christian movement had not yet separated itself from Judaism, the Galatians may not have distinguished clearly between the Jerusalem Church and the traditional image of the Holy City as the capital of Judaism. They would therefore suppose that in moving toward Jewish legalism

[13] See Ropes, *The Singular Problem of the Epistle to the Galatians;* Enslin, *Christian Beginnings,* pp. 219–24; Munck, *Paul and the Salvation of Mankind,* chap. IV, 87–134.
[14] "The Myth of the Great Mother" in chap. 4.

they were moving into closer harmony with the Jerusalem Church. Paul had watered down the gospel for their benefit and in doing so had gone beyond his authority as a representative from Jerusalem (cf. 4:16).[15]

That the situation in Galatia was complicated by more than one deviation from Paul's gospel is evident from the reference to their biting and devouring one another (Galatians 5:15). Beside the enthusiasts for Jewish legalism there were some who were returning to pagan practices (4:8–11).[16] A third group to whom Paul refers as "You who are spiritual" (6:1; cf. "You who desire to be under the Law" 4:21) were moving toward libertinism (5:13–6:10). They understood Paul's doctrine of freedom to mean that, since they were now in possession of the Spirit, they possessed the secret of immortality and were under no moral restraints. In a thoroughly selfish fashion, proud of their superiority over their brethren, they were using their "freedom as an opportunity for the flesh" (5:13). When the disturbing news of these developments in the Galatian Churches reached Paul it is small wonder that Paul confessed "I could wish to be present with you now and to change my tone, for I am perplexed about you" (4:20).

The Argument of the Letter   Among the letters of Paul, Galatians is unique in the abruptness with which Paul plunges into the main issue. There are no felicitations, no prayers of thanks, no compliments, only the formal grace and peace. Indeed the first point of his argument intrudes itself into the formal opening: "Paul an apostle—not from men nor through man, but through Jesus Christ and God the Father, who raised him from the dead." For the first two chapters Paul bolsters this claim that his authority and his gospel came not from men but through Christ from God.

The argument of Galatians advances in three movements. The first two chapters argue the validity of Paul's gospel which is based on the fact that he did not "receive it from man, nor was I taught it, but it

[15] Munck, *Paul and the Salvation of Mankind*, p. 100.
[16] It is possible to interpret this passage to mean that their interest in circumcision and such other matters of Jewish practice as festal observances was so colored by their pagan background as to amount to a form of paganism. It refers, at any rate, to a syncretism in which paganism was involved.

246246246246246

came through a revelation of Jesus Christ" (1:12). The innovations
from Judaism which the Galatians were introducing amounted to another gospel. Probably we should see in the reference to "an angel
from heaven" (1:8) the influence of the widespread interest in angels
in Asia Minor which found a point of contact with Jewish angelology.
Some over-enthusiastic members of the Galatian churches, already
enamoured of Judaism, were claiming angelic authority for modifying
Paul's teaching in the direction of legalism.

When taken with the puzzling statement in 5:11, the words in 1:8,
"But even if we . . . should preach to you a gospel contrary to that
which we preached to you," imply that some of the Galatians were
claiming the authority of Paul for their new gospel. Perhaps they
were representing it as an esoteric teaching suited only for those who
were ready for it.

We must keep in mind that we do not know the communication that
came to Paul which is in the background of this letter. We can only
guess the problems to which Paul alludes here. The "spirituals" to
whom Paul speaks in 6:1ff. who felt themselves above the moral restraints in the Law would be likely to represent their position as an
esoteric teaching. The deviations from Paul's gospel to which he is
speaking in the opening paragraphs, at any rate, were probably made
in more than one direction.

In three ways Paul defends his gospel. First, he is an Apostle of
Christ and is therefore a primary authority in interpreting the gospel.[17]
To prove that he did receive his apostleship from Christ he recalled to
the Galatians the story of his experience on the Damascus Road
(1:11–24). Like Jeremiah and Isaiah in ancient times God had chosen
him from birth, and in due time had, by revealing Christ to him,
called him to preach to the gentiles. Not for three years did he visit
Jerusalem; therefore his call to apostleship could not have come from
the Apostles there.

In the second place, Paul argued, the Jerusalem Apostles—Peter,
James, and John—had approved his gospel (2:1–10). Not that the
validity of his gospel depended upon their approval, but since they
"added nothing" to him and proffered "the right hand of fellowship"

<hr />

[17] See "The Conversion According to Paul" in chap. 6.

they could not now be quoted against Paul. With their acceptance of Paul's mission, furthermore, the unity of the Church was preserved, and he was not running in vain.

There still remained, however, the problem of the relation between the Jewish and gentile Christians in such ticklish matters as eating together (2:11–21). We must remember that in becoming "believers" the Jews did not regard themselves in any way outside the Jewish Commonwealth. Since the gentiles by not being circumcised were still outside of Judaism, how did the traditional and legal strictures against such matters as eating with gentiles apply to the relations of the Jewish Christians to their gentile brethren? Whether this specific problem had arisen in Galatia is not clear, but the problem permits Paul to introduce his speech to Peter in 2:14–21, which is the real purpose in relating the episode at Antioch.

Whether Peter's withdrawal from table fellowship with the gentiles occurred before or after the meeting at Jerusalem is unimportant because the issue here is different.[18] We may forgive Peter if all the logical consequences of Paul's gospel to the gentiles were not immediately apparent to him. Accepting the gentiles into the Church without bringing them through the gateway of Judaism was to raise issues over which Christianity was to battle for a long while. That the Apostles agreed with Paul in principle does not mean that they were always either theoretically or emotionally prepared to accept the logical consequences of that agreement. But we are not to suppose that they were the source of the trouble among Paul's churches in Galatia or elsewhere. The same difficulties which beset Peter and Barnabas in Antioch would be felt between the Jewish and gentile members of Paul's churches anywhere.

The purpose for which Paul related his argument with Peter and Barnabas was therefore to introduce the speech, which in turn provided a transition to the second main part of the argument of the letter. Paul's speech to Peter, in fact, contains the thesis of the second movement of the letter: Faith in Jesus Christ is not something added to the Law; it replaces the Law. Because faith has now replaced the Law, to cling to certain aspects of the Law is to nullify the grace of

18 Cf. Lake, *The Earlier Epistles of St. Paul,* pp. 293–97.

God that comes through faith. In the second movement of the letter (3:1–5:10) Paul supports this thesis by an argument involving three premises: The gift of the Spirit; the promise to Abraham; and the curse of the Law.

In the first instance Paul appeals directly to the experience of the Galatians. The gift of the Spirit had come to them through faith and not because they had kept the Law. Why then should they want to return to the Law? Paul follows this appeal to personal experience with an argument to show that the Law was never intended to be the true basis of man's relation to God. Abraham, the father of the Jewish race, had received righteousness by faith four hundred and thirty years before the Law was given; therefore, "it is men of faith who are the sons of Abraham" (3:7). That the gentiles are included is clear from the promise God made to Abraham that "in thee shall all the nations be blest" (3:8). That this promise is realized through Christ Paul shows by an argument based on the singular number of the word "offspring" (Greek: *spermati*). Christ is the offspring of Abraham through whom God's blessing comes to the gentiles.

In the meantime the Law could do nothing but condemn man; but Christ has removed the curse of the Law. Paul fortifies this statement by a combination of Scriptural quotations: "Cursed be every one who does not abide by all things written in the book of the law, and do them" (Deuteronomy 27:26). Man has not kept the Law; therefore he is under a curse. That the Law was not intended to produce righteousness follows from the statement that "He who through faith is righteous shall live" (Habakkuk 2:4), and this faith has no relation to the Law for "He who does them shall live by them" (Leviticus 18:5). But how does Christ bring the blessing of Abraham? By taking the curse upon himself: "Cursed be everyone who hangs on a tree" (Deuteronomy 21:23).

In answer to the obvious question as to why, if it could not be a way to righteousness, the Law was given at all, Paul replies that it was an interim provision until Christ should come. It was like the slave guardian who must watch over the heir until he comes of age. Now that Christ has come the believer is of age and free from the guardian. To turn back to circumcision and the observations of the Law is to return to guardianship of the slave. For the gentile Galatians to assume the burden of the Law would be akin to returning to the slavery of their former pagan worship of the "elemental spirits"[19] because the Law had been mediated by angels and therefore belongs to the old order of the present evil age. (Cf. Romans 2:12–16.)

After a personal appeal to their former loyalty to him, Paul brings his argument to a climax with an allegory based on Abraham's two sons (Genesis 16:15; 21:2, 9). It was not the son of Hagar, the slave, who became Abraham's heir, but the son of the freewoman. Through Christ the children of Abraham by faith are heirs of the promise to Abraham and are free. Those who insist on remaining under the Law, like Hagar's son Ishmael, cannot be heirs of Abraham but will be cast out. In 5:1–10 Paul concludes his argument. The Galatians are free; let them remain so by relying on "faith working through love" rather than on circumcision which would place them under obligation to the whole Law. "I have confidence in the Lord that you will take no other view than mine" (5:10) brings this movement of the letter to a close.

Paul turns briefly but pointedly to one further problem before ending his message. In the third and final movement of the letter Paul addresses a group that seems to have carried the idea of freedom from the Law to the extremes of haughty selfishness and libertinism (5:11–6:10). Christian freedom requires the believer to walk by the Spirit which is contrary to the desires of the flesh. They are "through love" to "be servants of one another." For the whole law is fulfilled in one word, "You shall love your neighbor as yourself" (5:13–14). Paul then gives a list of the works of the flesh and contrasts it with the fruits of the Spirit (5:19–23).

The Galatians are to walk by the Spirit, helping one another, and not grow weary in well-doing. In the conclusion which Paul added in his own handwriting, he turns once more to the issue of circumcision and concludes with the words, "For neither is circumcision anything, nor uncircumcision, but a new creation" (6:15). Although the arguments are to us strange, the issue of circumcision which occasioned it

---

[19] On the meaning of this phrase and its connection with angels, see Burton, *The Epistle to the Galatians, International Critical Commentary,* pp. 510–18.

forgotten, and some of the circumstances to which he alludes unknown to us, the letter to the Galatians is one of the most important of Paul's letters. Paul's doctrines of freedom in the Spirit, the morality of love rather than law, and salvation by faith set forth here remain at the center of the Christian Faith.

To Macedonia

There are three letters from Paul to churches in Macedonia, two to Thessalonica and one to Philippi. Although separated by some time in writing, these letters display a similarity of background that justifies their being treated together. That there are no major problems such as those in Galatia and Corinth to occasion the writing of these letters is a tribute to the constancy and stability of the Macedonian Christians. It may be significant that Philippians and I Thessalonians are the only two letters in which Paul exhorts his readers to continue what they are doing "more and more" (Philippians 1:9; I Thessalonians 4:1, 10).[20]

The Letters to Thessalonica   Unless Galatians was written from Antioch after Paul's first tour into the Galatian province, the Thessalonian letters are the oldest letters we have from Paul. They were written not long after Paul came from Macedonia into Achaia for the first time. According to Acts 18:5 Timothy came from Macedonia to rejoin Paul in Corinth, which was the occasion for writing I Thessalonians (I Thessalonians 3:6).

The relationship of the two letters to one another constitutes a problem which has caused some scholars to believe that II Thessalonians was written in imitation of I Thessalonians by a later hand.[21]

[20] The words which this phrase translates occur in other letters but not with this implication.

[21] Probably the best more recent statement of the case against the authenticity of II Thessalonians is Enslin, *Christian Beginnings,* pp. 241–44. The weight of scholarly opinion, however, is in favor of its genuineness. See Lake, *The Earlier Epistle of St. Paul,* pp. 77–101. Professor Lake gives a good account of the theory which Professor Harnack first presented in a paper to the Berlin Academy that the two Thessalonian letters were addressed to two different groups in Thessalonica, one gentile and the other Jewish. Cf. James Everett Frame, *The Epistles of St. Paul to the Thessalonians, International*

The problem consists principally in reconciling the two different views of eschatology in the two letters, and in explaining the remarkable similarity, which amounts in places to a paraphrase. At the same time the second letter lacks the warmth and personal touch of the first. In addition the reference to "a letter purporting to be from us" (II Thessalonians 2:2) and the words, "This is the mark in every letter of mine" (3:17) have seemed to some to be an attempt to authenticate a letter written by someone else in the name of Paul.

The first of these problems, concerning the return of Christ at the end of the present age, can easily be exaggerated. In I Thessalonians 4:13–5:11 "The day of the Lord" is pictured as coming "like a thief in the night," but in II Thessalonians 2:1–12 there must first be a rebellion and "the man of lawlessness" must be revealed.[22] In the first place, Paul is writing in the two passages to two different problems and presents those aspects of his teaching which apply to each. The two pictures of the end of time, in the second place, are not contradictory. The suddenness and unexpectedness of the end are not uncommonly found in apocalyptic writings in conjunction with details of the preceding events. (Cf. Mark 13:4–37.)[23]

As to the literary similarity, it should be noted that II Thessalonians parallels I Thessalonians less than has sometimes been implied.[24] The language and character of II Thessalonians are so characteristic of Paul that the similarities it bears to the first letter are better explained as due to the fact that they were written about the same time.

The similarities between the two letters may be explained by supposing that Paul read again his copy of the first letter to see what they had misunderstood in it when news reached him of the distress of the Thessalonian Christians (2:2). He may therefore be alluding to the first letter in the enigmatic phrase, "or by letter purporting to be from

---

Critical Commentary, pp. 39–54; Moffatt, *An Introduction to the Literature of the New Testament,* pp. 76–82.

[22] Cf. Klausner, *From Jesus to Paul,* pp. 238–39.

[23] Attempts to identify the "man of lawlessness" with the myth of *Nero redivivus* or Caligula (Cf. II Thess. 2:4 with Josephus, *Ant.,* XVIII, 8), the former of which would require the letter to be dated not earlier than 70 A.D. and therefore after the death of Paul, have been almost universally abandoned in recent years. Cf. Lake, *The Earlier Epistles of St. Paul,* pp. 78–79.

[24] For an analysis of the literary relationships see Frame, *Thessalonians,* pp. 45–51.

us" (2:2). The whole clause is difficult and perhaps should be translated: "nor be alarmed either by spirit or word or letter as though we had said that the day of the Lord is now present."[25] The suggestion of a possible forged letter is not as definite in the Greek as it is in the usual translation; spirit, word, and letter are correlatives and are equally possible sources for the misunderstanding of Paul.

That the second letter lacks the personal warmth—to the extent that it actually does—is probaby because it is shorter and, following so closely the first letter, was hurriedly written. Professor Weiss has attempted to revive the theory of Hugo Grotius that II Thessalonians was written before I Thessalonians and was delivered by Timothy on his visit to Thessalonica referred to in I Thessalonians 3:1-6.[26] Since the present arrangement of the two books in our canon is based on their relative length, such a theory is possible. That the persecution referred to in the past tense in I Thessalonians 2:14 is in the present tense in II Thessalonians 1:5 is probably the strongest argument for this theory. It does not, however, solve all the problems claimed for it and the reference to a previous letter in II Thessalonians 2:15 is virtually fatal to the theory.

Two reasons for the writing of I Thessalonians are apparent. The first is Paul's natural concern and anxiety for the newly founded church. As the result of a riot Paul had been forced to leave Thessalonica under circumstances that forbade his return for some time.[27] The opposition he had experienced was now directed against the church. Paul was writing to express his affection and concern and to encourage these new converts to continue faithful under persecution. Secondly, several problems had arisen in the church which called for further instruction and admonition.

Paul begins the letter with a profound thanksgiving for the faithfulness of the Thessalonians which has become a valuable example and testimony to the faith in Macedonia and Achaia (1:2-10). He recalls his own difficulties in Thessalonica and their loyalty to him and

[25] Cf. Lake, *The Earlier Epistles of St. Paul,* pp. 93-96; Frame, *Thessalonians,* pp. 246-48.
[26] Weiss, *Earliest Christianity,* I, 289-91. Cf. Moffatt, *An Introduction to the Literature of the New Testament,* p. 75.
[27] "Thessalonica and Beroea" in chap. 7.

compares their persecutions with those of the churches in Judea
(2:1–16). They have been warned that persecutions would come; they
are to follow his example and remain faithful. Paul has been anxious
to see them but as yet this is impossible, so he is writing this letter
(2:17–3:13).

Three problems, however, need correcting: 1) They are to continue
making moral progress: "as you learned from us how you ought to
live and to please God, just as you are doing, you do so more and
more" (4:1). 2) They are to avoid sexual immorality. Taking care
not to wrong their brothers, they must love one another (4:2–10).
3) In quietness and harmony they are to continue to work in their
vocations and avoid capitalizing on the charity of others.

Apparently some of the members of the church had died since Paul
had left and the Thessalonians were disturbed for them (4:13–18).
What would be the status of the deceased at the coming of Christ?
Paul assures them that "the dead in Christ will rise first" (4:16) and
they will be reunited. While he is on the subject of the coming of
Christ, Paul reminds them again that it will be "like a thief in the
night" (5:2); therefore, they are to be prepared for it; they are to
remain sober as "sons of the day" and "put on the breastplate of faith
and love, and for a helmet the hope of salvation" (5:8). With a brief
résumé of his exhortations, his benediction and request that the "letter
be read to all the brethren," Paul brings the letter to a close.

In his second letter Paul deals especially with two problems which
persisted among the Thessalonian Christians. Whether from a mis-
interpretation of his first letter or from some other source, the Thessalonians had acquired the notion that the day of the Lord had already
arrived. Apparently they thought that they had been left out; at any
rate, they were distraught. Also the problem of the idle had grown
more serious. Probably because they believed the end of the present
age so near, some had abandoned their jobs and were living at the
expense of the rest of the church.

After again expressing his thanks for the steadfastness of the Thessalonian Christians, and after reassuring them that their present sufferings will be vindicated "when the Lord Jesus is revealed from heaven"
(1:3–12), Paul comes quickly to the problem of the day of the Lord

(2:1–12): "let no one deceive you in any way; for that day will not come, unless the rebellion comes first, and the man of lawlessness is revealed" (2:3). Something "is restraining him now so that he may be revealed in his time" (2:6, 7). What or who it is that restrains the man of lawlessness may have been clear to the Thessalonians but is far from clear to us. Professor Munck has recently proposed the rather surprising theory that Paul himself was the one who was restraining these events of the end time; until his gentile mission was accomplished the end could not come.[28] The point of the passage is, however, that the day of the Lord cannot have come because the preceding events have not yet taken place. The Thessalonians have been chosen to be saved; they are therefore to "stand firm and hold to the traditions" which Paul had taught them (2:13–15).

The second problem, that of idleness, Paul had briefly mentioned in his first letter, but now it had become even more serious (3:6–15). The Thessalonians are to withdraw fellowship from those who persist in idleness. By earning his own bread Paul had set an example which they are to imitate. "If any one will not work, let him not eat" (3:10). A greeting and benediction added in Paul's own hand concludes the letter. Except for the teaching on eschatology these letters add little to our knowledge of Paul's thought, but the picture in these letters of the remarkable character and loyalty, as well as some of the problems of a congregation newly come from paganism, is an invaluable addition to our knowledge of the Early Church.

The Letter to Philippi   We have already observed the possibility that this letter was written from Ephesus rather than Rome, as the traditional view maintains.[29] It may, therefore, be earlier than the Corinthian letters.[30] Because of the obvious sudden break between 3:1 and 2, the question arises whether we have one letter or parts of more than one. The words in 3:1, "To write the same things to you is not irksome to me,"

[28] *St. Paul and the Salvation of Mankind,* pp. 36–42. Professor Munck is here following an interpretation revived by Oscar Cullmann which actually goes back to patristic writings.
[29] "Paul's Ephesian Imprisonment?" in chap. 7.
[30] See Duncan, *St. Paul's Ephesian Ministry,* pp. 290, 298–99.

seem to refer to a previous letter that Paul had written the Philippians. Also, attention is often called to the fact that Polycarp in his letter to the Philippians (3:2) refers to the *letters* that Paul had written them. Possibly two or more of Paul's letters have been put together to form our present letter. Several theories have sought to answer this problem. Because of the virulent attack on Paul's opponents which opens this section, some have found it difficult to believe that it could apply to Philippi and suppose that 3:2–4:1 is a fragment of a letter addressed to some other church.[31] More popular among recent scholars is the idea that 3:2–4:23 is an earlier letter gratefully acknowledging the arrival of Epaphroditus and that 1:1–3:1 is a letter which Paul sent with Epaphroditus as he later returned to Philippi.[32] A few scholars have suggested that the letter is composed of fragments of several letters.

While the division of Philippians into two or more letters solves some difficulties, there is not much substantial evidence to justify it. Polycarp may, for example, have been referring to the collected letters of Paul, and the reference to writing "the same things" in Philippians 3:1 may be explained in several ways. Certainly such an allusion is too frail evidence by itself to support the theory. If we were to cut apart Paul's letters wherever a sudden digression or change of thought appears, the resulting confusion of fragments would destroy all hope of reconstructing the order and circumstances of Paul's correspondence. If there were clear evidence of an earlier letter whose description fitted the contents of this section, we could feel justified in accepting the hypothesis of two letters as established.[33] Paul's expression of gratitude in 4:14–19 fits well with the reference to Epaphroditus in 2:25–30 and the allusion to those who "preach Christ from envy and rivalry" and "proclaim Christ out of partisanship, not sincerely but thinking to afflict me in my imprisonment" (1:15, 17) anticipates the sudden outburst in 3:2, "Look out for the dogs." We may feel justified therefore in treating Philippians as one letter.

[31] McNeile, *An Introduction to the Study of The New Testament,* pp. 90–92, but see Enslin, *Christian Beginnings,* pp. 281–82.
[32] See Goodspeed, *An Introduction to the New Testament,* pp. 90–92.
[33] Cf. Moffatt. *An Introduction to the Literature of the New Testament,* pp. 172–76.

The circumstances of Philippians are easy to recover from the letter itself. Upon learning of Paul's imprisonment the Philippians sent Epaphroditus with aid for him. Epaphroditus, who had remained to assist Paul, became seriously ill. News of his illness reached the Philippians, and Epaphroditus, hearing of their anxiety for his health, was distressed. Consequently, when Epaphroditus had recovered sufficiently to travel, Paul sent him home bearing the letter to thank the Philippians for their generous help and to explain why Paul had asked him to return to Philippi. In the letter Paul also indicated his intention to send Timothy to Philippi shortly and expressed the hope that he himself would be able to visit them soon. Counting the news of Paul's imprisonment, Epaphroditus' illness, and the Philippian Church's anxiety, no fewer than five trips between Paul's prison and Philippi had been made and two more, by Timothy and Paul, were anticipated.

The letter opens with one of the warmest expressions of thanksgiving and appreciation found anywhere in Paul's writings (1:3–11). There follows a brief reference to his imprisonment and his hope, for their sakes, that he will be released (1:12–26). In the exhortations that follow we may see the reflection of Paul's customary homilies delivered in the worship of his churches (1:27–2:18). He exhorts the Philippians to "stand firm in one spirit" (1:27) in the face of opposition and suffering. They are to follow the example of the humility of Christ who "being found in human form . . . humbled himself and became obedient unto death, even death on a cross" (2:8). They should "do all things without grumbling or questioning" (2:14) but rather with rejoicing.

Paul turns next to the immediate purpose of the letter (2:19–30). He hopes to send Timothy to visit the Philippians soon and possibly he can soon come also. This part of the letter closes with an explanation of the circumstances of Epaphroditus' return to Philippi.

The word "finally" in 3:1 begins what was probably intended to be the conclusion of the letter (unless, as some think, verse 1 is a fragment accidentally copied in here), but the letter moves on to what for us is its most valuable part. The vehement warning against "those who mutilate the flesh" (3:2) leads Paul to write the most revealing of his autobiographical passages (3:3–14). It is worth noting that each of the three important autobiographical passages in Paul's letters (Galatians 1:13–2:21; II Corinthians 11:22–12:10) occurs in connection with Paul's struggle with his opponents and begins with Paul's background as a loyal Jew. He is a "Hebrew born of Hebrews." In this passage, however, Paul goes farther into his own religious experience: all of his achievements under the Law and his advantages in Judaism he counted as loss for the sake of the righteousness "which is through faith in Christ" (3:9) in order "that I may know him and the power of his resurrection, and may share his sufferings, becoming like him in his death, that if possible I may attain the resurrection from the dead" (3:10–11). Paul has not reached his goal, but he is pursuing it "for the prize of the upward call of God in Christ Jesus" (3:14). In solemn tones he exhorts the Philippians to imitate him in this pursuit.

After a plea, in passing, for harmony between two women, Euodia and Syntyche, and a playful pun on the name of Synzygus (meaning yokefellow) whom he asks to help the women (to a reconciliation?), Paul returns once more to the refrain so prominent in this letter: "Rejoice in the Lord always; again I will say, Rejoice" (4:4). Another "finally" introduces one of the most appealing passages in Paul's writings:

> Finally, brethren, whatever is true, whatever is honorable, whatever is just, whatever is pure, whatever is lovely, whatever is gracious, if there is any excellence, if there is anything worthy of praise, think about these things (Philippians 4:8).

The stormy outburst, the frank revelation of his own spiritual experience and aspirations, and the homily are over; Paul returns to the primary purpose of his letter. In a brief but moving passage Paul expresses his gratitude for the generosity of the Philippians. His gratitude comes not from selfish concern for his own needs, for he has "learned the secret of facing plenty and hunger, abundance and want" (4:12). "But I seek the fruit which increases to your credit" (4:17). With the greetings and benediction this, the richest and most revealing of Paul's letters, comes to an end.

To Corinth

Although there was a church at Cenchreae (cf. Romans 16:1), the letters to Achaia which we have were addressed to the church in Corinth. The Corinthian correspondence is not only the most extensive in the collection of Paul's letters, but also in several ways the most important. With Romans and Galatians it comprises the source of most of our knowledge of Paul's thought. Yet unlike Romans and Galatians, the Corinthian letters afford us the best picture we have of a first century Christian church. That two of the most familiar and treasured chapters in the New Testament, The Hymn to Love, chapter 13, and on the resurrection, chapter 15, come from I Corinthians further indicates the importance of this correspondence.

How Many Letters? That Paul wrote to the Corinthians more than the two letters as they now stand in our New Testament is evident from his references to previous letters.[34] In I Corinthians 5:9-11 Paul mentions a letter dealing with the problem of associating with immoral men which he had previously written to Corinth. And in II Corinthians 2:3-4 and 7:8 he refers to a "severe letter," the description of which does not suit I Corinthians or the letter mentioned in I Corinthians 5:9-11. Are these letters entirely lost? Perhaps not. There is some evidence that parts of them may be embedded in the two letters that we have.

Between II Corinthians 6:13 and 14 there is a sudden and inexplicable break. A similar break occurs between 7:1 and 2. The intervening section warning against being "mismated with unbelievers" has nothing to do with what precedes or follows. When the section 6:14-7:1 is removed, however, the continuity of thought is restored. Paul is here expressing his deep feeling for the Corinthians and seeking to restore their former close relationship: "In return—I speak as to children—widen your hearts also" (6:13). "Open your hearts to us; we have wronged no one, we have corrupted no one, we have taken advantage of no one" (7:2). Clearly the section from 6:14 to 7:1 does not belong here. When we observe that the intruding section

[34] On Corinth and the circumstances of the letters see "The Province of Achaia" and "Letters from Ephesus" in chap. 7.

is concerned with a matter strikingly similar to that of the letter described in I Corinthians 5:9–11, it seems likely that this section is a fragment of the earlier letter.

In I Corinthians 5:9–11 Paul is seeking to correct a slight misunderstanding of the former letter and to reapply his exhortation to the situation with which he is now dealing. What appears to have happened is that a fragment of the first letter somehow became embedded here in II Corinthians. Professor Plummer has offered the objection to this theory that such a displacement in the middle of the letter and between sentences is difficult to explain.[35] If the manuscript had been torn apart, it is a surprising coincidence that it happened to part between sentences.

Whether the section in question comes between sentences or the phrases: "widen your hearts also" (6:13) and "Open your hearts to us" (7:2) are really, like 6:11, to be regarded as one sentence, the interruption is in the middle of a single thought and is more easily explained as an accident to the manuscript than a deliberate interruption of thought by Paul. If the scroll from which this letter was published was torn, it would probably part between pages. The clauses in question are short and in a manuscript there would be a natural tendency to end a clause on the page rather than carry a word over on the next page.

The opening and closing of the inserted letter may be missing because it was the copy preserved by the amanuensis which usually abbreviated the opening of the letter.[36] That no manuscript evidence exists for this insertion can be explained by supposing that the original collector of Paul's letters found the scroll containing II Corinthians badly damaged through long use and parted between what is now 6:13 and 7:2, and also found a worn copy of 6:14–7:1 lying beside it. Assuming it to be a part of the same scroll, he placed them together as they are today. He would not be so concerned with preserving the distinction among the several letters as he would in preserving the words of St. Paul.

[35] Alfred Plummer, *The Second Epistle of St. Paul to the Corinthians, International Critical Commentary* (New York: Charles Scribner's Sons, 1915), p. xxv.

[36] See Deissmann, *Light from the Ancient East,* pp. 235–36.

Another and more striking break in continuity occurs between II Corinthians 9:15 and 10:1. Except for the customary greetings and benediction 9:15 appears to be the close of the letter. The whole tone of the letter thus far has been conciliatory. There had been serious trouble in Corinth and Paul's leadership had been challenged; but the storm is over and Paul is seeking to renew the ties between him and the Corinthian Church. In chapters 8 and 9, furthermore, he is giving instructions regarding the collection for Jerusalem. What follows, then, in chapter 10 seems incredible. Suddenly Paul lashes out against his opposition as though the trouble was at its height.

That chapter 10 was written from Ephesus is strongly implied in the words, "So that we may preach the gospel in lands beyond you" (verse 16). Assuming that the "lands" refer to Italy and Spain (cf. Romans 1:15 and 15:28), in Macedonia they could hardly be spoken of as beyond Corinth. But it is clear from II Corinthians 7:5, 8:1, and 9:2 that that part of the letter was written from Macedonia. Since chapters 11–13 continue the severe invective of chapter 10, we are justified in assuming that chapters 10–13 are a separate letter from chapters 1–9. All that is lacking is the formal opening. This letter, like the fragment in 6:14–7:1, may have been published from the amanuensis' copy in which the opening lines were likely missing. If this assumption is valid, we have in these chapters the missing severe letter mentioned in II Corinthians 2:3–4 and 7:8. One objection which is sometimes raised to this theory is that there is in chapters 10–13 no mention of the offending person for whom in II Corinthians 2:5–11 Paul asks forgiveness. Apparently this person was at the bottom of the trouble in Corinth; therefore, it would be strange that Paul did not mention him in the preceding severe letter. How much of the beginning of what is now chapter 10 has been lost we do not know. Perhaps the offending person was mentioned in the lost sections. There may have been reasons connected with Paul's "painful visit"[37] why he chose not to make direct reference to the trouble maker. The difficulty is outweighed by the evidence in favor of the theory.

Another apparent difficulty has been seen in II Corinthians 12:18 where Titus apparently has fulfilled the mission which is still in the

---

[37] See "Letter from Ephesus" in chap. 7.

future in 8:16–18. If these passages refer to the same mission, chapters 10–13 are indeed a separate letter; but rather than the severe letter, it was one that was sent after II Corinthians 1–9.[38] That II Corinthians 12:18 refers to Titus' collection, however, is by no means certain. The evidence that chapters 10–13 comprise a separate letter that preceded the earlier part of II Corinthians outweighs this difficulty.

The following parallels between the two parts of II Corinthians are strong evidence that chapters 1–9 (except 6:14–7:1) are a later letter referring to the letter in chapters 10–13:[39]

Being ready to punish every disobedience, *when your obedience is complete* (II Corinthians 10:6).	For this is why I wrote, that I might test you and know *whether you are obedient in everything* (II Corinthians 2:9).
I warned those who sinned before and all the others, and I warn them now while absent, as I did when present on my second visit, that *If I come again I will not spare them* (II Corinthians 13:2).	But I call God to witness against me —*it was to spare you that I refrained from coming to Corinth* (II Corinthians 1:23).
I write this while I am away from you, in order that *when I come I may not have to be severe* in my use of the authority which the Lord has given me for building up and not for tearing down (II Corinthians 13:10).	And *I wrote as I did, so that when I came I might not be pained* by those who should have made me rejoice, for I felt sure of all of you, that my joy would be the joy of you all (II Corinthians 2:3).

In several other places in the Corinthian letters a sudden change of subject or hiatus indicates the possibility that further fragments from different letters have been joined. I Corinthians 9, which ill fits what precedes and what follows, furnishes a good example. Several scholars

---

[38] Lindsey P. Pherigo attempts on the basis of this conclusion a different reconstruction of the order of events in Paul's relations with Corinth. "Paul and the Corinthian Church," *Journal of Biblical Literature,* LXVIII, Part IV, December 1949, pp. 341–50.

[39] Italics are mine. For a comparison of further parallels and contrasts which point in this same direction see Plummer, *II Corinthians,* pp. xxvii–xxxvi.

have attempted elaborate reconstructions of the original letters by re-arranging these passages. Usually such reconstructions have concluded with more than four letters.[40] While there is nothing intrinsically improbable in the suggestion that Paul wrote more than four letters, yet nothing in the references within the letters or in what we know of the circumstances of his relations with Corinth requires more than four.

That some of these apparent fragments may belong with II Corinthians 6:14–7:1 as a part of the first letter and others to the severe letter is plausible; but because the discontinuity created by the presence of these other "fragments" is by no means as pronounced as it is in the instances we have examined and because they have failed to achieve a consensus among scholars, these reconstructions can be regarded as no more than attractive conjectures. In most instances a closer examination can detect an association of ideas which may have led Paul into the byways which appear to us as fragments. Such letters as Paul's, unlike conscious literary works, do not require and often do not display the virtue of logical and orderly progression of thought. Occasionally, too, Paul's fondness for paradoxes has created the impression of discontinuity where it does not actually exist.

The Corinthian correspondence does, however, include one other letter—a letter from Corinth to Paul. It is mentioned in I Corinthians 7:1 and some of its contents may be inferred from the repeated phrase, "now concerning . . ." here and in 7:25, 8:1, 12:1, and 16:1. In addition to this letter from Corinth Paul received oral reports from Corinth. "Chloe's people" (I Corinthians 1:11) had reported the quarreling over leadership with which the first part of I Corinthians is concerned. The last "conciliatory" letter followed the report of Titus that the crisis in Corinth was over (II Corinthians 7:6–7). Paul's own experience during the "painful visit" may have occasioned the third "severe" letter. How the news reached Paul which caused him to write the first letter we cannot tell. Perhaps Timothy had paid Corinth a visit and reported back to Paul (cf. I Corinthians 16:10–11; I Thessalonians 3:2, 6). Corinth was only a short sail from Ephesus so

[40] For a good discussion of these studies see McNeile, *An Introduction to the Study of the New Testament,* pp. 132–42. See also Weiss, *Earliest Christianity,* I, 323–57; B. W. Robinson, *The Life of Paul* (Chicago: University of Chicago Press, 1918), pp. 164–74.

that Paul would have no difficulty in keeping in touch with the church there.

We may reconstruct the communications between Paul and the Corinthians which involve his letters as follows:

1) Paul's first letter (II Corinthians 6:14–7:1) mentioned in I Corinthians 5:9–11 was written from Ephesus.
2) Chloe's people and a letter, perhaps brought by Stephanas, Fortunatus, and Achaicus, brought news of further trouble in Corinth.
3) Paul wrote a second letter which is our I Corinthians.
4) Paul started for Macedonia and stopped at Corinth for a brief visit (because of more unfavorable news?), but met with such a painful experience that he returned to Ephesus.
5) Paul wrote the "severe letter" contained in II Corinthians 10–13 and sent it by Titus, while he proceeded to Troas.
6) When Titus failed to appear in Troas, Paul went on to Macedonia where Titus met him with the good news that the trouble was over. Paul then wrote the "conciliatory letter" contained in II Corinthians 1:1–6:13; 7:2–9:15, after which he came to Corinth to begin his journey to Jerusalem with the collection.

The First Letter   How much of this letter remains in II Corinthians 6:14–7:1 is impossible to determine, but if Paul's allusion to it in I Corinthians 5:9–11 is an indication of its general contents, what we have may be all but the opening and closing. The theme is complete in itself. Yet Paul's practice in his other letters suggests that there probably was, beside the opening, a section which included thanksgiving and felicitations, and closing greetings. As Philemon shows, not all of Paul's letters were long. What we have, therefore, may be the body of the letter.

The theme of this letter is stated in the opening words: "Do not be mismated with unbelievers." There follows immediately a series of five rhetorical questions, all of which expect a negative answer. That Paul is not thinking of intermarriage with pagans here is evident in the terms of relationship he uses in these questions (cf. I Corinthians 7:12–16).

Taken together they form an impressive description of the ideal church: partnership, fellowship, accord, in common, and agreement. These relationships, so appropriate to believers with one another, must not obtain between the believer and the unbeliever or evil one. Because of just such a problem, the case of the incestuous man in I Corinthians 5:1–8, Paul recalled this letter to the attention of the Corinthians. Such passages as II Corinthians 11:15, 12:21, 13:2, 2:5–11, 7:10–12 indicate how serious this problem was in Corinth.

The contrasts in these questions are characteristic of the antitheses of the motif of the two ways in Jewish Wisdom literature. Righteousness, Light, Christ, believer, Temple of God provide a profile of the Christian; iniquity, darkness, Belial, and unbeliever picture the pagan. The mosaic of Old Testament quotations which follows in verses 16–18 is to show that, since the believers are the Temple of God, God will dwell with them if they separate themselves from evil. The exhortation drawn from these quotations concludes the passage:

Since we have these promises, beloved, let us cleanse ourselves from every defilement of body and spirit, and make holiness perfect in the fear of God (II Corinthians 7:1).

In the wickedest city of the Empire the Corinthian Christians had come upon a moral problem which in spite of this letter and the second one was to grow worse until it reached its climax in the bitter conflict that called forth Paul's third letter. When finally the conflict was over and the evil removed from their midst, the humbled and penitent believers in Corinth received Paul's fourth and final letter gratefully acknowledging the restoration of their fellowship. Such is the drama back of the Corinthian letters.

The Second Letter Paul's first letter to Corinth failed to solve the problem and in the meantime further problems had arisen. Word of these new developments reached Paul through Chloe's people (probably the personal servants of a prominent member in Corinth) and through a letter from the church. Paul takes up these problems in that order; therefore, the letter divides naturally into two parts between chapters

6 and 7 where he turns from the problems related by Chloe's people to those in the letter to him.

After the usual salutation and thanksgiving (1:1–9), Paul turns immediately to the problems reported by his visitors. The Corinthians are quarreling over their loyalty to various leaders (1:10–4:21). Four are named: Paul, Apollos, Cephas, and Christ. Possibly the words, "I belong to Christ," are a scribal gloss. Once written as a comment in the margin of a manuscript by a pious copyist, they may have been copied into the text by a later copyist who mistakenly supposed that they stood in the margin as a correction. Such glosses were not uncommon in the course of the history of the text of our New Testament. Neither the party of Cephas nor the party of Christ come in for attention in the discussion that follows.

The real problem seems to be between those who remained loyal to Paul and those who, dazzled by the brilliance of the Alexandrian Greek, Apollos, were childishly boasting of their new found wisdom. Paul's answer to them was that human leaders are only servants; their real loyalty is to Christ. Paul had preached to them in simplicity because this was what they needed. Nevertheless, he has wisdom to impart when they are ready for it. But it is not measured by the standards of worldly wisdom; it is "a secret and hidden wisdom of God" (2:7). As their childish boasting shows, the Corinthians are still not ready for true wisdom. They are immature and need "milk, not solid food" (3:2).

The second problem reported by Paul's visitors was a flagrant case of immorality: "A man is living with his father's wife" (5:1), yet the church is doing nothing about it! Paul orders the culprit to be delivered "to Satan for the destruction of the flesh, that his spirit may be saved in the day of the Lord Jesus" (5:5). Paul's mind is, however, still on the arrogance of the partisans of Apollos. If they are so wise, let them show it by cleansing the fellowship of this evil. He had written them against just such evil associations; let them heed his former letter.

A third problem, that of Christians haling one another into pagan courts, provided a further demonstration that their boast of superior wisdom was inappropriate. "Do you not know that we are to judge angels? How much more, matters pertaining to this life!" (6:3).

With a concluding warning against immoral associations Paul leaves these problems to turn his attention to the questions raised by the letter from Corinth.

The first of these questions concerned marriage and sex (7:1–40). Paul's apparently low opinion of marriage in this passage has provided difficulties for his interpreters. It certainly ran counter to Jewish tradition.[41] Three things, however, need to be kept in mind in understanding this chapter: 1) Paul's discussion of marriage is not a matter of morals. Paul knows no levels of morality; marriage is either moral or it is not, and if it is not he would never have made such concessions as he does in verses 9, 25, and 39. 2) Paul is well aware of the background of sexual license in Corinth. That Paul was familiar with pagan attitudes toward sex is shown by his reference to abstinence for periods of religious devotion. The idea of sexual abstinence as a preparation for cultic rites was a familiar practice in paganism and Paul allows it, with reservations, in the practice of the Corinthian Christians (verses 5–6). The high ideals of marital love were beyond those in whose environment sex was so commonly viewed from the standpoint of physical appetite rather than a sacred union of two personalities. As is shown by his treatment of the evil of prostitution in the preceding chapter (6:16), Paul is not unaware of the sacred significance of marriage. But the very fact that he had to point out this significance of sex as he did shows how little the Corinthians appreciated it. Elsewhere Paul could use the analogy of marriage to represent the relation between the Church and Christ. (Cf. II Corinthians 11:2, Romans 7:1–4, Ephesians 5:25–33.) 3) The controlling idea here—that the end of the age is so near and the urgency of spreading the gospel in preparation for it is so great that the normal pursuits of life must give place to the work of the Church—is clearly stated:

I think that in view of the impending distress it is well for a person to re-

[41] But cf. the Essenes, chap. 3 and note 82. Frank M. Cross, Jr., sees in this passage as well as in such passages as Luke 20:34–36 and Matthew 19:12 definite Essene characteristics. *The Ancient Library of Qumran and Modern Biblical Studies* (Garden City, New York: Doubleday and Company, Inc., 1958), pp. 71–74. How direct the connection is between these passages and the Essene movement, however, is an open question.

main as he is . . . I mean, brethren, the appointed time has grown very short; from now on, let those who have wives live as though they had none, and those who mourn as though they were not mourning, and those who rejoice as though they were not rejoicing, and those who buy as though they had no goods, and those who deal with the world as though they had no dealings with it. For the form of this world is passing away (I Corinthians 7:26, 29–31; cf. verses 32–35).

We should also note that Paul is careful to say that he does not have this teaching from the Lord (verses 12 and 25; cf. verses 10 and 40) and that even though the impending crisis of the end of the age made it appear expedient not to marry, they were not to place themselves in moral jeopardy thereby.

The second question which was raised by the letter from Corinth concerned food offered to idols. The problem, reported by Chloe's people, of those who were arrogant over their superior wisdom appears again here. The "wise" knew that "an idol has no real existence" (8:4) and, therefore, they did not scruple to eat the sacred meat that had been blessed by being offered to a pagan deity. Others, sharing the Jewish horror of such actions, strenuously objected. Paul met the problem with a timeless principle: "Therefore, if food is a cause of my brother's falling, I will never eat meat, lest I cause my brother to fall" (8:13).

Paul's own practices as an apostle furnished an illustration. He had a right to be supported by the churches which he served; "Nevertheless, we have not made use of this right, but we endure anything rather than put an obstacle in the way of the gospel of Christ" (9:12). The "wise" should rather be careful, lest their boasted freedom carry them into immorality or actual idolatry. "Therefore let any one who thinks that he stands take heed lest he fall" (10:12).

By contrasting pagan feasts with the Christian Eucharist Paul shows that the danger of idolatry is more real than the "wise" may have imagined. Idols are nothing, to be sure, but pagan worship is of demonic origin; therefore, to associate with pagan festivals and foods deliberately is to become a partner with demons. The Corinthians should buy their meat without asking questions; the food itself is not the issue; but to avoid hurting the conscience of others and courting

the danger of identifying themselves with paganism, they are not know-
ingly to eat pagan sacred food. "Give no offense to Jews or to Greeks
or to the church of God" (10:32).

Since this section lacks the introduction, "now concerning," it is
not clear whether the matters discussed in chapter 11 refer to questions
in the letter to Paul or go back to other reports he had received from
Corinth. Both matters have to do with practices in the worship of the
church. Women had been taking liberties with their new found freedom and appearing in the meetings with their heads uncovered. To
Paul the Jew this was too much; it was as much a disgrace as though
they had their heads shorn. Let the women wear veils.[42] Abuses had
developed also in the Lord's Supper. "Each one goes ahead with his
own meal, and one is hungry and another is drunk" (11:21). As Paul
has already shown in 10:16-17, the Eucharist is a solemn and sacred
matter: "For any one who eats and drinks without discerning the body
eats and drinks judgment upon himself" (11:29). This passage is
noteworthy because it furnishes us with the oldest account we have of
the institution of the Lord's Supper.

Paul turns next to the question of spiritual gifts which had been
raised by the letter to him (chapters 12-14). The problem was deli-
cate. On one hand, the childish pride manifested in the quarrel over
wisdom was showing itself in ecstatic gibberish which seized some of
the Corinthians at their meetings. Their frenzied experiences had
pagan roots and needed to be corrected. On the other hand, Paul himself had taught them about the gifts of the Holy Spirit and he must
not tread too roughly on the enthusiasm of these young converts. Paul's
handling of this problem is a model of diplomacy and understanding.

He begins by showing that such outbursts are not to be flaunted as
a mark of superiority because "there are varieties of gifts" (12:4).
What is more, a genuine gift of the Spirit works for the good of the
whole Body of Christ. Of what good is it to speak if no one understands
and is edified. Moreover, worship involves the mind as well as the
spirit. In the worship of the church there has to be intelligent communication. Otherwise, how can the listener "say the 'Amen' to your

---

[42] On the significance of the veil see Ramsay, *The Cities of St. Paul*, pp. 202-
205.

thanksgiving when he does not know what you are saying?" (14:16). "God is not a God of confusion but of peace . . . all things should be done decently and in order" (14:33, 40).

In the midst of this discussion—in a passage that has become one of the best loved chapters in the Bible—Paul proposes an even better solution. The "still more excellent way" of chapter 13 is the way of love (*agape*), without which all other gifts and achievements amount to nothing. Love is selfless, patient consideration for others; it is abiding where other gifts are ephemeral. Therefore, "make love your aim."

The final discussion of the letter serves as a summation of Paul's gospel (cf. Philippians 3:10–16). This great chapter on the resurrection may not have been called forth by any questions in the letter to Paul, yet the argument is pointed enough to suggest that the Corinthians needed instruction. Paul's teaching here is based on his own experience of the resurrection of Jesus on the Damascus Road. The resurrection is the goal of the Christian life: "If in this life we who are in Christ have only hope, we are of all men most to be pitied" (15:19). As for the nature of the resurrection, Paul introduces the idea of the "spiritual body" which is imperishable. What this spiritual body is he does not make clear except that it will be a body suited to a glorious new age to come. With the fervent hope of the imminent parousia still before his gaze, Paul discloses a mystery to those who live at the end of time: "We shall not all sleep, but we shall all be changed. . . . For this perishable nature must put on the imperishable" (15:51, 53).

That the collection for Jerusalem had been started some time prior to this letter is evident in the way Paul speaks of it in chapter 16. Apparently, from the words "Now concerning," the Corinthians had asked about the collection in their letter. Paul requests that it be accumulated in weekly installments so that the gift will be ready when he arrives. A few personal notes and greetings and Paul's closing in his own handwriting complete this his second longest letter.

The Third Letter The real problem that has precipitated the crisis in Corinth to which this letter is addressed largely eludes us. Behind Paul's sharp invectives and violent language we catch only shadowy glimpses

of the storm that was rocking the church. We need not assume that the
Corinthians had outside help in creating this situation; the two earlier
letters show that they did not need it. We will be justified in assuming
a connection between the trouble behind this letter and the difficulties
with the Apollos faction in the first four chapters of I Corinthians. That
there was a ring-leader behind Paul's opposition seems clear from the
reference in 11:4 to "some one" and the "one who has caused pain,"
whom Paul in the fourth letter (II Corinthians 2:5–11) asks the Corinthians to forgive. A number of manuscripts read "For he says" rather
than "For they say" in 10:10, which may be further evidence that Paul
has an individual in mind. It would be helpful if we could know why
Paul always refers to him in such an indefinite way.

It is interesting to note that while Paul's opponents impune his motives they appropriate Paul's personal claims for themselves: They are
Christ's (10:7); they commend themselves (cf. 10:18 with 11:18;
12:11; 3:1); they are Hebrews (11:22); they are servants of Christ
(11:23); they are apostles (11:5; 12:11); and "they work on the same
terms as we do" (11:12). The problems of immorality which we noticed in I Corinthians are also a part of the problem in this situation
(cf. 10:6; 12:21). Although there is in Corinth no tendency toward
adopting the Law with its requirement of circumcision such as there
was in Galatia, the problem here is not unlike that of the Galatian
"spirituals." Their repudiation of Paul's leadership is coupled with
serious immorality. We may wonder if the affair of the incestuous man
had something to do with the storm in Corinth.

Paul answers his opponents by insisting on his authority over the
Corinthians "which the Lord gave for building you up" (10:8). He
denies the charges of ulterior motives in the use of this authority (10:2;
11:7–11; 12:16–18). What these charges were we cannot guess; whatever they were, he intends to settle them with confidence when he is
present (10:2). Paul has a justifiable concern for the Corinthians, for
he betrothed them to Christ (11:2). His love for them he demonstrated
by preaching the gospel to them without cost to them, yet in this he
was misunderstood (11:7–11). But if his opponents want to boast, Paul
can boast too (11:16–12:12)! To Paul's "boast" we owe the very important list of his hardships in 11:23–33. Not only in hardships, but

also in visions and revelations Paul's apostleship has been proved; yet in reality his boast is in his weakness in order "that the power of Christ may rest upon me" (12:9).

Paul adds a final warning: He is coming for a third visit; let the Corinthians correct their errors. "I write this," he concludes, "while I am away from you, in order that when I come I may not have to be severe in my use of the authority which the Lord has given me for building up and not for tearing down" (13:10).

The Fourth Letter The severe letter had produced the desired effect and the culprit was being punished. In the final letter to Corinth Paul's joy over this news which Titus brought overflowed. The opening words are a profound blessing for God's comfort and a promise that as the Corinthians had shared his sufferings so they would share his comfort. In Asia Paul had come near to death, but as God had comforted him in the restoration of the Corinthians, so he had delivered him from death. An explanation was needed for Paul's change of plans about his visit to them. Regarding the chief offender Paul magnanimously asks that the Corinthians forgive and "reaffirm your love for him . . . any one whom you forgive, I also forgive" (2:8, 10).

Almost point by point Paul takes up the statements in his severe letter and either reverses them or restates them in a conciliatory tone. He will not commend himself; they are his "letter of recommendation" (3:2). Humbly he confesses that his "sufficiency is from God" (3:5). He is the minister of a new and more glorious covenant in the Spirit (3:6). "But we have this treasure in earthen vessels" (4:7). So that although afflicted and persecuted, Paul does not lose heart:

For this slight momentary affliction is preparing for us an eternal weight of glory beyond all comparison, because we look not to the things that are seen but to the things that are unseen; for the things that are seen are transient, but the things that are unseen are eternal (II Corinthians 4:17–18).

Paul's ministry, therefore, is one of reconciliation; God is making His appeal through Paul to reconcile the world through Christ to Himself (5:18–20). Paul then applies this ministry of reconciliation to his relations with the Corinthians because their reconciliation needs to become complete: "You are not restricted by us, but you are restricted in your own affections . . . widen your hearts also" (6:12, 13). Yet Paul rejoices that the Corinthians have repented, and Titus, too, rejoiced that the storm is over (7:7–16).

In chapters 8 and 9 Paul turns to the matters concerning the collection for Jerusalem. The Macedonian churches have insisted upon being included and have become an example of generosity for the Corinthians to follow (8:1–15). Titus and "the brother" will come to assist in this work. Because chapter 9 deals again with the same subject, repeating some matters as though they had not already been discussed in chapter 8, some scholars regard it as a separate note sent later to Corinth. That it is a separate short letter sent just before Paul left Macedonia for Corinth is quite possible, but there is nothing to preclude it from being a summary of the fourth letter, which repeats for emphasis the importance of the collection. That collection has become a symbol of the Corinthians' repentance. Verse 13 seems to refer beyond the collection to the concern of the whole letter—the renewed obedience of the Corinthians. In his final words we can almost hear Paul's great sigh of relief over their restoration: "Thanks be to God for his inexpressible gift!" (9:15).

To the Lycus Valley

Two of Paul's letters, and possibly three, were addressed to the triangle of cities situated in the Lycus Valley.[43] Although addressed to Colossae, the letter we know as Colossians was intended also for Laodicea (Colossians 4:16). From the description of Onesimus in Colossians 4:9 as "one of yourselves" it has been generally assumed that Philemon, which was written to Onesimus' owner, was also sent to Colossae. In Colossians 4:16 a "letter from Laodicea" is mentioned. As we shall see, this letter has been variously identified with Philemon, Ephesians, or an unknown letter that has since been lost.

The Letter to the Colossians　　Although a majority of scholars today regard this

---

[43] On these cities see "Cities of the Lycus Valley" in chap. 7.

letter as a genuine letter of Paul, there are still a number who harbor misgivings concerning its authenticity. The question arises for three reasons. 1) The style and vocabulary are different from Paul's other letters. 2) The philosophy is sometimes identified with the second-century gnosticism with which we are acquainted from the writings of Ireneaus, Tertullian and others. 3) The doctrine of Christ in this letter is presumed to be more advanced than that found in the other letters. Ephesians, of course, is left out of account in these comparisons because for similar reasons it is also suspected of being a later writing.

On closer examination, these objections are not serious. Other manifestly genuine letters of Paul have words unique to them among his writings. Differences in style are a precarious basis for judgment and in this instance can be accounted for by the differences in subject and situation.[44] The second objection has largely been abandoned in recent years. As we have seen gnosticism is a characteristic of a number of the popular religions of Paul's time and should not be regarded as a distinct and separate religion or philosophy.[45] We cannot be sure now, at any rate, just what the "philosophy" was that threatened the Colossian Church, but it must have been related to the popular angelolatry of Asia Minor and especially to the superstitious beliefs associated with the unusual natural phenomena in this area.[46] That the doctrine of Christ appears to be different in Colossians is to be expected because the rival claims of the pagan religions which Paul is opposing are different. Paul is nowhere in his letters writing systematic theology; he is seeking to demonstrate the exclusive sufficiency of Christ in terms intelligible to those to whom he writes.[47] Paul held a "high Christology"

[44] Cf. Edgar Johnson Goodspeed, *An Introduction to the New Testament* (Chicago: University of Chicago Press, 1937), p. 102.

[45] "Gnosticism" in chap. 4.

[46] "Cities of the Lycus Valley" in chap. 7. Professor Cross believes, however, that the Essenes are responsible for the errors referred to in Col. 2:16–23. *The Ancient Library of Qumran and Modern Biblical Studies,* p. 150 n. But it is difficult to account for Essene influence in a church so distant from Palestine and so predominantly gentile. Nothing in this passage requires more than a syncretism based on the elements of paganism and Judaism known to be present in that region. Enthusiasm for the Dead Sea Scrolls, like that for other discoveries, naturally invites investigators to try this new key in the locks of all New Testament problems, but we must not force the lock!

[47] Cf. Albert E. Barnett, *The New Testament, Its Making and Meaning* (New York: Abingdon-Cokesbury Press, 1946), p. 80. For opposite view see F. W.

from the time of his conversion, and although it is expressed in different terms, Paul's thought of Christ here is not basically different from that in such passages as Philippians 2:5–11; Romans 6:4; 8:3, 9, 18–39; Galatians 4:3–11; 5:6.

Rather than being an argument for a late date for Colossians, the treatment of the errors at Colossae is actually good evidence for its early origin and authenticity. That the Colossian Christians, recently converted from paganism, would bring into their new-found faith ideas and beliefs from their traditional religions is only to be expected. Such problems of syncretism in a religious climate such as was found in this area, far from taking years to develop, would arise almost immediately. What is noteworthy in Colossians is the patience with which Paul deals with the problem, which stands in sharp contrast to the vituperations of later writings against heresies of this kind. (Cf. II Peter 2:1–22; Jude, Irenaeus, *Against Heresies;* and Tertullian, *Against Marcion.*)

The coincidence of names in Colossians and Philemon[48] and the fact that Paul is sending Onesimus along with Tychicus, the bearer of the letter, suggest a close connection between this letter and Philemon. We may conclude that they were delivered at the same time by Tychicus and Onesimus. Both of them were written while Paul was in prison to a church which he had never visited. Epaphras, who was the leader of the Colossian Church and probably the founder of the three churches in Hierapolis, Laodicea, and Colossae, was in prison with Paul (Colossians 1:7; 4:12–13; and Philemon 23). We have already observed the likelihood that this imprisonment may have been in Ephesus.[49] It may be that Epaphras had come to report to Paul on the problems in the Colossian Church (1:8) and in some way became involved in the trouble for which Paul was imprisoned.

After the usual thanksgiving and prayer for the Colossians, Paul presents the exclusive claims of Christ who "is before all things, and

---

Beare, "Colossians," *Interpreter's Bible* (New York: Abingdon Press, 1955), XI, 142–45.

[48] Beside Paul and Timothy in the salutation there are seven persons named in both letters. Only two names in Philemon, Philemon and Apphia, are not in Colossians, and only three of those in Colossians, Tychicus, Justus, and Nympha, do not appear in Philemon.

[49] "Paul's Ephesian Imprisonment?" in chap. 7.

in him all things hold together" (1:17).[50] The "fullness of God" dwells in Christ and all things, including the Colossians, are reconciled to God by his blood. Paul has been made a minister of the Church, which is the Body of Christ. It is his task to make known this "mystery hidden for ages and generations but now made manifest to his saints" (1:26). Paul has a right therefore to admonish them. Apparently the Colossians were still paying obeisance to the daemons or demiurgi revered in the area. In typical pagan fashion they had added Christ to their list of intermediaries between them and the highest God, but they did not understand that faith in Christ involved dying to these "elemental spirits of the universe" (2:20).

Paul patiently explains that their salvation had come through Christ alone "who is the head of all rule and authority" (2:10). They are, therefore, to forsake all worship and regulations of their former paganism. Let them "seek the things that are above" (3:1) and "put to death" all immorality and selfishness. There are no longer any distinctions of race or class for "Christ is all, and in all." They have put on a new nature; from now on they must "put on love" (3:14) with all its attributes, doing "everything in the name of the Lord Jesus" (3:17). There follows a series of practical rules for Christian conduct in human relationships between husbands and wives, children and parents, and slaves and masters. The body of the letter ends with an exhortation to prayer and thanksgiving and the parting advice:

> Conduct yourselves wisely toward outsiders, making the most of the time. Let your speech always be gracious, seasoned with salt, so that you may know how you ought to answer every one (Colossians 4:5).

A few personal notes and greetings follow, and the enigmatic sentence, "And say to Archippus, 'See that you fulfill the ministry which you have received in the Lord' " (4:17). Archippus is included among those to whom the letter to Philemon is addressed. Is there a connection between this sentence and Philemon? Some scholars believe there

---

[50] Col. 1:15–20 appears to be an early Christian hymn. For a good analysis of the literary form of this passage see James M. Robinson, "A Formal Analysis of Colossians 1:15–20," *Journal of Biblical Literature*, LXXVI, Part IV, December 1957, 270–87.

is. The relation between these two letters is enough to require us to refer to Colossians in our discussion of Philemon.

The Letter to Philemon   The story of Philemon is familiar. According to the traditional version Onesimus, Philemon's slave, had run away and as often happened had stolen funds from his master with which to make good his escape. In some way he had come into contact with Paul and was converted. Now Paul was sending him home with this letter asking Philemon to forgive Onesimus and receive him back as a Christian brother. As for anything Onesimus may have stolen, Paul magnanimously writes, "Charge that to my account" (verse 18). Sending a runaway slave back to his master involved considerable risk for the slave because the master by law could punish him as he chose, could even take his life. To meet this danger Paul sent Tychicus to accompany Onesimus (Colossians 4:7–9).

A closer reading of the letter will show that there is more to the story than this and will help to explain why such a personal note, devoid of either doctrinal or ethical teaching, happened to be included in the collection of Paul's letters. The real burden of the letter is one of the broadest hints in history:

I would have been glad to keep him with me, in order that he might serve me on your behalf during my imprisonment for the gospel; but I preferred to do nothing without your consent in order that your goodness might not be by compulsion but of your own free will (verses 13–14).

What Paul really wants is to have Onesimus returned to him as a helper in the work of the gospel. Repeatedly he emphasizes his own imprisonment and, therefore, his need of Onesimus. That the letter is more than a personal note is clear from the address which includes, along with Philemon, Apphia, Archippus, and the Colossian church, and from the characteristic thanksgiving and greetings at the opening and close. We have already seen that there is a close connection between this letter and the one to Colossae. Probably they were both delivered at the same time.

Professor Knox has subjected these two letters to a thorough study in which he has at several points modified the traditional interpretation.[51] The owner of Onesimus, he contends, was not Philemon but Archippus in whose house the Colossian Church met. Paul's strange words in Colossians 4:17 are to enlist the support of the church in his request for Onesimus. On this theory, the letter is addressed to Philemon because he has succeeded Epaphras who is in prison with Paul as the leader of the churches in the Lycus Valley and can help influence Archippus to grant Paul's request. The language in verse 1 is ambiguous and it is not clear that Philemon is the host of the church or the one being addressed in the body of the letter. This theory, consequently, is very plausible.

Professor Knox carries his hypothesis further, however, to include the suggestion that Philemon is actually the "letter from Laodicea" referred to in Colossians 4:16. Philemon, he suggests, may have lived in Laodicea, the chief city of the district, and the letter was brought to him first and then was delivered to Archippus and the Colossian Church. The chief difficulty in this part of the hypothesis is that of explaining why Colossians was to be returned to Laodicea to be read. Why were they not both read at Laodicea at the same time?

Professor Goodspeed reverses the theory, making all of the addressees of this letter including Philemon, the owner of the slave, Laodiceans. The exchange of letters is therefore to enlist the aid of the nearby Colossian Church in obtaining Paul's request.[52] It is equally possible, however, that they are all Colossians and that the traditional view that both Philemon and Colossians were addressed to Colossae is to that extent correct. The exchange of letters with Laodicea is more likely to have had some connection with the main purpose of Colossians, the problem of pagan philosophy, than with the matter of the slave, Onesimus, which occupied only part of the closing section.[53]

---

[51] In his *Philemon among the Letters of Paul,* Professor Knox raises the question whether Onesimus had actually run away or had been sent to Paul on an errand. In the latter case, Paul is simply asking for him to be returned to him permanently. See pp. 17–18. It is clear from verses 11 and 18–19, however, that Onesimus is in some sort of trouble.

[52] See Goodspeed, *An Introduction to the New Testament,* pp. 119–120.

[53] Professor Knox offers the likely suggestion that the admonitions to slaves and masters are oblique references to Onesimus and his owner. *Philemon among the Letters of Paul,* pp. 36–45.

The letter to Philemon takes on added interest when we observe that in Ignatius' letter to the Ephesians the name Onesimus appears prominently as the Bishop of Ephesus.[54] Professor Knox has suggested that the tradition which identified this Onesimus as the person who is the subject of Philemon is correct.[55] Professor Goodspeed, following this suggestion, has offered the attractive hypothesis that Onesimus was responsible for the original collection of Paul's letters.[56] While these theories fall short of demonstration, there is no serious difficulty in their way and we may take them at least as plausible conjectures. If they are correct, they offer us a valuable chapter in the story of the developing New Testament and an appealing explanation of how such a short and personal note as Philemon came to be included in the canon.

The Question of Ephesians

Closely associated with Colossians in style, wording, ideas, and in the fact that Tychicus is the bearer, is another letter which we know as Ephesians. Its lofty description of the significance of Christ and its inspiring theme of oneness in Christ make this letter one of the important and influential books of the New Testament.

Destination and Authorship   The question of Ephesians arises from a textual problem in the first verse which, together with a combination of characteristics, make it impossible to determine with any certainty the circumstances and destination of this letter. The textual problem is simply that according to weighty manuscript and patristic evidence the words "in Ephesus" do not belong in the address.[57] So decisive is the evidence, in fact, that the *Revised Standard Version* has relegated the phrase to a footnote.

Certain characteristics within the letter itself add support to the

---

[54] See especially chapters 1–6. *The Apostolic Constitutions*, VII, 46, records a tradition that Philemon's servant Onesimus became the Bishop of Borea.

[55] Knox, *Philemon among the Letters of Paul*, pp. 71–108.

[56] Goodspeed, *An Introduction to the New Testament*, pp. 121–24.

[57] On this problem see T. K. Abbott, *The Epistles to the Ephesians and to the Colossians, International Critical Commentary* (New York: Charles Scribner's Sons, 1909), pp. i–ix.

conclusion that the letter was not written to Ephesus. It is the most general of all the letters in the Pauline collection. There are no specific problems in view. There are no closing greetings, no personal notes, such as those which are so characteristic of all of the other letters of Paul. That Paul was writing to a church which did not know him is clear from his words in 1:15 and 3:1–4. None of these things could be true of a letter from Paul to a church with which he had worked as long as he had at Ephesus.

Some of these observations, however, make it difficult to conceive any individual church to which this letter might be addressed. This difficulty has led a large number of scholars to doubt that the letter was written by Paul.[58] The arguments against Paul's authorship of Ephesians may be summed up in the following three objections: 1) The lack of personal references and characteristics of Paul's letters. 2) Its remarkable similarity—amounting at times to literary dependence —to Colossians while at the same time subtly differing in its theology. 3) Its differences in style and vocabulary, even more pronounced than Colossians, from Paul's other letters.[59]

In order to understand the question of Ephesians more clearly we must examine briefly these objections. The vocabulary of this letter does not offer a serious objection because, although there are a number of words here that do not appear elsewhere in Paul's letters, the same is true of other admittedly authentic letters. The question is one of degree; and since subject matter influences vocabulary, it is precarious to rest conclusions as to authorship on mere word counts. We must not judge in advance the size of Paul's vocabulary. The criticism of style, likewise, depends on judgments that are highly subjective. There are, in fact, differences within other individual letters of Paul that have led some enthusiasts for style criticism to cut them up into mosaics of dis-

---

[58] In his recent book, *The Key to Ephesians* (Chicago: The University of Chicago Press, 1956), Professor Goodspeed offers twenty-one reasons for believing that Ephesians was by a later writer. See also his *The Meaning of Ephesians* (Chicago: The University of Chicago Press, 1933).

[59] Good treatments of these problems may be found in Enslin, *Christian Beginnings*, pp. 293–98; B. W. Bacon, *An Introduction to the New Testament* (New York: The Macmillan Company, 1902); pp. 113–121; McNeile, *An Introduction to the Study of the New Testament*, pp. 165–77; Goodspeed, *An Introduction to the New Testament*, pp. 222–39.

parate materials that attribute to the "final compiler" an incredible editorial ingenuity. Unless other more decisive objections can be sustained against Paul's authorship of this letter, these objections have little weight.[60]

The alleged differences in theology rest largely on an exegesis of passages in Ephesians and their counterpart in other letters which on grounds quite independent of this problem may be questioned. Preconceptions of the evolutionary growth of the Church's institutions and organization, the tendency to "modernize" Paul, and questionable assumptions concerning the rise and development of heresies have exerted unwarranted influence on this question. Paul's doctrine of Christ, which is the principal issue, arose not from a theory but from an experience. It could, therefore, find expression, according to the situation, in various ways. Not infrequently we can find back of the figures he uses certain characteristic apocalyptic ideas and terms.[61]

That Ephesians shows the characteristics of a general letter without personal greetings and local references, and at the same time displays a remarkable literary dependence upon Colossians and Paul's other letters has led Professor Goodspeed to formulate the hypothesis that it was written as an introduction to the published letters of Paul by the original collector.[62] The theory has several attractive features. In the first place, it takes seriously the problem, faced by all those who deny the Pauline authorship of this letter, that Ephesians is by external evidence one of the best attested of Paul's letters. The earliest writings of the Apostolic Fathers as well as the later Epistles of the New Testament reflect its influence.[63] In the second place, it attempts an explanation of the fact that Ephesians contains material not only from Colossians[64] but also from all the other letters of Paul and that it con-

---

[60] Cf. Ernest Findlay Scott, *The Literature of the New Testament* (New York: Columbia University Press, 1932), pp. 179–80.

[61] Cf. Bacon, *An Introduction to the New Testament*, pp. 118–21.

[62] This theory is to be found in a number of his writings. The most recent and complete is *The Key to Ephesians*. The main part of this work consists of a valuable comparison of Ephesians with Colossians and the rest of Paul's letters by means of parallel columns. Cf. his *The Meaning of Ephesians* for a similar study of the literary relationships.

[63] See Abbott, *Ephesians and Colossians*, pp. ix–xiii.

[64] For detailed analyses of the relationship of Ephesians and Colossians see Moffatt, *An Introduction to the Literature of the New Testament*, pp. 375–81.

tains little else. If the collector was Onesimus, as Professor Goodspeed supposes, the theory gains a romantic appeal.

The theory is, nevertheless, not without difficulties.[65] That Paul in his letters repeats himself frequently we have already observed.[66] For another person to compile a work from Paul's writings as consistent and noble as Ephesians would require much greater genius than for Paul to have done it himself. Although the words "in Ephesus" do not belong in the opening verse, the grammar virtually requires some such phrase.[67] This theory would rule out any specific addressee and therefore cannot explain the grammatical construction here. Finally, we may raise the question as to whether or not Professor Goodspeed has actually succeeded in explaining how this letter, if not by Paul, could so quickly gain such general acceptance and such wide influence.[68] When all is considered, it seems to me that less difficulty lies in the way of accepting Paul's authorship of Ephesians than in any attempt to cut the Gordian knot by assigning the letter to a later author.

But if we regard the letter as genuine, the question of occasion and destination remains. Among those who accept the genuineness of Ephesians the most popular explanation of the question is some form of the theory advanced long ago by Archbishop Usher that it was written as a circular letter. The original idea that a blank was left in the copies which Tychicus carried into which the name of each recipient church was supplied has lost favor because there is no evidence of such a practice in ancient letter writing.[69] Without the blank theory, the difficulty

---

[65] For a criticism of Professor Goodspeed's theory see F. W. Beare, "Ephesians," *Interpreter's Bible*, X, 603.

[66] Indeed, this trait is not difficult to illustrate from the works of some of our more prolific modern writers.

[67] Every theory that denies to Paul the authorship of Ephesians has still to meet the objections to such theories raised by Professor Bacon. See *op. cit.*, pp. 116–17.

[68] See McNeile, *An Introduction to the Study of the New Testament*, p. 176 and Bacon, *An Introduction to the New Testament*, p. 115.

[69] W. J. Conybeare and J. S. Howson in their justly famous classic, *The Life and Epistles of St. Paul* (New York: Charles Scribner's Sons, 1892), pp. 396–98, adopted this suggestion with modifications and explained the later title, Ephesians, as due to the fact that the copy which came into the collection was found in Ephesus. "And this designation of the Epistle would the more readily prevail, from the natural feeling that St. Paul must have written *some* Epistle to so great a Church of his own founding as Ephesus" (p. 397). I know of no

of explaining why no textual evidence of other addressees in manuscripts of this letter has survived remains an obstacle to the circular
letter theory.

Another suggestion, that our letter is "the letter from Laodicea," has
commended itself to some scholars.[70] The real basis for this theory is
in the oldest evidence for the addressee of Ephesians. It is Tertullian's
remark with reference to Marcion that, "I here pass over discussion
about another epistle, which we hold to have been written to the Ephesians, but the heretics to the Laodiceans." A little farther on Tertullian
takes up the matter again, "We have it on the true tradition of the
church, that this epistle was sent to the Ephesians, not to the Laodiceans. Marcion, however, was very desirous of giving it the new
title. . . ."[71] That the letter is more general and lacks the personal
greetings of Colossians or Romans, both of which were also written to
churches which Paul had never visited, provides a serious difficulty for
this theory.[72] Yet it is hard to imagine a reason why Marcion should
alter the title of this letter, and "it is not likely that Marcion drew the
inference from Col. 4:16, which does not speak of an epistle *to,* but
an epistle *from* Laodicea."[73]

Every proposed solution offers its difficulties and none can be accepted without reservations. We are left, therefore, with the following
facts: 1) This letter was known very early in three forms, one without
any locality in the address, one addressed to the Laodiceans, and one,
which was later than the other two, addressed to Ephesus. 2) As we
have it, the letter, devoid of personal and local references, has the appearance of a circular letter which echoes ideas and phrases from Paul's

---

better explanation of the final prevalence of this obviously incorrect title than
this last sentence.

[70] Professor Bacon has adopted this view. See *An Introduction to the New
Testament,* pp. 115–16.

[71] *Against Marcion,* V, 11, 17. Quoted from *Ante-Nicene Christian Library,*
VII, trans. Peter Holmes (Edinburgh: T. & T. Clark, 1868), p. 430. Notice
that Tertullian only knows that the letter was addressed to the Ephesians by
tradition, not by the reading of the text. Cf. Abbott, *Ephesians and Colossians,*
p. ii. The association of the address to Laodicea with the heretics would be
sufficient to cause its rejection by the orthodox church.

[72] The suggestion that what we have is a version of the original letter which
was later edited for general circulation is difficult and has not won much support. See McNeile, *An Introduction to the Study of the New Testament,* p. 177.

[73] Bacon, *An Introduction to the New Testament,* p. 115.

other letters, especially Colossians. 3) Its influence and acceptance as a genuine letter of Paul are early and well attested.

The enigma of Ephesians remains. Certainly it was not addressed to Ephesus. Unless we reject the Pauline authorship, the letter was certainly written at the same time and place as Colossians, which as we have seen was probably Ephesus (cf. Ephesians 6:20–22 with Colossians 4:7–10). Thus, the tradition that associated this letter in some way with Ephesus may have arisen because the amanuensis' copy was used by the collector of Paul's letters. We have seen that at least nine churches in Asia outside of Ephesus were likely founded by Paul's co-workers. That Paul would seek to communicate with the rest of them as he did with Colossae is most probable and that he should do so by means of a general letter carried from one church to another by a messenger such as Tychicus is not unlikely. It seems equally probable that there is some connection between this letter and "the letter from Laodicea" referred to in Colossians 4:16, and that in this connection lies the explanation of Marcion's title for the letter. Further than this we cannot go. Until perhaps some fortunate discovery furnishes us a new key, the question of Ephesians remains unanswered.

The Content The theme of Ephesians is oneness in Christ. The letter falls into two parts: the first celebrating the one new man in Christ (chapters 1–3) and the second describing the practical and ethical consequences of this new existence (chapters 4–6). The first begins by blessing God that by the coming of Christ He has made known to us . . . the mystery of his will" (1:9) which is "to unite all things in him" i.e., Christ (1:10). God has shown His power in raising Christ from the dead and placing him over all earthly authority (1:19–22). The gentile believer who was dead in sins has also been made alive with Christ through faith (2:1–9). Because Christ has also abolished the "law of commandments and ordinances" and "has broken down the dividing wall of hostility,"[74] he has made the Jew and gentile one

---

[74] Because the "dividing wall" apparently refers to the boundary of the Court of the Gentiles at the Temple in Jerusalem, some scholars believe this verse refers to its destruction by Titus in 70 A.D. But the phrase as a symbol of hostility would have more meaning if the wall were still standing. The destruc-

"that he might create in himself one new man in place of the two,"
and reconcile "both to God in one body through the cross" (2:14–16).

Paul was made a minister of this gospel, which had been hidden in
former times and revealed to the holy apostles and prophets, "to preach
to the Gentiles the unsearchable riches of Christ" (3:1–8). This section
reaches its climax with a prayer that the readers may be strengthened
through the Spirit,

and that Christ may dwell in your hearts through faith; that you, being
rooted and grounded in love, may have power to comprehend with all the
saints what is the breadth and length and height and depth, and to know
the love of Christ which surpasses knowledge, that you may be filled with
all the fullness of God (3:17–19).

A benediction closes the section.

Paul opens the "practical" section by begging his readers "to lead a
life worthy of the calling to which you have been called" (4:1). There
follows a series of exhortations to live and work in unity, harmony and
love—to fulfill one's assigned ministry "until we all attain to the unity
of the faith and of the knowledge of the Son of God, to mature manhood, to the measure of the stature of the fullness of Christ" (4:13).
They must "no longer live as the Gentiles do," (4:17) but avoid all
immorality of their former lives; they are to forgive one another "as
God in Christ forgave" them; they are to "be imitators of God, as beloved children" (5:1). Being "children of light" and "wise," they must
avoid the deeds of darkness and foolishness (5:7–18). Thankfulness
and worship in the Spirit is to take the place of drunkenness (5:19–20).
There follows in 5:21–6:9 an essay on obedience: Wives must obey
their husbands and husbands are to love their wives (for marriage is a
symbol of "Christ and the Church"); children must obey their parents
and fathers must "not provoke your children to anger, but bring them
up in the discipline and instruction of the Lord"; slaves must obey
their masters and masters are to treat their slaves with a good will, remembering that they too have a Master in heaven.

In a dramatic analogy of the panoply of a Roman soldier Paul

---

tion of the Temple hardly resulted in a union of Jews and Gentiles! That Christ
is the way to true oneness is Paul's point.

brings the letter to a climax calling on his readers to put "on the whole armor of God, that you may be able to stand against the wiles of the devil" (6:10–17). An exhortation to continual prayer, including a prayer for him, a personal note concerning Tychicus, the bearer of the letter, and a benediction conclude the letter.

To Rome

At the beginning of the collection of Paul's letters in the New Testament stands his great letter to the Romans. It belongs here not only because it is the longest of his letters but also because it is, for its influence on theology, the most important. That it was written from Corinth during Paul's last visit there is beyond question. In his closing personal remarks Paul indicates that he is ready to depart for Jerusalem "with aid for the saints" (15:25). We learn from Acts 20:2–21:17 and II Corinthians 9:1–5 that it was in Corinth that the collection of this "aid" was completed and his journey to Jerusalem begun. In anticipation of his plan to go by way of Rome to Spain Paul writes this letter to the Christians at Rome.

Two problems require our attention before we turn to the purpose and content of Romans. The first concerns the variations in the text and the second has to do with the relation of the final chapter to the rest of the letter. Although it is an exceedingly complicated question, the first of these problems does not seriously affect our understanding of Romans and therefore need occupy us only briefly.

A Textual Problem   There is good evidence from
                             patristic writings that in the
second century a version of Romans existed which lacked chapters 15 and 16.[75] Although no extant manuscripts contain this shorter form of Romans, some of them do place the doxology usually found in 16:25–27 at the end of chapter 14 and one places it at the end of chapter 15. A few others either omit the doxology altogether or contain it both

[75] Sanday and Headlam, *Romans,* pp. lxxxv–xcviii, provide a good study of this problem. It was written, however, before the discovery of the important Chester Beatty papyrus. For a good, concise statement of the matter taking this discovery into account see Enslin, *Christian Beginnings,* pp. 264–68 and McNeile, *An Introduction to the New Testament,* pp. 154–58.

at the end of chapters 14 and 16. Two manuscripts also show that an edition of the letter existed without the words "in Rome" in 1:7, 15.

These facts have given rise to a number of conjectures. Assuming that the shorter form of the letter also lacked the words "in Rome," some scholars have suggested that Paul wrote a circular letter which he later enlarged to send to Rome. Others believe either that the Church edited Romans for general use or that Marcion shortened it.[76] No good reasons have been offered, however, for Marcion's objection to these chapters. That the ending of the shorter form breaks into a paragraph and interrupts a unit of thought makes it doubtful that the shorter version was original or intentional.[77] Probably the shorter form was the result of pages being lost from the end of a manuscript. The wear and tear on ancient manuscripts may account for the existence of more than one New Testament problem.

Many scholars suspect that the doxology in 16:25–27 is not a part of the original letter. According to the list of Paul's letters in the Muratorian fragment Romans once stood at the end of the collection.[78] The doxology may have been added as a suitable conclusion for the Pauline collection, which would explain its appearance in the three different places where one or another form of this letter ended. The deletion of the words "in Rome" remains a mystery. That it is the result of editing the letter for general use, though not without difficulties, perhaps is as good an answer as any.

A Letter to Ephesus? That the oldest manuscript of this letter, the Chester Beatty papyrus, places the doxology (16:25–27) at the end of Romans 15 indicates that some early manuscripts did not contain chapter 16. The evidence within the chapter itself that it does not belong to Romans is virtually conclusive. That Phoebe would be moving from

[76] See Lake, *The Earlier Epistles of St. Paul,* pp. 350–61. This entire chapter (VI) provides an authoritative study of the textual problems of Romans.

[77] That there is any connection between the shorter form and the omission of the words "in Rome" in 1:7, 15 is conjectural. Theories of a circular letter built on such a connection are therefore precarious.

[78] The list, which counted the Corinthians and Thessalonians as one letter each in order to reduce the number to seven, also separated Philemon, I Timothy, II Timothy, and Titus from the rest of Paul's letters because they were regarded as personal rather than church letters.

Cenchreae, the eastern port of Corinth, to Rome, while not impossible, is unlikely. The warning against deceivers and trouble makers in verses 17–20 not only goes against the whole tone of Romans, but raises the question of how Paul learned of this danger in Rome. Far more serious, however, is the difficulty of explaining the long list of greetings in verses 3–15 addressed to a distant church which Paul had never visited. More than twenty-eight persons (twenty-six by name) are specifically mentioned in these greetings.

All of these characteristics would be most natural in a letter addressed to Ephesus, which was a short sail across the Aegean Sea from Cenchreae. Several things in this chapter, in fact, definitely point to Ephesus. The last we knew of Prisca and Aquila they were in Ephesus and were hosts to a church there (cf. I Corinthians 16:19 with Romans 16:5, Acts 18:18, 26). To be sure, Romans was probably written after the death of Claudius, whose edict expelling the Jews from Rome would no longer be in force. Prisca and Aquila may therefore have returned to Rome, but this is unlikely. Epaenetus is mentioned as "the first convert in Asia for Christ" (verse 5); Andronicus and Junias are called "kinsmen" and "fellow prisoners" (verse 7). These greetings are not addressed to casual acquaintances but to people with whom Paul had lived and worked. To suppose that all of these had so recently migrated to Rome is to multiply coincidences beyond belief.

The warning in verses 17–20, so difficult to understand if addressed to Rome, suits very well the kind of problems Paul's churches in Asia Minor encountered. We must conclude, therefore, that 16:1–23 is a brief letter of introduction for Phoebe the deaconess who is moving from Cenchreae to Ephesus.

That this letter became attached to Romans indicates that they were probably both written from Corinth at the same time and were placed in circulation together from the amanuensis' copy.[79] The process of

---

[79] This question and the fact that greeting persons by name was apparently unusual for Paul (only one other instance occurs in his extant letters; cf. Colossians 4:15) has caused Professor Knox to doubt that this note is genuine. See "Romans," *Interpreter's Bible*, IX, 366–68. His arguments seem to me to be hypercritical. The difference in the purpose of this letter is sufficient to explain the greetings. Its preservation would be guaranteed both by the warning in verses 17–20 and the veneration which was later accorded companions of Paul, so many of whom are named here. The letter is typical of its kind. See

forming the Pauline collection was probably not as simple as it is sometimes pictured and it likely advanced in stages with one or two letters
at a time enjoying a limited circulation before they were all brought
together in one corpus. That some time in this process these two letters
were joined should not surprise us when we remember that the Corinthian letters were joined into one, as were the letters to the Thessalonians, in order to bring the collection to the appropriate number
of seven. Probably because the opening and closing of some of them
had been lost, the Corinthian letters were never restored to their full
number. The same is undoubtedly true of Romans and this note of
introduction.

The Content   From both the introductory
                                       and concluding paragraphs
we learn the purpose of this letter. In 1:8–15 Paul explains his desire
to visit the Romans. It is to impart to them "some spiritual gift to
strengthen" them (verse 11) "in order that I may reap some harvest
among you as well as among the rest of the Gentiles" (verse 13). That
he does not address the Romans as a church has suggested to some
scholars that there was no organized church in Rome and that Paul
hoped to organize the loose fellowship into a church.[80] But the inference is weakened by the fact that Ephesians, Colossians, and Philippians similarly omit the word "church" in the address.

In the closing paragraphs Paul returns to the reasons for his interest
in Rome. "I hope," he writes, "to see you in passing as I go to Spain,
and to be sped on my journey there by you, once I have enjoyed your
company for a little" (15:24). A little farther on he repeats the hope
more positively: "I shall go on by way of you to Spain" (verse 28).
His purpose is clear: he is enlisting the support and endorsement of the
Roman Christians for his proposed Spanish mission (cf. 10:14–17).[81]
The Spanish mission is itself a step toward a still larger goal. The
winning of the gentiles will finally result in the saving of the Jews as
well: "Now I am speaking to you Gentiles. Inasmuch then as I am an

---

Deissmann, *Light from the Ancient East,* pp. 197, 234–36, and notes. Cf.
Goodspeed, *An Introduction to the New Testament,* pp. 85–87. Letters of introduction were not unheard of among Paul's churches. See II Cor. 3:1–3.
    [80] Sanday and Headlam, *Romans,* xxviii.
    [81] Cf. Weinel, *St. Paul, The Man and his Work,* p. 287.

apostle to the Gentiles, I magnify my ministry in order to make my fellow Jews jealous, and thus save some of them" (Romans 11:13–14).

Yet there is a deeper motive for the letter. He is also concerned for the Romans. As he implies in 1:15 there is still room for further evangelization of Rome. Underneath these concerns is Paul's deep concern for the unity of the Church. He is not simply unburdening himself to these comparative strangers when he writes of the indebtedness of the gentiles to the Jews (15:27) and asks them to join with him in prayer for the success of his "service for Jerusalem." The Roman Christians are involved in the outcome. The apostle to the gentiles must include the gentiles of Rome in bringing "about obedience to the faith . . . among all the Gentiles" (1:5–6; cf. 15:15–16). The waiting community of the people of the Kingdom of God are and must be "one body in Christ" (12:4–5).

From such phrases as, "among you as well as among the rest of the Gentiles" (1:13; cf. 1:5–6) and in the fact that throughout his discussion of the place of the Israelites in God's program of redemption he refers to them in the third person we may conclude that the Roman Christians were mostly gentile. That some Jews were included among them, however, is evident in Paul's words, "Do you not know, brethren —for I am speaking to those who know the law . . ." (7:1). Romans has often been compared with Galatians as a calmer, more carefully reasoned statement of the same argument. There are similarities but the differences are also impressive. In Romans there is no defense of Paul's apostleship such as that which occupies a third of Galatians. Not only is Romans a more dispassionate statement of his thought, but the question of the Law and of circumcision is different. The question in Romans is not that of circumcising the gentiles to bring them under the Law, but of the futility on the part of the Jew of trusting in circumcision and the Law. The body of the letter sets forth the nature of Paul's gospel and the reasons for the urgency of proclaiming it throughout the gentile world.[82]

In 1:16–17 Paul states the thesis of the letter: The gospel "is the

---

[82] We should note that the section on the relation of the gentile mission to the salvation of Israel (chaps. 9–11) is not a parenthesis but a conclusion to his argument in the preceding chapters.

power of God for salvation to every one who has faith, to the Jew first and also to the Greek. For in it the righteousness of God is revealed through faith for faith; as it is written, 'He who through faith is righteous shall live.' " In developing this thesis he begins with the gentiles, who "though they know God's decrees" (1:32; cf. 1:19–21; 2:14–15) have not obeyed them. In a long "bill of particulars" Paul lists the grossest sort of sins as evidence (1:24–32). The Jew, likewise, although he has been circumcised and possesses the Law, has disobeyed. A series of sharp rhetorical questions emphasize the nature and extent of this disobedience. From these observations Paul draws his conclusion: "For there is no distinction; since all have sinned and fall short of the glory of God" (3:22–23; cf. 2:12). "All men," therefore, "both Jews and Greeks, are under the power of sin" (3:9).

True righteousness comes, as it did to Abraham, by faith (chapter 4). Those who "share the faith of Abraham," though gentiles, are his true descendants and heirs of God's promise made to him. This righteousness has been made available by the death of Christ to those who by faith are identified with him. Paul uses a number of terms and figures here: The believer is "justified by his blood" (5:9); he is "reconciled to God by the death of his Son" (verse 10); "As by one man's [Adam's] disobedience many were made sinners, so by one man's [Christ's] obedience many will be made righteous" (verse 19). But this grace of God is not a license to sin, for in baptism the believer has participated in the death of Christ and has been raised to "walk in newness of life" (6:4). He is no longer a slave of sin but of God (6:20–23); sin must not—and need not—be allowed to rule him because through the Spirit he is possessed of a new moral power. The Law exists therefore not as way to righteousness, and therefore a way to receive the promise; it was given to show the true state of affairs within man (chapter 7). Throughout our mortal existence the Law reveals the sin that dwells within us and God's judgment upon that sin.

By faith, then, the believer is free from condemnation. "For the law of the Spirit of life in Christ Jesus has set me free from the law of sin and death" (8:2). As "heirs of God and fellow heirs with Christ" (8:17) the believers await their fulfillment in the coming glory when all creation shall be redeemed "from its bondage to decay" (8:21). They are therefore "more than conquerors":

For I am sure that neither death, nor life, nor angels, nor principalities, nor things present, nor things to come, nor powers, nor height, nor depth, nor anything else in all creation, will be able to separate us from the love of God in Christ Jesus our Lord (8:38–39).

There follows in chapters 9–11 an involved discussion of the place of Israel in the new denouement of God's program. In an amazing spirit of self-offering Paul reveals the depth of his concern for his people: "For I could wish that I myself were accursed and cut off from Christ for the sake of my brethren, my kinsmen by race" (9:3). Yet Paul's hope for Israel runs high. Their transgression has set them aside for the time being, but "through their transgression salvation has come to the Gentiles, so as to make Israel jealous" (11:11); "a hardening has come upon part of Israel, until the full number of the Gentiles come in, and so all Israel will be saved" (11:25).

The conclusion of this long exposition of what Paul means by the gospel is: "God has consigned all men to disobedience, that he may have mercy upon all" (11:32). Paul closes this section with one of his most inspiring doxologies and turns to the ethical consequences of his gospel.

In a number of places the ethical exhortations of chapters 12–15 echo the Sermon on the Mount. Certainly this is one of Paul's finest passages on the practical issues of Christianity. The believer is to offer himself as a living sacrifice unto God (12:1). Each member is faithfully to fulfill his own function in the life of the church. He is to "let love be genuine" (12:9) and bless his enemies. The Christian must be "subject to the governing authorities" (13:1) and pay his taxes while he awaits the salvation of the new age. Members of the church are to be tolerant and considerate, respecting the scruples and opinions of others. "We who are strong ought to bear with the failings of the weak, and not to please ourselves" (15:1). With a brief benediction Paul turns again to his plans to visit Rome on his way to Spain. Finally, the benediction: "The God of peace be with you all. Amen." So ends the greatest and most influential letter ever written.

Paul and the Pastoral Epistles

There remain in the Pauline collection three letters which were addressed not to churches but to two of Paul's assistants, Timothy and Titus. Because they were written to church leaders and deal with matters concerning the administration of churches, they have since the eighteenth century been called Pastoral Epistles. The difficulty is that there are strong reasons for suspecting that these letters, at least as we now have them, were not from the hand of Paul. Scholarly opinion is, in fact, almost unanimous in regarding these Epistles as the product of a later period.[83] Without entering too deeply into the technical problems involved we may summarize the reasons for this opinion in the following four arguments:[84]

1) The vocabulary and style of these letters differ too greatly from the rest of Paul's letters to be explained by differences in subject matter and circumstances. We have already observed that linguistic arguments are risky and not always convincing, but in this instance the evidence is so strong as to be virtually decisive. The difference in vocabulary between the Pastoral Epistles on the one hand and the ten letters of Paul on the other hand is approximately twice as great as the greatest difference among the ten letters.[85] Among the differences in vocabulary, furthermore, are particles, prepositions and the like which are tell-tales of a writer's style. In contrast to the ten letters of Paul many of the words peculiar to the Pastorals in the New Testament are found in later writings such as those of the Apostolic Fathers. The language of the Pastorals, in other words, is that of the second century.

2) Several important words which the Pastorals have in common with the letters of Paul are used in a strikingly different sense. The word faith, for example, which Paul uses in a dynamic sense is used in the Pastorals as a substantive referring to a body of doctrine. As the word is used here it is much closer to what Paul calls tradition.

[83] But see Lock, *The Pastoral Epistles, The International Critical Commentary,* pp. xxix–xxxi and note.

[84] For a thorough and detailed study of this problem see P. N. Harrison, *The Problem of the Pastoral Epistles* (Oxford University Press, Humphrey Milford, 1921).

[85] How imposing this difference is can be seen in the text of the Pastorals reprinted in Harrison, Appendix IV, following p. 184, in which the words not found in the other letters of Paul are printed in red.

3) It is impossible to fit the references to Paul's life and movements in the Pastorals into his circumstances known to us from Acts and his own letters. The difficulty cannot be removed by any theory of his release from prison in Rome and return to the Aegean area because Acts makes it clear that when he left for Jerusalem with the collection for the church there he was leaving that part of the world for the last time (Acts 20:25, 38); and because some of the personal notes, if they belong in the same letter as they stand, contradict one another (cf. II Timothy 4:11 with 21). If these Epistles came from the close of Paul's life, it is difficult to understand how, after Timothy had been with Paul from the time of his Galatian mission, Paul could still write, "Let no one despise your youth" (I Timothy 4:12; cf. 5:1–2; II Timothy 2:22).

4) The organization and life of the Church reflected in the pastorals are more static and highly developed than was true in Paul's day. This argument is probably the weakest of the four. It is easy to underestimate the organization Paul gave his churches. Bishops and deacons are mentioned in Philippians 1:1 and the numerous references to the various offices in the life of his churches point to a definite structure. The difference is real, nevertheless, and along with the change in emphasis on eschatology, as well as the strong polemic against heresies unlike anything we find in Paul's other letters, adds support to the other arguments against Paul's authorship of these Epistles.

There are several passages, however, which manifest the vocabulary and style characteristic of Paul's writing. Because of this fact several scholars are convinced that there are a number of fragments of Paul's letters embedded in these Epistles. Some of these passages are echoes of passages in the other letters, but some of them are new material yet so characteristically Pauline that they must represent fragments of his letters which are otherwise lost. These latter passages appear to be fragments of personal notes written at different times and under different circumstances by Paul to Titus and Timothy which provided the basis of our present Pastoral Epistles.[86]

[86] This hypothesis is fully discussed and the fragments are analyzed in Harrison, *The Problem of the Pastoral Epistles*, Part III, 87–135. The location of these fragments in the life of Paul has been attempted with interesting results

If this assumption is correct the discrepancy which we observed between II Timothy 4:11 and 21 is caused by bringing together fragments from different letters. Also, the present form of the Epistles being addressed to Timothy and Titus is explained. As they now stand the Pastorals are literary Epistles rather than letters. Two themes dominate these documents: The responsibility of church leaders to guard against heresies and moral laxity and proper qualifications for church officers. In more modern terms they might be called pastoral handbooks.

This conclusion does not reflect on the value or authority of the Pastoral Epistles as a part of the canon of the New Testament. On the contrary, that they come from a period later than Paul makes them especially valuable for a knowledge of the life and history of the Church in the later period of New Testament times. Their relation to Paul and his successors and their orthodoxy fully assured their place in the canon. We are concerned with the problem only as it relates to the study of Paul. Literary conventions in ancient times were far different from ours.[87] There were no prefaces, footnotes, quotation marks, and the like to indicate the literary structure or sources of such documents. Perhaps it would not be too far-fetched, in the analogy of modern practice, to describe the pastorals as posthumous editions expanded and revised with an anthology of quotations from the author's other works and published to bring the Apostle's teaching and authority to bear upon the critical problems of a later time.

In modern practice these documents would bear two names—that of Paul and the unknown editor-author who published them in their present form. As it is, the editor-author, having accomplished his purpose, was content to be lost in anonymity, leaving to Paul the full credit not only for the personal notes which would otherwise have been lost but also for the ideas, which surely belonged to him throughout the documents.

---

in Duncan, *St. Paul's Ephesian Ministry*, pp. 184–225, and with different conclusions, in Bacon, *The Story of St. Paul,* pp. 198, 221–22, 375–79, *passim.* For opposite opinion see Moffatt, *An Introduction to the Literature of the New Testament,* pp. 414–15 and Enslin, *Christian Beginnings,* pp. 306–307.

[87] For good discussions of this question see F. C. Baur, *Paul the Apostle of Jesus Christ,* trans. from 2nd ed. by Edward Zeller, rev. by Alan Menzies (London: Williams and Norgate, 1876), p. 110 and Harrison, *The Problem of the Pastoral Epistles,* pp. 8–13.

Thus we conclude our survey of the collection of Paul's correspondence. As ancient collections of letters go, it is not large; yet no correspondence, ancient or modern, has shown such greatness or exerted such influence. One reason for that influence—probably the chief reason—is that Paul's letters are the oldest and greatest interpretations of Jesus.

9 we do impart wisdom...

Yet among the mature we do impart wisdom, although
it is not a wisdom of this age or of the
rulers of this age, who are doomed to pass
away. But we impart a secret and hidden wisdom of
God, which God decreed before the ages
for our glorification. (I Corinthians 2:6–7)

Although Paul was not a systematic theologian and wrote nothing that can be classified as systematic theology, in the subsequent history of the Church no one else has exerted so great an influence on the development of that discipline. This influence of his letters is one of the reasons for their importance. Scattered throughout his correspondence are found the foundation stones upon which the great doctrinal systems of Christianity have been built. The primary purpose of our study has been to approach a better understanding of them by placing Paul's letters in their proper setting in his life and background. Yet the understanding of Paul requires of us one more step: We must attempt to assemble his ideas in an orderly arrangement in order to see them in perspective.

Such an undertaking is not without its dangers. We need, therefore, to keep several facts in mind: 1) Paul is writing to specific people in specific situations, and what he says is to be understood, insofar as we are capable of doing so, as he expected those people to understand it. Failure to interpret Paul in this way can easily lead to the discovery of inconsistencies and incongruities which may not actually exist. The basic pattern of Paul's thinking, which we may call his theology, is to

296

be discovered in his incidental instruction of the churches on issues that confronted them at the time.

2) Paul's thinking does not stand complete in his letters. Again and again he refers to the instruction that he had given his churches in person. (Cf. I Thessalonians 2:1–13; 3:4; 4:1–12; II Thessalonians 2:5–6, 15; I Corinthians 2:1–6; 4:16–17; 11:2, 23; 15:1–3, and others.) Although he is in both Ephesians (4:20–21) and Colossians (1:7; 2:7) writing to churches with which he has not had personal contact, Paul assumes that his readers have been taught the traditions of Jesus. We can only surmise what was included in these traditions (cf. Romans 15:15). What he writes, therefore, presupposes and intends to supplement and reinforce teaching that is lost to us.[1] If we could know, for example, what lies back of Paul's words in II Thessalonians 2:6, "and you know what is restraining him now . . .," one of the most familiar of the insoluble problems in the letters would disappear.

3) In assembling statements from various places in Paul's letters into a topical system there is a danger that not only the *ad hoc* nature of the statements will be forgotten, but that the new, artificial context of the "system" will replace the genuine context of the disparate materials and impose a meaning upon Paul's words quite foreign to his intention. The fresh vividness of Paul's insights can easily be lost when his words are stretched on the Procrustean bed of a system. When his thoughts are understood in their context, however, they do display an underlying unity that in each instance carries us back to the meaning and significance of Paul's experience on the Damascus Road.

In this chapter we cannot attempt to construct a theology of Paul. Such an undertaking would require a book in itself.[2] We shall rather

[1] Cf. Weinel, *St. Paul*, p. 187.

[2] The literature on this subject is vast and any list of suggested readings must represent an arbitrary selection. The following books will at least introduce the reader to the subject: C. H. Dodd, *The Meaning of Paul for Today*, Living Age Books (New York: Meridian Books, 1957); Archibald M. Hunter, *Interpreting Paul's Gospel* (Philadelphia: The Westminster Press, 1954); Harris Franklin Rall, *According to Paul* (New York: Charles Scribner's Sons, 1945); William Baird, *Paul's Message and Mission* (New York: Abingdon Press, 1960); C. A. Anderson Scott, *St. Paul the Man and Teacher* (London: Cambridge University Press, 1936). More technical treatments of Paul's thought will be found in: John A. T. Robinson, *The Body*, Studies in Biblical Theology

survey some of the main themes of his teaching as they display themselves in his letters. By this means we may be able to gain a clearer conception of his "gospel" and of the "tradition," "instructions," "commands," and "exhortations" by which Paul sought to edify his churches.

In a sense Paul's words to the Corinthians, "I decided to know nothing among you except Jesus Christ and him crucified" (I Corinthians 2:2) are true of all of his preaching and teaching; for Christ made the difference between Saul the Pharisee and Paul the Apostle of Jesus Christ. Beyond the traditional beliefs of Judaism which for Paul are still valid, Paul's theology is Christological—it is an exposition of the meaning of Christ for the faith and destiny of the believer (II Corinthians 4:5). To study Paul's thought is to study his teaching concerning Christ Jesus.[3]

Because of his experience on the Damascus Road Paul's view of Jesus always began with the resurrection. From that perspective Paul looked in both directions: backward to Jesus' passion and earthly life; and forward to his vivid consciousness of Christ's living presence; and finally to the future "revealing of our Lord Jesus Christ" (I Corinthians 1:7) at the end of the present evil age. Our survey of Paul's teaching, therefore, will follow the order of these three views of Jesus.

In its backward look Paul's view of Jesus is essentially the same as that of the Gospels: It is dominated by the passion and resurrection. In their interest in the crucifixion and resurrection his letters, in contrast to the Gospels, give the impression of an almost complete neglect of the earthly ministry of Jesus. In spite of this impression the foundation of Paul's teaching is his backward look to the earthly ministry of Jesus. The occasional nature of his letters, as we shall see, has obscured from us the extent of his interest in the life and teachings of Jesus.

No. 5 (Naperville, Ill.: Alec R. Allenson, Inc., 1957); C. A. Anderson Scott, *Christianity According to St. Paul* (London: Cambridge University Press, 1927); W. D. Davies, *Paul and Rabbinic Judasim* (London: S. P. C. K., 1958). Albert Schweitzer, *The Mysticism of Paul the Apostle*, trans. William Montgomery (New York: The Macmillan Company, 1960). Older but still important are: Weiss, *Earliest Christianity*, II, chaps. XIV–XXI; Alfred E. Garvie, *Studies of Paul and his Gospel* (London: Hodder and Stoughton, 1911). Besides such studies as these, there are numerous books and articles on special aspects of Paul's thought.

[3] Cf. F. C. Porter, *The Mind of Christ in Paul* (New York: Charles Scribner's Sons, 1930).

"Christ from a Human Point of View"

In I Corinthians 11:23 and again in 15:3 Paul refers his readers to traditions he had delivered to them which he had also received. The first of these concerns the Last Supper and the second is a resume of Jesus' passion and resurrection. Clearly these traditions are a part of the body of tradition which Paul had in common with the rest of the Church and which as a part of his work in founding churches he patiently taught to his new converts. Such passages as these show that Paul's neglect of the earthly life of Jesus, so commonly assumed, can be easily exaggerated.

That Paul's comparative silence concerning the earthly Jesus was deliberate is sometimes inferred from his statement: "Even though we once regarded Christ from a human point of view, we regard him thus no longer" (II Corinthians 5:16). This passage has provoked a number of questions which are not easy to answer, but at least this much is clear: Paul is comparing relationships. There was a time when the believer's relationship with Jesus was "from the human point of view," but with the passion and resurrection that earthly relationship came to an end. Since by being "in Christ" the believer had become "a new creation" the relationship among believers is also no longer "from the human point of view," but has changed in the same way as has their relationship with Christ. Yet the new relationship does not ignore the former one. The believer's new relationship with Christ and consequently with his fellow believers exists precisely because Christ once came "in the likeness of sinful flesh" (Romans 8:3) and made it possible.

If the new relationship of the believers "in Christ" is founded on the "Event" of the earthly Jesus, it follows that Paul's apparent neglect of Jesus' earthly career cannot be the substitution of a mystical "Christ of faith" for the "Jesus of history" who no longer had any meaning for him. A simpler explanation is to be found in the nature of the letters. Paul takes for granted his readers' knowledge of the tradition of Jesus and refers to that tradition only where it serves to make his point.[4]

If this explanation is correct, it is evident that in order to under-

_____
[4] Professor Hunter offers a similar explanation followed by a brief but im-

stand Paul we must endeavor insofar as possible to discover what the tradition was which Paul imparted to his churches and which lies in the immediate background of his letters. A careful examination of the letters will show that the task is not as forbidding as it might seem.

"Born in the Likeness of Men"   In nearly a dozen passages Paul refers to the advent and lineage of Jesus. In several of these passages Paul refers to the pre-existence of Jesus as a matter that is apparently familiar to his readers. Although the pattern of thought in these passages is strikingly similar to such well-known passages as John 1:1–3 and Hebrews 1:2–3, Paul is not promulgating a doctrine but in each instance is seeking to solve a problem or to present some practical exhortations.

In order to exhort the Philippians to "do nothing from selfishness or conceit, but in humility count others better than yourselves" (2:3) Paul introduces the longest and most important of these passages, Philippians 2:5–11.[5] "Christ Jesus, who, though he was in the form of God . . . emptied himself, taking the form of a servant, being born in the likeness of men," and "became obedient unto death," (2:5–8) is the supreme example of humility. In II Corinthians 8:9 "the grace of our Lord Jesus Christ, that though he was rich, yet for your sake he became poor, so that by his poverty you might become rich" becomes the example of generosity which the Corinthians should follow in making their contributions to the collection for the Jerusalem Church. Here again is the same picture of the pre-existent Christ laying aside his heavenly glory and position to assume the humility of his earthly life for the redemption of mankind.

Two passages carry the thought further to include Christ's role in the creation and support of the cosmos. The first of these is introduced in Paul's discussion of the question of eating food offered to idols. It represents the Christian's "knowledge" that "although there may be

---

pressive summary of Paul's information concerning the earthly Jesus, *Interpreting Paul's Gospel*, pp. 56–58. See also Deissmann, *Paul*, pp. 195–97 and notes.

[5] In the nineteenth century this passage gave rise to an important theory of the Incarnation known as kenosis, from the verb (*ekenosen*) translated "emptied." For an excellent exposition of the passage see Grant, *An Introduction to New Testament Thought*, pp. 232–36.

so-called gods . . . yet for us there is one God, the Father, from whom are all things and for whom we exist, and one Lord, Jesus Christ, through whom are all things and through whom we exist" (I Corinthians 8:5–6). The parallelism of the attributive clauses is striking and reminds us of the words in John 1:3: "all things were made through him" and in Hebrews 1:2: "through whom also he created the world." The statement represents the "knowledge" of the men "of knowledge" in Corinth for whom eating food offered to idols presented no problem; therefore, Paul is merely quoting a teaching already familiar to the Corinthians. The point of his argument is that "not all possess this knowledge" (8:7); in exercising their freedom, the strong are consequently under obligation to consider the faith of the weak.

The second of these passages, the Christological hymn in Colossians 1:15–20, was written to demonstrate the exclusive claims of Christ as opposed to the syncretistic "philosophy" to which Colossians were prone in order that they might "continue in the faith, stable and steadfast, not shifting from the hope of the gospel which you heard" (1:23). Two statements in this passage express the idea of Christ's pre-existence and role in creation: "He is the image of the invisible God (cf. Hebrews 1:3), the firstborn of all creation; for in him all things were created . . . all things were created through him and for him," and "He is before all things, and in him all things hold together" (1:15–17). Two further passages, when read in the light of the passages we have observed, also imply the descent of Christ from a heavenly pre-existence: "But when the time had fully come, God sent forth his Son, born of woman, born under the law, to redeem those who were under the law, so that we might receive adoption as sons" (Galatians 4:4–5); and "sending his own Son in the likeness of sinful flesh and for sin, he condemned sin in the flesh" (Romans 8:3).

Thus we can see that Paul's teaching on the nativity of Jesus presents as high a Christology as can be found anywhere in the New Testament. Although it goes farther, Paul's thought is akin to the rabbinic notion that among the seven things that existed before the creation of the world was the name of the Messiah.[6] When we remember that the "name" in ancient times was supposed in some way to participate in

---

[6] The notion probably came from apocalyptic thought. See I *Enoch*, XLVIII, 2–3.

the reality of that for which it stood (hence the Jewish refusal to pronounce the sacred name of God), we can see that in his doctrine of
Christ's pre-existence Paul was not departing so far from Judaism as
it might seem.[7] The Torah, however, was also one of the seven things
before creation, and it may be that here as elsewhere Paul is deliberately setting Christ in the place of the Torah.[8] Certainly Paul would
not agree that the Torah antedated creation, for in Galatians 3:17 he
emphatically states that it came four hundred and thirty years after
Abraham. Paul saw in Jesus the revelation of the great mystery of
God's plan for the redemption of mankind—a mystery which had been
kept hidden in the secret councils of God (Ephesians 3:9–11) until
"the time had fully come." Christ is the "wisdom of God, which God
decreed before the ages for our glorification" (I Corinthians 2:7).

In his references to the advent Paul did not neglect the humanity
of Jesus. Although "he is before all things" (Colossians 1:17), he was
nevertheless "born of woman, born under the law" (Galatians 4:4).
Reminiscent of the genealogies of Matthew 1:1–16 and Luke 3:23–38
is Paul's statement: "who was descended from David according to the
flesh" (Romans 1:3). Jesus came "in the likeness of sinful flesh" (Romans 8:3). One of the distinctions of the Israelites is that "of their
race, according to the flesh, is the Christ," (Romans 9:5) who "became a servant to the circumcised to show God's truthfulness, in order
to confirm the promises given to the patriarchs" (Romans 15:8). This
last quotation and the labored exegesis in Galatians 3:16–19, whereby
Paul attempts to show that the word offspring in God's promise to
Abraham actually refers to Christ, associate the coming of Jesus with
Old Testament prophecy in a way that reminds us of Matthew's emphasis on Jesus' fulfillment of "what the Lord had spoken by the
prophet" (cf. Matthew 1:22; 2:5, 15, 17, 23). In these incidental
references Paul discloses that he is no less familiar than other New
Testament writers with the traditions concerning the origin of Jesus
both according to the flesh and as the Son of God.

[7] On the significance of the name see Silva New, "The Name, Baptism, and
the Laying on of Hands," Foakes Jackson and Lake, *The Beginnings of Christianity*, V, 121–40.
[8] "The Conversion According to Paul" in chap. 6. Cf. Davies, *Paul and
Rabbinic Judaism*, pp. 147–76.

"One Man's Obedience"   If we look in Paul's letters
                                   for what we may call "sto-
ries of Jesus" we find that, except for a few events associated with
the passion, there are none. Yet Paul frequently points to Jesus as the
example for Christian living in a way that presumes his readers' knowledge of the life of Jesus. Professor Deissmann has observed, "The
earthly life of Jesus, then, was appreciated by Paul, at least in the
letters that have come down to us, more for its character as a whole,
than for its details."[9] Only in the sense that he does not relate or refer
to specific events in the life of Jesus can we speak of his neglect of the
earthly Jesus. In Paul's letters the moral example of Jesus is brought
before the reader again and again. Although we cannot reconstruct a
"Life of Jesus" from the letters, we can gain a clear picture of his
character.

Beside the crucifixion, burial, and resurrection Paul mentions two
events in Jesus' life. In connection with abuses that had grown up in
Corinth in the observance of the Lord's Supper Paul recalls to the
mind of the Corinthians what he had taught them. There follows in
I Corinthians 11:23-26 the oldest account we have of the Last Supper.
From this we learn that Jesus was betrayed and that on the same night
he had presided at the meal which became the model and antecedent
of the Christian Eucharist (cf. I Corinthians 10:16-17, 21).

In Romans 5:19 Paul contrasts the disobedience of Adam as the beginning of sin with the obedience of Jesus as the source of righteousness. Strictly speaking "obedience" here refers to Jesus' submission to
the cross as the divinely ordained role of the Messiah. Paul uses obedience with the same meaning in the phrase "became obedient unto
death" (Philippians 2:8). It was the earthly Jesus, nevertheless, who
by submitting to the cross obeyed the will of God; and in Romans
15:2-3 Paul points again to that obedience as an example of how we
ought "not to please ourselves. . . . For Christ did not please himself."

The healing ministry of Jesus lies back of the "signs and wonders
and mighty works" by which Paul had manifested to the Corinthians
the "signs of a true apostle" (II Corinthians 12:12). These "signs"
were done in the name of Jesus (cf. Acts 19:11-13) and as Peter in-

[9] *Paul*, p. 195.

dicated in his explanation of the healing of the lame man at the gate of the Temple these "mighty works" were the continuation in his name of the healings of Jesus (Acts 3:11-16; cf. 10:38). The Corinthians were certainly aware that the "signs of a true apostle" were signs because of their relation to Jesus' own mighty works.

Most of Paul's allusions to the life of Jesus appeal to his example for Christian living. The believer is destined "to be conformed to the image of his Son" (Romans 8:29). Paul can speak therefore of putting "on the Lord Jesus Christ" (Romans 13:14), or urge the Corinthians to "be imitators of me" as he reminds them "of my ways in Christ" (I Corinthians 4:16-17). Later in the same letter he repeats the exhortation: "Be imitators of me, as I am of Christ" (I Corinthians 11:1). To the Colossians he wrote: "As therefore you received Christ Jesus the Lord, so live in him . . . just as you were taught" (Colossians 2:6-7). And his highest commendation of the Thessalonian believers was: "And you became imitators of us and of the Lord" (I Thessalonians 1:6). Paul can even speak of fulfilling "the law of Christ" (Galatians 6:2; cf. I Corinthians 9:21).

Paul assumes that his readers know the character of Jesus whom they are to imitate. Yet he incidentally refers to several aspects of Jesus' life in a way that provides a significant profile of Jesus. Although "for our sake" he was "made . . . to be sin," he "knew no sin" (II Corinthians 5:21). Paul appealed for obedience from the troublesome Corinthians "by the meekness and gentleness of Christ" (II Corinthians 10:1). In the great Christological hymn which we have already noted in Philippians 2:5-11 the "human form" of Jesus furnishes Paul with the supreme example of that kind of humility which looks "not only to his own interests, but also to the interests of others." To the Asian Christians who were surrounded by the vicious immorality of the gentiles he wrote "You did not so learn Christ!" (Ephesians 4:20). Clearly "the new nature, created after the likeness of God in true righteousness and holiness" in the next sentence (verse 24) has as its model the Christ whom they had learned. In Ephesians 4:13 the goal of "mature manhood" which Paul sets before his readers is described as "the measure of the stature of the fullness of Christ."

In the final analysis the character of Jesus can be summed up in the one word love. Thus, Paul admonishes his readers to "walk in love, as Christ loved us" (Ephesians 5:2; cf. verses 25). That the "incentive of love" in Philippians 2:1 refers to the life of Jesus is clear from the description of the coming of Christ Jesus that follows. One of Paul's most vivid descriptions of the motivation of his own life consists of the simple words: "For the love of Christ controls us" (II Corinthians 5:14). Because he is an imitator of Christ, that he therefore does not seek his "own advantage" (I Corinthians 10:33). To be "in accord with Christ Jesus" is to live in "harmony with one another" (Romans 15:5). Certainly Christ is the model for Paul's great Hymn to Love in I Corinthians 13.

We should scarcely expect to find in these occasional letters the stories of Jesus which occupy so much of the attention of the writers of the Gospels. But we do find the deep and indelible impression of the character and quality of his life on the pages of every one of Paul's letters. The description of Jesus we have gleaned from those letters is an expansion of the words of the speech recorded of Peter in Acts 10:34–43: "He went about doing good and healing all that were oppressed by the devil, for God was with him."

"Remembering the Words of the Lord Jesus" Far more prominent than the references in Paul's letters to the life and character of Jesus is the influence of Jesus' teaching as recorded in the Synoptic Gospels. The reader who will take the trouble to compare Paul's letters with the Gospels will be amazed to find how extensive are the parallels.[10] That Paul seldom quotes Jesus directly does not indicate that he is unable to do so or that he is unaware of the parallels between his admonitions and the teaching of Jesus. In his letters Paul is not instructing his churches in the teaching of Jesus; he is presupposing the instructions they have already received and admonishing them on that basis.

[10] Many of these parallels are indicated in the cross references in most Bibles but the careful reader will find many others. Several studies of these parallels have been written. Some have undoubtedly gone too far in finding similarities that are quite remote. The data used in this chapter, however, have been taken from materials compiled in my classes. See Appendix 2. Cf. the brief but valuable survey of this matter in Davies, *Paul and Rabbinic Judaism,* pp. 136–46.

Paul introduces the longest and most direct parallel to the Synoptic Gospels, the words of Jesus at the Last Supper, with the reminder that it was what he had "delivered" to them. The command of Jesus in I Corinthians 7:10–11, however, Paul is apparently giving to the Corinthians for the first time. Although his words are a free paraphrase Paul identifies them as a charge from the Lord and clearly refers to the saying recorded in Mark 10:11–12.

In several places Paul quotes the traditions of Jesus without identifying them as such. It is interesting to note that in these instances he parallels the Synoptic Gospels more closely than he does in the charge concerning divorce in which he is expressly citing words of Jesus (cf. I Corinthians 9:14 with Matthew 10:10). It may be worthwhile to compare these traditions with their Synoptic parallels:

Romans 2:6a	*Matthew 16:27b*
For he will render to every man according to his works (cf. Proverbs 24:12).	And then he will repay every man for what he has done.

Romans 2:21a	*Matthew 23:3b*
You then who teach others, will you not teach yourself?	For they preach, but do not practice (cf. Luke 11:46).

Romans 12:14	*Luke 6:28b*
Bless those who persecute you; bless and do not curse them.	Bless those who curse you, pray for those who abuse you.

Romans 14:13a	*Matthew 7:1*
Then let us no more pass judgment on one another (cf. I Corinthians 4:5).	Judge not, that you be not judged (cf. Luke 6:37).

I Corinthians 13:2b	*Matthew 17:20b*
And if I have all faith, so as to remove mountains.	If you have faith as a grain of mustard seed, you will say to this mountain, "Move hence to yonder place," and it will move.

Philippians 2:15c	*Matthew 5:14*
Among whom you shine as lights in the world.	You are the light of the world.

Philippians 4:6a	*Matthew 6:25a*
Have no anxiety about anything.	Do not be anxious about your life (cf. Luke 12:22)

I Thessalonians 5:13b	*Mark 9:50c*
Be at peace among yourselves (cf. Romans 12:18 and 14:19).	And be at peace with one another.

Romans 13:9b	*Matthew 22:39*
You shall love your neighbor as yourself (cf. Galatians 5:14; I Thessalonians 4:9; Leviticus 19:18).	You shall love your neighbor as yourself (Mark 12:31 and Luke 10:27).

That the first and last of these parallels are quotations from the Old Testament suggests the possibility that in these instances Paul is not quoting from the tradition and that the parallels are coincidental. The suggestion is very unlikely because the quotations, especially the latter, are too deeply embedded in the tradition and too much a part of Paul's interpretation of Jesus to be mere coincidence. There are in the letters a few quotations from the Old Testament parallel to the Gospel tradition which, however, may have come from a stock of Old Testament passages common to the writers of the New Testament.[11]

In many instances the similarities between his letters and the Gospels are probably the result of "the mind of Christ" in Paul. We must remember that Paul and Jesus shared a background in Judaism with its vast store of ethical teaching, but what Paul took from that background was controlled by his understanding of Jesus. Because of his sense of being in Christ and his profound understanding of him, Paul could write commands and exhortations in the name of the Lord Jesus in

[11] For a good recent study of the collection of the Old Testament passages used by New Testament writers, following to a somewhat different conclusion a course of investigation pursued a number of years ago by Rendel Harris, see C. H. Dodd, *According to the Scriptures*, (New York: Charles Scribner's Sons, 1953).

which, in spite of their similarity to the Gospels, he was not citing any specific saying of Jesus.[12] In I Corinthians 4:10, for example, Paul writes sarcastically, "We are fools for Christ's sake, but you are wise in Christ. We are weak, but you are strong. You are held in honor, but we in disrepute," which recalls the words of Jesus in Matthew 10:24, "A disciple is not above his teacher, nor a servant above his master." (Cf. II Corinthians 8:9 with Matthew 8:20; II Corinthians 10:12 with Matthew 7:1; II Corinthians 11:13-15 with Matthew 24:5, 23-26; Galatians 5:17 with Matthew 7:24 ff.; Ephesians 4:25 with Matthew 5:37.)

The parallels between Paul's letters and the Gospels are for the most part, however, too numerous and too close to be accounted for by coincidences of thought. The range of topics covered is also impressive. In the majority of these parallels Paul makes no attempt to quote or paraphrase the words of Jesus but seems to assume that the readers know them. What Paul writes in these passages is in the nature of *midrashim* or commentaries on the tradition. Indeed, much that is in Paul's letters furnishes a good example of apostolic interpretations of the teaching of Jesus. It will be worthwhile for us to observe a few of these passages:

Not every one who says to me, "Lord, Lord," shall enter the kingdom of heaven, but he who does the will of my Father who is in heaven (Matthew 7:21).

For it is not the hearers of the law who are righteous before God, but the doers of the law who will be justified. When Gentiles who have not the law do by nature what the law requires, they are a law to themselves, even though they do not have the law. . . . While their conscience also bears witness and their conflicting thoughts accuse or perhaps excuse them on that day when, according to my gospel, God judges the secrets of men by Christ Jesus (Romans 2:13-16).

No one can serve two masters; for either he will hate the one and love the other, or he will be devoted to the one and despise the other. You cannot serve God and mammon (Matthew 6:24).

[12] Cf. Enslin, *The Ethics of Paul*, pp. 112-16.

Do you not know that if you yield yourselves to any one as obedient slaves, you are slaves of the one whom you obey, either of sin, which leads to death, or of obedience, which leads to righteousness? But thanks be to God, that you who were once slaves of sin have become obedient from the heart to the standard of teaching to which you were committed, and, having been set free from sin, have become slaves of righteousness (Romans 6:16–18).

Render therefore to Caesar the things that are Caesar's, and to God the things that are God's (Matthew 22:21).

Let every person be subject to the governing authorities. For there is no authority except from God, and those that exist have been instituted by God. Therefore he who resists the authorities resists what God has appointed, and those who resist will incur judgment. Therefore one must be subject, not only to avoid God's wrath but also for the sake of conscience. For the same reason you also pay taxes, for the authorities are ministers of God, attending to this very thing. Pay all of them their dues, taxes to whom taxes are due, revenue to whom revenue is due, respect to whom respect is due, honor to whom honor is due (Romans 13:1–2, 5–7).

The kingdom of God is as if a man should scatter seed upon the ground, and should sleep and rise night and day, and the seed should sprout and grow, he knows not how. The earth produces of itself, first the blade, then the ear, then the full grain in the ear. But when the grain is ripe, at once he puts in the sickle, because the harvest has come (Mark 4:26–29).

You foolish man! What you sow does not come to life unless it dies. And what you sow is not the body which is to be, but a bare kernel, perhaps of wheat or of some other grain.

.   .   .

So is it with the resurrection of the dead. What is sown is perishable, what is raised is imperishable. It is sown in dishonor, it is raised in glory. It is sown in weakness, it is raised in power. It is sown a physical body, it is raised a spiritual body. If there is a physical body, there is also a spiritual body (I Corinthians 15:36–37, 42–44).

"Jesus Died and Rose Again"   The crucifixion and resurrection are for Paul two parts of one divine act for the salvation of mankind. Although he frequently speaks of the crucifixion without referring to the resurrection it is just as clear that he has the resurrection in mind as it is that he is

including Jesus' death in his references to the resurrection. These references are elliptical expressions for the one great fact in which for Paul the meaning and significance of Jesus are to be found.

That Jesus died by crucifixion is important for Paul's thought. He shows the significance of the mode of Jesus' death in the argument which we have already noted concerning the curse upon "one who hangs on a tree" (Galatians 3:13),[13] and in the emphasis he places upon it in several other passages (Galatians 3:1; I Corinthians 1:17, 18, 23; 2:2, *passim*). Paul can refer to the crucifixion, nevertheless, in a number of ways: He speaks of it as suffering (Romans 8:17; II Corinthians 1:5) and as "Christ's afflictions" (Colossians 1:24). In a number of instances he simply uses the word death or the verb died. Several times he refers to the cross or blood of Christ. In I Corinthians 5:7 he writes, "For Christ, our paschal lamb, has been sacrificed," and in Ephesians 5:2 he describes Christ as the one who "gave himself up for us, a fragrant offering and sacrifice to God." Once he speaks of Jesus as having been killed (I Thessalonians 2:15).

In this last passage, which is reminiscent of the closing sentences of Stephen's speech (Acts 7:52), Paul charges the Jews with the responsibility for the death of Jesus. The ultimate responsibility for crucifying "the Lord of glory," however, he places on "the rulers of this age" (I Corinthians 2:8). Whether "the rulers" are the demonic powers who are in control of the present evil age or are the human rulers, the term refers to the action of Roman authorities. Therefore, although he mentions none of them by name, Paul knows of Judas' betrayal of Jesus (I Corinthians 11:23), his arrest and examination by priests and elders under Caiaphas the high priest (I Thessalonians 2:14–15), and his condemnation by Pilate (I Corinthians 2:8). Three times he alludes to the burial of Jesus (I Corinthians 15:4; Romans 6:4; Colossians 2:12). Jesus was not the unwilling victim of an evil deed. His death was according to the Scriptures (I Corinthians 15:3) and the purpose of God who "gave him up for us all" (Romans 8:32). Jesus was "obedient unto death" (Philippians 2:8) and revealed his love by giving "himself up for us" (Ephesians 5:2; Galatians 1:4).

On the resurrection Paul could speak from first hand. Here he took

---

[13] "The Persecution According to Paul" in chap 6.

his place with the original Apostles: "Have I not seen Jesus our Lord?" (I Corinthians 9:1). We have already examined in some detail Paul's record in I Corinthians 15:4–8 of the appearances of the Risen Lord.[14] Paul's statement that Jesus appeared first to Peter corresponds to the tradition in Mark 16:7 (cf. Luke 24:34). As in Acts, most of the references in Paul's letters describe Jesus' resurrection in the passive voice: God had raised him from the dead. The ascension and exaltation of Jesus to be seated at the right hand of God, which receives considerable emphasis in Luke and Acts, Paul mentions several times (cf. Romans 8:34; Ephesians 1:20; Philippians 2:9; Colossians 3:1 with Luke 22:69; 24:51; Acts 1:9–10; 2:33; 5:31 *passim;* also Mark 14:62; Matthew 26:64).

Although he shares the conviction of Jesus' exaltation, Paul emphasizes the presence of the living Christ in his Church and in the believer. Such was his own experience. Through his experience on the Damascus Road the life of Jesus, which reached its climax in the crucifixion, became for Paul—more than a matter of external history—a fact of his own inner experience. He was no longer a spectator; he was a participant:

For I through the Law died to the law, that I might live to God. I have been crucified with Christ; it is no longer I who live, but Christ who lives in me; and the life I now live in the flesh I live by faith in the Son of God, who loved me and gave himself for me (Galatians 2:19–20).

In this experience the "Jesus of history" and the "Christ of Faith" meet. Yet they are the same person; Paul's relationship has changed. Before the fateful event on the Damascus Road he could despise the earthly Jesus and persecute his followers, but the Risen Christ had taken Paul captive. As a result he is "a slave of Jesus Christ"; and because he is, he can no longer regard the earthly Jesus "from a human point of view." Paul is no less interested than are the writers of the Gospels in the "historical Jesus"; he, like them, is interested in Jesus not as a mere human teacher who had been killed but as the living Christ—as God's climactic act for the salvation of mankind. The earthly ministry of Jesus remains an essential part of that story.

[14] "The Conversion According to Paul" in chap. 6.

"We Regard Him Thus No Longer"

The change in Paul's relationship to Christ changed all of his other relationships. As "a new creation" (II Corinthians 5:17) he stood in a new relationship to God and the Law, to his fellowmen—his own people the Jews and the gentiles, and to himself. To understand what the living presence of Christ meant to Paul we must examine these relationships.

"Under the Power of Sin"   To understand the change in relationships which Christ brings about we must first observe what is wrong with the old relationships. Paul's answer to this question is in the word estrangement. Thus he reminds the Colossians that they "once were estranged and hostile in mind, doing evil deeds" (Colossians 1:21). In Ephesians 2:12 he summarizes the plight of the gentiles before conversion: "You were at that time separated from Christ, alienated from the commonwealth of Israel, and strangers to the covenants of promise, having no hope and without God in the world."

The source of this estrangement is sin. The word is in the singular because it refers not to particular actions or misdeeds but to a state of being or spiritual condition. Indeed, Paul goes farther and refers to it as a power or force which holds sway in the world. It is interesting to note that he never makes use of the traditional concept of Satan to explain the power of sin. Satan will have a role in the events preceding the end of time (II Thessalonians 2:9); he or his ministers occasionally hinder Paul (II Corinthians 2:11; 11:14–15; I Thessalonians 2:18); he tempts persons who expose themselves to him (I Corinthians 7:5); and he may destroy the flesh of one who submits to him (I Corinthians 5:5), but when Paul deals with the hostile forces which hold the world in their grip he uses more abstract terms such as "the prince of the power of the air" (Ephesians 2:2; cf. Colossians 2:15). In his descriptions of the condition of sin Paul chooses his terms in order to contrast it with the condition of being in Christ. Thus, in contrast to the gospel which "is the power of God for salvation to every one who has faith, the Jew first and also to the Greek" (Romans 1:16), all men, "both Jews and Greeks, are under the power of sin" (Romans 3:9); the believers who were once "slaves of sin" are now "slaves of righteousness" (Romans 6:18-20); Christ "has delivered us from the dominion of darkness and transferred us to the kingdom of his beloved Son" (Colossians 1:13); "The law of the Spirit of life in Christ Jesus has set me free from the law of sin and death" (Romans 8:2).

The cause of this sinful condition Paul describes in various ways. In Romans 5:12-21 he is contrasting the entrance of sin into the world with the coming of righteousness. To demonstrate this contrast he focuses attention on two men—Adam and Jesus Christ. Sin, which is an alien power, gained entrance through Adam, and "by one man's disobedience many were made sinners" (verse 19). Adam here is the representative man; back of this passage is the Hebrew concept of the solidarity of the race.[15] Because all men participate in the disobedience of Adam they also come under the power of sin and death. Adam becomes a negative type of Christ who by his obedience reversed the process.

Earlier in this same letter, however, Paul writes as though men deliberately place themselves under the power of sin. So he describes the gentiles: "Men who by their wickedness suppress the truth . . . are without excuse; for although they knew God they did not honor him as God. . . . Therefore God gave them up in the lusts of their hearts . . ." (Romans 1:18-24). The Jew is in no better circumstance, for although he has the Law he is unfaithful to it. "There is no distinction; since all have sinned and fall short of the glory of God" (Romans 3:22-23). In Galatians 4:3 he uses an analogy that points to a demonic source for the power of sin: "We were slaves to the elemental spirits of the universe."

From one point of view the Law itself is a source of the power of sin:

What then shall we say? That the law is sin? By no means! Yet, if it had not been for the law, I should not have known sin. I should not have known what it is to covet if the law had not said, "You shall not covet." But sin, finding opportunity in the commandment, wrought in me all kinds of covetousness. Apart from the law sin lies dead. I was once alive apart from the

---

[15] Cf. Kee and Young, *Understanding the New Testament,* p. 271.

law, but when the commandment came, sin revived and I died; the very commandment which promised life proved to be death to me. For sin, finding opportunity in the commandment, deceived me and by it killed me (Romans 7:7–11).

In Paul's discussion of sin the problem of the Law is never very far from the immediate background. Even the gentiles "show that what the law requires is written on their hearts" (Romans 2:15). Paul's attitude toward the Law differed radically from that of orthodox Judaism. As we have already seen, his acceptance of Jesus as the Messiah involved the conclusion that the Law had been set aside; the age of the Law had come to an end.[16] To explain this fact Paul reasoned that the Law, far from being the means of salvation, was an interim provision which, "since through the law comes knowledge of sin" (Romans 3:20), was added because of transgressions (Galatians 3:19). The Law is a part of this present age and must disappear with it: "the law is binding on a person only during his life" (Romans 7:1).

It is clear that this theory of the Law represented a decisive change for Paul. He was speaking from the Pharisaical point of view when he said of himself, "as to righteousness under the law blameless" (Philippians 3:6); but as a Christian he confessed, "When the commandment came, sin revived and I died" (Romans 7:9). He discarded the rabbinic idea that the Law was among the seven things created before the world (Galatians 3:17). And the notion that the Law was mediated by angels (cf. Galatians 3:19; Acts 7:53; Hebrews 2:2), which was probably based on the Septuagint reading of Deuteronomy 33:2, did not represent for Paul the transcendence of God but the subordinate position of the Law. By a *reductio ad absurdum* he rejected the casuistry of the Oral Law by which the Law was brought within reach of human achievement: If man is to be saved by the Law, "he is bound to keep the whole law" (Galatians 5:3; cf. 3:10). Since no man can do that, the Law does not save but condemns all men.

One further difficulty with the Law is that if it were possible to achieve righteousness thereby it would become an occasion for boasting (Romans 3:27) and therefore a barrier between man and God (cf.

---

[16] "The Conversion According to Paul," chap. 6.

Romans 4:2-5). Thus Paul could write: "You are severed from Christ, you who would be justified by the law" (Galatians 5:4). Man's estrangement, therefore, the Law is powerless to overcome. It cannot deliver man from the power of sin, and if it could, it would only replace sin as a new cause of estrangement.

Of what purpose, then, is the Law? As a Jew Paul cannot discard the Law or say that it is sin: "The law is holy" (Romans 7:12). It is "the law of God" (7:22) and was given therefore as a part of His divine purpose. At least three purposes of the Law are discernible in Paul's interpretation: 1) It is the revelation of sin: "Sin indeed was in the world before the law was given, but sin is not counted where there is no law" (Romans 5:13; cf. 4:15). The Law is, therefore, the basis of God's judgment upon sin.

2) It is to arouse the power of sin to its full capacity "in order that sin might be shown to be sin, and through the commandment might become sinful beyond measure" (Romans 7:13; cf. 5:20). The Law is not thereby the cause of sin. By stirring up the latent forces of sin it not only exposes the power of sin for what it is, but it also shows that sin gains its hold on man through the flesh (Romans 7:14, 18). To illustrate this point Paul significantly uses the one commandment in the Decalogue which deals with motives rather than overt actions. By forbidding covetousness the Law fanned into a flame the latent covetousness in Paul's flesh. That the word flesh does not refer to what we would call the material body as distinguished from the soul can be seen in Paul's inclusion among the "works of the flesh" such evils as "jealousy, anger, selfishness, dissension, party spirit" (Galatians 5:19-20).[17] The flesh is the person oriented to this transient, evil world; the body, in contrast, is the person oriented toward the world as God's creation and therefore open to the influences of God. Flesh is man as a "mere human being" and therefore through sin has become man in his estrangement. Thus in the midst of his argument for the resurrection Paul can declare: "flesh and blood cannot inherit the

[17] The question of the meaning of such terms as flesh, body, soul, and spirit is too involved and technical to discuss here. An excellent study of these terms will be found in Robinson, *The Body.* For the meaning of the word "flesh," see especially pp. 17-33.

kingdom of God, nor does the perishable inherit the imperishable" (I Corinthians 15:50).

3) The Law was our pedagogue "until Christ came" (Galatians 3:24). It has kept us "under restraint until faith should be revealed" (verse 23). The figure is that of the strict discipline of the gentleman's son under a trusted slave until the son reaches his majority. Until in the coming of Christ the new age began to enter history the Law was given to provide a moral discipline and at the same time, paradoxically, to reveal the ultimate futility of all such disciplines and therefore to prepare for the coming of Christ.

The Law, therefore, defines the nature of man's estrangement and reveals its source. The consequence of this estrangement is death (Romans 5:12-14; 6:23). Because of sin man participates in the "bondage to decay" (Romans 8:21) which holds all of creation in its grip. "The form of this world is passing away" (I Corinthians 7:31), and the man of flesh will pass with it, for to "set the mind on the flesh is death" (Romans 8:6). Under the power of sin man is therefore without the hope of the resurrection and the age to come in the Kingdom of God. Indeed, the man under the power of sin is already "dead through trespasses and sins" (Ephesians 2:1). And "the sting of death is sin, and the power of sin is the law" (I Corinthians 15:56).

"Righteousness Based on Faith"   Paul's interpretation of Jesus differs in several important respects from all of the traditional images of the Anointed Deliverer in whose coming the promised new age would be realized.[18] To be sure, the word Christ which he uses so constantly is a Greek translation of the Hebrew word Messiah, but for Paul it carries none of the political overtones usually associated with it. Jesus "was descended from David according to the flesh" (Romans 1:3), but the ancient dream of a restoration of the monarchy by a scion of David is completely absent.

Although Paul fervently awaited the return of Jesus to usher in the general resurrection and the new age, in his description of that hope several of the traditional lineaments of the apocalyptic Son of Man are

---

[18] Cf. Weiss, *Earliest Christianity*, II, 448-52.

conspicuously absent. The catastrophic events, the avenging of Israel upon her enemies, and the narrow nationalism which were so familiar in the apocalypses have been replaced by the cross, the abrogation of the Law, the inclusion of the gentiles and the new life in the Spirit. It was not the traditional concepts of the Messiah or the apocalyptic Son of Man that shaped Paul's picture of Jesus; it was Jesus who shaped his picture of the Messiah.

For Paul the deliverance wrought by Christ was far more profound than anything in the Jewish messianic expectations. Israel had always understood that the calamities which befell her were permitted by God because of her sins. Repentance and new obedience were therefore the pre-conditions of divine deliverance. To this end faithful Jews, desiring to be members of the righteous remnant to whom the Kingdom would come, rigorously applied themselves to keeping the Law. Of such had been Paul the Pharisee. But from Jesus he learned that man must first be delivered from the inward tyranny of the power of sin before he could be delivered finally from outward tyrannies and political oppression. This was the deliverance which Jesus through his crucifixion and resurrection had accomplished. Against the tyranny of the power of sin the Law was helpless.

As we have seen, one of the convictions to which Paul had come as a result of his revelation on the Damascus Road was that the Law could not—and was never intended to—gain for man the righteousness that would overcome his estrangement from God. Through Christ "God has done what the law, weakened by the flesh, could not do" (Romans 8:3). In Paul's thinking Christ had superseded the Law and had taken its place. To understand what this means we must remember that the Law (Torah) included more than the commandments; it embraced the whole substance of the revelation of God to man.[19] For Judaism, therefore, it was the Covenant, the basis of man's relationship to God. The Commandments were, of course, the heart of the revelation, and by keeping them the faithful Jew hoped to achieve the righteousness which was the condition for deliverance and the coming reign of God.

[19] For a discussion of the relation of the Torah to law see Samuel Sandmel *The Genius of Paul* (New York: Farrar, Straus & Cudahy, 1958), pp. 46–60.

The Law, however, had only succeeded in placing man under its curse (Galatians 3:10–12); because of it man stands under condemnation. In Christ God has therefore given man a new revelation and a Deliverer. "The righteousness of God has been manifested apart from law, although the law and the prophets bear witness to it" (Romans 3:21). Since God has shown "his love for us in that while we were yet sinners Christ died for us" (Romans 5:8), Christ has brought about a new covenant, a new relationship with God. Man's estrangement has been overcome.

The key to this new relationship is in Christ's identification with man and man's identification with Him. Thus Christ delivered man from the curse of the Law by taking the curse of the Law upon himself (Galatians 3:13). The claim of the Law upon man was broken thereby because when Christ was raised from the dead and "designated Son of God" (Romans 1:4) the Law was brought to an end.[20]

The Law is a part of the temporal order and exercises its authority only over those who belong to that order. In a characteristic rabbinic argument Paul demonstrates this fact: "a married woman is bound by law to her husband as long as he lives; but if her husband dies she is discharged from the law concerning the husband" (Romans 7:2). From this principle Paul concludes, "you have died to the law through the body of Christ" (7:4). Since through his death and resurrection Christ broke the curse of the Law, the believer by his identification in the body of Christ is also freed from the curse and condemnation of the Law. The power of sin which has through the flesh gained control of man also belongs to this present evil age. In dying with Christ the believer therefore dies to the flesh; he is now "dead to sin and alive to God in Christ Jesus" (Romans 6:11).

The positive side of this experience is central in Paul's thought. His encounter with the Risen Lord became more to him than proof of Jesus' resurrection and messiahship. It became an experience within Paul. He was not only a witness but also a participant. By being in Christ he, too, had been resurrected. From that time he sought to

[20] Professor C. C. Everett makes this idea the basis of Paul's entire theory of the atonement; see *The Gospel of Paul* (Boston: Houghton Mifflin Company, 1893).

"share his sufferings, becoming like him in his death, that if possible I may attain the resurrection from the dead" (Philippians 3:10-11). He is therefore "a new creation" (II Corinthians 5:17); he can now "walk in newness of life" for "it is no longer I who live, but Christ who lives in me" (Galatians 2:20). Dying with Christ to the Law and to the power of sin made possible his resurrection to life in Christ; and because through faith he was in Christ, Christ was in him.

In describing the believer's new life in the Spirit Paul is following the pattern of thought expressed by Ezekiel.

I will sprinkle clean water upon you, and you shall be clean from all your uncleannesses, and from all your idols I will cleanse you. A new heart I will give you, and a new spirit I will put within you; and I will take out of your flesh the heart of stone and give you a heart of flesh. And I will put my spirit within you, and cause you to walk in my statutes and be careful to observe my ordinances (Ezekiel 36:25-27).

With the coming of Christ came also the great outpouring of God's Spirit promised by Joel (2:28-29; cf. Acts 2:17-18). To be in Christ is therefore to have the Spirit dwelling within—it is to live by the Spirit. Hence the new life of righteousness is the gift of the Spirit. Because of the intimate connection between being in Christ and the gift of the Spirit Paul could speak indiscriminately of the Spirit of God and the Spirit of Christ. This life in the Spirit is all a part of the "new creation" brought about by the resurrection of Christ. The "new covenant" predicted by Jeremiah (31:31-34) had become a reality.

But this change is not automatic; it is realized only by faith. So Paul interprets the quotation from Habakkuk 2:4: "He who through faith is righteous shall live" (Romans 1:17; Galatians 3:11). True righteousness "depends on faith" (Romans 4:16; Philippians 3:9) and is therefore a gift of God's grace. Faith is here something more than intellectual assent; in obedient trust it is the full commitment of the person to God.

Faith, according to Paul, is the act whereby a man identifies himself with Christ, becomes actually one with him in nature, and is thus enabled to die and rise again with him. Faith is thus the indispensable, and at the same time the all-sufficient, condition of salvation.[21]

Through this experience the believer is redeemed (the term [Greek: *apolutroo*] refers to the manumission of slaves) from slavery to the power of sin; having died to the Law he is no longer under its sentence of death. Being raised to a new life of righteousness in Christ he has been reconciled to God; his estrangement is over and God has adopted him as a son:

For all who are led by the Spirit of God are sons of God. For you did not receive the spirit of slavery to fall back into fear, but you have received the spirit of sonship. When we cry, "Abba! Father!" it is the Spirit himself bearing witness with our spirit that we are children of God, and if children, then heirs, heirs of God and fellow heirs with Christ, provided we suffer with him in order that we may also be glorified with him (Romans 8:14–17).

"The Whole Structure Is Joined Together"

Paul appears to picture Christ's deliverance as a highly individualistic and intimately personal experience. In this regard it is not unlike the "salvation" experienced in the mystery religions, but here the similarity ends. Paul's religion was far from individualistic. On the contrary, because of its relation to the living presence of Christ, the Church occupies a central place in his thought.[22] Nor is the believer's relation to the Church a sequel to salvation. Rather, at the very point where the believer's experience of identification with the death and resurrection of Christ is most personal, the Church is involved. Thus Paul can write: "Likewise, my brethren, you have died to the law through the body of Christ, so that you may belong to one another, to him who has been raised from the dead in order that we may bear fruit for God" (Romans 7:4). In his very oneness with Christ by which his redemption is realized the believer becomes one with the Church.

[21] A. C. McGiffert, *A History of Christianity in the Apostolic Age* (New York: Charles Scribner's Sons, 1917), p. 141.

[22] On Paul's doctrine of the Church see the excellent chapters in Weiss, *Earliest Christianity*, ch. XXI, 615–51 and Robinson, *The Body*, chap. 3, 49–83.

The word *church* translated from the Greek *ecclesia* (from which we derive our word ecclesiastical and its cognates) means *called out* or *assembled*. It refers, therefore, to the community of the faithful who belong to and are waiting for the Kingdom of God. The meaning of the term suggests its connection with Isaiah's concept of the righteous remnant to whom God will bring deliverance and restoration (Isaiah 1:25–26; 10:20–27; cf. Romans 9:27–28). The Church is therefore the true continuity of God's chosen people, the heirs of His promise made to Abraham, and the instrument and object of God's action within history.

As the new Israel the Church, however, knows no racial or national boundaries: "It is men of faith who are the sons of Abraham" (Galatians 3:7). In Christ God has acted to create from both Jews and Gentiles a new people for Himself (Ephesians 2:13–15). So Paul wrote to the Ephesian gentiles:

So then you are no longer strangers and sojourners, but you are fellow citizens with the saints and members of the household of God, built upon the foundation of the apostles and prophets, Christ Jesus himself being the chief cornerstone, in whom the whole structure is joined together and grows into a holy temple in the Lord; in whom you also are built into it for a dwelling place of God in the Spirit (Ephesians 2:19–22).

In Paul's most significant statements about the nature and meaning of the Church he seldom uses the term. The heart of his concept of the Church is expressed in I Corinthians 12:27: "Now you are the body of Christ and individually members of it." The word members here (Greek: *mele*) refers to a limb or organ of the human body. The same word occurs in his question earlier in this letter, "Do you not know that your bodies are members of Christ?" (I Corinthians 6:15). The new life in Christ is therefore a corporate existence of all believers united in him as one living organism.

For Paul, then, the living presence of Christ is bound up with his life in the Church. Unlike the guilds or societies of devotees of the mystery religions, the Church is not a mere fellowship of those who have had a similar religious experience. It constitutes the continuing experience itself. The believer is not a member of the Church because he is saved. But rather in his dying and rising in Christ by which he is delivered from the power of sin he is already in the Church; they are two aspects of the same experience. So Paul could exhort the Colossians to "let the peace of Christ rule in your hearts, to which indeed you were called in the one body" (3:15).

When he said "It is no longer I who live, but Christ who lives in me" (Galatians 2:20), Paul was not speaking as a solitary mystic of an ineffable experience which separated him from his fellowmen. He predicated the same experience of the Colossians: "For you have died, and your life is hid with Christ in God. When Christ who is our life appears, then you also will appear with him in glory" (Colossians 3:3–4). Significantly, the pronouns in these sentences are plural while the word life is singular.

Union with Christ means, therefore, union with one another. This idea is most clearly expressed in Romans 12:5: "So we, though many, are one body in Christ, and individually members one of another" (cf. Ephesians 4:25). When the Corinthians became embroiled in strife and division, Paul pleaded with them that there "be no discord in the body, but that the members may have the same care for one another. If one member suffers, all suffer together" (I Corinthians 12:25–26). On a new and profound level the ancient idea of corporate personality is revived in the solidarity of the community of the faithful in Christ.

We observed at the beginning of this section that Paul's change of relationship with Christ changed all of his other relationships. The key to this change is his participation in the body of Christ by which he was united with his fellow believers in the new creation. According to the flesh Paul, like Christ, was an Israelite but he had "died to the flesh," and therefore the advantage he had as an Israelite he "counted as loss" (Philippians 3:7). The new Israel under the New Covenant had replaced the old Israel and only to the extent that Paul's kinsmen by race were also children of Abraham; by faith was Paul bound to them in the unity of the people of God (Romans 11:1–7).[23] The

---

[23] There is an element of paradox in Paul's thinking here, for although the true people of God are the new Israel by faith, he retained his status in the commonwealth of the old Israel and remained under the discipline of the

same is true of the gentiles: "For there is no distinction between Jew and Greek" (Romans 10:12). To those outside the body of Christ, Paul was an Apostle; he was "under obligation" to them to preach the gospel that they might be saved (cf. Romans 1:14; 10:14–17; 11:13–14). He could neither ignore nor withdraw from them in self-righteous superiority; rather his lifelong responsibility was to them: "I have made myself a slave to all, that I might win the more" (I Corinthians 9:19). His membership in the body of Christ brought him into a new and closer relationship with his fellow believers, and it also placed him under a new and deeper obligation to the rest of the world: "So we are ambassadors for Christ, God making his appeal through us" (II Corinthians 5:20).

That the emphasis in his letters is on the presence of Christ in the Church rather than on Christ's exaltation does not mean that the exaltation is extraneous to Paul's thought. The exaltation has made possible Christ's presence in the believers (Ephesians 1:20–23). Indeed, because of his union with the exalted Christ the believer is also exalted:

But God, who is rich in mercy, out of the great love with which he loved us, even when we were dead through our trespasses, made us alive together with Christ (by grace you have been saved), and raised us up with him, and made us sit with him in the heavenly places in Christ Jesus (Ephesians 2:4–6).

In several places Paul uses the analogy of a building to describe the Church: "Do you not know that you are God's temple and that God's Spirit dwells in you?" (I Corinthians 3:16; cf. 3:9, 6:19, II Corinthians 6:16, Ephesians 2:19–22). The analogy suggests two things: The process of building or growth which is taking place in the Church (cf. Ephesians 4:12, 16; Colossians 2:19), and the functional importance to the whole of the various parts or members of the Church. This last idea has great practical importance for Paul's churches.

To end the contention in the Corinthian Church over spiritual gifts

---

synagogues which in most instances were not a part of the new Israel. He never lost sight, in other words, of the continuity between the two. Cf. Rom. 3:1–2 with 9.

he wrote in I Corinthians chapter 12 his longest treatise on this theme. In this passage Paul is endeavoring by means of the analogy of the harmonious function of the organs of the human body to press home two points: The first is that the believer's function in the Church is to serve the common good and contribute to the service for which the Church is responsible. The second point is that the members must not be self-seeking but concerned for one another, for "if one member suffers, all suffer together" (verse 26). "There are varieties of gifts, but the same Spirit" (verse 4). In Romans 12:4–8 and Ephesians 4:11–16 Paul uses the same analogy of the interdependence of the various parts of the body to admonish the believers to be stable and zealous in performing their assigned functions and exercising their Spirit-given minintries in the work of the Church.

The emphasis on the corporeity of the Church in Christ, like the mystical absorption of the soul in the divine, seems to spell the end of individuality. Although occasional verses such as II Corinthians 3:18 and Galatians 3:28, when isolated from their contexts, might be so interpreted, yet even a casual reading of Paul's letters will show that this is not true. The force of his ethical admonitions lies in their appeal to the individual's will and sense of responsibility. Nor is this ethical appeal to the individual due to the fact that his union with Christ is incomplete or that he is still "in the flesh." Paul's emphasis on the peculiar role of each member in the total life of the Church will not allow such an explanation (cf. I Corinthians 12:27–30). It is these very individual differences among the members, in fact, that make the body possible: "If all were a single organ, where would the body be?" (I Corinthians 12:19).

Paul's thought actually moves in the opposite direction from classical mysticism. Just as by being freed from slavery to the power of sin and becoming a slave of God he finds his true freedom, so in his oneness with Christ in the Church, paradoxically, the believer discovers his true individuality. This truth can be seen in Paul's treatment of the sacraments of baptism and the Eucharist, or as he calls it, the Lord's Supper. We cannot go into the intricate problems concerning Paul's treatment of these sacraments. It will be sufficient to observe their bearing on the believer's relation to the Church.

Baptism is an individual act; it is the expression of individual religious experience. This fact is recognized in Paul's words: "for as many of you as were baptized into Christ have put on Christ" (Galatians 3:27). In Romans 6:3–11 (also Colossians 2:12) baptism is the sacramental expression of the believer's death and resurrection in Christ, which is an individual, personal experience.[24] Yet the meaning of this very act culminates in the Church: "For by one Spirit we were all baptized into one body" (I Corinthians 12:13). The Church is present, in fact, in the entire action. The proclamation of the Church led the candidate into faith (Romans 10:14–17), the Church through its ministry administers the baptism[25] and in "putting on Christ" the believer becomes a part of the Church.

The Eucharist, on the other hand, is the action of a community. Everything about it suggests the fellowship of the Church:

The cup of blessing which we bless, is it not a participation in the blood of Christ? The bread which we break, is it not a participation in the body of Christ? Because there is one loaf, we who are many are one body, for we all partake of the same loaf (I Corinthians 10:16–17).[26]

This quotation shows how realistically Paul viewed the sacraments. His concern in this chapter is with the grave danger that the Corinthians by willfully eating meat offered to idols would be united to the demons who fostered idol worship among the pagans. The principle is the same as that in the Eucharist; therefore "you cannot partake of the table of the Lord and the table of demons" (I Corinthians 10:21).

Probably the Eucharist goes back ultimately to the figure of the Messianic Banquet. It points to the eschatological realization of the Kingdom of God, and is therefore an anticipation of the perfect fellowship of the new age. But apart from the genuine individuality of the participants it would be meaningless. Significantly, Paul's recital of the

---

[24] For Paul baptism also still retained its older meaning of a lustration for purification from sin (cf. I Cor. 6:11).

[25] From the prevalence of the passive verb it is clear that baptism in Christianity was not, as it apparently was in Judaism, self-administered. Cf. I Cor. 1:14–17.

[26] On the bread as a symbol of the unity of the Church see *The Didache*, 9, 4.

tradition of the Last Supper was in connection with an abuse that was destroying the fellowship (I Corinthians 11:17–34). True individuality is realized in the unity of consideration for others. Until the members yield themselves in love to the oneness of the Church the fellowship is broken, the "body and blood of the Lord" is profaned, and the undiscerning person "eats and drinks judgment upon himself" (verse 29). "That is why many of you are weak and ill, and some have died" (verse 30).

In the Eucharist, the nature and meaning of the Church have their most profound expression. It recalls the whole drama of Christ's self-offering for his Church and the life of the Church in him. It is the expression of the believers' corporate "participation in the body of Christ" (I Corinthians 10:16). Here the believers "assemble as a church" (I Corinthians 11:18), but it is precisely here that the individual becomes important; his love and concern for others become most essential to the life of the Church.

"I Press Toward the Mark"   Although they had "died to sin" and were raised to new life in Christ Jesus, the members of Paul's churches were far from perfect. As to his own life Paul confesses: "So then, I of myself serve the law of God with my mind, but with my flesh I serve the law of sin" (7:25; cf. Philippians 3:12). Such is the paradox of the Christian life. The believer lives between two worlds—the present evil age and the age to come—and he is a part of both.

It is significant how often Paul puts his statements concerning the new status of the believer in the form of admonitions: "If then you have been raised with Christ, seek the things that are above" (Colossians 3:1). In Romans 6:6–7 he writes, "We know that our old self was crucified with him so that the sinful body might be destroyed, and we might no longer be enslaved to sin. For he who has died is freed from sin." Yet five verses later he writes, "Let not sin therefore reign in your mortal bodies." And although as believers they are in Christ he exhorts them to "put on the Lord Jesus Christ, and make no provision for the flesh to gratify its desires" (13:14). Similarly, in Colossians 3:3 he writes, "For you have died, and your life is hid with Christ in God." And two verses later he adds, "Put to death therefore what is earthly in you: immorality, impurity, passion, evil desires, and covetousness, which is idolatry."

Salvation in one sense is a process: "For if while we were enemies we were reconciled to God by the death of his Son, much more, now that we are reconciled, shall we be saved by his life" (Romans 5:10; cf. Colossians 3:9). Paul's admonitions are therefore "to become what you are" in Christ. As his vivid picture in Romans 7:7–25 shows, the life of the believer is a battle between the flesh which, although in the throes of death, still seeks control and the Spirit which is the new life in the believer. But the believer, unlike the one who struggles for righteousness under the Law, is not waging the battle in his own strength: "For we are his workmanship, created in Christ Jesus for good works" (Ephesians 2:10); "For God is at work in you, both to will and to work for his good pleasure" (Philippians 2:13).

We have seen how Paul's relationship with Christ changed his relationship to the Church, his fellowmen, and the world; here we see how Christ changed Paul's relationship to himself. He had died to self and was alive to God, but the change was still in process. He was confident, nevertheless, of its outcome: "So we do not lose heart. Though our outer nature is wasting away, our inner nature is being renewed every day" (II Corinthians 4:16). Therefore, he could boast: "I can do all things in him who strengthens me" (Philippians 4:13). So in refusing to remove the "thorn in the flesh" the Lord had assured him, "My grace is sufficient for you, for my power is made perfect in weakness" (II Corinthians 12:9). In Paul's view this same relationship to self is true of every believer. In dying and rising with Christ the believers are not their own; they were bought with a price (I Corinthians 6:19–20). Paul frequently calls them saints (*hagioi*); they are holy people in the sense that they have been "set apart" for Christ.

Paul's ethical admonitions are addressed, then, to the paradoxical situation in which the believer finds himself. The orientation of Paul's ethics can be seen in the question, "How can we who died to sin still live in it?" (Romans 6:2). His is not therefore in the strict sense of the word an ethical system.[27] He did not address his admonitions to

---

[27] For a thorough study of Paul's ethical teaching see Enslin, *The Ethics of Paul;* also Weiss, *Earliest Christianity,* II, 546–94.

"the unspiritual man," for the "unspiritual man does not receive the
gifts of the Spirit of God, for they are folly to him" (I Corinthians
2:14). Not universal principles but the will of God formed the
foundation of Paul's moral teaching. Yet the precepts of that teaching
are universally valid and all men will be judged by the same standard
of the will of God for men which underlies them.

The question is one of motivation. Paul saw that man had not been
able to live according to the light he had (Romans 1:18–20; 2:12–14),
therefore what man needed was not more knowledge but the power
to do what he knew he ought to do. To the extent that God's Law
could be known from nature man had proved himself incapable of
obeying it. Consequently, Paul addressed himself to those who by faith
possessed the Spirit and therefore had available the power to respond
in obedience to God's demands. We are not to assume, of course, that
Paul had no concern for the evils in society around him or that his
ethics are irrelevant to the needs of society.[28] The Church as the
presence of Christ in the world must, on the contrary, do battle on
all levels with evil wherever it is encountered (cf. Ephesians 6:11–12).
But "the weapons of our warfare are not worldly but have divine
power to destroy strongholds" (II Corinthians 10:4).

We must remember also that in his letters Paul is addressing himself not to mankind in general but to the particular needs of those
who are already in the body of Christ. Except for occasional references
such as Romans 1–2 and the reference to "the governing authorities"
in Romans 13:1–7, he speaks of the relation of the Church to the
world only in terms of the gospel. This may be due partly to his vivid
expectation of an early end of the present evil age and partly to the
ad hoc nature of his letters. But the Church's proclamation of the
gospel is not calling the world to come under the rule of God with
whom otherwise it has nothing to do. Rather it is a call to faith by
which a new relationship with God is established. In Paul's view the
world stands always under the rule of God, but because of disobedience

---

[28] On the question of the social relevance of Paul's ethics see Amos N.
Wilder, "Kerygma, Eschatology and Social Ethics" in W. D. Davies and D.
Daube, ed., *The Background of the New Testament and Its Eschatology* (Lon-
don: Cambridge University Press, 1956), pp. 509–536.

it stands under that rule as judgment; it is "storing up wrath . . . on the day of wrath" (Romans 2:5). In this sense, therefore, the ethics of Paul are an expression of the universal demands of the rule of God and as such, to the extent to which they apply, are relevant to all mankind.

Paul's immediate purpose in his letters, nevertheless, was to meet the moral needs of the churches. The believers are called upon to make use of the moral power available to them in the Spirit. In at least three ways Paul offers his moral guidance:

1) The believer is to "put to death therefore what is earthly in you" (Colossians 3:5). Referring to his own self discipline as an example he writes, "I pummel my body and subdue it, lest after preaching to others I myself should be disqualified" (I Corinthians 9:27). The Stoic would find such language familiar, but the context is quite different. Such self mastery is possible to the believer not through his own will power but because he has already been mastered by the superior power of Christ. In the struggle between the old life of flesh and the new life of the Spirit he is to place himself under the power of the Spirit by denying the insistent but invalid claims of the flesh.

2) The believers are to "be imitators of me, as I am of Christ" (I Corinthians 11:1). In his own life as well as in his teaching Paul proposed to set before his churches the positive example of Christ. Here, as in the lists of vices and virtues and homely rules of conduct (cf. Galatians 5:19–23; Colossians 3:18–4:1), we can see that Paul's admonitions do not deal in mere abstractions. We have already observed how he cited Jesus as an example for faithful living; we should also note that the majority of his allusions to the tradition of Jesus' teaching are by way of moral instruction. Paul was keenly aware of the need of his Christians, many of whom were so newly won from paganism, for elementary moral instruction.

3) As the true foundation for Christianity Paul exhorted his readers to "make love your aim" (I Corinthians 14:1). As he explained to the Romans:

. . . he who loves his neighbor has fulfilled the law. The commandments, "You shall not commit adultery, You shall not kill, You shall not steal, You

shall not covet," and any other commandment, are summed up in this sentence, "You shall love your neighbor as yourself." Love does no wrong to a
neighbor; therefore love is the fulfilling of the law (Romans 13:8–10; cf.
Galatians 5:13–14).

"As God's love has been poured into our hearts through the Holy
Spirit" (Romans 5:5) and "controls us" (II Corinthians 5:14) so the
believer is to make love the basis of all his actions and relationships
(cf. Galatians 5:13). In this the believer is simply carrying out the life
of the Spirit, for "the fruit of the Spirit is love . . ." (Galatians 5:22).

In a word, Paul's ethic is "faith working through love" (Galatians
5:6); it is God's love in Christ coming to expression in and through
the believer. The ethic of Paul is a "Christian ethic" in that it is addressed to those who in Christ are willingly committed to the rule of
God and possess the power to "walk by the Spirit" (Galatians 5:16).
Addressed to particular people under particular circumstances, his admonitions contain a number of elements which no longer apply, but
underneath these time conditioned exhortations are timeless principles
by which Christians of every age have guided their lives. To what more
timeless exhortation can we turn than such words as these:

Finally, brethren, whatever is true, whatever is honorable, whatever is just,
whatever is pure, whatever is lovely, whatever is gracious, if there is any excellence, if there is anything worthy of praise, think about these things
(Philippians 4:8).

"So Shall We always Be with the Lord"

We have seen that from the moral standpoint the believer's
deliverance from the power of sin is not complete. The same is true
of his whole situation. As Paul represents it, redemption will not be
complete until this present evil age has ended and the Church has
realized its hope in the age to come. At the beginning of this study
we observed Paul's fervent belief that the new age was near at hand.
This hope illuminates all his letters and is not so much a separate
idea as it is the prevailing assumption in all of his thinking about
Jesus.[29] Although he freely uses apocalyptic figures, we look in vain

[29] See Weiss, *Earliest Christianity*, II, 526–45. For an excellent monograph

for his description of the new age replete with the detailed imagery characteristic of apocalyptic writings. Paul is content with one great thought: In the new age his union with Christ will forever be complete. The triumph of Christ in the eschatological new age is therefore the third view of Jesus which in this chapter we are examining.

"To Wait for His Son from Heaven"   Although the Church is now the body of Christ and knows his living presence within itself, it is in another sense the community of the faithful, righteous remnant waiting for the coming Kingdom of God. Paul represents it more personally as a waiting for the coming of Christ (cf. I Thessalonians 1:10; 2:19). The word *parousia*, commonly used to refer to the coming of Christ, suggests the figure of the arrival of a king to assume his throne and represents an element of standard Jewish eschatological imagery.

Closely associated with the coming of Christ is the final Judgment. In Romans 2:16 God is the Judge, but in II Corinthians 5:10 Paul speaks of "the judgment seat of Christ." Both the idea of a judgment executed by the Messiah and the picture of God as the final Judge are to be found in Jewish apocalyptic literature. Paul probably is not, however, making a distinction here but simply using the terms freely to refer to a universal judgment at the end of the age.

According to I Corinthians 6:2 the "saints" will have a share in judging the world. Yet the believers themselves will come under judgment (I Corinthians 1:8; 4:5; II Corinthians 5:10; Romans 14:10). Even though the issue of the Christian's judgment is not "the wrath" which is reserved for the wicked and hostile powers in control of this present age, he may find that his "work is burned up . . . though he himself will be saved, but only as through fire" (I Corinthians 3:15; cf. 11:32).

That the final judgment and the arrival of the new age will represent the complete triumph of God through Christ Paul makes clear in I Corinthians 15:28: "When all things are subjected to him, then the

---

on the present day relevance of New Testament eschatology see John A. T. Robinson, *In the End, God* (London: James Clarke, 1950).

Son himself will also be subjected to him who put all things under him, that God may be everything to every one." (Cf. Philippians 2:10–11; Ephesians 1:9–10.) In Romans 11:32 Paul's language suggests a doctrine of universalism: "For God has consigned all men to disobedience, that he may have mercy upon all." Such passages as Romans 2:8–9; 6:21–23; Philippians 3:19; II Thessalonians 2:12; and especially II Thessalonians 1:9, "They shall suffer the punishment of eternal destruction and exclusion from the presence of the Lord and from the glory of his might" present a different view.

In several places Paul speaks as though he expects Christ's coming at any time. According to I Thessalonians 5:2–4 that day will arrive "like a thief in the night" (cf. Romans 13:11; I Corinthians 7:29–31; Philippians 3:20). Certain prior conditions appear in several passages. The most familiar of these prior conditions is the revelation of the "lawless one" whom "the Lord Jesus will slay" (II Thessalonians 2:3–12). There is, however, one other such condition.[30] In Romans 11:25–26 the "full number" of the gentiles and subsequently all Israel must be saved before the end. Yet Paul sees the "hope" rapidly drawing closer, and in longing closes I Corinthians (16:22) with the characteristic early Christian prayer, *Maranatha,* "Our Lord, come!"

In referring to the events of the end Paul uses several other characteristically apocalyptic figures such as the judgment fire (I Corinthians 3:13), the archangel's call (I Thessalonians 4:16), the last trumpet (I Corinthians 15:52; I Thessalonians 4:16), and meeting the Lord in the air (I Thessalonians 4:17; cf. Daniel 7:13–14). Paul makes rather free use of traditional apocalyptic language and shares with the rest of the Church of his day the vivid hope of the sudden arrival of the new age of the Kingdom of God.[31] But he has no organized scheme of his own to add; nor is he deeply concerned with any time-table of final events. The final, perfect realization of his oneness with Christ is his real concern.

---

[30] This fact has considerable bearing on the question of the authenticity of II Thessalonians. The difference in eschatology between it and I Thessalonians is paralleled elsewhere in Paul's letters. See "Letters to Thessalonica" in chap. 8.

[31] On the development in eschatological thought in first century Christianity see my "Changing Ideas in New Testament Eschatology," *The Harvard Theological Review,* L, January 1957, pp. 21–36.

"Christ the First Fruits"   In virtually all of Paul's
references to the coming
new age Jesus occupies the center. Even in his use of conventional
apocalyptic figures his thought is controlled by his encounter with Jesus
on the Damascus Road. Nowhere is this more evident than in his
teaching on the final resurrection. It is noteworthy that Paul does not
appeal to the traditional Pharisaical arguments for this belief. The
actual basis of his whole argument in I Corinthians 15, the *locus
classicus* of his teaching on this subject, is his own witness to the resurrection of Jesus.

Since Christ is the "first fruit" of the resurrection, the believers'
resurrection is not only equally certain, it will be of the same kind (cf.
I Corinthians 6:14; I Thessalonians 4:14–16). The resurrection, in
other words, has already begun with Jesus; he is the first sheaf of the
eschatological harvest (I Corinthians 15:23–24; cf. Matthew 9:37.
The figure is taken from the Old Testament offering of the first of the
harvest. See Exodus 22:29; Leviticus 2:12; Numbers 18:12; Deuteronomy 18:4). The "spiritual body" for which he argues so laboriously
—which because it is "spiritual" is nonetheless to be understood as a
real body—is unquestionably an indirect description of Jesus as in his
conversion experience Paul had seen him.

In this passage the emphasis falls on the word imperishable. Thus,
the change to an imperishable body must also be made by those who
by being alive at his coming avoid death: "For this perishable nature
must put on the imperishable, and this mortal nature must put on immortality" (I Corinthians 15:53). That the imperishable body means
more than simply indestructibility Paul shows by his reference to being
"glorified with him" (Romans 8:17; II Corinthians 4:17; Colossians
3:4). The believers share therefore not only Christ's resurrection but
his exaltation (Ephesians 2:6). Paul's glowing hope reaches out to embrace all creation: "For the creation waits with eager longing for the
revealing of the sons of God . . . because the creation itself will be
set free from its bondage to decay" (Romans 8:19–21). Finally death
will be conquered. "The last enemy to be destroyed is death" (I Corinthians 15:26).

From the day Paul encountered him on the Damascus Road and

learned that Jesus of Nazareth was indeed the Messiah, through all the toils, tribulations, and cares of his incredible ministry Paul was possessed of one great passion: to "be with Christ" (Philippians 1:23) by whose living presence within him Paul had labored and had endured more than all of the other apostles. In his influence on Christian thought during the succeeding centuries, in his timeless ethical principles, in the inspiration of his indefatigable labors and devotion to Christ Paul stands alone. He is par excellence The Apostle of Jesus Christ.

appendices

ON THE CHRONOLOGY OF PAUL

Among the most difficult and uncertain elements in the story of Paul is chronology. In spite of the Delphi inscription which provides a close date for the proconsulship of Gallio, there are actually no fixed dates for a chronology of Paul's life (see "The Corinthian Church" in chapter 7). There are, to be sure, several points of contact with persons and events which we can check from other sources, but in each instance the date is open to question. Thus, the chronology of Paul requires decisions regarding the date of the expulsion of the Jews from Rome by Claudius, the famine in Jerusalem, the tenure of Gallio's proconsulship in Corinth and at what point in the stay in the city of each of them Paul appeared before him, and the accession of Festus to the procuratorship in Jerusalem.

Establishing a fixed date from which to reckon would by no means solve the problem. There is the question, for example, of how to interpret Luke's indefinite temporal phrases. In a few places Luke does supply definite information: Paul was a year and six months in Corinth (Acts 18:11); he was at least two years and three months in Ephesus (19:8, 10); and he spent three months in Corinth on his last visit. But what does he mean by such phrases as "about that time" in 19:23 or "no little time" in 14:28? Does the phrase "But when two years had elapsed" (24:27) refer to Paul's imprisonment or to Felix's tenure of office? From Galatians 1:18 we can supply three years for the "many days" of Acts 9:23, but there is no clue to the lapse of time on his journeys and little more as to the time spent in the cities of Galatia and Macedonia.

The meaning of the three years in Galatians 1:18 is clear, but do the fourteen years in 2:1 include these three years or should they be added? To such questions must be added the larger question of the relation of Acts to Paul's letters. Our decision as to whether to relate the Jerusalem visit in Galatians 2:1–10 with Acts 11:30; 12:25, or with Acts 15:1–29, or with Acts 18:22–19:1 will radically affect the chronology of Paul's life. Any chronological scheme for the life of Paul must therefore be tentative. (For a comparison of scholarly opinions on this question see the chart in Moffatt, *An Introduction to the New Testament*, pp. 62–63. Reprinted in Kepler, *Contemporary Thinking about Paul*, pp. 158–159.) Fortunately, we need not decide all of these chronological questions in order to understand him. I have therefore deliberately avoided dates in discussing Paul's letters and most of the events of his life. For what it may be worth, however, the following is my own estimate of the approximate dates of the key events:

A.D.		
	10–15	Paul's birth
	25–30	His arrival in Jerusalem
	31–33	His conversion
	34–36	His first visit to Jerusalem
	44–46	Famine in Jerusalem
	44–47	The Jerusalem Council
	50–52	Paul in Corinth (18 months)
	52–56	Paul in Ephesus (approximately three years)
	55–58	His final voyage to Jerusalem with the collection; his arrest and imprisonment (two years)
	57–60	The voyage to Rome
	62–68	Paul's death

2

PAUL AND THE SYNOPTIC TRADITION

In a course designed to study the life and letters of Paul within the larger context of their place in the development and expansion of the primitive Church my students have cooperated in compiling extensive lists of parallels between the Pauline Corpus and the Gospels. Some of the results of those studies are significant enough to warrant being included here. Such a project as this can be neither exact nor exhaustive. Enthusiasm for finding parallels easily leads to comparisons that are far-fetched and concern to produce a convincing list can lead to the omission of valid material.

No attempt is made in this list to distinguish the four kinds of material indicated in the discussion of Paul's use of the Tradition (see "Remembering the Words of the Lord Jesus" in chapter 9) : the more or less direct quotation, the midrash, the coincidental quotations from the Old Testament, and the coincidences resulting from the common background and ethical outlook of Jesus and Paul. The following list is confined to the sayings of Jesus according to the Synoptic Gospels and is condensed from a larger list.

	Romans	*Synoptic Gospels*
The evil within man	1:28–31	Mark 7:20–23 and parallel
On judging one another *vs.* God's judgment	2:1, 6–11. Cf. 14:10, 13	Matt. 7:1–2 and parallel; Matt. 16:27; 25:31–46; Luke 8:15. Cf. Ps. 62:12
Hearers *vs.* doers	2:13, 21	Matt. 7:21; 23:3–4 and parallel
True Jews and true circumcision	2:27–28. Cf. 4:11	Matt. 3:9; 12:41 and parallel
The Law upheld	3:31	Matt. 5:17

339

	Romans	*Synoptic Gospels*
Rejoicing in persecution	5:3	Matt. 5:12 and parallel
Serving two masters	6:16	Matt. 6:24 and parallel
Rewards and punishments	6:23	Matt. 25:46
A reference to the Garden of Gethsemane or the Lord's Prayer?	8:15	Mark 14:36 and parallel; Matt. 6:9 and parallel
God knows the hearts of men	8:27	Luke 16:15
God vindicates His own	8:33	Luke 18:1–8
Confessing Christ	10:9	Matt. 10:32 and parallel. Cf. Mark 8:38
Refusing to see or hear	11:7–10	Matt. 13:13–15
The elder Brother?	11:15	Luke 15:25–32
The time of the gentiles	11:25	Luke 21:24
The perfect will of God	12:2	Matt. 5:48 and parallel. Cf. Matt. 13:22
Bless persecutors	12:14, 19–20	Matt. 5:44 and parallel
Live in peace	12:18 *passim*	Mark 9:50
Pride and love of high position	12:3	Matt. 10:24 and parallel. Cf. Luke 14:11
Not repaying evil for evil	12:17	Matt. 5:38–42 and parallel
Obey authorities	13:1–7	Mark 12:13–17 and parallels
The law of love	13:8–10. Cf. Gal. 5:14–15	Mark 12:28–34 and parallels. Cf. Matt. 19:19
Be ready for the parousia	13:11	Mark 13:33–37 and parallels
Living to the Lord	14:8	Luke 20:38
Causing others to stumble	14:13	Mark 9:42–48 and parallels
Unclean food	14:14	Mark 7:15 and parallel

	Romans	*Synoptic Gospels*
False prophets	16:17	Matt. 7:15
Being guileless	16:19	Matt. 10:16
The defeat of Satan	16:20	Luke 10:17–20
	I Corinthians	
Revealing of the Son of Man	1:7	Luke 17:30
Jews demand signs	1:22	Mark 8:11–12 and parallels
The true sign	1:23	Luke 7:18–23
The disciple is not above his master	4:8–13	Matt. 10:24
Delivering one to Satan	5:5	Luke 22:31
Beware of leaven	5:6	Mark 8:15 and parallels
Saints will judge the world	6:2	Matt. 19:28
Church discipline and law suits	6:1–8	Matt. 5:25, 39–40 and parallel; Matt. 18:16–17
Marriage	6:16	Mark 10:7–8 and parallel
Special gifts	7:7	Matt. 19:11
Divorce	7:10	Mark 10:11 and parallels; Matt. 5:32
Slave of Christ	7:22	Matt. 6:24 and parallel
Earthly ties and the Kingdom of God	7:29–35	Matt. 10:37–38 and parallel. Cf. Luke 10:38–42
Offending the weak	8:12	Mark 9:42–48 and parallels
The laborer deserves his wages	9:4, 6–14	Matt. 10:10 and parallel
The Eucharist and the Last Supper	10:16–17; 11:23–25	Mark 14:22–25 and parallels
Eat what is set before you	10:27	Luke 10:8
Calling Jesus Lord	12:3	Matt. 16:17
Faith to move mountains	13:2	Mark 11:22–23 and parallels

	I Corinthians	*Synoptic Gospels*
Supremacy of love	13:13	Mark 12:31 and parallels
Childlikeness	14:20	Mark 9:36 and parallels
Conquest of the enemies of Christ	15:25–27	Mark 12:35–37 and parallels. Cf. Matt. 28:18
The analogy of seed and the plant	15:36–37. Cf. vss. 42–43	Mark 4:26–29. Cf. Matt. 13:43
	II Corinthians	
Day of Judgment	5:10	Matt. 16:27; 25:31–46; Luke 8:15
Living for Christ	5:15	Matt. 10:37–38 and parallel
Ambassadors for Christ	5:20	Mark 6:6–11 and parallels
Christ was made sin for us	5:21 Cf. vss. 14–15	Mark 10:45 and parallel
Losing one's life and gaining it	6:4–10	Mark 8:34–37 and parallels
Jesus' poverty	8:9	Matt. 8:20 and parallel
The measure of a gift	8:12	Mark 12:41–44 and parallel
God's providence	9:8	Matt. 6:30–33 and parallel
Spiritual weapons	10:4	Luke 11:21–22. Cf. Mark 3:27 and parallel
Judging one another	10:12	Matt. 7:1 and parallel
Whom the Lord commends	10:18	Matt. 7:21–23 and parallel
False leaders	11:13–15	Mark 13:5–6 and parallels; Matt. 24:5, 23–26 and parallel

	II Corinthians	Synoptic Gospels
Enduring for Christ's sake	12:10	Matt. 10:18
Two or three witnesses	13:1	Matt. 18:16
Christ speaking in an apostle	13:3	Matt. 10:20 and parallel
	Galatians	
Christ gave himself for our sins	1:4	Mark 10:45 and parallel
No justification by the Law	2:16	Matt. 5:20
The Law and the coming of Christ	3:24	Matt. 5:17
Serving one another	5:13	Mark 10:42–45 and parallels
Love of neighbors	5:14	Mark 12:31 and parallels
The flesh *vs.* the spirit	5:17	Matt. 6:24 and parallel
Restore the fallen in humility	6:1	Matt. 7:3–5
Sowing and reaping	6:7–8	Matt. 13:24–30
The harvest	6:9	Mark 4:26–29; Matt. 24:13
	Ephesians	
The eyes of your hearts	1:18	Matt. 6:22–23
All things subjected to Christ	1:22	Matt. 28:18
Christ at the right hand of God	1:20	Matt. 19:28
The foundation of Christ and the apostles	2:20	Matt. 16:18; Mark 12:10 and parallels
The new revelation	3:4	Matt. 13:16–17 and parallel
On meekness	4:2	Matt. 5:5
Truthfulness	4:25	Matt. 5:36
Evil mouth	4:29	Matt. 15:10
Grieving the Holy Spirit	4:30	Mark 3:29 and parallels
Forgive one another	4:32	Matt. 18:21–35 and parallel
Imitators of God	5:1	Matt. 5:45, 48

	Ephesians	*Synoptic Gospels*
Purity in speech	5:4	Matt. 12:35–37 and parallel
Children of light	5:8	Matt. 5:14–16
Marriage	5:31	Mark 10:7–8 and parallels
Honor thy father and mother	6:2	Mark 7:10; Matt. 15:4; Luke 18:20
Slaves and masters	6:6–9	Matt. 24:45–51 and parallel
The power of darkness	6:12	Luke 22:53
Spiritual armor	6:14	Luke 12:35
Persistent prayer	6:18	Luke 18:1–8; 11:5–9. Cf. Mark 14:38 and parallels
	Philippians	
Witness through persecution	1:12	Mark 13:9–13 and parallels
Christ's humility and obedience unto death	2:5–11	Mark 9:12; Matt. 20:28; 26:39, 42; Luke 22:27
Lights in the world	2:15	Matt. 5:14–16
Forsaking all for Christ	3:7	Matt. 13:44
The book of life	4:3	Luke 10:20
Be not anxious	4:6	Matt. 6:25–34 and parallel
	Colossians	
Hope in heaven	1:5	Matt. 6:19–20 and parallel
The gospel preached throughout the world	1:6, 23	Mark 13:10 and parallel
Hidden treasures	2:3	Matt. 13:44
Triumph over demonic powers	2:15	Mark 3:23–30 and parallels. Cf. Luke 10:18
Set the mind on things above	3:2	Matt. 6:19–21, 33 and parallel

	Colossians	*Synoptic Gospels*
Forgive one another	3:13	Mark 11:25 and parallels
Act wisely toward outsiders	4:5	Luke 16:1–9
	I Thessalonians	
Killing the prophets	2:15	Matt. 23:37 and parallel
Christ coming in glory	2:19; 4:16	Mark 8:38 and parallels; Mark 13:26 and parallels
Rejecting God	4:8	Luke 10:16
Love one another	4:9	Mark 12:31 and parallels
The sudden coming of Christ and judgment	5:2–3	Mark 13:17 and parallels; Matt. 24:42–44 and parallel. Cf. Matt. 25:1–13
Sons of light	5:5–7	Matt. 5:14–16. Cf. 25:1–13
Be at peace with one another	5:13	Mark 9:50
Do not render evil for evil	5:15	Matt. 5:38–48 and parallel
Persistent prayer	5:17	Luke 18:1–8. Cf. 11:5–9
	II Thessalonians	
The coming of the Lord	1:7	Mark 8:38 and parallels; Mark 13:26 and parallels
The punishment of the wicked	1:9	Matt. 25:30, 46
Desecration of the Temple	2:4	Mark 13:14; Matt. 24:15
False Christs and signs and wonders	2:9	Mark 13:22 and parallel
Church discipline	3:6, 14	Matt. 18:17
On work	3:6–13	Matt. 24:45–51 and parallel; Matt. 21:28–32. Cf. Matt. 9:37–38 and parallel

ın∂ex . . .

*Boldface numerals indicate pages on which
major discussion appears.*

a

Abraham, 248, 249, 290, 302, 321,
322
Achaia, 208, 209, **210–215**, 226, 242,
250, 252, 258
Acts, 7, 8, 11, 13–17, 19, 25, 34, 35,
43–47, 49–51, 56, 57, 75, 86,
109, 111, **117–122**, 125–135,
137–140, 145, 148, 150, 151,
154–160, 163–165, 167, 169–
179, 182, 183, 185–219, 225,
227, 230, 232, 243, 244, 255,
285, 293, 303–305, 310, 311,
314, 319
Adam, 290, 313
Agelaus, 80
Akibar, 38, 59
Alexander the Great, 28, 32, 44, 48,
70–75, 78, 79, 88, 90, 91,
122, 189, 207, 216, 217
Alexander Jannaeus, 33, 53
Alexandria, 39, 48, 60, 71, 91, 92,
124, 128, 184
Amoraim, 35
Amyntas, 189
Ananias, 56, 164, 174, 175, 176
Andrew, 10
Andronicus, 287
Antigones, 72
Antigonus Gonatas, 72
Antioch, 44, 120, 147, 158, 159, 178,
179, 182, 183, **184–186**, 187,
188, 190, 191, 192, 197, 200,
201, 202, 204, 215, 221, 242,
243, 244, 247, 250

Antiochus Epiphanes, 32, 44, 48, **77,**
78, 124, 128
Antiochus the Great, 32, 48, 80, 123
Antipas, 34
Antipater, 81, 126, 190
Antony, Mark, 83, 84, 85, 123, 205
Aphrodite, 211
Apollos, 119, 169, 184, 214, 215, 265,
270
Apostle to gentiles, 8, 122, 172, 173
Apostolic Christianity, 17
Apostolic Decrees, 198, 199
Apostolic Fathers, 5, 6, 8, 15, 117,
280, 292
Apuleius, 101, 106
Aquila, 49, 54, 55, 86, 213, 215, 217,
219, 287
Archelaeus, 34
Archippus, 275, 276, 277
Aretas, 119, 175
Argives, 123
Aristotle, 70, 73, 74
Artaxerxes, 29
Asidaeans (See Hasidim), 43
Atargatis-Hadad, 105
Athenadorus, 94, 125
Athens, 49, 80, 94, 124, 191, 195, 210
Attis, 103, 104
Augustine, 6, 9
Augustus (Octavian), 70, 79–85, 88,
90, 123, 125

B

Babylon, 28–30, 44, 46, 47, 71
Bacon, B. W., 157, 162, 279, 280, 281,
282, 294